Oxford Studies in Social History
General Editor: Keith Thomas

The Holy Household

1. **The Perlach Square in Winter**, attributed to Heinrich Vogtherr, c. 1541, Städtische Kunstsammlungen Augsburg. On the right, Councillors leave the town hall dressed in rich furs. Above them is the town hall balcony and below it, the *Pranger* (stocks) where criminals are exhibited. In the background in front of the Perlach tower, marketwomen sell goods which craftsmen and women purchase; in the foreground, peasant women offer produce for sale. Note the plaits of the unmarried girls and the wimples of the married women. In the centre middle ground a richly-dressed patrician woman and her daughters are followed by their maidservant. (The artist has distorted the arrangement of the buildings.)

The Holy Household

Women and Morals,
in Reformation Augsburg

LYNDAL ROPER

CLARENDON PRESS · OXFORD

*This book has been printed digitally and produced in a standard specification
in order to ensure its continuing availability*

OXFORD
UNIVERSITY PRESS

Great Clarendon Street, Oxford OX2 6DP

Oxford University Press is a department of the University of Oxford.
It furthers the University's objective of excellence in research, scholarship,
and education by publishing worldwide in

Oxford New York

Auckland Bangkok Buenos Aires Cape Town Chennai
Dar es Salaam Delhi Hong Kong Istanbul Karachi Kolkata
Kuala Lumpur Madrid Melbourne Mexico City Mumbai Nairobi
São Paulo Shanghai Singapore Taipei Tokyo Toronto

with an associated company in Berlin

Oxford is a registered trade mark of Oxford University Press
in the UK and in certain other countries

Published in the United States
by Oxford University Press Inc., New York

ISBN 0-19-821769-2
ISBN 0-19-820280-6 (pbk)

ACKNOWLEDGEMENTS

My thanks, first of all, to the Women's Movement, without which this book could not have been written. In particular, the London Feminist History Group, the Oxford Women's History Group, the Oxford Feminist Theory Group, the Feminist Early Modern Historians' Group, the London Women's History Seminar, and History Workshop have all given me friendship and inspiration over the years.

This book began in Australia, where Charles Zika first persuaded me to be interested in magic and religion. In Germany, Professor Heiko Oberman at Tübingen guided the work initially, and I am most grateful for his continued advice. The members of the Tübingen Sonderforschungsprojekt Stadt und Reformation welcomed and encouraged me, and I've learnt much from Dr Ingrid Bátori, who had faith in an Australian's unlikely project. At Ulm, Dr Specker of the city archive and the archival staff were very helpful, and the late Herr Strobel, historian of Pfuhl, helped me to decipher sixteenth-century handwriting. I am particularly grateful to all the staff of the archive at Augsburg, especially to Dr Wolfram Baer, the late Herr Thomas Mayr, and Herr Günter Schubert. Hans Wilhelm, Katarina Sieh, Peter Lipburger, and Jürgen Kraus, with whom I worked at Augsburg, not only shared information but made archival life fun. I am indebted to Drs Elfriede and Friedrich Blendinger for their suggestions of sources and questions to explore, and for their hospitality. My special thanks to Hans and Rita Pion-Wilhelm and to the late Herr Anselm Wilhelm and Frau Wilhelm, who all helped me to love Augsburg.

I would like to acknowledge the financial assistance and help of the Deutscher Akademischer Austauschdienst, the University of London Central Research Fund, the University Women's Federation of Australia, Caltex Australia, the German Historical Institute, the British Government Commonwealth scholarship scheme, Merton College, Oxford, King's College, London, and Royal Holloway and Bedford New College, London. Three months at the

Humanities Research Centre in Canberra attending the 'Feminism and the Humanities' series helped me to start rethinking the book. The many friends who helped with advice and support made writing this book a pleasure. Léonie Archer, Michael Baxandall, Maxine Berg, Mrs A. Bloch, Tom Brady, Philip Broadhead, Miranda Chaytor, Anna Clark, Trish Crawford, Henry Cohn, Anna Davin, Natalie Davis, the late Walter Groos, Stuart Hall, Elaine Hobby, Judith Herrin, Olwen Hufton, Bill Kent, Rolf Kiessling, Hans Joachim Köhler, Peter Lang, Micha Lewin, Mrs Elisabeth Lintelo, Jill Matthews, Jim Mitchell, Olaf Mörke, Maria Müller, Jinty Nelson, Maggie Pelling, Mike Roper, Ailsa Roper, Cath Roper, Stan Roper, Hans Christoph Rublack, David Sabean, Raphael Samuel, Pat Simons, Anne Summers, Carol Willock, Merry Wiesner, Heide Wunder, and Charles Zika all came up with ideas which have found their way into this book. None of them, of course, is to blame for its faults. Keith Thomas twice read the manuscript with enormous care: his sharp eye and perceptive comments have helped refine its argument. Ruth Harris critiqued the thesis from cover to cover and cheered me on with international phone calls. Bob Scribner was a perfect supervisor and critic, giving me 'free rein' but helping me pull it all together when I could not see how to—I hope his patience will be rewarded. Barbara Taylor generously read the entire book several times, made editorial suggestions throughout, argued with me, and gave me the determination to get it right. Guy Boanas read and heard endless drafts and pre-drafts, gave constant love and encouragement, and even solved my software problems when he should have been doing his own research. He gives the lie to a pessimistic view of the household workshop; and so the book is for him.

L.R.

London
1988

CONTENTS

LIST OF PLATES

LIST OF TABLES

GRAPH

Introduction

THE Reformation burst on the world in chiliastic expectation, alight with the message of salvation by faith alone, with dreams of a world to be set aright by the avenging horsemen of the Apocalypse. How did this revolutionary evangelicalism become transformed into the consoling, socially conservative pieties of Protestant guildsfolk? How was it possible for a gospel which preached the spiritual equality of all Christians, male and female, rich and poor, and even denied the need for a priesthood, to become the bulwark of a secular order based on hierarchy? How could a religion which began by exulting in the prophetic talents poured out on daughters as well as upon sons come to view women almost exclusively as wives, whose sphere it was to be subordinate to their husbands and instructed by their preachers? My central claim is that the moral ethic of the urban Reformation, both as a religious credo and a social movement, must be understood as a theology of gender. Hitherto, the effects of the Reformation on women have been viewed as largely beneficial: the positive evaluation of marriage and of women as wives, and the doctrine of the priesthood of all believers have been adduced to argue that women's status improved.[1] More speculatively, Protestantism has even been identified as the spiritual soil from which progressive feminism later drew its strength.[2] Such a genealogy implicitly allies Protestantism with the forces of progressivism, individualism, and modernization. This book argues that such a presentation of the Reformation's legacy is a profound misreading of the Reformation itself.

[1] R. Bainton, *Women of the Reformation in Germany and Italy* (Minneapolis, 1971); S. Ozment, *When Fathers Ruled: Family Life in Reformation Europe* (Cambridge, Mass., 1983).
[2] R. Evans, *The Feminist Movement in Germany 1894–1933* (London, 1976), who argues that the peculiar character of state-dominated religion in Germany helped to weaken feminism in Germany.

The heritage of Protestantism for women was deeply ambiguous, and could lead either to an affirmation of female piety or to a renewed patriarchalism. In German towns, as the Reformation was institutionalized, the values of evangelical moralism were harnessed to an older conservative tradition which defined women as wives in submission to their husbands. Not even a distinctive feminine mode of religious experience, such as we see in Catholic saints' and Marian cults, or in the extreme hyperpiety of saintly widows, lived on in early mainstream evangelicalism.[3] Far from endorsing independent spiritual lives for women, the institutionalized Reformation was most successful when it most insisted on a vision of women's incorporation within the household under the leadership of their husbands.

This conclusion is at first surprising. Puritan prophetesses, French Calvinist noblewomen, women members of the English Civil War sects are familiar to us as activists in their movements, leading and prophesying. And indeed, in the first phase of the Reformation in the heady days of the 1520s, women were to be found writing pamphlets,[4] countering critics with the argument: 'If they say . . . Paul says women should be silent, I answer, But don't you know that he also says (Galatians 3) that in Christ there is neither man nor woman';[5] even threatening that 'perhaps a hundred women will write against [the papists]'.[6] They cited biblical heroines like Judith and Deborah or historical exemplars from the early Church, creating a lineage which would justify their bold attacks on the most respected church authorities. With its affirmation of Isaiah's prophecy of the spirit flowing to daughters as well as to sons, Protestantism seemed to secure a platform for women outside the papist ecclesiastical structures.

But this moment was brief. Of the women pamphleteers, all but Katharina Schütz, wife of the Strasbourg preacher Mattheus Zell, had laid down their pens by the 1530s. Even her career

---

[3] See also, on Lutheran thought, M. Wiesner, 'Luther and Women: The Death of Two Marys', in J. Obelkevich *et al.* (eds.), *Disciplines of Faith* (London, 1987).

[4] See P. Russell, *Lay Theology in the Reformation: Popular Pamphleteers in Southwest Germany 1521–1525* (Cambridge, 1986), pp. 185–211.

[5] 'moecht man sagen . . . Paulus sagt die weyber sollent schweigen. Antwort ich Weisst aber nit auch das er sagt Galat iii Jn Christo ist weder man nach [*sic*] weyb . . .': Katharina Schützinn, *Entschuldigung Katharina Schützinn für M. Matthes Zellen jren Eegemahel* [Strasbourg, W. Köpfel, 1524], fo. c/ii'.

[6] Argula von Grumbach, quoted in Russell, *Lay Theology*, p. 196.

reveals how far urban evangelicalism had moved from its initial enthusiasm for female polemicists of the Reformation. An increasingly marginal figure, she came to be regarded by the city preachers as a nuisance with an evil tongue. Interestingly, she dared to form close friendships and kinships with spiritualists and other religious radicals, associations which further deepened the antagonism between her and the city clergy and authorities, and bear witness to the impossibility of containing her religiosity solely within the intellectual confines of the established evangelical movement.[7] Urban Protestantism, once embedded in the certainties of household moralism, could not furnish a mode for women's public action, or even at first a distinctly feminine register of piety. Women could not speak from within the intellectual heritage of urban communalism, nor could they make the language of civic righteousness their own.

Why? In order to understand the conservative shift in the Reformation's message to women we must explore the dynamics of the craft workshops which became the nurturing soil of populist Protestantism. These myriad craft workshops, where work-place and dwelling-place were identical, and where each member knew their sexual and social place, were urban Protestantism's home ground. It is in this wider sense that we can speak of the 'family': a grouping which included servants, apprentices, and journeymen. It will be argued that as the Reformation staked out its views on marriage, sexuality, and prostitution—the territory it so effectively made its own—so it mapped out an agenda for reform of relations between the sexes.

Heir to the master craftsmen's own politics, articulated by their guilds, the politics of the Reformation gave voice to the interests and perceptions of the married craftsmen who ruled over their wives and organized the household's subordinate labour force of men and women. In a real sense, therefore, as the Reformation was domesticated—as it closed convents and encouraged nuns to marry, as it lauded the married state exemplified by the craft couple, and as it execrated the prostitute—so it was accomplished through a politics of reinscribing women within the 'family'.

*

[7] Ibid.; M. Chrisman, 'Women and the Reformation in Strasbourg 1490–1530', *Archiv für Reformationsgeschichte*, 63 (1972), 143–68; Bainton, *Women of the Reformation*.

This book sets out to describe the Reformation's effects on marriage and family as it was implemented in a single town, Augsburg. Augsburg has been chosen because, with Strasbourg and Nuremberg, it was one of the three premier cities of southern Germany. Its religious history is an interestingly fractured one, with an early Lutheranism being succeeded by a more morally centred evangelicalism, influenced by theologians like Zwingli and Bucer. There were in addition supporters of several Anabaptist sects in the city, while after 1548 Catholicism was reintroduced and Jesuit influence began to grow. Evangelical moralism and its alternatives were therefore well represented in the town, a clash which allows the contours of the evangelical movement to emerge more clearly. The city also has an outstanding collection of criminal records and punishment books, eloquent testimony to the Council's project of disciplining its citizenry. These afford a rare opportunity to explore not only the priorities of guild and Council, but also the impact of evangelical moralism on the men and women who lived through the years of the Reformation.

But this domestication of the Reformation was a gradual, historical process. It took place through a shifting balance of forces during the sixteenth century. In order to see how it took place, and how its constituency was created, we need first to understand the nature of the city and the chronology of the Reformation. Chapter 1 explores the implementation of the Reformation and the sources of its support in the realities of the household workshop, each headed by a master guildsman. The second chapter will show how this evangelical household moralism was articulated in Augsburg, and how urban politics were transformed as a guild-influenced Reformation gained support in the town. These politics were spelt out above all in the processes of ordinance-making and enforcement of statutes, as evangelicals tried to create the kingdom of God through discipline. Prostitutes in particular came to symbolize the wickedness which the evangelicals wished to eradicate, and the third chapter describes the Council's attempt to abolish prostitution altogether. Marriage was to be the only place for sexual relations, and in the fourth chapter we see how the Council tried to ensure that marriage was the foundation of social and sexual order. But, as Chapter 5 will show, the more the Council tried to uphold marriage, and the more it intervened in disorderly marriages, punishing violent husbands and cautioning shrewish wives, the more it exposed the fragility of the patriarchal order it wished to reinforce. The last chapter explores the fate of the group of women who could not be incorporated into this civic, evangelical moralism which viewed women as wives: nuns. Subject to ecclesiastical rather than urban authorities alone, monks and nuns had always occupied an ambiguous position in urban culture. Yet though male monasteries rapidly succumbed to the Reformation, as monks left to take up other professions, became evangelical preachers, or else travelled to Catholic areas, convents offered the one institutional focus of real and lasting opposition to the triumph of evangelical moralism in the town. Godly order, the ethic which redrew the ideals of wifehood and mastership, and was imagined to underwrite the social stability of the town, was determinedly contested by these female outsiders to urban culture.

Gender relations, as this book will argue, far from being tangentially affected by the Reformation, were at the crux of the Reformation itself.[8] The conservative rewriting of the Reformation movement's message around a politics of women's role in marriage and household was the key to its successful implementation and establishment.

[8] For a powerful demonstration of the centrality of gender relations in class formation, see L. Davidoff and C. Hall, *Family Fortunes* (London, 1987).

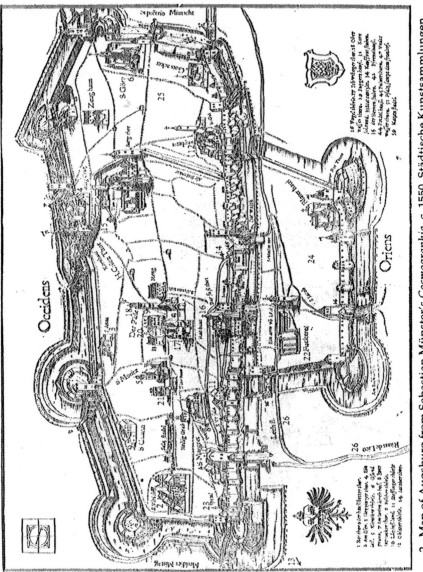

2. Map of Augsburg from Sebastian Münster's *Cosmographia*, c. 1550, Städtische Kunstsammlungen Augsburg.

1. Cathedral of Our Lady; 2. St Ulric and Afra; 3. St Anna's; 4. Holy Cross; 5. St Maurice's; 6. St George's; 7. Franciscan monastery; 8. Dominican monastery; 9. St Katherine's convent (Dominican); 10. St Margaret's convent (Dominican); 11. St Ursula's convent (Dominican); 12. St Stephen's foundation; 13. St Nicholas's convent (Benedictine); 14. St Clare on the Horbruck's convent (Franciscan); 15. St Martin's convent (Franciscan); 16. Maria Stern's convent (Franciscan); 17. town hall; 18. Perlach watch tower; 19. *Herrenstube*; 20. *Kaufleutestube*; 21. Fugger houses; 22. *Fuggerei*; 23. hospital of the Holy Ghost; 24. St Jakob's suburb; 25. Our Lady's suburb; 26. Lech river

1

The Domestication of the Reformation

Augsburg

One of the largest and most powerful of the southern German cities, with a population of over 30,000, Augsburg on the eve of the Reformation ranked in importance with Strasbourg and Nuremberg. Though it had little countryside directly subject to it, Augsburg dominated the surrounding region, acting as a magnet of employment for serving-women and young men and as a market for peasant produce. The movement between town and country might be two-way, for while the city's spires and elegant buildings could entice local nobility into the town, the rich burghers increasingly began to invest in country estates where they might ape noble retirement. So also the conception of the city itself oscillated between images of enclosure and openness. The Council could describe itself in 1537 as the leader of citizens 'within a ringed wall', and indeed, maintenance and expansion of its walled defences and bastions were to become a dominant concern of civic policy during the anxious 1540s.[1] But it was also a proud and outgoing centre of commerce, whose traders had long dealt with Venice and other Italian merchants, had interests in mines across Europe as far as England, and had even explored outside Europe, with an outpost in Venezuela. Despite its invocation of a bounded, protected collectivity, many Council members had travelled far afield and trade interests linked the

---

[1] J. Kraus, *Das Militärwesen der Reichsstadt Augsburg 1548–1806* (Augsburg, 1980), pp. 354 f.

city inescapably to the wider world—even the city's meat supply depended on Hungarian cattle.[2]

Within the city, space and buildings articulated an outer semblance of order. The force of the two rivers at whose junction the city stood—the Lech and Wertach—was harnessed and turned to make the city profitable, so that small canals from the Lech channelled its energy through the Lech quarter, providing the power for machines and water for domestic use. These streams were an image of local wealth so current to Augsburgers that it was to provide the theme for the bronze fountain erected in 1594 which now stands on the main city square, capped by a proud Caesar gesturing at the town hall, the centre of political power.[3] Below him, four river gods, two male and two female, watch the play of water. Just as the river gods represent the female Wertach and the minor Singold stream while the male figures stand for the Lech and its urban tributary the Brunnenbach, the fountain suggests that two opposed forces, masculinity and femininity, are here joined in ordered, creative balance.

Politically and symbolically, the heart of the city was the square outside the town hall, near the Perlach, the city watch-tower at whose base stood the Council church of St Peter. From the balcony on the town hall, proclamations would be read and here the Emperor himself might appear. At the annual oath-swearings, where citizens renewed their mutual oath of loyalty to the Council, this square was the central assembly point. Here it was too that the guilds had first secured political power for themselves, massing on the square outside the town hall in 1368

---

[2] G. Gottlieb *et al.* (eds.), *Geschichte der Stadt Augsburg*, 2nd edn. (Stuttgart, 1985); F. W. Roth, *Augsburgs Reformationsgeschichte*, 4 vols. (vol. i: 2nd edn., Munich, 1901; vols. ii–iv: Munich, 1904–11); *Welt im Umbruch: Augsburg zwischen Renaissance und Barock*, 3 vols. (Augsburg, 1980, 1981); J. Strieder, *Zur Genesis des modernen Kapitalismus: Forschungen zur Entstehung der grossen bürgerlichen Kapitalvermögen am Ausgang des Mittelalters und zu Beginn der Neuzeit, zunächst in Augsburg*, 2nd edn. (Munich 1935); W. Zorn, *Augsburg: Geschichte einer deutschen Stadt*, 2nd edn. (Augsburg, 1972); J. Hartung, 'Die Belastung des augsburgischen Grosskapitals durch die Vermögenssteuer des 16. Jahrhunderts', *Jahrbuch für Gesetzgebung, Verwaltung und Volkswirtschaft (Schmollers Jahrbuch)*, 19 (1895), 1165–90.

[3] B. Bushart, 'Kunst und Stadtbild', in Gottlieb, *Geschichte der Stadt Augsburg*; B. Bushart, 'Die Augsburger Brunnen und Denkmale um 1600', *Welt im Umbruch*, iii; H. Friedel, *Bronzebilddokumente in Augsburg 1589–1606: Bild und Urbanität* (Augsburg, 1974).

to demand guild representation. At military musters the square was again a central rallying-point, and its situation next to the watch-tower, from where the great storm-bell signifying danger to the town would be rung, made it at once the most vulnerable and powerful civic territory. In military and political terms, the square was male space. Women had to stay indoors when the storm-bell rang, and they were not politically active citizens nor did they take part in the oath-swearings. The councillors, pictured in the painting by Heinrich Vogtherr in their warm, black furs processing out of the Council on to the square after a meeting, were all male; for in this urban republic only men could embody political authority.[4]

Yet at normal times this same square would be filled with the mixed-sex bustle of market-day, with women's high-pitched voices calling their wares, and tradeswomen and servant-girls gossiping and vying for bargains. Here too they might cast a glance at the evil-doers displayed in the stocks on the town hall—men and women who were guilty of thieving or of procuring and prostitution. Held up to shame and ignominy at the political heart of the city, with a statement of their misdeeds read out over them, those who had offended against the rules of property and the sexual order publicly lost their honour and were expelled from the town.

Parallel to the secular logic of space, there was a sacred topography. Towards the north the town was dominated by the cathedral, a rival focus of power whose land and administrative responsibilities extended far beyond the city. Nestling in its shadows were the lodgings of many clerics; and here prostitutes were well practised in seeking clients. The six parish churches of the city, associated with education and involving lay people, gave one logic of organization, but superimposed on this were the houses of the orders, Dominicans, Benedictines, Carmelites, Franciscans, and Augustinians, who had both male and female houses dotted around the city.[5] In size and magnificence, the counterweight to the cathedral was the great Benedictine church

---

[4] L. Roper, '"The Common Man", "the Common Good", "Common Women": Gender and Meaning in the German Reformation Commune', *Social History*, 12/1 (1987), 1–22.

[5] R. Kiessling, *Bürgerliche Gesellschaft und Kirche in Augsburg im Spätmittelalter* (Augsburg, 1971), pp. 31–41.

of St Ulric and St Afra, the chief saints of the town, newly rebuilt and visited by the Emperor Maximilian. Here was a great concentration of sacred local power, for the church housed not only relics of St Ulric, the Bishop of Augsburg, but the bones of St Simpert and St Digna, together with 'many other pious virgins of the company of Sts Hilaria and Afra' and a tomb containing the body of St Afra herself. Sacred power, unlike political authority, could be imagined in both male and female forms. The city itself was protected by St Afra, a powerful local saint. The daughter of the King of Cyprus, forced to flee after the death of her father, she had come as a pagan and prostitute with her mother in response to a prophecy that she would do great things in Augsburg. This saying, so the story runs, she interpreted as meaning that they would make a great killing as whores in the city. However, Bishop Narcissus visited the house and converted the women to Christianity, and they later died martyrs' deaths.[6] Her cult, with its promise of redemption for even the most sinful and shamed woman, represented a rather different understanding of sin and womanhood from that of the Reformation which we will explore.

But though the civic buildings and churches embodied a strong sense of local pride and unity, the city was becoming increasingly divided. The elaborate, new Italianate palaces of the merchant and patrician élite were dotted around the central area of the city, with their flat, painted façades concealing inner colonnaded courtyards and impressive private apartments. Buildings to be handed down within the family 'forever', they were reminiscent of noble seats. The private gardens filled 'with rare costly plants' in which rich burghers used to relax in St Jacob's suburb stood amongst tradesmen's shops.[7] The fabled wealth of such families as the Fugger, Welser, and Baumgartner, built on international trading connections, was in sharp contrast to the cramped working conditions of the local-based craftsmen, crowded along

    [6] *Ursprung und Anfang Augsburgs*, [Augsburg, Johann Bämler, 14]83, bound with Hagiologium of St Ulric and St Afra; *Die Chroniken der deutschen Städte vom 14. bis ins 16. Jahrhundert*, 36 vols. (Leipzig, 1865–1931), iv. 290, 295; ibid. xxv. 302–3.

    [7] P. von Stetten d. Ä., *Geschichte der Heiligen Römischen Reichs Freyen Stadt Augsburg* 2 vols. (Frankfurt and Leipzig, 1743–58), pp. 120 f.; P. Hecker, 'Der Augsburger Bürgermeister Jakob Herbrot und der Sturz des zünftigen Regiments in Augsburg', *ZHVS* 1 (1874), 34–98, 49.

the Lech canals in the upper city for water-based machinery, or spread out through St Jacob's suburb and beyond the cathedral in Our Lady's suburb where water was scarce. These were the areas where the weavers predominated, numerically the largest trade in the town; and they were the group which was to play such a central role in the introduction of the Reformation.[8]

The Reformation in Augsburg

In Augsburg, interest in the ideas of Luther can be discerned from at least 1518, when the reformer visited the city, and from then on evangelical preaching gradually won the movement more supporters. However, two major political alignments can be discerned which determined the Reformation's character. The first, radical alignment culminated in the Reformation disturbances of 1524–5, which constituted there (as in the other large cities where they occurred) the single major threat to the city's ruling élite of merchants, patricians, and upper guildsmen. A series of 'evangelical incidents', where pro-Reformation radicals engaged in direct action—by throwing blessed salt in holy water, or tearing mass-books—to show that the old religion's objects had no sacral power, took place. The Council retaliated with the banishment of one of the perceived instigators, the evangelical monk Schilling; but this finally culminated in a major riot. The men who gathered on the city square to demand the return of the 'evangelical monk', banished by the city Council for his incendiary pro-Reformation sermons, were a mixture of evangelical guildsmen, day-labourers, and, as the chroniclers of the event grimly noted, poor weavers. To the chroniclers, the content of the evangelical monk's sermons was less noteworthy than what they took to be its underlying menace: the explosive

---

[8] Gottlieb, *Geschichte der Stadt Augsburg*; B. Roeck, *Bäcker, Brot und Getreide in Augsburg* (Augsburg, 1987); D. Schröder, *Augsburg* (Historischer Atlas von Bayern, x, *Schwaben*; Munich, 1975); P. Broadhead, 'Internal Politics and Civic Society in Augsburg during the Era of the Early Reformation', Ph.D. thesis (Kent, 1981); E. Piper, *Der Stadtplan als Grundriss der Gesellschaft: Topographie und Sozialstruktur in Augsburg und Florenz um 1500* (Frankfurt, 1982).

alliance he uncorked of poor guildsmen and day-labourers, united in anger against the heathen Council.[9] What worried chroniclers and Council alike was that the anger of the evangelicals at the banishment of Schilling could rapidly turn to a hatred of 'the big jacks', as the artist-chronicler Jörg Preu described them, who fleeced the poor and persisted in the old godless religion of the money-grubbing monks.[10] The fear that the evangelicals' protest raised was partly a throw-back to the older guild struggles of 1368 and to the ever-present worry that 'the poor weavers' would erupt into open discontent—a powder keg the Council and even one philanthropist had sought to defuse by providing them with free town-baked bread during the famines of the previous decade.[11] The 1524–5 disturbances were so alarming because they embodied a perceived alliance not only between peasants and townsfolk, but between poor guildsmen, weavers, and others and those with no political voice at all—day-labourers, journeymen, and other non-guildsmen—against the merchants and patricians, the rich and politically powerful.

In Augsburg, politics was played out within a careful equilibrium of patrician and guild power. With their seventeen guilds, each sending twelve representatives to the Great Council, the guilds had a clear majority over the patricians in the widest assembly. This majority was whittled down in the Small Council which held more actual power, for there one or two representatives from each guild (the guild masters) were balanced against eight patricians.[12] Patrician representation was most striking amongst the high offices, and one of the two mayors of the city was always a patrician. Patrician blood alone, however, did not circumscribe the élite: Augsburg's social élite was a cohesive combination of rich merchant families and older patricians who intermarried and shared the *Herrenstube*. Unlike

---

[9] Roper, 'The Common Man'; Roth, *Augsburgs Reformationsgeschichte*, i; Broadhead, 'Internal Politics', pp. 124–60; P. Broadhead, 'Politics and Expediency in the Augsburg Reformation', in P. Newman Brooks (ed.), *Reformation Principle and Practice: Essays in Honour of Arthur Geoffrey Dickens* (London, 1980); W. Vogt, 'Johann Schilling der Barfüssermönch und der Aufstand in Augsburg im Jahre 1524', *ZHVS* 6 (1879), 1–32.

[10] *Chroniken der deutschen Städte*, xxix, Preu.

[11] Ibid. xxv, Rem, p. 77.

[12] There were 2 representatives each from the major guilds: merchants', weavers', salt-dealers', pedlars', and butchers'; 1 each from the others.

in other towns such as Ulm, involvement in trade did not tarnish an individual's social prestige, so that in Augsburg there was a far more immediate recognition of the importance of trade and money in the town's policies.[13]

A number of upper craftsmen were incorporated, though to a lesser extent, by their occupation of positions within the town's political élite, as guild masters and judges, high-ranking office-holders and mayors. Members of the rich guilds of the merchants and salt-dealers were especially prominent, in part because the time needed to devote to politics simply could not be spared by poorer masters who needed to earn a precarious living. Some of these guild politicians were merchants and traders rather than trade workers; but none the less, even middling guildsmen would have felt some sense of incorporation in town government by virtue of voting for, or acting as, one of the 'Twelve' for their guild. Co-option of these guild members, and those beneath them, was vital to the city's stability. In 1524 it was only by mobilizing the ranks of the middling, respectable guildsmen, the members of the Great Council, against this perceived rebellion that the Council was able to cling to power. Thus having assured itself of guild support, the Council executed two weavers on the Perlach square before dawn in secrecy—an improbable scapegoating which limited the damage caused by the riots, symbolically restored the Council's power in the heart of the city, and singled out two insignificant weavers who held no powerful position in the guilds.[14] In other cities, like Erfurt and Memmingen, where stability could not be re-created so readily, Councils had to give way for a time to a government of peasants and poor townsfolk.

The broad stratum of masters, which the revolt of 1524 threatened to fragment along lines of wealth, was only a fraction

[13] K. Sieh-Burens, *Oligarchie, Konfession und Politik im 16. Jahrhundert: Zur sozialen Verflechtung der Augsburger Bürgermeister und Stadtpfleger 1518-1618* (Munich, 1986); K. Sieh-Burens, 'Die Augsburger Stadtverfassung um 1500', *ZHVS* 77 (1983), 125-49; I. Bátori, *Die Reichsstadt Augsburg im 18. Jahrhundert: Verfassung, Finanzen und Reformversuche* (Göttingen, 1969); P. Dirr, 'Studien zur Geschichte der Augsburger Zunftverfassung 1368-1548', *ZHVS* 39 (1913), 144-243; P. Dirr, 'Kaufleutezunft und Kaufleutestube in Augsburg zur Zeit des Zunftregiments (1368-1548)', *ZHVS* 35 (1909), 133-51.

[14] Roper, 'The Common Man'; Broadhead, 'Internal Politics', Vogt, 'Johann Schilling'; Roth, *Augsburgs Reformationsgeschichte*, i.

of the city's population. At a total of just above 3,800 in 1536, guild members made up around a tenth of the populace.[15] The workshop households at whose head most stood would have accounted for over half the population;[16] for the total number of households listed in the tax-book for 1540 was slightly over 7,000.[17] The tessellated series of dependent workers, such as married weavers who worked in master weavers' enterprises, stretched the net of guild domination yet further through the city. The masters clung firmly to the rights and privileges which made

[15] A. Gasser, *Annales de vetustate originis, amoenitate situs . . .* (Scriptores Rerum Germanicarum, ed. G. Menck, 3 vols.: Leipzig 1728-30; vol. i, no. xvii), p. 1801, yields a total of 3,803. See also P. von Stetten, *Geschichte der Heiligen Römischen Reichs Freyen Stadt Augsburg*, p. 339. (However, see Roeck, *Bäcker, Brot und Getreide in Augsburg*, p. 176, for a listing taken from a chronicle of Clemens Jäger, yielding a total of 3,964 guild members. Jäger notes 175 merchants whereas other sources list 75, and 395 'Kramer' where others list 335. We shall follow Gasser's figures. Jäger's numbers are a mistaken overestimate, since the merchants' guild was declining at this time and numbered only 36 in 1539 as members left it for the patriciate: O. Mörke and K. Sieh, 'Gesellschaftliche Führungsgruppen', in Gottlieb, *Geschichte der Stadt Augsburg*, p. 302.) It is not clear whether either figure included widows. For recent literature on Augsburg's population size, see Roeck, *Bäcker, Brot und Getreide in Augsburg*, pp. 66-82; B. Rajkay, 'Die Bevölkerungsentwicklung von 1500 bis 1648', in Gottlieb, *Geschichte der Stadt Augsburg*; M. C. Paas, *Population Change, Labour Supply and Agriculture in Augsburg 1480-1618* (New York, 1981); J. Jahn, 'Augsburgs Einwohnerzahl im 16. Jahrhundert: Ein statistischer Versuch', *Zeitschrift des Vereins für bayerische Landesgeschichte*, 39 (1976), 379-96.

[16] Cf., however, K. Schulz, *Handwerksgesellen und Lohnarbeiter: Untersuchungen zur oberrheinischen und oberdeutschen Stadtgeschichte des 14. bis 17. Jahrhunderts* (Sigmaringen, 1985), who argues that in other towns some non-masters enjoyed both guild rights and citizenship. The figures from the muster list of 1539 yield a total of 4,293 male householding citizens. Some of these would have been patricians (and non-guildsmen); some, preachers; some, members of non-guild crafts; but since we know that there were 3,803 guildsmen in 1536, and reliable population estimates place population totals at about 30,000-40,000 inhabitants, it follows that although there were some guild members who were not masters of their craft-guild, there was only a small minority of non-master guildsmen.

[17] There were 7,155 taxpayers in 1540: J. Hartung, 'Die Augsburger Vermögenssteuer und die Entwicklung der Besitzverhältnisse im 16. Jahrhundert', *Schmollers Jahrbuch*, 19 (1895), 867-83, 171, 177. Tax was levied by household. On tax in Augsburg, see C. P. Clasen, *Die Augsburger Steuerbücher um 1600* (Augsburg, 1976); and on social structure, see F. Blendinger, 'Versuch einer Bestimmung der Mittelschicht in der Reichsstadt Augsburg vom Ende des 14. bis zum Anfang des 18. Jahrhunderts', in E. Maschke and J. Sydow (eds.), *Städtische Mittelschichten* (Stuttgart, 1972); Kiessling, *Bürgerliche Gesellschaft*; C. P. Clasen, 'Arm und Reich in Augsburg vor dem Dreissigjährigen Krieg', in Gottlieb, *Geschichte der Stadt Augsburg*.

them citizens and safeguarded their livelihoods against the predations of competitors and 'unskilled' workers who were not masters. These guildsmen were certainly not a majority of Augsburg's inhabitants; and numbers of day-labourers and servants remained stubbornly unincorporated into the household-workshop system.[18]

But the guildsmen were far from being a homogeneous group. In a city where the twin pressures of rapid economic expansion and periodic decline were creating ever more visible divisions of wealth, between the Italianate palaces of the fabulously rich merchants on the one hand and the single-room hovels of the poor master weavers on the other, these perceived wealth differences threatened to replace a sense of shared privilege and civic belonging among the guild masters with a politics of 'those who had nothing', as the tax-book phrase put it. Such a grouping would cut across the alliance of privilege of the masters to create an alliance of deprivation between poor guildsfolk, day-labourers, and journeymen. This was the spectre which alarmed the Council in 1524, and made it so uncertain of the loyalty of its own citizens that it severely stretched the civic purse by stationing foreign mercenaries in the town to keep order for some time after the serious riots were over.[19]

In 1524—and indeed throughout Germany in 1525—Reformation had been allied with disorder. But by the mid-1530s it was Protestant phrases which the Council mouthed, and Reformation evangelicalism which underpinned the civic order itself. This shift—the domestication of the Reformation—has long been recognized as one of the central sixteenth-century developments. But what has gone unrecognized is the centrality of the politics of marriage to this process. By promising a religion of wedded life and a politics of the control of marriage, the evangelical message recruited substantial portions of the guildsfolk for a Reformation which favoured them, and which gave powerful articulation to the craft values of order, discipline, and the authority of the master.

The transformation of message was mirrored by an alteration

---

[18] See Schulz, *Handwerksgesellen und Lohnarbeiter*, and Tables 1.1 and 1.2 below.

[19] Broadhead, 'Internal Politics', pp. 137, 124-57.

in the movement's public face. The early Reformation radicals who took the lead—hotheads who tore prayer-books, sprinkled blessed salt in the font, and bearded the Catholic monks—tended either to be journeymen who lacked the settled securities of masterhood, or poor weavers.[20] This was an inversion of customary social precedence which the Lutherans found embarrassing. But even in the mid-1520s the preachers began to boast of their loyalty to the Council, and by the later 1520s an alliance was taking shape between the new urban Reformation preachers—who increasingly owed their appointments to the Council—and the city's political élite.[21] By the mid-1530s the movement's leaders were substantial men who were masters and household heads. Some of the early radicals, disillusioned with mainstream evangelicalism, found their way into the Anabaptist sects which enjoyed significant minority support in the town.[22] In 1527 Augsburg was the meeting-place for a large assembly of Anabaptists from all over the region, but persecution followed, and though Augsburg did not go so far as to execute any Anabaptists, the Council periodically rounded up Anabaptist meetings in the town and expelled or imprisoned attenders.[23]

Mainstream evangelicalism too, however, was no longer one movement; and the history of these years is pockmarked by the tensions between the dwindling Lutheran faction and the more radical clergy who found favour with most guildsfolk, influenced by the Swiss urban theologian Huldrich Zwingli and the Strasbourg

[20] See e.g. StadtAA, Urg. 9 May 1524, Ulrich Richsner (weaver); 10 May 1524, Peter Scheppach (weaver); 10 June 1524, Franz Laminit ('Teschenmacher'); 6 Aug. 1524, comment of Hans Schwaier (weaver); H. Lutz, *Conrad Peutinger: Beiträge zu einer politischen Biographie* (Augsburg, 1958), p. 227, Georg Fischer (baker's journeyman).

[21] On Augsburg's clergy, see H. Wiedemann, *Augsburger Pfarrerbuch* (Nuremberg, 1962).

[22] e.g. Bartholome Nussfelder, who ripped a Franciscan monk's Latin prayer-book during a Reformation 'disturbance', and was named as a 'vorsteer' by Anabaptists during the trials of 1528. See the brief biography in J. Wilhelm, *Augsburger Wandmalerei 1368-1530: Künstler, Handwerker und Zunft* (Augsburg, 1983), pp. 539-40.

[23] On Anabaptism in Augsburg, see F. Roth, 'Zur Geschichte der Wiedertäufer in Oberschwaben', *ZHVS* 27 (1900), 1-45; 28 (1901), 1-154; F. Uhland, *Täufertum und Obrigkeit in Augsburg im 16. Jahrhundert* (Tübingen, 1972). On Schwenckfeld in Augsburg, see *Corpus Schwenckfeldianorum*, ed. C. Hartranft et al., 19 vols. (Leizpig and Pennsburg 1907-61).

preacher Martin Bucer. A very important refrain in reformed theology, far more central than it was to Lutheranism, was the reform of morals and the upholding of discipline through the use of church bans and civic punishment.[24] The resonance this theme found in Augsburg may well account for the growing strength of the reformed faction.

Preachers, Pamphleteers, and Civic Moralism

The principles of evangelical moralism and guild ideals could form a powerful partnership. Its epitome was the Protestant married household, which, slow as it was to gain acceptance, could stand as a living rebuke to what guildsmen perceived as the licentiousness of the luxury-loving monks. Though differently accented, the message of the preachers and evangelical pamphleteers had much in common with civic attitudes towards the differences between men and women and the nature of sexuality. For the evangelical preachers, their status as married men was emblematic of their incorporation into the town as citizens, subject to the same moral code and law as any other citizen. Chaste and married, the reformed clergy strove to present themselves as exemplars of wedded life, while the unmarried Catholic priests, who had claimed moral superiority as the virginal godly caste, were unmasked as representing all that was dissolute and immoral. To guild eyes too, the old papist monks were targets of ridicule and symbols of godlessness because they did not head households but, like the sexually immature and licensed journeymen, banded together in brotherhoods. Priests were seen as guilty of every kind of sexual sin. They were accused of the sins of luxury and idleness which always accompanied sexual sins—an interesting hangover from medieval concepts of the aetiology of sin—and this vision was not weakened by such incidents as the discovery of Dominicans playing bowls in the monastery when the Council's commission arrived to seize the building in 1534.[25]

The idle, lecherous monk was a stock figure of Reformation polemic, translated into visual terms as a stout, tonsured figure,

[24] W. Köhler, *Zürcher Ehegericht und Genfer Konsistorium*, 2 vols. (Leipzig, 1932, 1942).

[25] K. Wolfart, *Die Augsburger Reformation in den Jahren 1533-1534* (Leipzig, 1901), p. 110 n. 4; *Chroniken der deutschen Städte*, xxiii, Sender, p. 391.

consorting with prostitutes or, worse, seducing respectable womenfolk.[26] In pamphlet literature, the topic of confession focused the issue of clerical lasciviousness most directly. Imagined nearly exclusively as an encounter between female penitent and cleric, it was the major propagandist vehicle for fears of monkish sexuality. So polemicists like Johannes Strauss would speculate on the reasons why women spent two hours at confession, or retail stories like that of the woman who praised the cleric 'who had shriven her like no cleric had ever done before'.[27]

Such propaganda drew heavily on a vein of misogyny. The women, far from being mere passive victims of their clerical interlocutors, were seen as willing accomplices in their seduction, and the scandal which resulted was damaging not so much to the women themselves as to their fathers or husbands, whose reputations were held to be impugned. In fact, at another level, the priest was imagined as interrogating the women about their husbands' sexual behaviour, thus criticizing and scrutinizing male sexuality. The imagined alliance of women and clerics was threatening indeed.

The themes of pamphlet literature were paralleled in everyday gossip and insult. The campaign against prostitution and the trials of individual prostitutes who visited priests further fuelled the identification of priests as the whore-masters of the town;[28] while the trial of a group of homosexuals, which lasted from 1533 to 1534 and which involved a cleric, made clerical sexuality seem not only undisciplined but 'perverse', 'against nature' as the indictment put it.[29] What particularly galled evangelicals was that clerics, subject to religious and not to civic law, often tended to be dealt with more leniently and were immune from civic correction—and in this case too, the cleric was not even forced to give evidence in person. The trials would have brought to

---

[26] R. W. Scribner, *For the Sake of Simple Folk* (Cambridge, 1981).

[27] S. Ozment, *The Reformation in the Cities: The Appeal of Protestantism to Sixteenth Century Germany and Switzerland* (New Haven and London, 1975), pp. 53–4.

[28] e.g. StadtAA, Reichsstadt, Urg. 14 July 1533, Agnes Veiheler; Urg. 7 Feb. 1534, Elisabeth Guterman; Urg. 22 Dec. 1533, Anna Lindenmair; Urg. 27 Feb. 1532, Ursula 'medlin'; Urg. 16 Dec. 1532, Margaret Rupfenvogel; Urg. 27 Feb. 1532, Kunigund Schwaier; Strafbuch des Rats II, fo. 75', 2 Sept. 1536, Ursula Vaigler.

[29] Ibid., Urg. 1 May 1532, Christoff Schmid; Urg. 1 Dec. 1533, Michel Will; Urg. 19 Mar. 1534 (Ausruf), Michel Will. See also Conclusion below.

memory an earlier occasion on which several priests, known to have had homosexual relationships, were hung in a cage from the Perlach and left to die—a gruesome punishment which circumvented the ban on secular authority judging clerics since technically no hand had been laid on them.[30]

These suspicions became the staple of insult on both sides of the religious divide. In 1523, when women remonstrated with a priest who was commending the virtues of the prayer Salve Regina, he referred to one as 'schone frau', a prostitute, and she retorted that the 'schone frauen' were all with the priests, and that the bishop was the greatest whore-master of them all.[31] The ambiguity of 'courtesan', meaning both papal courtier and courtesan, could be nicely turned against the clergy, and it was cleverly used in a pamphlet of 1523 against 'the courtesans and servants of the temple'.[32] By extension, Catholic women could be slandered as prostitutes or concubines: in another exchange, a woman who insulted a man as a 'Lutheran dog' (*lutherischer Hund*) was branded a 'priest's whore' (*Pfaffenhur*).[33]

However, if the 'old papists' could be branded as sexually delinquent, the new clergy did not become immune from sexual scandal simply by taking wives. Indeed, a reformed priest who had lived with a concubine did not automatically make her or himself respectable by getting married. Marriage in sixteenth-century Germany involved a series of stages, not just a ceremony in a church, and there were a number of points at which married clergy had to demand recognition of their married status. Of these, acceptance by a guild was one of the most critical, for guilds normally regarded priests' offspring as illegitimate and hence ineligible for admission. Guild membership could be transferred from wife to husband and was inherited by all a craftsman's legitimate children. Consequently, in the early days of Reformation influence in Augsburg, guilds were compelled to reach a view on clerical marriage because they had to adjudicate at least three issues: First, did the alleged 'marriage' confer those

[30] *Chroniken der deutschen Städte*, v, Zink, p. 67, 1409.
[31] StadtAA, Reichsstadt, Urg. 28 Oct. 1523 (testimony).
[32] *Von dem Pfründmarkt der Curtisanen und Tempelknechten* (n.p., 1521; *Die Flugschriften des frühen 16. Jahrhunderts*, Microfiche series, ed. H. J. Köhler (Zug, 1978-), no. 279/796); *Der Curtisan vnd pfrunde fresser*, [Augsburg? 1522].
[33] StadtAA, Reichsstadt, Urg. 5 Apr. 1526, Jörg Othmar.

guild rights which a man attained either at or through marriage? Second, was the alleged marriage in fact a sexual liaison, itself enough to disqualify someone from guild membership? Third, were children of the union to be counted as legitimate and therefore as potential members of the guild once they reached adulthood or got married? Because the guild's collective honour depended symbolically on the members' reputation for sexual probity and legitimate birth, the decision concerned the standing of the guild itself and the reputation of all its members.

In Augsburg, this issue was one of the submerged grievances in the serious riots of 1524: the daughter of Utz Richsner, weaver and evangelical pamphleteer, had married a priest who now wished to take up the membership of the weavers' guild which passed to him by virtue of the marriage. The weavers' guild rejected his request, a decision which was tantamount to classing Richsner's daughter as a *Pfaffenhur*. The question was discussed at the tavern meetings out of which the uprising of 1524 was planned,[34] and eventually the Council itself moved to defuse the issue. It authorized Anthoni Bimel, the guild master, to make a payment of 20 gulden to Richsner's son-in-law for a moratorium (*stilstannd*) in the matter.[35]

Gossip could be used to good effect against Protestant clergy too. One woman who did casual work as a prostitute let it be widely known that the prior of the Carmelites, a prominent evangelical, had promised to marry her;[36] and Urbanus Rhegius had to defend himself against gossip from Catholic sympathizers that he had had an adulterous affair.[37] But these proved passing embarrassments. In the early years, Protestants managed to capture the high ground of civic moralism, successfully representing themselves as the guardians of righteousness and the spokesmen of married morality.

---

[34] Ibid., Urg. 6 Oct. 1524, Lienhart Knoringer; Urg. 11 Sept. 1524, Hans Kag.

[35] Ibid., BMB 1524, fo. 77ʳ: '20 fl munz auch Anthonien Bimeln, so er von wegen ains Erbern Rats, des Richsners tochterman vmb stillstannd willen der Zunftgerechtigkait, bezalt, vnd ausgeben hat'.

[36] Ibid., Urg. 9 Aug. 1533, Elisabeth Schwarz.

[37] *Chroniken der deutschen Städte*, xxix, Preu, pp. 34–45, 1527.

The Institutionalization of the Reformation

The second important phase of the Reformation occurred as an open alignment of Council and Reformation gradually ensued in response to constant political pressure from the preachers. In Augsburg this process was accomplished in two stages between 1534 and 1537. Until 1534 the Council's policies on the issue of Reformation had been guided by the counsels of its civic secretary, the humanist and Catholic Conrad Peutinger. Sensitive to the need to retain the imperial favour which had furthered the city's trading interests and protected its independence, Peutinger favoured a 'middle way' which would keep the city loyal to the Emperor while not alienating the ever-growing group of evangelicals.[38] This strategy of temporizing, however, could not long contain the militant fervour of evangelicals who wanted a thoroughgoing urban Reformation. Annual elections afforded an important means of pressing for political change, and preachers such as Michael Keller drew the religious issue directly into politics. The success of the simple weaver Mang Seitz, and his rise to mayorship, must in part be attributed to his known Zwinglian leanings;[39] and though he too followed a moderate course, the tide of popular opinion was evident. A hesitant Reformation was introduced in 1534 in response to shrewd clerical lobbying and guild and popular pressure.[40]

The election of the Zwinglians Hans Welser, a patrician who had hardly any experience in politics, and Mang Seitz to the key positions of mayors in 1537 set the seal on the institutionalization of the Reformation. During 1537 the Reformation was fully introduced. Catholic churches were shut, several convents and monasteries were finally wound up, and—most importantly—the institutions of the Discipline Lords and Marriage Court were set up. These twin institutions, whose operations will be described in the next chapter, were typical of reformed upper German cities: Basle had introduced a Marriage Court in 1529,

---

[38] Lutz, *Conrad Peutinger*; Broadhead, 'Politics and Expediency'; Roth, *Augsburgs Reformationsgeschichte*.

[39] See Sieh-Burens, *Oligarchie, Konfession und Politik*, p. 135. Wolfgang Rehlinger, also mayor for the first time in 1534, was unusually young.

[40] See Broadhead, 'Politics and Expediency'; Wolfart, *Die Augsburger Reformation*.

Zurich in 1526, Strasbourg in 1529, and Ulm in 1531.[41] They enabled the Council to wrest authority over marriage and sexuality from the Church, and to exercise a far closer control over the household and the sexual comportment of those within it than had ever existed before. This was what the Zwinglian preachers had long been demanding; but the institutions were firmly civic and no church ban was envisaged—an exclusion to which they could scarcely object since their rise to respectability had been based on lauding the Council's duty and power to 'punish wickedness and do all that is necessary for good Pollicey and government'.[42]

More difficult to establish is whether this programme of moral regeneration was a guild demand, since Council records from these years are particularly sparse and guild records patchy at best in Augsburg. We might guess at its attraction from the accusation that during one of his visits to the city, the upper German Zwinglian reformer Amrosius Blarer attempted to stir up trouble by calling on guild masters to press for a church ban.[43] There is no evidence that he found any success in a town which now had its own Discipline Lords; but his assumption that it would be guildsmen who would look favourably on demands for moral discipline illustrates the strength of this constituency. The programme of the Discipline Ordinance certainly accorded with guild values.[44] The ideal of marriage which it put into practice, and the hierarchy of discipline within the household— subordination of children to parents, servants to masters, and women to men—was not new, but it was based on the old guild ideal of the household. The new supervision of sexual behaviour was merely more far-reaching than the guilds had even been able

---

[41] Köhler, *Zürcher Ehegericht und Genfer Konsistorium*. See also on Strasbourg, J. Abray, *The People's Reformation: Magistrates, Clergy and Commons 1500-1598* (London, 1985), pp. 188 f.; and on Esslingen, H. C. Rublack, 'Reformatorische Bewegung und städtische Kirchenpolitik', in I. Bátori (ed.), *Städtische Gesellschaft und Reformation* (Stuttgart, 1980), pp. 218 f. For a different view, see H. Schilling, '"History of Crime" or "History of Sin"? Some Reflections on the Social History of Early Modern Church Discipline', in E. Kouri and T. Scott (eds.), *Politics and Society in Reformation Europe* (London, 1987).

[42] Roth, *Augsburgs Reformationsgeschichte*, ii, Beilage I, p. 272, 10 Haupt Articul from the preachers, 1534, published 1535.

[43] Köhler, *Zürcher Ehegericht und Genfer Konsistorium*, ii. 318.

[44] For text, see *Ains Erbern Rats | der Stat Augspurg | Zucht vnd Pollicey Ordnung*, Augsburg, 1537.

to exercise over their members. Moreover, the six new Discipline Lords, three each from the Small Council and the Great Council, gave an important sphere of power to men who had not acted as embodiments of Council justice before. With its strong guild representation, it drew these political outsiders more closely into the ambit of power. They were paid for their attendance too, so that ordinary guildsmen as well as patricians could serve their term.[45]

However, the institutionalization of the Reformation did not result in a complete resolution of the tensions between guildsmen and patricians, rich and poor. The early 1540s seemed to herald a reprise of the conflicts of 1524 when Jakob Herbrot of the furriers' guild led a movement against the patriciate, newly enlarged in 1538-9 to replenish its diminishing bloodstock. Herbrot himself remains a somewhat shadowy figure. Execrated by his enemies as the offspring of the Devil, his talents were so prodigious as to warrant diabolic explanation.[46] The centre of his political power was the *Kaufleutestube*, an organization of merchants and members of various guilds in contradistinction to both the *Herrenstube* of the merchants and patriciate, and the exclusive guild of the merchants. This organization struck at the heart of the stable consensus among the élite, for it threatened to detach leading merchants and guildsmen from their alignment with the patriciate. Herbrot recruited enormous support amongst guildsfolk for this stand and for his forthright reformed evangelicalism, and by 1540 he had risen from political obscurity to become guildmaster and member of the Small Council. Just five years later Herbrot became mayor.[47]

[45] Köhler, *Zürcher Ehegericht und Genfer Konsistorium*, ii. 305-6. According to the 'Execution-Ordnung der Strafherren', they were to receive 6 kreuzer per sitting, 'Dieweil dises ambt mhue und vleiss ervordert, auch vil gelegen daran sein will.' Köhler provides a summary of this 'Execution Ordinance', now missing from the Augsburg archive.

[46] See the extraordinary contemporary attack on Herbrot, 'Panurgus haist ainer, der sich weder scheucht noch schempt, alle böse stück zu thun', printed in *Chroniken der deutschen Städte*, xxxii. 424-9.

[47] StadtAA, Reichsstadt, Ratsämterlisten 1536-48, computer print-out of this source from the Sonderforschungsbereich Z2, Tübingen; Sieh-Burens, *Oligarchie, Konfession und Politik*, esp. pp. 109-15; Hecker, 'Der Augsburger Bürgermeister Jakob Herbrot'; Strieder, *Zur Genesis des modernen Kapitalismus*. For examples of his own writing, evidencing his evangelical views at a time of great personal and civic crisis, see P. Hecker, 'Die Correspondenz der Stadt Augsburg mit Karl V im Ausgang des Schmalkaldischen Krieges', *ZHVS* 1 (1874), 257-309.

But if the guildsmen who supported him saw him as one of their own, they were mistaken. Herbrot was a successful long-distance trader in furs rather than an archetypal craftsman, and he apparently acted as a monopolistic capitalist, buying out many of the smaller leather-workers and creating his following at least partly through a system of clientage and indebtedness and through money dealings. This was indeed a quirky choice as the spokesperson of a guild-based populism. None the less, his political influence was considerable, and if not the architect he was one of the chief financial backers of the policy of resistance to the Emperor and alliance with the Schmalkaldic League of Protestant independent cities and principalities. After the war he was to be blamed by a Catholic patrician faction for having single-handedly wrought the city's destruction by following a reckless and godless policy.[48] Such an accusation, which must be partly understood as an attempt to lay blame exclusively on one individual and to minimize the involvement of other members of the élite, none the less illustrates the extent to which Herbrot's dominance was felt by the élite as a braggart interruption to a noble civic tradition. And while it is true that the pragmatist Herbrot did clever deals with some members of the patriciate, buying off Anton Fugger and even engaging in peace negotiations with the Emperor, the underlying contours of his politics were felt to be aggressively pro-guild and pro-reform. This was the policy which marked the final break with the conciliationist, middle-way policies of Peutinger and ushered in the triumph of the Protestant guild ethic.

Herbrot soon learned to work with parts of the élite, and the changes of the 1540s did not topple the old patrician–merchant alliance. None the less, the Councils of the late 1530s and 1540s were more closely identified with the guilds than ever before.[49] Guild domination seemed complete when in 1546 the Protestant city watched a convoy of several major Catholic merchants and patricians leave town a few months before the invasion of the Emperor's Catholic forces, the Council shrewdly winking at their

[48] See *Chroniken der deutschen Städte*, xxxii. 115–49. This memorial of 1548 was anonymous and called for the abolition of the guild government.

[49] For a different interpretation of this period, laying greater emphasis on continuities, see Sieh-Burens, *Oligarchie, Konfession und Politik*.

dereliction of civic duty in return for loans.[50] While the troops of the Protestant Schmalkaldic League massed beyond the town, and anxiety increased within it, the Council's proclamations were triumphalist: it exulted in how, 'through the industrious and steady proclamation of the Word of God together with well-taken ordinances everyone has been turned to God, and has turned away from all evil living'.[51] Yet the godly city had still not been perfected. The same ordinance, issued in the heady days before war broke out, went on to remark on 'the dangerous times, which are without doubt caused by our sins and transgression', and called for a renewed campaign against 'an excess of eating, drinking, gormandizing, disputing, beating, indiscipline, blasphemy, and vices of this kind amongst the common man'.[52] But now the vision might be realized, for now at last the city was purified of the ungodly, the Catholic 'big jacks' who did not share the proud guild vision of a network of allied and independent godly cities, but saw their world as bound instead by trade connections and banking interests to the wider universe of the Empire.[53]

To the Emperor Charles V too, the guildsmen of southern Germany constituted the section of the population which was to blame for both the Protestant heresy and the political disobedience which had culminated in the revolt of 1546 against him. In consequence, it was their political institutions which bore

[50] Roth, *Augsburgs Reformationsgeschichte*, iii. 362–3; Gasser, *Annales*, p. 1841; Hecker, 'Der Augsburger Bürgermeister Jakob Herbrot', p. 52.

[51] StadtAAugs, Reichsstadt, Schätze 16, fo. 113ᵛ, 26 June 1546: 'durch des emsig vleissig vnnd stette verkhundungen des wortt Gottis sampt gutt furgenumner ordnung menigclich zu Gott bekeret, vnd von allen ärgerlichen leben abgestannden sein'. Interestingly, this period also saw attempts to spread the Reformation (and Council jurisdiction) over monastic lands in the countryside: Roth, *Augsburgs Reformationsgeschichte*, iii. 398 f.

[52] 'auch die gefärlich Zeit vnnd leuft, die on Zwiffel von vnnser sunden vnd vbertrettung wegen vber vnns verhenngt werden . . .', 'ain solcher vberfluss von essen, trinnckhen, vberfullen, zanckhen, schlagen, vnzucht, gottslestern vnd dergleichen lasster bey dem gemainen Man . . .': StadtAA, Reichsstadt, Schätze 16, fo. 113ᵛ.

[53] When the city had been defeated, and Herbrot himself feared for his life, it was the attempts of the patrician Claudius Peutinger to tell the Council 'wie man sich mit der Straf und in ander Weg gegen dem gemainen Mann halten soll' that grated most: Peutinger's imputation that the Council and Herbrot had lost control of discipline in the community was an insult which struck at the core of the civic righteousness ideal. See Hecker, 'Die Correspondenz der Stadt Augsburg', pp. 298 f., letter of Herbrot to Anton Fugger, 3 Mar. 1547.

the brunt of his victorious wrath. In 1548, in the wake of the city's defeat by the Emperor and its occupation by imperial troops, the guilds were abolished, their political representation on the Council was revoked, and their proud guild-houses and trade insignia were crassly inventoried and sold by a civic official.[54] Only merchants and patricians were to hold important office, and Catholics were to receive far greater political representation than their numbers warranted.[55] The craft masters' domination of urban politics was, it would seem, over.

However, though the new constitution imposed by Charles V seemed to put the merchant-patrician élite firmly in the saddle, the need to maintain craft prosperity and nurture social cohesion in the town won out over sectarian revenge and, for a time, over militant re-Catholicization. The élite was itself split on the religious issue, and it needed in any case to reach some accommodation with the important stratum of craft masters if it was to secure stability and religious peace, let alone carry out the massive task of administering the minutiae of trade regulation which the new constitution entrusted to it. These desiderata influenced the ebb and flow of Council policy during the unsettled years of the later sixteenth century, as the flimsy compromise of Protestant and Catholic councillors tried to weather religious riots and looming revolt.[56] In 1552, during the revolt of the princes, Herbrot returned and a craft regime was established for a few brief months:[57] a return to the old guild constitution was a rallying cry which still had power to alarm. Yet despite the demise of the guilds, a guild-influenced policy can be discerned in its proclamations and economic regulations. Above all, essential continuities with the guild regime are evident in its ongoing surveillance of sexuality and marriage. The Councils of the late sixteenth and even early seventeenth centuries continued to make redactions of the Discipline Ordinance of 1537, which was the

[54] *Chroniken der deutschen Städte*, vii, P. H. Mair, pp. 149–58.
[55] Sieh-Burens, *Oligarchie, Konfession und Politik*, pp. 33 f.
[56] See Roth, *Augsburgs Reformationsgeschichte*, iv; H. Immenkötter, 'Kirche zwischen Reformation und Parität', in Gottlieb, *Geschichte der Stadt Augsburg*; P. Warmbrunn, *Zwei Konfessionen in einer Stadt: Das Zusammenleben von Katholiken und Protestanten in den paritätischen Reichsstädten Augsburg, Biberach, Ravensburg und Dinkelsbühl von 1548–1648* (Wiesbaden, 1983).
[57] Roth, *Augsburgs Reformationsgeschichte*, iv; Hecker, 'Der Augsburger Bürgermeister Jakob Herbrot', pp. 85 f.

corner-stone of Reformation guild-influenced moralism.[58] They persisted in hunting out adulterers, punishing prostitutes, and warning reprobates. Even a religiously fractured citizenry could unite around that powerful vision of an ordered, godly household.

The crucial years of the Reformation are the period with which this book is chiefly concerned. The 1530s and 1540s were the decades which established the politics of marriage and household and aligned them squarely with craft values. Protestant praise of work, marriage, and orderly relations was a powerful sacralization of values long held by guildsmen, and it was the more compelling because it preached the orderly world which sixteenth-century Augsburgers felt to be disintegrating beneath their feet. The fragile alliance that evangelicalism formed of craftsmen and their dependants could be yoked—if uneasily—in support of the politics of the merchant-patrician élite. This is precisely what happened in the later part of the century, and it explains the enduring authority of the guilds' policies on marriage, and their nostrums on economic regulation. The Marriage Court did not outlast the reintroduction of Catholicism after 1548, but the Discipline Lords continued to patrol the lives of Augsburgers. The policies on marriage, family, and the economy drawn up during those decades, and the socially stable alliances formed, were to outlive the Reformation in Augsburg itself, lasting through the years of Counter-Reformation and Jesuit influence.

THE HOUSEHOLD WORKSHOP

To understand the attraction of evangelical civic righteousness, and the ideology of the appropriate roles of men and women which accompanied it, we need to understand the work relations and household ideal in which it was grounded.[59] The concept

---

[58] See StadtAA, Reichsstadt, Fasz. Zuchtordnungen 1553 and 1618.

[59] On the Reformation as petty bourgeois ideology, see R. W. Scribner, 'Reorientating the Reformation', *History Workshop Journal*, 14 (1982), 2–22; T. Brady, *Ruling Class, Regime and Reformation at Strasbourg 1520–1555* (Leiden, 1978); C. Friedrichs, 'Capitalism, Mobility and Class Formation', *Past and Present*, 69 (1975), 24–49.

of order as articulated in the Discipline Ordinance of 1537 had at its core the threefold relations of subordination within the household: of wife to husband, children to parents, and servants to masters. These the Council represented as constitutive of the urban order. And when the Council came to define its own political legitimacy in the same document, it was to the image of fatherhood that it was drawn. Like a father, the Council watched over and disciplined its subject children. For the Council, social, economic, and political relations were always conceived of within the frame of the household. Underpinning its own legitimacy was an array of seemingly self-contained household units.[60]

Such a vision of the polity could also appear to be at one with the town's economic structure. In theory, and in terms of actual population numbers, Augsburg's economy was dominated by a myriad of small household-based workshops. In this, Augsburg was like every other early modern city. But, as elsewhere, wealth was not distributed evenly across these scattered enterprises. The capital accumulations for which Augsburg was famous were concentrated in the hands of a small number of merchant traders, closely linked with patricians, whose largely kinship-related firms also bore a loose resemblance to the family workshop.

But while the wealth of such merchants dominated the civic landscape, and tales of their doings in places as far away as Venezuela entered the proud civic mythology, the mass of Augsburgers depended on small, local, house-based enterprises. Numerically the weavers predominated: in 1536 their guild boasted 1,451 members, when the next most numerous guild, that of the smiths, counted a mere 341. Augsburg stood within the vast weaving triangle of southern Swabia, so that regionally too, textiles dominated the local economy.[61] The crises of the cotton- and fustian-weaving industries were to colour the city's poor-relief strategies and threaten its political stability throughout the century. As we saw, rumours in 1524 that 'the weavers were murmuring' were enough to set the city fathers' nerves on edge and cause them to call in reports from local spies.

[60] *Ains Erbern Rats | der Stat Augspurg | Zucht vnd Pollicey Ordnung.*
[61] C. P. Clasen, *Die Augsburger Weber: Leistungen und Krisen des Textilgewerbes um 1600* (Augsburg, 1981); id., 'Arm und Reich in Augsburg' and 'Armenfürsorge im 16. Jahrhundert', both in Gottlieb, *Geschichte der Stadt Augsburg*.

Alongside weavers were cloth-cutters, tailors, and patchers, who seem to have produced chiefly for the local market. Fish, meat, and food provisions, together with small retailing of all kinds, formed another important sector of the town's economy. Some, like the cattle market, involved long-distance trade as herds of cattle were brought into the town from places as far away as Hungary; others, like the provision of fresh herbs and vegetables, concerned only local peasants and market-women. In addition to the town's large population, there were numbers of travelling tradespeople who also required provisions, while the many local and imperial diets Augsburg hosted during the century attracted a regular crowd of visiting dignitaries. Metalworking trades occupied a sizeable number of workshops in Augsburg; and though the trade could not yet rival that of Nuremberg, its prestige was growing. There were tanning and leather workshops which made good use of the hides of the cattle brought in for slaughter, and fur industries which imported more exotic skins. The production of luxury goods became increasingly significant during the sixteenth century as the concentration of both lay and clerical wealth in the city and its distinguished visitors created a substantial market.[62] The armour, ceremonial swords, and muskets for which Augsburg became famous; the baroquely elaborate fine gold and silver cups, plates, and beakers; or the printed books, missals, and woodcuts which have all survived in today's museums and which bear the city's proud *Stadtpir* emblem, are only the most enduring evidence of this production of luxury goods.[63]

All of these industries were based on varieties of the household workshop, where work-place and dwelling-place were the same. Each unit was led by a master and his wife, and he co-ordinated the labour of apprentices, journeymen, and servants who lived

---

[62] H. Kellenbenz, 'Wirtschaftsleben der Blütezeit', in Gottlieb, *Geschichte der Stadt Augsburg*.

[63] A. von Reitzenstein, 'Die Plattner von Augsburg', in H. Rinn (ed.), *Augusta* (Augsburg, 1955); O. Gamber, 'Besteller, Erzeuger und Liefernormen des Augsburger Harnisches', in *Welt im Umbruch*, iii; J. F. Hayward, 'Blank- und Feuerwaffen und sonstige Arbeiten aus unedlen Metallen', in *Welt im Umbruch*, ii; B. Thomas, 'Augsburger Harnische und Stangenwaffen', in *Welt im Umbruch*, ii, and Katalog, pp. 487–537; H. Seling, *Die Kunst der Augsburger Goldschmiede 1529–1868: Meister, Marken, Werke*, 3 vols. (Munich, 1980); J. Bellot, 'Humanismus—Bildungswesen—Buchdruck und Verlagsgeschichte', in Gottlieb, *Geschichte der Stadt Augsburg*.

on the premises. The produce of the small work-force was sold either from a market-stand or from the workshop direct. At all stages of production, from the purchase of the raw materials through the use of tools to the sale of the product, the workshop master controlled the process and led his independent enterprise. The vision of the independent master running his small workshop was central to the self-understanding of early modern townsfolk.

Indeed, so vital was the maintenance of the independent craft household to civic stability that the Councils of the second half of the century invested an enormous measure of capital and policy-making in shoring up the fragile weavers' workshops against the predations of outwork and the putting-out system. By far the largest trade in the city, numbering nearly five times as many masters as the next largest group, the weavers might at any time form a political bloc which could threaten the stability of any civic government. At once the backbone of the town's economy in numerical terms, and the archetypal small-workshop trade, weaving was also economically most vulnerable; and after the halcyon days of the 1530s, when weavers were offered cut-price citizenship to move to the town, the trade was in almost continual crisis by the second half of the century. The vast project of maintaining the weaving industry as a set of independent master-headed workshops had to be accomplished by strict regulation of the number of looms each workshop might run, thus spreading the misery as evenly as possible. When even this failed to prevent weavers from succumbing to debt and pawning their production of cloth in advance, the city itself became a megacapitalist: the trade purchased the entire production of the city and sold the cloth direct, advancing loans for raw materials from the profits.[64] Such a stunningly extensive underwriting of a failing industry can only be understood in terms of the compelling social need to anchor the series of independent workshops, ensuring their masters' continuing 'independence' from the monopolies that were to emerge in other towns, such as in seventeenth-century Nördlingen, where one family dominated the entire weaving trade.[65] As this example of the

---

[64] Clasen, *Die Augsburger Weber*, esp. pp. 286–307.
[65] C. Friedrichs, *Urban Society in an Age of War: Nördlingen 1580–1720* (Princeton, 1979); and cf. also Wilhelm, *Augsburger Wandmalerei*, pp. 66–71, on the eclipse of the small artist's workshop by larger concerns.

weaving trade suggests, a large part of the power of the household ideal stemmed not only from its capacity to depict ordinary people's experience of domestic and work relations, but, paradoxically, from its ability to evoke a world which had passed away.

The Sexual Economy of the Household

We cannot understand the power of the independent household-workshop Utopia if we grasp it in terms of work relations alone. In the household-workshop ideal, a sexual economy mirrored the productive economy. Marriage was the boundary around which distinctions of status and function were organized. The master of the workshop, whose mark stamped its products, had to be a married man. A master who had never been married was a contradiction, a dishonourable figure whose leadership abilities and sexual competence were deeply suspect. As the watchmakers complained of the 'unmarried master' Georg Roll, whom they refused to recognize: if he were allowed to employ journeymen 'the young serving-folk would be strengthened in all naughtiness; good manly discipline would be suppressed and hindered'.[66] They were ultimately successful in having him booted out of town. Only the adult married masters could elect their guild representatives or vote for civic office-holders.[67] The connection between political capacity and marriage was taken so seriously that a late fifteenth-century Council decree had even stipulated that only those currently married could hold urban office—a provision that would have disqualified all widowers. The master's wife was thus guarantor of her husband's achieved adult masculinity: she proved his masterhood, while at the same time being responsible for the food, light, bedding, heat, water, and other domestic needs of the shop's small labour force. With his own self-contained business, the master incorporated within himself financial independence, public honour, sexual maturity, and political adulthood.

[66] StadtAA, Reichsstadt, HWA Uhrmacher 1544–1602, fos. 87 ff.; HWA Schmiede 1530–69, pp. 659 ff. (and note esp. pp. 675 ff., 695 ff.); RB 35, 1566, 1567; M. Bobinger, *Kunstuhrmacher in Alt-Augsburg* (Augsburg, 1969).

[67] Sieh-Burens, 'Die Augsburger Stadtverfassung um 1500', p. 129. Those in receipt of alms, and criminals and debtors were also excluded.

Set apart from the master and mistress were the journeymen, apprentices, and servants, who were all in theory unmarried. An apprentice would learn his chosen trade for a period, then work a mandatory number of years as a trained but still subordinate workman obedient to the instructions of the master, and then, finally, make his masterpiece, marry, and set up a workshop of his own. Until that day, however, sexual immaturity was a manifestation of the journeyman's subordination. For many, that day would never arrive: probably around as many as a fifth of Augsburg's population never married. Instead, the sexuality of young men was given an approved outlet in the brothel, which married men were supposed not to enter. Sexual intercourse did not confer authority there. In rowdy groups, young men could affirm their masculinity and their bonds with each other as they whiled away evenings in the town-run brothel. Young women's passage to sexual adulthood, by contrast, was far more perilous. Both servant-women sent to town to save for a dowry, and local daughters had to guard their honour against the errant eye of a master and keep the riotous attentions of the men of the house within bounds, while at the same time attracting the eligible

 marriage partner who alone could provide a route out of household servitude.[68]

Marriage was not only emblematic of the difference between authority and subordination; it was also the most important route for social advancement. Properly negotiated, it could enable a foreign, prospectless journeyman to become a substantial citizen-master. All he needed to do was to find a widow or guildsdaughter who could confer on him the trade rights and citizenship without which he could not hope to be a master. If the trade allowed outsiders to purchase those rights, a wife with means would help him to do so. And at marriage, sons and daughters both stood to inherit a share of property from their parents which would allow them to set up on their own. Those who married had clear material advantages over those who did not.

[68] See C. Klapisch-Zuber, 'Female Celibacy and Service in Florence in the Fifteenth Century', in her *Women, Family and Ritual in Renaissance Italy* (Chicago, 1985); ead., 'Women Servants in Florence during the Fourteenth and Fifteenth Centuries', in B. Hanawalt (ed.), *Women and Work in Preindustrial Europe* (Bloomington, 1986); M. Wiesner, *Working Women in Renaissance Germany* (New Brunswick, 1986), pp. 83–92.

· But this coherently articulated order of the household, where each individual knew his or her sexual and economic place, was disintegrating. Indeed, for the army of day-labourers, permanent servants, itinerants, and improvident craftsfolk it had probably never meshed with the reality of their lives. In the sixteenth century the twin pressures of economic growth and mid-century decline worked to place the household ideal under extreme stress. In the developing metalwork trades, where new skills were being refined and craftsmen like Desiderius Helmschmid were winning an international reputation for their large commission work,[69] several workshops might collaborate on a single order. As these enterprises grew, the smiths determined that the only limit to be placed on the number of journeymen and apprentices a master might keep was the capacity of the premises.[70] This was a clear attempt to forestall masters setting up a chain of separate, dependent workshops. The lack of controls on numbers, however, would certainly have encouraged the growth of large concerns more removed from the ideal of the compact, simple hierarchies of the household: Desiderius Helmschmid employed no fewer than four adult journeymen.[71] Some trades responded to restrictions on numbers by using other workshops to produce part of a product for them: the furniture-makers appear to have tried to use widows' workshops in this way.[72]

Figures drawn from the military muster, which listed every male citizen with a duty to bear arms for the defence of the city, and all adult journeymen who might be asked to fight, bear this out (see Table 1.1).[73] Workshop size was predominantly small, though these figures do not reveal numbers of women servants or children able to contribute to the labour of the household. Less than a quarter of the households listed employed any live-in adult males at all. Tiny enterprises, they managed on a very small male adult labour force. A number, of course, may well have employed

---

[69] Gamber, 'Besteller, Erzeuger und Liefernormen des Augsburger Harnisches'.

[70] StadtAA, Reichsstadt, HWO/B, 25 July 1549, fos. 94–248ᵛ (Schlosser etc.); 23 July 1549, fos. 239–241ᵛ (Kesselhamer, Kupferschmid, etc.).

[71] Ibid., Fasz. Musterregister I, 1520–39, Muster 1539.

[72] Ibid., HWA Kistler 1548–66, fos. 155 ff., 202 ff., 399 ff., petitions 30 July 1560, Thomas Heyss and Vorgeher and Verordneten responses, and Bartholome Weishaupt, 1556.

[73] On the muster as a source, see Kraus, *Das Militärwesen der Reichsstadt Augsburg*, pp. 74–137.

City and Reformation

TABLE 1.1. *Size of workshops 1539 (Muster List)*

| | No. of unmarried manservants | | | | | | Total no. of households |
	0	1	2	3	4	4 +	(inc. widows)
Quarter 1	426	129	84	21	7	4	671
Quarter 2	772	137	68	13	4	5	999
Quarter 3	531	125	54	17	7	—	734
Quarter 4	209	95	25	12	—	2	343
St Jacob (5)*	1282	63	9	5	—	—	1359
St Cross/ St George (6)	456	114	82	23	5	2	682
St Steffan (7)	212	46	13	4	2	1	278
TOTAL**	3888	709	335	95	25	14	5066
Comparable figures for 1619[a]	4488	902	407	96	22	19	

Note: *Since the detailed figures for this suburb are incomplete, I have made simple projections on the basis of the half of the suburb which does survive and the crude totals for the whole suburb.

**My totals differ slightly from the contemporary totals which are occasionally mathematically unreliable.

[a]B. Roeck, *Bäcker, Brot und Getreide in Augsburg*. (Sigmaringen, 1987), p. 166.

male workers, some of them married, who lived in their own households instead of under the master's roof. Of those who did employ and house unmarried male workers, most employed only one, but another sizeable group employed two; and a significant minority housed and employed three, four, or even more journeymen. Masons, brickmakers, and linen-bleachers tended to be the employers of the larger groups of adult male workers, housing five or even a dozen men in enterprises far removed from the cohesive family-workshop unit.[74] Precisely those trades which were growing in importance in the sixteenth century, the gunsmiths', watchmakers', locksmiths', and copper-smiths', were comparatively large employers: as figures for 1615 show, on average each was employing at least one or two adult journeymen at a time when the majority of masters employed no journeymen

[74] StadtAA, Reichsstadt, Fasz. Musterregister I, 1520–39, Muster 1539; and Clasen, 'Arm und Reich in Augsburg', p. 332.

at all.[75] The considerable number of houses with two, three, or more adult male employees would have been crowded enterprises, once we include the equal numbers of apprentices who might be expected to work in such establishments and maidservants and children.[76] Such large groupings may well have strained the conceptual boundaries of the household workshop, whose harmony relied on the blending of familial and work-related patterns of subordination. Young adult men in particular, with diminishing chances of independence, did not always happily subject themselves to the authority of another man. And the patterns of working relations which they reveal were to remain little changed into the next century: figures from 1619 show a broadly similar distribution of journeymen.

Crisis also undermined the workshop. The bleaker economic conditions of the later sixteenth century caused some masters to become immiserated, forcing them to pawn their produce in advance in return for the raw materials they could not afford, and thus falling into the cycle of economic dependence which was anathema to the guild ideal of the independent master. We know that many guildsmen in other cities were in fact day-labourers or workers in others' shops; and some guilds were dominated by these workers.[77] As the century wore on, population increased and growth stagnated; the Augsburg guilds reacted to crisis by trying to restrict the numbers who might

---

[75] Ibid.

[76] Clasen is able to give numbers of children and servants of both sexes for weavers in 1601: *Die Augsburger Weber*, pp. 51–67. He finds that 1,009 *Gesellen* and 143 weavers' sons were working in Augsburg weaver households in 1615, a number which fell to 755 by 1619, assuming the 1619 list is complete (pp. 105–10). By contrast, a total of 2,595 servants of both sexes were employed in 1601. If this ratio can be a rough guide, it would suggest that the total number of those employed was certainly more than double the number of *Gesellen*.

[77] Schulz, *Handwerksgesellen und Lohnarbeiter*, pp. 49 ff. It is hard to arrive at exact figures or calculate changes for Augsburg. Comparing guild numbers to total numbers of taxpayers does not reveal marked changes; but these figures must be used with caution because of differences in calculation methods. A 1475 survey of guildsmen listed 2,238 (excluding widows), while there were 4,485 taxpayers in the same year (Kiessling, *Bürgerliche Gesellschaft*, pp. 44 ff.). In 1540 there were 7,155 taxpayers, though there were 3,803 guild members in 1536 (Hartung, 'Die Belastung des augsburgischen Grosskapitals'). In 1610, 5,523 individuals listed a trade, just over 50% of the 10,285 taxpayers, while 30% gave no trade or were day-labourers (Clasen, 'Arm und Reich in Augsburg'). However, it is unclear how many of those who provided a trade to describe themselves in 1610 were in fact independent masters; some may have been working for others.

become masters and set up their own competitive workshops.
In an application of the theory that wealth was essentially finite
and space limited, guildsmen argued that the correct way to
proceed was by careful allocation of resources within the guild
and exclusion of those without. At some point during the century
most guilds imposed a complete temporary ban on new
admissions apart from the sons and sons-in-law of masters, and
increased the costs of entry to the trade or lengthened the
qualifying periods.[78] The consequence of all these measures—
as indeed of the growth of the prosperous larger concerns—was
to create a group of journeymen who either could not hope to
marry or else faced lifetimes as married, dependent
journeymen—a violation of the neat hierarchies the household
was meant to guarantee. Furthermore, for day-labourers and poor
guildsmen the income from a joint venture was no longer
sufficient to secure a family's livelihood.[79] Women had to
scrimp together some extra income outside the home—often in an
entirely different business—if the household were to feed itself. In
such uncertain times it was not surprising that it was marriage which
became the subject of debate for all these diffuse transformations.

Guilds

For the male masters the guilds were a powerful vehicle for
articulating unease, for affirming their corporate sense of identity,
and protecting their interests.[80] What is remarkable is the extent
to which work and sexuality were inseparable in the language
of honour that was axiomatic to that sense of corporate identity.
Honour, the greatest collective possession of a craft, could be
imperilled in two ways: through work and through sexual
comportment. Through its rules the craft sought to preserve its
status and the collective honour of its members. Beadles,

---

[78] See StadtAA, Reichsstadt, HWA Schmiede 1530–69, fo. 575ʳ; HWA
Uhrmacher 1544–1602, fos. 111ʳ ff.; provisions of trade-regulation in HWO/B
and HWO/C; and e.g. Clasen, *Die Augsburger Weber*, pp. 107 f., for applications
by weavers for trade rights—in 1556 some complained they had worked for 16,
20, or 22 years. See also R. Wissell, *Des alten Handwerks Recht und Gewohnheit*,
2 vols. (Berlin, 1929), i. 192 ff.

[79] Broadhead, 'Internal Politics', pp. 76–83.

[80] Wiesner, *Working Women*, pp. 32 ff., for a similar argument.

hangmen, knackers, and brothel-keepers were accounted dishonourable because of the nature of the work they undertook, and in some towns millers and even linen-weavers might join this list.[81] Contact with such dishonourables threatened to pollute the individual with the same dishonour. Thus, two young apprentices trembled for their honour because they had conversed too freely with the knacker's wife; while it took the entire guild of carpenters to repair the gallows, so that all the guild members would share the stain of dishonour brought about by contact with the instruments of hanging.[82] In such a world it was vital to celebrate the honour of the craft, and to insist on the dignity which practising the arts of the trade brought its members.

A system of behavioural supervision more stringent in its demands than even that of the pre-Reformation Council could be turned against masters who offended against collective honour by such misbehaviour as working with those who were reputed dishonourable, living with a woman out of wedlock, or deserting a wife. These reprobates, or *Störer* as they might be known—a word which captures the perception of their behaviour as a disruption of guild respectability in both its sexual and economic aspects—could be expelled from the guild. Their sexual misdealings were regarded no less seriously than infringements of work practices. But though guilds also disciplined their members for rowdy behaviour on guild premises and for swearing, other types of non-marital sexual episodes, such as visiting prostitutes or violence within marriage, do not seem to have aroused such intense concern. Only when a guild master's behaviour publicly shattered a marriage and injured the household workshop—when he committed one of the sexual 'public sins' as they were known—was the honour of the guild outraged, and hence the guild brought down its collective vengeance on the miscreant. For this reason too, guilds jealously guarded the

---

[81] F. Glenzdorf and F. Treichel, *Henker, Schinder und arme Sünder*, 2 vols. (Bad Münster, 1970); Wissell, *Des alten Handwerks Recht und Gewohnheit*, i. 67 f.; K. Lorenzen-Schmidt, 'Beleidigungen in schleswig-holsteinischen Städten im 16. Jahrhundert, soziale Norm und soziale Kontrolle in Städtegesellschaften', *Kieler Blätter zur Volkskunde*, 10 (1978), 5–20.

[82] StadtAA, Reichsstadt, HWA Sailer, 10 Apr. 1555; Schätze 63, Paul Hector Mair Memorialbuch, fo. 3ʳ.

requirement that all members should be of legitimate birth.[83] This provision was tested to the limit by the contrary pull of guild privilege if a guildswoman married a tradesman of non-legitimate birth and sought to gain his admission to the guild. Under pressure from the Council, guilds would often relent. More important than these occasional concessions, however, was the guild's public insistence, enshrined in its regulations, that all its members were of legitimate birth and thus as far removed from the taint of bastardy as possible. Because guild honour could only be competitively affirmed, each craft had to be watchful lest it decline into dishonour, becoming like the parody guild of pimps, whores, bastards, and vagabonds that popular fable loved to burlesque.

Honour had to be demonstrated and displayed in public form. Most guilds boasted guild-houses, in whose parlours weddings, dances, and other festivities might be staged or drinks shared. Their rooms were decorated with showy guild plate, memorial tablets depicting the coat of arms of each guild member, and guild insignia in ape-aristocratic fashion.[84] In a city church, a chapel or donated window of a corporate guild could rival even the showy munificence of a single patrician family.

What was this vision of honour and ideology of workshop which meant so much to tradesfolk; and which, as we have seen, continued to colour Council policies long after the abolition of the guilds? The masters' world-view was not a capitalist vision of limitlessly expanding wealth. Indeed, Weber's thesis that Protestantism embodied the spirit of capitalism profoundly misrepresents the nature of evangelicalism's appeal.[85] Urban Protestantism found its main support among the middling guildsfolk, and indeed, it has been argued that it was essentially a petty-bourgeois movement, giving voice not to the values of expansive entrepreneurial capitalism, but to an essentially conservative moralism based on the husbanding of limited resources. Guild policy and evangelical moralism alike were

---

[83] Wissell, *Des alten Handwerks Recht und Gewohnheit*, i. 248 f.; Wiesner, *Working Women*, pp. 152 f.

[84] See inventories of guild-houses, *Chroniken der deutschen Städte*, xxxii (Paul Hector Mair), pp. 149–58.

[85] Max Weber, *The Protestant Ethic and the Spirit of Capitalism*, trans. Talcott Parsons (New York, 1958).

rooted in the conviction that wealth was essentially limited. Civic policy therefore had to be a matter of conserving the existing wealth and superintending its division.[86] To the master tradesmen, Augsburg's ills were caused by the influx of outsiders who took houses, were improvident, sponged off poor-relief, and overmanned the trades. The cure for the city's plight was to restrict numbers settling in the town, prevent the poor and foreigners from marrying, and close the trades to outsiders.

This prescription could be compelling not only to the masters, but also to those men on the margins of masterhood: journeymen and apprentices who hoped to become masters themselves one day, either by somehow scrounging together the substantial sum of money demanded for the mastership fees or by a lucky marriage to a tradesdaughter or widow. Marriage functioned as an integrative social fantasy: always a potential groom, a non-master could be incorporated into a trade-based vision of defence of privilege and the household workshop because he too might one day marry a widow. And where journeymen's own associations did establish a robust identity of their own, sometimes even leading to strikes against their employers (witness the furriers in the fifteenth century at Strasbourg),[87] these forms of political organization could be vitiated by their perceived stage within the life cycle. Journeymen's associations were often loosely attached to guild premises, and journeymen were subject to guild discipline by their masters. As individuals, journeymen were in theory unmarried and pre-adult.[88] Marriage marked the threshold over which they would step into maturity. Consequently, the grievances of journeymen and apprentices could seem to relate to their position in the life cycle, their problems to be resolved individually as each man came of age and, at his wedding, crossed the divide which symbolically separated the feast-tables of the masters from those of his old mates. Marriage thus served to mask the relations of ongoing

---

[86] e.g. StadtAA, Reichsstadt, Schätze 16, fo. 143ᵛ, 26 Aug. 1562.

[87] G. Strauss, *Manifestations of Discontent on the Eve of the Reformation* (Indiana, 1971), pp. 130 ff.; and see W. Reininghaus, 'Frühformen der Gesellengilden in Augsburg im 14. Jahrhundert', *ZHVS* 77 (1983), 68–89, esp. p. 87 for *Aufstand* of journeymen in Augsburg in 1426.

[88] Even in fourteenth-century Augsburg, however, there were occasional married journeymen: Reininghaus, 'Frühformen der Gesellengilden', p. 83.

structural difference between masters and non-masters by making
them appear to be issues of social age.

While the ideology of the household workshop effectively
seemed to subsume—and to some degree silence—the interests
of working non-masters, it similarly alienated women's interests.
Women were not 'masters' in the full sense, even as widows, and
they neither voted nor were able to be guild masters in the
pre-1548 constitution (or trade officers thereafter). This guild
conception of household was thus not only exclusive in class
terms. It was a male vision, enunciated and developed by men,
whose interests could be—and sometimes were—at odds with
those of the women of the trade. Yet, like journeymen, women
too could have a stake in the household system which protected
the trade status of a tradesdaughter or widow, and allowed even
a servant-woman to long for the good marriage which would
ultimately make her a mistress. In the next section we shall discuss
how this ideology of the workshop was a male ideology, grounded
in a sexual division of labour which was held to be 'natural'.
This division of labour within the household simultaneously created
and reinforced the role felt appropriate to women.

Craft, Gender, and Labour

Central to the ideal of the household workshop was the concept
of marriage as a working as well as a sexual partnership. Just as
the sexual roles of men and women were complementary and
different, so too the working roles of men and women in turn
distinguished and created sexual difference. The ideology of the
craft household powerfully represented the interests of husband
and wife as harmonious. The good of the enterprise was the aim
of both, and man and wife co-operated in the processes of
production. This is a compelling Utopia of the convergence of
male and female labour. Its attraction lives on in the pages of Alice
Clark's *Working Life of Women in the Seventeenth Century*
(1919), for whom women's incorporation in the labours of the
workshop freed them from household drudgery, ennobling them
through the dignity of productive work.[89] For historians of the

---

[89] A. Clark, *Working Life of Women in the Seventeenth Century* (London, 1919;
2nd edn. with introduction by M. Chaytor and J. Lewis, London, 1982). See also M.
Howell, *Women, Production and Patriarchy in Late Medieval Cities* (Chicago, 1986).

nineteenth century the pre-industrial epoch can seem to represent an Eden which did not yet know the distinctions between public and private, man's sphere and woman's realm. Because there was no division between work-place and dwelling-place, child care could seem to be a shared responsibility of men and women, barely distinguishable from the supervision of the other, larger workshop hands.

This vision was firmly articulated in Council rhetoric. When the Council cautioned misbehaving couples who were not living peaceably together, it would instruct them to 'work faithfully with each other', or warn a wife that she should 'help her husband with his sustenance'.[90] Sustenance is an evocative word, resonant both with the concept of financial support and that of feeding and nourishment. As such it straddles the divide between labour within the workshop and what we might term housework—the labour of cooking, cleaning, and caring for a workshop labour force.[91] The primacy of its emphasis on feeding serves to enhance the importance of the woman's contribution rather than seeing it as not real work in the genuine sense. And just as husband and wife were thought to work together, so also in the craft milieu their property was usually jointly owned. In contradistinction to the marriages of rich merchants and patricians, where prospective husband and wife carefully reserved their separate inheritances and specified dowry, matching, and morning gifts so that the distinct claims of each on the estate would be clear, guildsfolk who married for the first time simply 'put their goods together', as the civic secretary Franz Kötzler described their practice.[92] In all property deals, whether of guildsmen or patricians, the wife would customarily be named as co-vendor or co-purchaser, an apparent expression of the co-operative venture of the household. In marriage, it would seem, the craft world gave material expression to the gospel dictum that husband and wife were one flesh, one indivisible unity.[93]

---

[90] e.g. StadtAA, Reichsstadt, Prot. der Zuchtherren V, fo. 78, 12 July 1544; IV, fo. 20, 30 Dec. 1542; III, fo. 139, 5 July 1542.

[91] L. Roper, 'Housework and Livelihood: Towards the *Alltagsgeschichte* of Women', *German History*, 2 (1985), 3–9.

[92] StadtAA, Reichsstadt, Fasz. Sammlung von Ordnungen, Statuten und Privilegien.

[93] For further detail on property relations in Augsburg, see my 'Gender and Property in Sixteenth Century Augsburg', forthcoming.

But this language was a partial description at best. Beneath the ideology of labour which did not distinguish between men's and women's work was another, relentlessly gendered, conception of labour. Within the household there were divisions of duty not only by rank and marital status, but by sex. These distinctions were anchored and expressed by the different work-lives of men and women.

The most obvious difference between men's and women's labour was women's greater responsibility for domestic labour and child care. So 'naturally' was child care considered to be part of a woman's domain that it is hardly mentioned in our sources and barely even surfaces in descriptions of the role proper to women, who were persistently addressed as wives rather than mothers. The little we can discover about child care suggests that it was difficult to distinguish from co-ordination of the labour forces of the household: as soon as possible the young child went on errands or took part in work processes within the household. Child care, however, as distinct from domestic labour and the generalized duties of wifehood, had yet to develop its own discourses in civic culture.[94]

We can, however, identify the importance of domestic tasks in the running of the workshop. One way of doing so is to examine the masons' trade, which had a very different organization from most crafts. Unlike the other firmly workshop-based trades, masons were expected to live in their own married households and work daily with a gang and master. Consequently, the difference between their pay and that of a live-in journeyman can suggest the amount a master saved by having his workers reside in the shop. It has been established that a mason would have earned an annual maximum of about 21 gulden in 1475; yet journeymen at the same period stood to earn only between 3 and 9 gulden a year. Some of the differential is accounted for by the free board and lodging which the journeyman received; some, by the fact that wage-rates did not have to suffice for a family but only for an individual. The master's wife and servants provided the domestic services thought necessary for a male worker, part of his unpaid 'real wage'. Masons' ordinances, too,

---

[94] L. Roper, 'Work, Marriage and Sexuality: Women in Reformation Augsburg', Ph.D. thesis (London, 1985), pp. 38 ff.

allow us to make women's invisible economic contribution yet clearer. Civic wage-rates from 1516 show that, in the summer, masons were to be paid 32 pence, journeymen masons with trade rights, 24 pence, and others, 18 pence. But if the master provided food for his workers, he could subtract 8, 6, and 4 pence for each category of worker—between a quarter and a third of their wages. Since meat cost only 3 pence per pound, a canny master should have made a profit—a saving achieved through the invisible labour of the women who provided the food.[95]

Such labour was also affected by the gradual transformations within the economy. A workshop with up to ten workers (permitted by the carpenters), or with as many workers as the premises could hold—the only restriction placed on numbers by the smiths—entailed different work for women.[96] As workshops grew in size and more journeymen and apprentices lived in the shop, so also the volume of work involved in washing, cooking, heating, and lighting for these labourers increased; while the amount of time available for involvement in production processes decreased. Yet economic change did not invariably confine women to domestic labour: contrary developments increased the numbers of married workers who did not have workshops of their own, which meant that there were also numbers of households where the menfolk earned only journeymen's wages but had somehow to nourish a family.[97] Women had to stretch the household income of these families by picking up odd bits of work, labour which was no longer contained within a joint household enterprise. For instance, in the smiths' trade, no fewer

---

[95] J. Hartung, 'Die Augsburger Zuschlagsteuer von Jahre 1475: Ein Beitrag zur Geschichte des städtischen Steuerwesens sowie der socialen und Einkommensverhältnisse am Ausgang des Mittelalters', *Schmollers Jahrbuch*, 19 (1895), 95-136; StadtAA, Reichsstadt, HWO/A, fo. 72ᵛ (wage-rates); fo. 71ᵛ (price of meat). See also for wages and prices, M. Elsas, *Umriss einer Geschichte der Preise und Löhne in Deutschland vom ausgehenden Mittelalter bis zum Beginn des neunzehnten Jahrhunderts*, 2 vols. (Leiden, 1936); U. Dirlmeier, *Untersuchungen zu Einkommensverhältnissen und Lebenshaltungskosten in oberdeutschen Städten des Spätmittelalters* (Heidelberg, 1978); Piper, *Der Stadtplan*, esp. pp. 61-71.

[96] StadtAA, Reichsstadt, HWO/B, fos. 49ᵛ ff. (carpenters); HWO/B, 23 July 1549, fos. 239ʳ-241ᵛ; 25 July 1549, fos. 294-248ᵛ (smiths); and six 'knecht' allowed by furriers, HWO/A, fo. 33ᵛ, St. Kath. Abend, 1505.

[97] Schulz, *Handwerksgesellen und Lohnarbeiter*; Wiesner, *Working Women*, pp. 13 f.; S. Karant Nunn, *Zwickau in Transition, 1500-1547: The Reformation as an Agent of Change* (Columbus, 1987), pp. 69 f.

than nineteen men who married between 1563 and 1569 were
described as smiths, but their names do not appear in the trade's
own list of those who had trade rights and therefore master
status.[98] Working for other masters, they and their wives would
have needed extra income to support themselves on a
journeyman's wage.

Men and women were trained from youth for different kinds
of work. While the young apprentice or journeyman learnt the
secrets of the trade he would expect to practise for the rest of
his life, young women mostly either worked as servants or
remained in the household, where what training they had might
only remotely relate to the work of the enterprise they joined
on marriage. Their work lacked the definition of that of their
brothers. As the trade restrictions on the labour of 'servants' in
the lace-making and purse-making trades make plain, a servant's
work could often stretch to include labour in the production
processes.[99] A cheaper, more flexible source of labour than that
of a male, she could be trained to help out where needed. But
her skills remained auxiliary. At the end of her indentured term
she had no recognized induction in the arts of a trade, and her
next post would most likely be with a master of a different craft
altogether. And should there be an over-supply of labour in a
trade, the overseers of that craft would seek to stem male
disgruntlement by trading off female work against male privilege.
Involved in a dispute which raged across the whole of southern
Germany, the belt-makers' trade tried to counteract the tendency
of masters to use cheap and flexible servant-women in place of
yet more journeymen by fining any master who set 'one or more
maids to do the work which it is fitting for journeymen to
do'.[100] Ring-makers in Nuremberg, too, tried to prevent maids
working in their trade.[101] But these trades acted by safeguarding
the young men whose journeymen's organization was loosely
attached to the guild's own. True to its nature as a union of male
interests, it protected its own future constituency against the

[98] StadtAA, Reichsstadt, Schätze 46b, Schmiedezunftbuch, entries for
1532–69 compared with Hochzeitsprotokolle I, 1563–69.

[99] Ibid., HWO/B, 5 June 1549, fos. 174 ff. (Nestler); 170 ff. (Seckler).

[100] Ibid., HWO/C, 1558, fo. 234; Schulz, *Handwerksgesellen und
Lohnarbeiter.*

[101] Wiesner, *Working Women*, pp. 166 f.

unorganized serving-women, who had no institution to voice their disparate interests. Where a guild would recognize an obligation to women—as the butchers' guild did when it conceded the right to make sausages to guild widows; or when the hat-makers or needleworkers reserved certain tasks to those women with trade rights—it made distinctions among women.[102] But these concessions were made solely on the basis of the women's relationship to male guild members. Even then, trades would often prefer the privileges of male foreign workers to those of guildsdaughters: a tradesdaughter's earnings did not rival those of a journeyman, and for her there was no assured progression from working as a subordinate to working as a skilled craftsman.

Beneath the façade of the gender-neutral conception of work as 'sustenance', there were in reality careful divisions of task and skill within workshops which served to underline women's adjunctive role within production.[103] Amongst the bakers, women set out the loaves. Butchers' wives boiled tripe and bones; fishwives sold from the market-stalls by the Perlach tower; and weavers' wives were among the vast army of spinners who worked in and around Augsburg to keep the weavers' looms busy.[104] Clearly, in a bustling workshop the niceties of such distinctions might not always be honoured. More important,

[102] StadtAA, Reichsstadt, HWO/B, 24 Dec. 1549, fos. 372 ff. (Metzger); HWO/C, 5 June 1549, fos. 249 ff. (Nadler).

[103] For different interpretations from that adopted here of women's work in this period, see, amongst others, Wiesner, *Working Women*; Howell, *Women, Production and Patriarchy*; M. Wensky, *Die Stellung der Frau in der stadtkölnischen Wirtschaft im Spätmittelalter* (Vienna, 1980); K. Wesoly, 'Der weibliche Bevölkerungsanteil in spätmittelalterlichen und frühneuzeitlichen Städten und die Betätigung von Frauen in zünftigen Handwerk (insbesondere am Mittel- und Oberrhein)', *Zeitschrift für Geschichte des Oberrheins*, 128 (1980), 69–117; J. Quaetert, 'The Shaping of Women's Work in Manufacturing Guilds, Households, and the State in Central Europe 1648–1870', *American Historical Review*, 90/5 (1985), 1122–48; H. Wunder, 'Zur Stellung der Frau im Arbeitsleben und in der Gesellschaft des 15.–18. Jahrhunderts', *Geschichtsdidaktik*, 3 (1981), 239–52.

[104] StadtAA, Reichsstadt, HWA Metzger 1417–1554, fos. 202 f.; 251 f., 11 Oct. 1557; Urg. 2 May 1527, Hans Geyger (wife described as making and selling sausage); Prot. der Dreizehn VI, fo. 140ʳ, 3 May 1541 (women selling fish); and for more detail, Roper, 'Work, Marriage and Sexuality'; Clasen, *Die Augsburger Weber*. For women's separate tasks in mining, see C. Vanja, 'Bergarbeiterinnen: Zur Geschichte der Frauenarbeit im Bergbau, Hütten- und Salinenwesen seit dem späten Mittelalter, I: Spätes Mittelalter und frühe Neuzeit', *Der Anschnitt*, 39 (1987), 2–15.

however, was the belief that there were certain tasks which 'it is not fitting for women to do', and the fiction that women were not inducted into the secrets of the trade. These were powerful ways of marking out the differences between women and men. One weaver complained that his wife held up his weaving because she did not keep up the pace finishing off the cloths. This was women's work, and it did not occur to him or to the Council members to whom he told this story that he should have turned his hand to cloth-finishing himself.[105] Indeed, the claim that women did not know and could not learn the mysterious arts of a trade could be a mark of a trade's honour and exclusiveness. So the goldsmiths averred with self-conscious pride that 'women understand nothing of the goldsmiths' work, and do not know when jewels, gold or silver are good and true, for the goldsmiths' craft is not considered to be the least but the greatest craft', explicitly tying the trade's honour to its exclusion of womenfolk.[106]

Indeed, it could even be argued that it was amongst the metal trades, where there were no limitations on the numbers of apprentices and journeymen who might be taken on, that gender differentials and the exclusion of women went furthest.[107] Women servants were less likely to have to double as extra metalworkers, while, conversely, the larger numbers of household members to be cared for increased the domestic tasks of the womenfolk. The metal trades stipulated some of the longest apprenticeships and qualifying work-periods of any trade: provisions which both increased the male monopoly on an occult, intricate skill and guaranteed a large dependent labour force on which the masters could draw. As the most prestigious group of trades within Augsburg, gradually surpassing even the wealthy salt-merchants, they were also the most masculine.[108]

---

[105] StadtAA, Reichsstadt, Urg. 17 Apr. 1541, Simon Streib (stored 1542).

[106] 'frawen, versteen sich nichtz auf der goldschmid arbait. wissen auch nit, wan Edelstain gold oder Silber guet vnd gerecht sei, dan das goldschmids handtwerckh, nit das geringst sonder das maist geachtet wurdt': ibid., Goldschmiede 1532–80, 1550.

[107] For an interpretation similarly focusing on the differences between trades, see M. Berg, 'Women's Work, Mechanisation and the Early Phases of Industrialisation in England', in P. Joyce (ed.), *The Historical Meanings of Work* (Cambridge, 1987). I am grateful to her for the opportunity to read this in draft.

[108] StadtAA, Reichsstadt, HWO/B, 15 Mar. 1550, fos. 311 ff.; 23 July 1549, fos. 239 ff.; 2 Dec. 1549, fos. 294 ff.; HWO/C fos. 412 ff.

Brewing, by contrast, which had originally been a skill associated with women, was less easy to characterize as a male secret. Training was brief, but by the second half of the century this was counterbalanced by the very hefty admission fee: a full 21 gulden.[109] Male barber-surgeons defended their monopoly on healing, traditionally a woman's province, by linking their capacity to formal qualifications. Maria Marquart spoke of 'the gift and skill which has been given to me by God', and stressed her experience of thirty-three years; Barbara Karg wrote of the sixty years' experience in healing sick people which she and her mother had between them, using the skill which she 'had received from God the Almighty and the instruction of a learned medico'.[110] The claim that their wisdom had a divine source was an attempt to invoke a higher authority than a human trade organization in a craft still unsure of success in treating patients. But it was also a measure of their exclusion from the trade, the lack of recognition of their informal 'experience', and the unavailability to them of the powerful arguments from guild precedent, the mode of argumentation which male petitioners most commonly employed.

Unlike Cologne, which, remarkably, had three women's guilds for silk-makers, yarn-makers, and gold-spinners, Augsburg had no women's guilds and few trades where women could undertake a recognized training or apprenticeship.[111] In only a few months a woman might qualify as a folder of cloth in the city mangle; or she could learn to sew, an accomplishment she could use in the household or to earn extra cash for outside orders.[112] All these industries, however, were hand-to-mouth expedients— none involved the establishment of a workshop or the long-term employment of others. Consequently, women's special skills lacked the recognition which men's training brought to their labour. Adjunctive skills, quickly learnt and readily adaptable to other trades, women's abilities could seem to be natural feminine

[109] Ibid., HWO/B, 26 Mar. 1549, fos. 93 ff.
[110] Ibid., HWA Bader und Barbiere 1535–80, 20 Oct. 1571; before 17 July 1571 and reply 17 July 1571.
[111] Howell, *Women, Production and Patriarchy*; Wensky, *Die Stellung der Frau in der Stadtkölnischen Wirtschaft*.
[112] StadtAA, Reichsstadt, HWO/B, 31 Jan. 1549, fo. 13ʳ, Zemenleger-inordnung; Urg. 14 Aug. 1533, Magdalena Bauman, payment for apprenticeship in sewing.

traits rather than carefully acquired knowledge. So the Council in Augsburg, as in Munich, Frankfurt, Memmingen, and Nuremberg, appointed respectably married women to carry out the task of supervising midwives, a duty the Augsburg Council considered such matrons as naturally qualified to undertake without special training, despite their protests to the contrary.[113] Similarly, women were responsible in most trades for the work of buying and selling, skills which were largely trade-neutral.[114]

Because women were not able to become guild masters in their own right but entered into the status of mistress of a workshop only through marriage to a craftmaster, their economic opportunities were always circumscribed within a position of subordination. Though they could trade separately from their husbands and could work outside the household, these forms of work were small-scale. A woman needed a husband to secure comfortable economic survival. To an extent this need was mirrored by the master's need of a wife to help run the workshop and qualify him as a master, but for the man, marriage brought authority, recognition, and independence. As the wife of a well-off master a woman might gain some 'high labour status', but this was entirely dependent on her relationship with him.[115]

At every point, women's work was affected by the guild organization which neither protected their interests nor represented them. The jealous tentacles of guild regulation stretched over most enterprises a woman might undertake, and if she were thought to be running her own business or, worse, taking custom from established trade masters, she was ordered to desist. Hans Vogel Blind's wife, who sold old clothes, found herself in hot water with the tailors' guild when she successfully started to patch the clothes, selling reconditioned garments at cheap prices. Even though her husband was blind and could not earn enough as a master craftsman to support the household, the guild would not relent: protection of the guild monopoly over a skill which might otherwise have faced stiff competition from

[113] Ibid., RB 19./II, 17 Oct. 1545, fo. 39ʳ; 9 Dec. 1545, fo. 65ᵛ: the wives of Anthoni Welser and Ambrosi Jung asked to be excused since they considered themselves 'too ignorant', but the Council refused this request. See also Wiesner, *Working Women*, pp. 55 ff.

[114] Ibid. 111–48.

[115] For a different view, see Howell, *Women, Production and Patriarchy*.

needle-wise women was too important to allow a charitable precedent.[116]

As a result, non-widowed women found most economic possibility in trades where guild control was weakest. Tent-making, silk-weaving, and veil-making were among the newer trades which lacked a trade structure and therefore provided opportunities for women. But as their economic importance grew, so they fell under the jealous eye of the trades; and under the guise of regulation, male control was instituted over each of these industries during the course of the sixteenth century. In its wake, women were gradually edged out.[117] Such moves were animated not only by their ostensible justification—the need for quality control over products which would bear the city's mark—but by the need of settled masters with orderly households to be given a secure share of the market. This was an argument which once again rendered invisible women's separate economic needs outside the household unit.

Widowhood

Even as a widow, a woman did not escape the constraints of the guild system. Although on widowhood a woman inherited her husband's guild rights and might lead a workshop enterprise, she was still not able to elect her guild representatives, and her 'right' to run the business was subject to restriction. Some widows overcame these disabilities and increased the fortunes left to them: Appollonia Mair, for instance, was so successful as a tanner that she petitioned the Council for a central trade shop. Nor was she merely keeping the business on until her son came of age: in its counter-supplication, the trade mentioned that Mair's son already had one of the sought-after shops. Between 1535 and 1539 the civic glazier was a woman, and between 1544 and 1549 the 'Agstin', successor to a man of the same name, appears in the civic accounts as the city cooper.[118]

[116] StadtAA, Reichsstadt, HWO/A, fos. 108ʳ-ᵛ; and see also RB 19, fo. 32ʳ, 24 Feb. 1545.

[117] Clasen, *Die Augsburger Weber*, pp. 130-3, 323 ff.

[118] StadtAA, Reichsstadt, HWA Lederer 1548-1654, 1557, Appollonia Mair; BMB lists under 'Gemain Ausgaben' payments in 1544 to Stadthafnerin; 1533-9, the suffix '-in' denotes the female form of a name. However, women's name-forms alone provide no clue as to their marital status or involvement in trade: the same

However, both economic factors and explicit regulation militated against widows. Goldsmiths refused point-blank to permit women to continue their husbands' workshops, a stipulation which they justified by appeal to the craft's prestige.[119] Other trades reserved particular types of work for widows, but these were usually the least remunerative: so the butchers allowed widows a monopoly on sausage-making, a poorly paid task which left them reliant on male butchers for their raw materials. Even this was too near an approximation to an independent business. In 1548 the Council agreed that in future women could sell only from their houses and not from the lucrative benches in the meat market in the centre of town. Women seem to have been entirely excluded from the long-distance trade in meat, the most profitable sector of the trade.[120]

Even in those trades where guild regulation did not restrict widows' work, few widows appear to have been able to continue their husbands' enterprises. In Augsburg, as in most early modern German towns, households headed by women accounted for between 10 and 20 per cent of all households.[121] Yet a list of guildsfolk drawn up in 1475, incomplete though it is, reveals that almost no guild approached this figure, while the total proportion of widows in guilds was a mere 5 per cent.[122] Even this handful of widows may have been noted as possessing trade rights rather than practising the trade. And for the millers and painters, the only crafts where it is possible to reconstruct how many widows

woman may be variously called Anna Matheisin, Hans Matheisin, Hans Matheisin wittib (Hans Matheis's widow), die Matheisin Metzgerin, Anna Matheisin Metzgerin ('butcheress'), and so forth (examples from StadtAA, Reichsstadt, HWA Metzger 1417–1554, petitions 1550–3). The form 'Anna Matheisin Metzgerin' does not prove that a woman was running a workshop; it may merely indicate that the woman's husband was a butcher. Here, however, we know from indications in the sources that the women were widows and were receiving commissions from the Council. Stadtglaserin; 1540–9, Stadtschefflerin.

[119] StadtAA, Reichsstadt, HWA Goldschmiede 1532–80, 1567.

[120] Ibid., Schätze 16, fo 57', 20 Oct. 1539; RB 21/II, fo. 79', 4 Oct. 1548; and see Roper, 'Work, Marriage and Sexuality', pp. 63 ff.

[121] For Augsburg, I am grateful for the information supplied by Olaf Mörke, Sonderforschungsbereich Z2, on the basis of analysis of the Augsburg tax-books. See K. Lorenzen-Schmidt, 'Zur Stellung der Frauen in der frühneuzeitlichen Städtegesellschaft Schleswigs und Holsteins', *Archiv für Kulturgeschichte*, 63 (1982), 317–99; the figures in Wesoly, 'Der weibliche Bevölkerungsanteil', range from 16% to 25%.

[122] Roper, 'Work, Marriage and Sexuality', p. 66.

TABLE 1.2. *Widows and workshops 1539*

	Widows	Widows with unmarried male workers	Unmarried male workers	Male citizens	Non-citizens
Quarter 1	121	13	424	550	19
Quarter 2	217	1	359	782	14
Quarter 3	89	5	312	645	19
Quarter 4	37	3	201	306	9
St Jacob (5)	185	1	96	1174	20
St Cross/ St George (6)	75	9	380	607	—
St Steffan (7)	49	2	104	229	—
TOTAL	773	34	1876	4293	81

continued their dead husbands' businesses, an interesting pattern emerges. Those whose husbands were most wealthy tended to be most successful, while the poorer widows seem to have succumbed to the demands of creditors and the difficulties of being legally obliged to employ a journeyman in the workshop. Their male master counterparts could dispense with this drain on their income when times were bad.[123]

This pattern is borne out by an examination of the military muster of 1539 (see Table 1.2). Widows made up 10 per cent of those included in the muster, but they were scattered very unevenly across the town. Quarter 2 contained the highest proportion of windows—16 per cent—and about a third of the overall total. This area, criss-crossed by many canals and dominated by small household workshops, was extremely mixed, containing some of the city's poorest inhabitants as well as some rich citizens. Area 5, St Jacob's suburb, was the largest in terms of soldiers and housed a fair number of widows. But the small number of unmarried sons and journeymen indicates that few, if any, of these widows could have been employing the mandatory journeymen and continuing workshops. Hardly any widows were to be found in the parishes of St George and St Stephan, regions populated by craftsfolk and small weavers in particular. As a group then, few widows could have been

[123] Ibid. 67 ff; Wilhelm, *Augsburger Wandmalerei.*

continuing workshops. From studies of other early modern towns we know that widows were over-represented in the poorer sections of the population.[124] Only a total of thirty-four women (mostly widows) were listed as employing menservants; and several of these were patrician women rather than tradeswomen. Since all trades demanded that at least one journeyman was needed to continue a workshop, it follows that only a handful of widows—perhaps thirty at most in a city of some 30,000 inhabitants and nearly 4,000 guildsmen in 1536—could actually have been continuing husbands' workshops. Some widows may have continued workshops with the aid of their sons, but in that case the son would normally have been liable to military duties in the same informal way as the menservants, and would therefore appear in the muster. Thus, the much-vaunted right to continue a workshop was, it would seem, a theoretical privilege rather than a provision which was of use to the majority of widows.[125] Its primary function lay as part of a marriage strategy, protecting the workshop until the widow remarried and transferred her guild and citizenship rights to a new husband.

Widows remained as subject as other women to the nexus of sexual status and gender. In a trade organization where only a limited number of individuals might reach master status, protecting widows' rights to work so that they need not be forced into remarriage could, like the rights of masters' daughters and servants, be represented as a curtailment of young men's opportunities to enter the guild. Such arguments lay close to the surface of many guild justifications of their conduct towards widows. So, when she petitioned the goldsmiths' guild to allow her to continue her husband's workshop during the Imperial Diet, the widow of Joachim Nitzel was told that she would be unable,

---

[124] In Augsburg, we know that 19% of those receiving civic alms from 1544 through 1558 to 1568 were widows, a figure which rose to 30% in 1576, and is even more striking given that children accounted for 55-60% of the rest of the paupers (C. P. Clasen, 'Armenfürsorge in Augsburg vor dem Dreissigjährigen Krieg', *ZHVS* 78 (1984), 65-115, here p. 88). For widows' poor economic position in other towns, see Lorenzen-Schmidt, 'Zur Stellung der Frau'; A. Winter, 'Studien zur sozialen Situation der Frauen in der Stadt Trier nach der Steuerliste von 1364', *Kurtrierisches Jahrbuch*, 15 (1975), 20-45; H. Rüthing, *Höxter um 1500: Analyse einer Stadtgesellschaft* (Paderborn, 1986), pp. 363 f.

[125] For similar findings, see Rüthing, *Höxter um 1500*, pp. 360 ff.

by reason of her sex, to control her journeymen, and that she lacked the necessary skills because she had not been trained through the craft. In a parting shot, the goldsmiths alleged that granting Nitzlin's petition would encourage others to demand the same rights—and with more justification, for Nitzlin was young and comfortably off, while other widows were poor. Someone, they hinted darkly, was putting her up to it. Dismissing the seriousness of her intentions, they implied that her widowhood was just a cover for some untrained young man to make a profit. They made it clear that, by reason of her youth, Nitzlin was to be classed as a future wife not as a widow.[126] Suspicion of the sexually mature, rich and fertile, yet unhusbanded woman who might ally herself with the young man they imagined to be behind her complaint, colours their writing. Female sexuality, once loosened from the patriarchal bond of the husband, can never provide true authority for the workshop. If not all guilds took such a dim view of female capacity, gossip about widows and fear of their untamed sexuality was common currency. As one widow wrote just a few months after the death of her husband: [it was] 'the evil talk, which I sometimes have to endure in my widowhood', which led her to consider remarriage.[127]

The other side of this coin was the stock-in-trade of many a popular pamphlet and verse, the powerful widow who married again and who could lord it over a young man.[128] Presented as sexually voracious and repulsive, she was to be feared because she had triumphed over the man—an inversion which, ironically, the guilds' own regulations fostered. Many decreed that a journeyman who married a trade widow but had not completed his training and years of experience should be banned from buying and selling until he fulfilled guild requirements.[129] In the

---

[126] StadtAA, Reichsstadt, HWA Goldschmiede 1532-80, 1550, widow of Joachim Nitzel. In fact she won her claim (RB 24./II fo. 3ʳ, 9 Aug. 1550); but 5 years later the list of members included no widows (HWA Goldschmiede, 1555). See also Seling, *Die Kunst der Augsburger Goldschmiede*, iii. 37.

[127] StadtAA, Reichsstadt, HWA Schmiede 1530-69, 1568, widow of Hans Jäger.

[128] See e.g. H. Sachs, *Ein Rat zwischen einem Alten man vnd jungen gesellen dreyer heyrat halben*, Nuremberg, G. Merckel, [1560?]; and see also M. Geisberg, *The German Single-Leaf Woodcut 1500-1550*, 4 vols. (New York, 1974), iv. 1270, Virgil Solis; A. Stewart, *Unequal Lovers: A Study of Unequal Couples in Northern Art* (New York, 1977).

[129] e.g. StadtAA, Reichsstadt, RB 16, fo. 146ᵛ, 3 July 1538 (Tuchscherer); HWA Schneider 1443-1564, 2 Sept. 1559, Hans Kuefer; HWA Lederer 1548-1654, 6 Jan. 1556, Peter Keil.

interim, his wife was to undertake this work and head the workshop. Similarly, such a young master was reliant on the continuing goodwill of his wife and any stepchildren to enable him to retain use of the workshop after her death. The repellent images of the unequal couples—old men and young women; old women and young men—play on this theme of inappropriate sexuality. Its lasting attraction in the bourgeois and petty-bourgeois urban world should be sought, however, not only in its relation to 'reality', but in its teasing-out of ambivalences within the workshop ideal. Here, sexual life and economic function were poorly coupled. In the mismatch of sexuality and wealth, this culture played with the absurdities and channellings which the household-workshop regimen of work, labour, sex, and money demanded.

It should now be apparent that a theology which was nourished by guild ideals of household and family, and which insisted on the certainties of the household order, was unlikely to disturb views of female inferiority, despite evangelicalism's belief in women's spiritual equality. Resting on a male-defined and -articulated notion of hierarchy, both social and sexual, the household Utopia was able to unite rich and poor, master and aspirant journeyman, around a vision of male authority in marriage and labour. We can see the force of this vision in a seemingly minor passage in the great Discipline Ordinance of 1537, dealing with the rights and duties of servants. Just as the ordinance was concerned to establish right-relations between fatherly Council and citizenry, master and journeymen, husband and wife, so also it set out the role of servants. Appealing to the vow which servants undertook at the start of their contract, the ordinance exhorted them to fulfil their contract and forbade them to take another post in the city for two years if they left before term. This measure was aimed at preventing servants from transferring from one master to another, or wheedling more money out of a mean employer; and it would have seriously limited servants' ability to negotiate better conditions and wages.[130]

---

[130] *Ains Erbern Rats | der Stat Augspurg | Zucht vnd Pollicey Ordnung*, fos. b ii^r-^{v}.

Similarly, just a few years later the Council tightened the time-honoured practice of offering servants cut-price citizenship: in future, only those servants who had served ten years in not more than two or three posts, and were considered 'good' servants, should be offered this prize.[131] Clearly intended to encourage a stable, subservient attitude on the part of servants, the ordinance viewed them as obedient children who might earn their civic inheritance through good work and a respectful demeanour. Conversely, masters and mistresses were reminded not to be too coarse to their servants and to treat them in a 'fitting' fashion, phrases which nicely catch the essential resonances of standing and status, and which were also used to describe the proper relation between wife and husband.[132] They underline the imagined gulf between servant and master—imaginary rather than real, because servants might often be related to their masters, and the labour they performed in the household workshop might sometimes be similar to that undertaken by the male journeymen and apprentices.

Although the sex of the servant is specified as male or female, and though it may well have been meant to refer to journeymen and apprentices, the overall drift of the passage seems to be aimed primarily at servants, predominant amongst whom were women. Women servants certainly clogged the courts with complaints about dismissal, and were criticized by their employers for their incompetent ways.[133] Such a thoroughgoing attempt to discipline a group of workers and to tie them by law to a particular position would have been far less easy to carry out against journeymen or apprentices; and it was only possible because servant-women lacked an organization of their own or a recognition of skill. The serving woman, the member of the household workshop who had least rights and fewest prospects, was also the most thoroughly 'ordered' by the guild vision. As wife, widow, or as servant, women's lives were circumscribed by the household workshop in which they were subordinate. The theology which sacralized those relations, and imagined a civic haven in which the household would be restored to its mythical, ordered past, was a powerful vision of salvation for urban craftsmen.

[131] StadtAA, Reichsstadt, Schätze 16, fos. 94ʳ-ᵛ, 1544.
[132] *Ains Erbern Rats | der Stat Augspurg | Zucht vnd Pollicey Ordnung.* fo. b/iiᵛ.
[133] StadtAA, Reichsstadt, Prot. der Zuchtherren.

2

The Politics of Sin

THE Discipline Ordinance of 1537, the most important institutional legacy of the Reformation in Augsburg, marked not only a transfer of control over marriage and morals from the Church to the civic Council, but the codification of a new psychology of sin and a distinctive language of crime—all the more powerful for being an uneasy amalgam of religious and secular traditions. The new code carried with it a kind of secular theology of gender which articulated the ideal differences between men and women, locating them in different duties, work responsibilities, and psychologies.

In its definition of sexual differences, the new rhetoric of paternal moralism rapidly developed into a new understanding of paternal power in the political sphere. As the Council assumed a far greater role in policing those who lived within the city walls, it developed a conception of its own authority which was at once more sophisticated and made far wider claims for its own jurisdiction. This aggressive interpretation of the scope of its authority found dramatic expression when, in January 1537, the Council sent the old Catholic clergy packing and locked several churches—a flagrant violation of the bishop's authority which he was powerless to stop. Yet, paradoxically, it was not only the Church which felt the pinch of this extension of the Council's jurisdiction, but the guilds. The power of the guilds suffered a significant eclipse, even though the Reformation's institutionalization was accomplished to most guildsmen's applause (apart from those reactionary craftsmen mocked by the evangelical painter and chronicler Jörg Preu because they feared the loss of the lucrative ecclesiastical commissions). We shall explore how this came about, and then show how the new organs of moral control, the Discipline Lords and the Marriage Court, became integrated into civic institutions and advanced the careers of the men who staffed them.

HOUSEHOLD MORALISM

Perhaps the most striking feature of evangelical urban moralism in this period is its determined pessimism about human nature, coupled with a view of all human relationships—and especially those between man and wife—as being structured around authority and submission. For both preachers and Council, the role of authority in creating a moral citizenry was crucial: the preachers spoke of the need for the Council to punish the evil-doers, and the Council spoke of 'the human will which is unfortunately more inclined to evil than to good'.[1] Consequently, the subtle task of training the will fell primarily to the authorities, not to the individual. The human will was not to be 'harnessed too tightly', but on the other hand should not be allowed 'too much space and opportunity, so that it should not give rise to sins and evils'.[2] The imagery of harnessing, restricting, and fencing came naturally to this understanding of the will, and 'discipline' became a central term of both secular and religious discourse.

The emphasis on discipline brought with it a secular demonology of categories of people who were identified as disruptive. Prime among these were young people, the shiftless, and adulterers. Lay and reformed values now concurred in presenting the orderly married estate as normative, and each of these varieties of evil-livers affronted marriage and escaped the settled confines of the household ideal. Young unmarried men had previously been permitted the sexual licence of brothel visits; and it was the horseplay of youth, engaging in door-knockings, noisily singing in the New Year and prising money from their hearers, dancing, or taking leading roles in carnival frolics, which was to come under fire from the reformers.[3] 'The youth' were

---

[1] StadtAA, Reichsstadt, Schätze 16, fo. 48ᵛ, n.d.: 'dem menschlichen willenn, der laider mer zum pösenn dann guten genaigt seien'; and cf., on the role of education and discipline, G. Strauss, 'Success and Failure in the German Reformation', *Past and Present*, 67 (1975), 30–63.

[2] StadtAA, Reichsstadt, Schätze 16, fo. 48ᵛ: 'Raum vnnd Lufft lassen, damit zu Sunnden vnnd lastern nit ursach gegeben wurd'. See also ibid., fo. 54ʳ, 22 Dec. 1540, against the youth who 'lebt vnd gebaret mit gelassnen Zaum'. This mandate was also to be read from pulpits.

[3] Ibid., throughout. Cf. the youth gangs of Italian towns, who used coarse language and caused disturbances: C. de la Roncière, 'Tuscan Notables on the Eve of the Renaissance', in P. Ariès and G. Duby (eds.), *A History of Private Life*, ii (Cambridge, Mass., 1988).

no longer seen as meriting a certain licence because of their age, but were viewed as sexually and morally anarchic. In 1540 the Council complained (in a mandate both proclaimed and read from the pulpit) 'that the youth are seldom and infrequently brought up in the fear of God and in good habits any more', while, in a submission to the Council, the preachers complained of the irresponsible marriage promises made by young people under the influence of drink, urging that the young were bringing marriage into disrepute.[4] Consequently, young people's courtship rituals and young men's processions and popular culture increasingly became a target of Council mandates. Sexually mature and virile, yet unable to head households of their own, the demeanour of the young men who had to live this contradiction began to be seen as threatening, portending a serious attack on marriage itself. As we have seen, there were tensions enough in the difficult labour relations between masters and young journeymen. Yet these hostilities were transformed into a set of concerns about youth, and young people's insubordination was read as the result of bad upbringing within the family, not as an expression of class hostility.

The mixture of religious and secular concerns on which the positive ideal of the household drew can be seen clearly in the Poor Law Ordinances, designed to deal with the shiftless. Introduced in 1522 at the time of the Reformation's first successes in Augsburg, the Poor Law was modified through the course of the century. Its original impetus was civic rather than evangelical, and it was paralleled by many other Poor Laws introduced throughout European towns in the first decades of the century. But it rapidly became a powerful vehicle for articulating a clearer conception of the distinct duties of each male and female member of the household, in productive as well as in affective relations. Increasingly, it was coloured by evangelical concerns; but, like the Discipline Ordinance, this provided a foundation which the

---

[4] 'das die Jugennt so seltten vnd wenig mer. Inn der forcht Gottes vnnd gutenn sitten vfferzogen würd': StadtAA, Reichsstadt, Schätze 16, fo. 54ʳ, 22 Dec. 1540; and see also ibid., fo. 101ᵛ, 20 June 1545, on 'Simetfeuer, Abenddenz vnnd Rayengesang'; 'das die Torichte, ainfeltige Jugent hinderrugks vnd Ausserhalb Irer Elltern oder Phlegeren offtermals mit lustigen begreifflichen worten hinder gang oder etwan hinter dem wein | vnd in wingklen vberredet . . .': Lit. 1534, Nachtrag 36.

post-Reformation Councils were easily able to incorporate.[5] The original ordinance made it plain that the man of the household's duty was to provide for his wife and children: if he failed to do so and the family had to rely on poor-relief, he was to wear the civic symbol (the *Stadtpir*) as a visible badge of his fecklessness.[6] To reinforce the message, by mid-century a man had to wear the sign even if, though he could not support wife and children, he earned enough for his own keep.[7] Household responsibilities, particularly so far as spending money was concerned, became areas of grave Council interest—thus in 1534 a group of a dozen weavers involved in a gaming-ring were admonished and punished for the irresponsible behaviour which left their wives and children in penury.[8] Nor was the Council's response in this case exceptional—throughout the 1530s and 1540s the Council was ready to intervene in marital disputes where there was a danger that a husband's reckless spending imperilled the material welfare of his wife and child. Drunkenness, which the Council saw as a mainly male problem, was viewed in terms of failure to provide and was considered to be perverse 'spending' on oneself—a suspicion of lower-class male conviviality so intense that it led to proposals that the poor be given food and relief in kind rather than money.[9]

The woman was to assist the man in the work of his craft, to organize child care, and to keep house. In public rhetoric she was nearly always addressed as a 'wife' (usually *Frau*; occasionally *Weib*), in terms of her economic and emotional relationship to a man, seldom as 'mother'. Indeed, '*Mutter*' usually refers to the reproductive organs of the female body, to the uterus in particular.[10] Seen as a wife rather than as a mother, her duty of sustenance

---

[5] On the Ordinance of 1541, see C. P. Clasen, 'Armenfürsorge in Augsburg vor dem Dreissigjährigen Krieg', *ZHVS* 78 (1984), 65–115, esp. pp. 69 f.

[6] StadtAA, Reichsstadt, Ratserlasse 1507–99, 27 Mar. 1522.

[7] Ibid., Schätze 63, fos. 184ʳ–185ᵛ, 9 Feb. 1550.

[8] Ibid., Urg. 23 Oct. 1534, Hans Schmid, Ulrich Eberlin; Urg. 30 Oct. 1534, Christian Vitschman, Hans Rorer; Urg. 31 Oct. 1534, Hans Peichelstain, Mathis Trauter; Urg. Do. nach Simonis et Jude 1534, Bartholome Seiz; and cf. Schätze 16, Hagk, fo. 50ᵛ, 14 Aug. 1540, against 'Essen Trincken vnnd Borgen Bey den Wirttenn'.

[9] Ibid., Schätze 16, fo. 60ᵛ, 1541.

[10] H. Heimberger, 'Schwangerschaft, Geburt und Frauenkrankheiten in der mittelalterlichen Volksmedizin', *Württembergisches Jahrbuch für Volkskunde*, 8 (1951), 111–22.

was played down. Consequently, though it was assumed that she too could earn money to supplement her keep by spinning, it was realized that this poorly paid work would hardly stretch to keep a family. If her husband was not in town or if she were a widow, she could receive supplementary doles for her children. Excused from the burden of providing, she could more readily escape the opprobrium of shiftlessness heaped on her husband. It was men rather than women whom the Council blamed for overburdening the system; a scapegoating which preserved unchallenged the unequal earning capacities of women and men.

Increasingly the Poor Law became identified with evangelical conceptions of charity and statements of the proper order in the household because it raised the question of who was deserving. It made a clear distinction between civic charity and the haphazard devotional charity of the pre-Reformation period, distributed to the worthy and unworthy alike because all were equally capable of praying for the donor's soul. Reformed charity was given to the 'house poor' (*hausarm*), not to the indigent—a word which nicely imagined them as confined within their houses. The categories most deserving of charitable support were the *hausarme* widows and orphans, or as the evangelical preacher Musculus described them, 'poor daughters, who must perish on account of poverty, and come into danger, poor boys who would otherwise be ruined through indiscipline . . .'—all those within households which lacked male support.[11] Even after the reintroduction of Catholicism, the values of moral living and discipline lived on in the ordinance: by 1568 only those who had fallen into poverty because of sickness and not because of 'insufferable housekeeping' were to be given alms. The language of capitalist investment now began to be applied to charity, and the same mandate went on to state that 'many good-hearted Christians who otherwise would be very inclined to give their alms generously here, disburse the same in other places, because experience teaches them that this fund is far from the best to

---

[11] 'Hausarm': StadtAA, Reichsstadt, Ratserlasse 1507–99, 27 Mar. 1522; 'hausarmen wittben vnnd waisen, Arme dochter, die armut halb muessen verligen, vnd zu schaden geratten, Arme khnaben die sonst zuchtloss mussen verderben': ibid., Lit. July–Dec. 1538, no. 10, Musculus.

invest it'.[12] Only the production of disciplined, careful housekeepers could provide the profit for such charitable investment. But in the early years it was a concept of charity which could make evangelicals appear uncharitable—somewhat testily, the Council was driven to justify its refusal to help foreign vagrants (those individuals who were not householders) on the grounds that the papists' seeming largesse had been dissipated on useless people (*unnützer leut*).[13] Moreover, the Council's notions of how the 'deserving poor' ought to behave did not square with the real possibilities of people's lives—male wages also were often insufficient to keep a family, and most households relied on the labour of women and children.[14]

THE NATURE OF SIN

For the evangelicals, convinced of humankind's disorderly, ungodly instincts, the ideal of the orderly household within the righteous city had to be realized by firm discipline as well as through inculcating a vision of the pious, deserving Augsburger. The concept of 'firm discipline', understood in the metaphors of constraint, led to a bureaucratic reorganization in which the disciplining duties of each court and Council body should be clearly articulated. The Discipline Lords' duties were to police the Ordinance of 1537, administering fines and small prison sentences for fornication, adultery, violent behaviour, and the like. Difficult cases— or those which demanded a more severe punishment— were to be referred to the Council. The Discipline Court outlived the Reformation, and Discipline Ordinances continued to be published and extended well into the following century in patrician-led, biconfessional Augsburg, becoming

[12] 'vil gutt herzigen Christen so sonsten ganz genaigt weren Jr Almusen daher reichlich zugeben dasselb an ander ortt wenden, dieweil Jnen die Erfarung zuerkennen gibt, das Es dis orts bey vilen nit am bösten angelegt wurdet': ibid., Schätze 63, fos. 197^{r-v}.

[13] Ibid., Schätze 16, fos. 73^r-74^r, 14 May 1542.

[14] See P. Broadhead, 'Internal Politics and Civic Society in Augsburg during the Era of the Early Reformation 1518-1537', Ph.D. thesis (Kent, 1981), pp. 76-83.

thoroughly integrated into the city administration.[15] In addition, a host of smaller authorities were instituted: in 1529 the Butchers' Punishment Lords were created (a court whose precise functions are unclear, but which apparently dealt with both trade offences and general offences of disorderly behaviour), and the following decades saw a vast increase in the numbers of *Einunger* (members of a disciplining and adjudicatory body dealing with petty offences), new Iron Lords who dealt with prisoners, and Poor Law administrators.[16]

This plethora of bodies and authorities, each with a somewhat roughly described remit, were a way of ensuring that ordinances were implemented: as the rhyme that one civic official had stamped on to the leather cover of a punishment book put it:

> There never was an ordinance so fine,
> That without policing it wouldn't decline.[17]

Law in Augsburg was a confused accretion of ordinance, tradition, and precedent increasingly influenced by imperial law and the Roman law learnt by the city's lawyers. The original local law code of 1276 was still in force in theory, but many of its provisions were simply ignored, and the Council tended to proceed by issuing new ordinances and attempting to square its practice with imperial and Roman law where it could. Not until a good deal later in the century did it even attempt to overhaul the law code and produce a coherent law-book.[18]

Yet while the Discipline Court outlasted the Reformation, the other major institutional innovation of the Reformation, the Marriage Court, was apparently suspended in 1546, and it was not to be reinstated until the Protestant restoration during the

---

[15] Discipline Ordinances in StadtAA, Reichsstadt, Schätze 36; and Fasz. Zuchtordnungen. On discipline in the later sixteenth and seventeenth centuries, see L. Lenk, *Augsburger Bürgertum im Späthumanismus und Frühbarock (1580–1700)* (Augsburg, 1968)

[16] StadtAA, Reichsstadt, Ratsämterlisten 1520–35, 1536–48; W. Köhler, *Zücher Ehegericht und Genfer Konsistorium* 2 vols. (Leipzig, 1932, 1942), ii. 280–322.

[17] 'Kain Ordnung was noch nie so schon | Huelt man nit drob Sy müsst zergon': StadtAA, Reichsstadt, Prot. der Zuchtherren IV, 1542, cover.

[18] E. Liedl, *Gerichtsverfassung und Zivilprozess der freien Reichsstadt Augsburg* (Augsburg, 1958); R. Schmidt, 'Das Stadtbuch von 1276', in G. Gottlieb *et al.* (eds.), *Geschichte der Stadt Augsburg*, 2nd edn. (Stuttgart, 1985).

Swedish occupation in 1632.[19] This court was a civil court rather than a disciplining authority, and it dealt with pleas for divorce, claims for loss of virginity and child support, and cases of disputed marriage promises. It was at one level simply an administrative reform, an urbanized version of what had been an ecclesiastical court, and its establishment could be seen in terms of the Council's duty to act as an emergency bishop, creating a cheaper, simpler, and more accessible court for its citizens in the vacuum of power created by the Reformation's advance. But its links with Council authority were very direct, for appeals from the Marriage Court's decisions could pass only to the Small Council, and the court was ordered to seek advice from the Council's own advocates.[20] Indeed, it was essentially a civic Protestant understanding of marriage which determined the new court's proceedings and which ultimately made its incorporation into biconfessional Augsburg an impossibility. As we shall see, however, the changes in the control of marriage which accompanied its establishment did prove more enduring.

In addition to these two authorities, the resources of the Council itself, and its processes of criminal interrogation, torture, and punishment, began increasingly to be put at the service of the moralization of the community. In place of the somewhat haphazard modes of punishment of the pre-Reformation city, where offenders such as pimps, prostitutes, and procurers were simply banished on St Gall's Day[21] and particularly abhorrent sexual offenders were exiled or punished, the reformed Council

---

[19] This is where the protocols of the Ehegerichtsbuch break off (StadtAA, Reichsstadt, Ehegerichtsbuch 1537–46). StadtAA, Reichsstadt, Fasz. Ehegericht 1548–78, I, contains several cases from 1548 which had been 'suspended' and are now to be settled. Note, however, Liedl, *Gerichtsverfassung und Zivilprozess*, who wrongly states (p. 64) that the Marriage Court continued until 1632. Köhler believes the court continued until 1548 (*Zürcher Ehegericht und Genfer Konsistorium*, ii. 293); but he does not appear to have seen the Ehegerichtsbuch, and relied instead on Fasz. Ehegericht, I.

[20] On the details of procedure, see Köhler, *Zürcher Ehegericht und Genfer Konsistorium*, ii. 290–3 (summary of StadtAA, Reichsstadt, Ehegerichtsbuch 1537–46, fos. 1ʳ–4ᵛ, seventeenth-century transcription in Fasz. Ehegericht, I). The Council's legal 'doctors', Pius Peutinger and Lucas Ulstat, sat with the Marriage Court at its inception: StadtAA, Ratsbuch 16, fo. 135ʳ, 6 Dec. 1537.

[21] Even this punishment could be eased. See *Die Chroniken der deutschen Städte vom 14. bis ins 16. Jahrhundert*, 36 vols. (Leipzig, 1862–1931), xxiii, Sender, p. 72, who says that in 1499 the Galli exile procedures were modified so that the offenders were exiled secretly instead of being publicly shamed.

introduced a consistent and co-ordinated structure of authority which aimed to let no offender escape detection and punishment. Punishments ranged from short prison sentences and fines, which the Discipline Lords could order, to longer periods of imprisonment and to exiling, maiming, or even execution, which only the Council could impose.[22] This integrated system of moral control also survived the Reformation: in 1558, in relation to adultery, the Council decreed that anyone found in a suspicious place or with suspicious people should be admonished; and if detected a second time, should swear an oath 'that you did not commit or complete in deed any dishonourable act with the person N.'; and if there were reason for doubting his or her word, or any other suspicious circumstances, then the Discipline Lords—or the Council—should even have discretionary powers to administer corporal punishment (*am leib*).[23] The intensity of supervision of public and private space which this ordinance presumed was if anything more complete than that created in reformed Augsburg.

The hierarchy of sexual offences under the new, reformed dispensation was also very different from that of the ecclesiastical ranking of sexual sins which preceded it. Exercised through confession, the discipline of the pre-Reformation Church had encouraged the individual to examine his or her intentions, desires, and fantasies. Sin was understood to reside in the individual's concupiscence rather than in the particular form of

---

[22] There were 'Execution Ordinances' detailing precisely how the *Zuchtherren* were to enforce the ordinances. The Execution Ordinance for 1537 is no longer extant in the city archive, though Walter Köhler was able to use it. (See *Zürcher Ehegericht und Genfer Konsistorium*, ii. 304–13, for his summary of its contents.) Several transcriptions of the Execution Ordinance for 1553 are, however, available (StadtAA, Reichsstadt, Schätze ad 36/5, 36/3). Further light is thrown on the workings of the Discipline Lords by the Ein- und Ausgabebuch der Zuchtherren, 8 Oct. 1537–Dec. 1557 (presumably a 'clean copy' made from pre-existing records); and the more systematic Ausgeb der Zuchtherren, 1558 (StadtAA, Reichsstadt). From these it is apparent that the demands on notarial services generated by the authority's business were such that a post was created. It is also apparent that sums reaching as much as 2 gulden in 1558 were being paid to *Kundschafter* (what Köhler refers to as spies) for information concerning offences and offenders. This money was often administered by the *Stadtvogt*, who also sat with the Discipline Lords.

[23] StadtAA, Reichsstadt, Ratsbuch 30./II, fos. 80ʳ⁻ᵛ, 29 Oct. 1558, and transcribed in Zucht- und Executionsordnung 1553, Schätze ad 36/5, fo. 37ᵛ. I am grateful to Katarina Sieh-Burens for the Ratsbuch reference.

the offence itself. Thus, in several confessional manuals, married couples were exhorted to examine their own sexual deportment, and to uncover the sinful aspects of their own lusts even within the marital relationship. So all-important was the state of desire to an adjudication of sin that lust for one's spouse could become an act of adultery; while intercourse with one's spouse while enacting a fantasy of him or her as another lover could be counted a lesser sin. Masturbation, the 'secret sin', which could not be understood as an offence which injured another person, was one of the most abhorred sins: the quintessential sin of fantasy, it represented the epitome of sinfulness as a hidden state of mind which demanded continual self-examination and constant confession under the direction of the model priest, whose archaeological skills were needed to unearth sin.[24] Moral perfectionism was a pursuit which could be endlessly refined, and its perfection was the preserve of a spiritual élite. The fine, abstruse distinctions of the confessional manuals were hopelessly optimistic in their estimate of what an ordinary parish confessor or friar could either carry out or expect of his penitents. Even so, the model of sin as a function of desire which underlay the institution of confession was common currency. The attraction of indulgences lay in their seeming spiritual–materialist capacity[25] to atone for guilt, even for those sins which had not been uncovered by the searchlight of what must often have been cursory confessional sessions. No matter how some theologians might caution against too great a trust in indulgences at the cost of a true and full confession, there were many preachers who urged the effectiveness of indulgences and intercessionary prayer to the saints or by the community of fellow-Christians.

[24] See e.g. *Der spiegel des sünders*, Augsburg, A. Sorg, 1480, and *Beichtbuchlin*, Augsburg, Valentin Schlosser, 1491; and T. Tentler, *Sin and Confession on the Eve of the Reformation* (Princeton, 1977). For a very different analysis of the concept of sin in the pre-Reformation Church, see J. Bossy, *Christianity in the West 1400-1700* (Oxford, 1985), pp. 35–42; and for another view, L. G. Duggan, 'Fear and Confession on the Eve of the Reformation', *Archiv für Reformationsgeschichte*, 75 (1982), 153–75.

[25] On the concept of 'crypto-materialism', see R. W. Scribner, 'Cosmic Order and Daily Life: Sacred and Secular in Pre-Industrial German Society', in K. von Greyerz (ed.), *Religion and Society in Early Modern Europe* (London, 1984); and see R. Evans, 'Religion and Society in Modern Germany', *European Studies Review*, 12 (1982), 249–88 (here pp. 270 f.).

The city, however, had long operated with a rather differently accented language of sin. Grasping 'sin' in terms of particular categories of public offence—or as it termed them, the 'public sins' of adultery, blasphemy, gambling, and the like—it had no interest in individual intention. Indeed, the offence lay rather in its publicity, its affront to civic decency, a distinction nicely illustrated by the Discipline Ordinance of 1472's strictures against those living in illicit unions (those who 'by der vnstat vnd ledigkait sitzen'), rather than against fornication itself. The fairly brief discipline mandates of the late fifteenth century left this understanding of sin implicit. A series of particular injunctions spasmodically repeated, they lacked any articulation of the connections between the motley collection of public-order offences with which they dealt.[26] Guild disciplining procedures similarly concentrated on the 'public sins', such as known adultery, which led to disruption of the household workshop, or cursing and swearing and the like, all manifest misdeeds which tarnished the public honour of the guild and its members.

The new civic moralism of the 1530s was heir to these older civic and guild traditions,[27] and it shared its apprehension of sin as particular categories of act. Neither masturbation nor lustful marital sex figures in its lists of sins. Instead, the Discipline Ordinance of 1537 made marriage the corner-stone of its moral and religious universe, including a full-blooded affirmation of the positive ideal of married life. A pessimistic vision, it was coloured by a kind of millenarian expectation that God's punishing wrath would descend on the city. It expatiated on the essential coherence of the offences it wished to punish, defining them in simultaneously religious and civic terms: blasphemy and swearing were punishable because they showed 'the highest unthankfulness and insult which humans as creatures can show to their creator;

[26] For the 1472 Ordinance, see StadtAA, Reichsstadt, Schätze 36/1. For repetition of such mandates, see e.g. ibid., Ratsbuch 15, fo. 61ʳ, 20 Oct. 1498 (against those who dwell together 'zu der vnstät'); and Ratserlasse 1507-99, 11 Feb. 1520 (swearing and drunkenness), renewed 17 Jan. 1524; ibid. 23 May 1531 (disturbances to public order, etc.).

[27] The Carolina, the Imperial Criminal Code of 1532, may be another of the influences at work. However, it was far from being the model: it lacks the evangelical rhetoric or exposition of the connectedness of sin of the Augsburg Ordinance, its stipulated punishments differ from those of the Augsburg Ordinance, and the offences it names are slightly different: *Die Peinliche Gerichtsordnung Kaiser Karls V von 1532*, ed. A. Kaufman, 4th edn. (Stuttgart, 1975).

and it is also such a vice through which God might fairly be moved to anger and to punishment of the world'; gaming for money caused 'the destruction of friendly intentions, hate, envy, anger . . . and destruction in all honourable doings, and finally often leads to the destruction of body, life, honour and good'; it 'is contrary to God's command' and especially reprehensible when it caused 'lack or ruin to him, his wife or children's support'; and it warned all parents to bring up their children in discipline and the fear of God.[28]

Now, however, although the same sins called down the Council's wrath, the accent was different. The shift from the old Church's concern with secret sins of the heart to the Council's preoccupation with sinful acts which offended against marriage was, at one level, a difference of the spheres appropriate to each mode of discipline. Confessional discipline was well adapted to deal with the sins of desire and offences which, like masturbation, lacked a victim. But there is more than a contrast of modes here. The period saw a move away from individual confession to a collective, congregational acknowledgement of guilt followed by a general absolution. This shift was fuelled by a populist hatred of prurient, prying priests, and the move against private confession was an important element in the victory of Zwinglian preachers over their Lutheran rivals.[29] In reformed Augsburg, sexual discipline was in the hands of the Council and its courts. Protestant clergy, who had given up the weapon of the confessional, might issue advice, counsel, and reprimands, resorting to the ban only with Council involvement and approval. Lacking the sanction of private confession and absolution, such counsel was less intrusive and less coercive. Given by a married Protestant clergy, its sexual preoccupations, too, were different,

---

[28] 'die höchste vndanckbarkait vnd verletzung des menschen | als der Creatur wider jren Schöpffer anzaigt | auch ain sollich Laster ist | dadurch Got der Allmechtig nit vnbillich in vil wege erzürnnt vnd zur Straff vber die Welt bewegt würdt'; 'das dardurch nichts annders | dann zertrennung freündtlichs willens verhassung | neid | zorn | verirrung | vnd zerrüttung in allem Erbern thun vnd lassen | vnd also endtliche verderbung an Leib | leben | Ere vnd Gůt | vilfältig eruolgt' . . . deren Spile | die jme | seinen Weib vnd kinnden | an jrer Narung scheinbarlichen mangel oder verderben pringen mögen': *Ains Erbern Rats | der Stat Augspurg | Zucht vnd Pollicey Ordnung*, Augsburg, 1537, fos. a/iiiͬ, a/vͬ; and on the education of children, fo. b/iiͬ.

[29] F. Roth, *Augsburgs Reformationsgeschichte* 4 vols. (vol. i: 2nd edn., Munich, 1901; vols. ii–iv: Munich, 1904–11), ii. 194.

and it tended not to dwell so much on the perils of marital lust as to condemn adultery, loose living, and fornication. Now, for Council and preachers alike, the fact of the publicity or otherwise of the formerly named 'public sins' was immaterial: whether public knowledge or not, adultery and fornication were thought to destroy the fabric of the household.

Yet if sins were imagined to be particular acts of specific types, the new moralism was not without its own internal dynamic. Like the confessor, the Council also saw its task as being to extract a full confession of all the misdeeds an individual had committed, and to bring him or her to a sense of sinfulness. Repeatedly in the 1537 Ordinance, the Council was drawn to the image of fatherhood to describe its relation to its subjects. This image naturalized its assumption of power over the citizens, enabling it to speak of itself as wiser and more powerful, with a duty to lead and educate those in its charge.[30] At the same time it developed a typology of sinners, so that those who committed certain sinful acts began to be seen as fatally flawed by that sin. Vagabonds, whom the Council considered to be incorrigible, were imagined as a particular class of character and little interest was expressed in their mental worlds; but when it came to those who were the Council's subjects, or those whom it considered potentially respectable, the Council began to develop an aetiology of vice, locating the individual's 'fall', as it termed it in biblical tones, in his or her history. So Anna Ebeler was castigated for committing adultery and suspected of involvement in prostitution a few months later. But although the Council was anxious to reclaim her through education, it also saw her as tinged with a sinfulness which must now characterize all her acts; and refused to believe her vehement assertions that she had not committed 'sinful work'. Gretle Sailer, a 15-year-old girl whom the Council described as 'wise enough' despite her age, was interrogated at length because the Council assumed that her relatives and the company she kept would inevitably lead her into

---

[30] For examples of such turns of phrase, see *Ains Erbern Rats | der Stat Augspurg | Zucht vnd Pollicey Ordnung*, fo. a/ii^r: 'die vorgeenden Vätterlichen Ermanungen'; fo. a/ii^v: 'ermanet ain Erber Rat . . . trewlich | vätterlich | vnd mit gantzem ernst'; fo. b/iii^r: 'zum vätterlichsten vnd trewlichsten ersucht vnd ermanet haben'; fo. b/vi^r: 'Vnd hat ain Erber Rat die Straffen vnd | Censuren . . . so Vätterlich | mildt | vnd träglich Gesetzt'.

sin.[31] This was the rudimentary beginning of a half-articulated psychology of 'sinfulness' which tried both to explain and predict the sinner's errant behaviour while yet recognizing the potential, even amongst the respectable of Augsburg, for honour and decency to collapse and a 'fall' to occur.

POLITICAL AUTHORITY AND EVANGELICAL MORALISM

The entire Ordinance of 1537 was rooted in a dualistic conceptualization of relations of authority and submission. Providing an exhaustive catalogue of sin, the ordinance laboriously presented each category of crime as a variety of disobedience. Even gaming, somewhat improbably, transgressed God's command that 'no one should desire another's goods'.[32] Crime, instead of being understood as a breach of the communal civic peace (the tacit understanding which had underpinned pre-Reformation ordinances), was an offence against legitimate authority. Working carefully through sins of the word (blasphemy, perjury, slander), the ordinance moved on to anatomize the sins of the body: first, collective physical misbehaviour (gambling, drunkenness), then sins of sexual misuse of the body, and finally sins of violence and disorder (drawing weapons, fighting). Each was an injury towards a higher authority. But, in a kind of unconscious blasphemy, God and the Council became almost interchangeable as the Father who is offended. Indeed, so thoroughgoing was the articulation of the role of secular authority as the executor of God's commands, that there was little place for the reformed Church or the preachers in the ordinance: they could have no function in this narrow hierarchy of sacral and political power.

The image of power at the heart of the ordinance is that between husband and wife, the biblical metaphor so often used by theologians to expound the relationship between Christ and his Church. The husband should love his wife 'as his own flesh';

---

[31] StadtAA, Reichsstadt, Urg. 29–31 Mar. 1544, Anna Ebeler; and Prot. der Zuchtherren IV, fo. 165, 19 Dec. 1543; Urg. 8 Aug. 1542, Marg[gretle] Sailer.

[32] *Ains Erbern Rats | der Stat Augspurg | Zucht vnd Pollicey Ordnung*, Tfo. a/v[r].

she, in turn, 'should fear the husband, and have him before her eyes, and consider him to be her head'.[33] Wisdom, authority, and watchful benevolence on one side; respectful deference on the other: this was a compelling metaphor for the comportment which the Council wanted to encourage from its own citizenry. It also involved, of course, a claim to an exclusive and masterly kind of authority, a conception of the nature of urban political legitimacy which was fundamentally at odds with the communitarian understanding of the Council as the voice of the citizenry, even though the Council continued to attempt to combine both modes of discourse in its public pronouncements. What is interesting is that this claim to absolute authority was accomplished through spelling out the nature of masculinity and femininity in marriage. Moral politics provided the key to this political reorientation.

The reform of morals in Augsburg also marked a deeper shift in the control of marriage and mores from an uneasy duo of city and church authority to a near complete civic monopoly over discipline. Partly because of the weaknesses of the local Church, the extent of secularization was greater in Augsburg than in many towns: the city never permitted clerical representation on the Marriage Court or the Discipline Lords, nor did it regularly solicit the clergy's advice; and no system of independent, parish-based, church-run discipline made any headway in the town.[34] Even

[33] Ibid., fo. a/vi^v.

[34] Church representation was far greater in other towns: Köhler, *Zürcher Ehegericht und Genfer Konsistorium*, i, ii; and cf. the workings of the consistory in the communities described in D. Sabean, *Power in the Blood* (Cambridge, 1984). There are scattered references to attempts to establish a church-based 'discipline' in Augsburg: there is a brief 'proposal' on 'Von versümung vnd von vsschliesung von der kirchen' contained in StadtAA, Reichsstadt, Personenselekt, Varia, '*c*.1550', but this undated document is hardly a programme and it is doubtful whether it even stems from Augsburg. There is a mention of a church ban in *Bekandtnuss der Euangelischen Leer* | in *Zehen Haupt Articulen kürtzlich begriffen*, Augsburg, P. Ulhart, 1546, fo. a/iii^v—but it is unclear whether this was put into practice so soon before the war. Ambrosius Blarer's attempts to establish a church ban seem to have foundered. The Discipline Ordinance contains a near mockery of the congregational system of discipline, asking individuals first to warn those who sin in secret; but if there is no improvement, the sinner is to be immediately reported to the Council for punishment, and the informer is to be protected and given an honorarium (*Ains Erbern Rats* | *der Stat Augspurg* | *Zucht vnd Pollicey Ordnung*, fo. b/v^v). This is even justified by a vague appeal to 'our Lord in the Evangel': a reference to the passage in Matthew to which theologians appealed when they demanded a congregational system of discipline with threefold, secret, brotherly admonitions. Here it is used to support a secular, authoritarian system of discipline, while 'brotherly admonition' becomes the first stage of a paid informant's work.

the 1537 Church Ordinance's elaboration of the use of the ban proposed intense Council involvement.[35] The reform can thus be viewed as the culmination of a long struggle whose roots lay in the medieval conflict between church and civic government over the delineation of jurisdictions.[36] But it also signalled an important shift in political power within the city itself from guild to Council. This transformation pre-dated the abolition of the guilds by Charles V; yet, ironically, it was accomplished by one of the most fervently pro-guild Councils Augsburg had seen since 1368.[37] Because so many of the guild-books were destroyed in the aftermath of the 1548 settlement, it is impossible to reconstruct the precise functioning of guild discipline. It is clear, none the less, that guilds had enjoyed considerable power over their members, consistently disciplining them for minor-order offences and excluding those guilty of such major offences as bigamy, desertion, or even illegitimacy—whether or not punished by secular authority. The guild operated as a more perfect community within the city, its members' collective honour established competitively through reputation.[38]

---

[35] E. Sehling *et al.* (eds.), *Die evangelischen Kirchenordnungen, des 16. Jahrhunderts* (Leipzig, 1902-11), Bayern II, p. 54.

[36] See R. Kiessling, *Bürgerliche Gesellshaft und Kirche in Augsburg* (Augsburg, 1971), on this long-standing conflict.

[37] On the political history of the period, see Roth, *Augsburgs Reformationsgeschichte*, iii, iv; and K. Sieh-Burens, *Oligarchie, Konfession und Politik im 16. Jahrhundert* (Munich, 1986). Roth, however, and most other historians, would date centralization to the post-1548 regime, not to the reformed Council. The period 1537-48, so crucial to an understanding of Augsburg's later history, still lacks a modern historian.

[38] See R. Wissell, *Des alten Handwerks Recht und Gewohnheit*, 2 vols. (Berlin, 1929), for examples of such ordinances. For Augsburg, see StadtAA, Reichsstadt, HWA Goldschmiede 1532-80, 1529: 'Auch die gesellen vnnd leren knaben sich sonnst redlich vnnd Erber wie sich wol gepurt hallten söllen, sölche aber riffianer, vnpillich verschwender, Spiler, oder mit leichtvertigen frawen, behennckt wären, die soll kain maister vnnder vnns weder setzen noch denselben ainich arbait gebenn'; and the statute against admission of those of illegitimate birth which follows; punishment of 'Zucken' and 'rumor', Ledererordnung vor 1542, Bestand Handwerksordnungen, fo. 2ʳ; no illegitimates, Zünfte 245, Zunftbuch der Schlosser, Schmiede, und Schleifer 1453-1534; punishment of 'schelten', Zunftbuch der Schlosser, Artickel der Schlosser Gesellen, 13 Feb. 1535; Zunftbuch der Schuster 1457-99. Clearly many of the prohibitions, especially those concerning illegitimacy, were principles rather than practice; but the importance of these ordinances lies in their status as public claims of the guild as a group to collective honour.

Indeed, during the early years of the Reformation, before the establishment of the Discipline Court, guildsmen's moralism could turn against the Council's own policies and authority. 'Good morals' was the watchword of much early evangelical propaganda, but in place of Catholic confession it proposed shared, 'brotherly' correction, where, in accordance with the gospel, one should admonish one's brother-Christian for his sins. The morals of the rich and powerful must also be subject to such scrutiny, for they could equally damage the society. So Hans Kag, later executed for his part in the 1524 riots, averred he had wanted to admonish the mayor, Georg Vetter, in a friendly and brotherly fashion ('guotlich vnnd bruderlich') to get rid of his mistress.[39] The claim to be a 'brother' with the right to admonish this patrician and leading political figure as an equal did not go down well in a society in which the Council was increasingly presenting itself as an *Oberkeit*, an authority on a par with princes and dukes in the Imperial Diet which ruled over its subjects, whom it certainly did not see as brothers. So too, popular moralism could result in criticism of Council decisions. The demands of the rebels of 1524 included a plea for the 'release of the furrier', a man who had been imprisoned six years earlier for murdering his wife because of her infidelity.[40] In popular tradition, backed by legal precedent, there was considerable support for death as a penalty for adultery, a tradition on which Luther sometimes drew.[41] A husband who killed his wife or her seducer *in flagrante* was to be exonerated in a celebrated case in Ulm in 1528 after legal counsel had been sought from Nuremberg.[42] This kind of patriarchal moralism, which supported a man's rights over his wife's body even to the point of condoning her murder as a punishment for infidelity, could have extensive popular appeal amongst men, just as these groups also staunchly defended their right to 'chastise' their wives physically for any misdeeds.

[39] StadtAA, Reichsstadt, Urg. 11–12 Sept. 1524, Hans Kag.

[40] Broadhead, 'Internal Politics and Civic Society', p. 151.

[41] See F. Dahms, *Luther über Scheidung und Wiederverheirathung Geschiedener* (Berlin, 1859); and *D. Martin Luthers Werke* (Weimar, 1883–   ), iv, Tischreden 4499.

[42] See J. Baader, 'Nürnbergisches Rechtsgutachten über die Ermordung zweier Ehebrecher zu Ulm im Jahre 1528', *Anzeiger für Kunde der deutschen Vorzeit*, NF 11 (1864), 134–6.

Yet, though it was amongst guildsfolk that the most ardent supporters of the Reformation and evangelical moralism might be found, the new Discipline Ordinance increased the power of the Council not only at the expense of that of the Church, but also at that of the guilds. Just a year after the publication of the city Discipline Ordinance, a Discipline Ordinance for the guilds was composed by the Council. Its robust preface is an affirmation of Council authority against guild privilege:

When the honourable parlour and guild fellows survey the just, true freedoms and powers for the maintenance and furtherance of the common good, and consider the reason for matters, they will discover that they have sufficient in one authority, viz. the Council, and enough capacity for the punishment of faults, just as the firmament has sufficient in the sun, so that indeed it could not endure any addition. And in addition, because the parlour and guild fellows sit on the Council in any case and are ordained to punish the wicked and protect the pious . . .[43]

This was precisely the ambitious style of exclusive claims to authority familiar from the 1537 Ordinance. The mandate went on to point out that the Council had now forbidden guilds to punish any offences apart from competitive drinking (*Zutrinken*), gaming, cursing and verbal abuse, and public-order offences (*Frevel*). The ordinance explained that all four offences were to be punished if they were committed on guild premises; but the extent of guild subordination to Council authority was yet more apparent as the ordinance went on to advise that even serious cases within these categories were to be punished by Council authorities. Its obsessively precise demarcation of competences points to the sensitivity of the issue—as in, for instance, its bizarre prescription that when, however, '*zutrinken* and drunkenness lead to gorging [*fressen*] glass, candles or raw food, so that brutish [*vihische*] indiscipline is used, and the person seems or appears likely to cause his own death, then the Council should

---

[43] 'Wenn die erbern Stub vnnd Zunfftgnossen vff die rechte war vnnd zuerhaltung auch merung gemains nutz dienlichen freihait vnnd gerechtigkait sehen, vnnd den grund der sachen bedencken, so werden Si befinnden, das Si an ainer Oberkait Vnnd [*sic*] Straffung der Laster, das ist, an ainem erbern Rat so gnung haben als das firmanent an ainer Sonnen, der Es doch nit mer leiden mocht, Zumal weil die Stubgenossen on das im Rat sitzen, Vnnd zur Straff des pösen Vnnd beschirmung der frumen geordent seien . . .': StadtAA, Reichsstadt, Fasz. Ordnungen 54 (Zuchtordnungen), 'Straf vff den Stuben vnnd Zunnfftheusern belangend'. A copy of this ordinance, minus preamble, also exists in HWA Fischer 1429-1551, 3 July 1538.

punish'. The ordinance concluded by recognizing the right of the 'delegated six lords' (Discipline Lords) to make their own inquiries about 'each and every parlour and guild-house, in such a way that if they find that one or more of the four above-mentioned offences has been committed in the parlours or guild-houses, and had not been punished within eight days', then the Discipline Lords should have full power to punish. Curbing guild autonomy still further, it added that guild authorities who failed to punish offenders would themselves be disciplined—a measure which expressed a deep mistrust of the probity of guild officials. Indeed, to judge by the Weaver Journeymen's Ordinance of 1545, the limitations on guild authority were being drawn still tighter, for that ordinance recognized the Council's right to punish even those already disciplined internally by the guild.[44] The extension of Council jurisdiction to cover the entire city, subordinating even the vaunted independence of the guild enclaves to the 'inquiries' of the Discipline Lords, marked the claim of the new moral righteousness to be truly city-wide. It created, in theory at least, a unified body of subjects, subordinating not only the guildsmen to the demands of discipline, but bringing women and non-guildsfolk just as surely under its sway.

But the shift in power from guild to Council was not simply accomplished by Council fiat. Increasingly through the 1530s and 1540s, guildsmen themselves seem to have been attracted to the central forum of politics. By contrast, the traditional route to membership of the political establishment—steady progress through the ranks of the guild Twelve and Great Council membership, up through the position of guild master and inclusion in the Small Council, to be finally crowned after many years with a political post with some power—could seem less attractive. Jakob Herbrot, the parvenu furrier who burst on to the political scene in 1540, becoming head of his guild and a member of the Small Council, had not served a single year as a guild representative. His ascent from there to mayorship in five years was a remarkable case of accession to real political power without any apprenticeship in guild

---

[44] Ibid., HWO/ A, Knappenordnung, Policei Ordnung fos. 280^r-283^v, 21 Mar. 1545.

politics.[45] Nor, though he was the most extraordinary, was he the only craft politician to rise so rapidly in the 1540s. Men like Hans Schweiklin, who entered the Council in 1539 and became a treasurer in 1540 (a post which carried with it membership of the Thirteen, the Council's powerful inner group); Sebastian Seitz, who became a councillor in the same year and a tax-master in 1540, rising to become a keeper of seals in 1548; or Georg Oesterreicher, who joined the Council in 1545 and rose to become mayor a mere three years later, could boast similarly meteoric careers.[46] None had served a weary decade in guild politics: instead, they chose to invest their political ambitions directly in urban politics. A Council which seemed to be implementing a programme of evangelical reform grounded in guild values could well have appeared a more profitable and sympathetic arena than the gerontocracy of the guilds. A morally regenerate Council, which aimed to bring all the citizenry together as a community, and forced even the clergy to integrate themselves and take out citizenship, may have promised a more compelling Utopia than the fragmented, competitive honour system where each separate corporation fought for its standing and privilege. This shift in the centre of political gravity away from the guilds and even more firmly towards the Council may help to account for the failure of the guilds to mount a serious challenge to this invasion of their privileges—a failure which was to have devastating consequences when they were finally dissolved by order of the Emperor in 1548.

The growing participation of guildsmen in urban government during the 1540s can be traced at several levels. Amongst the Thirteen, the most powerful committee, the personality of the non-patrician Jakob Herbrot clearly stamped urban politics. But he operated within a ruling clique which, in numerical terms at least, hovered around the traditional ratio of eight guildsmen to five patricians. It was above all in the new offices—the Discipline

---

[45] Ibid., Ratsämterlisten 1536–48, Tübingen Sonderforschungsbereich computer print-out. On Herbrot, see Roth, *Augsburgs Reformationsgeschichte*, iii, iv; Sieh-Burens, *Oligarchie, Konfession und Politik*; P. Hecker, 'Der Augsburger Bürgermeister Jakob Herbrot und der Sturz des zünftigen Regiments in Augsburg', *ZHVS* 1 (1874), 34–98.

[46] StadtAA, Reichsstadt, Ratsämterlisten 1536–48, Tübingen Sonderforschungsbereich computer print-out.

Lords, the augmented *Einunger*, the Iron Lords, the Butchers' Lords, the Poor Law Lords, and, to a lesser extent, the Marriage Court judges—that the influx of guildsmen was evident. In a single year these new areas of government created over eighty new posts, most of which were filled by guildsmen—an exponential expansion of offices which must have done much to absorb the energies of any politically ambitious guildsman.[47] Their areas of responsibility—discipline, compromise, marital disputes, petty offences—had been the substance of the guilds' own original jurisdiction; and doubtless when they exercised their authority these men brought with them the values they had formed in the craft milieu.

Discipline Lords and Marriage Judges

Within this newly reorganized system of offices and career patterns, the Discipline Lords became rapidly entrenched. Nine of the fifteen men who entered the ruling clique of the Thirteen between 1539 and 1548 had served in the Discipline Lords.[48] A seat on this bench became an established phase of a political career for both guildsmen and patricians. The Lords itself, with its careful balance of members of the Small and Great Councils (according to its original constitution, half were to come from each), drew inexperienced guildsmen into urban politics and gave them the opportunity of working with members of the Small Council and even with senior politicians, of whom there was usually one nominated each year. Together, as they passed judgement in the name of the Council on those who came before them, they learnt the deportment of authority.

The Discipline Lords were firmly identified with evangelicalism. None of those who served up to 1548 is known to us as a Catholic, an extraordinary occurrence in a civic administration which still included some Catholics in its ranks. Yet strangely enough, the Marriage Court, which one might expect to be far more robustly evangelical because its very existence was a clear violation of ecclesiastical authority, does

---

[47] Ibid.
[48] Ibid.; and for membership of the Discipline Lords before 1542, see RB 1529-42.

not seem to have been so firmly Protestant. Two of those who served on it for many years, Leonhart Christof Rehlinger and Heinrich Rehlinger, were prominent (though not hard-line) Catholics by at least 1548.[49] This difference is illuminating, and it suggests that these two new institutions had markedly different characters.

These dissimilarities are borne out by an examination of the backgrounds of those who served on the two bodies. As Tables 2.1 and 2.2 demonstrate, whereas all the Marriage Court judges also served in the city court, of which the Marriage Court was a sub-court, only 60 per cent of those who served as Discipline Lords could draw on court experience.[50] The collective court experience of Marriage Court judges appears even more marked if we consider the length of time they served on the civic court: over three-quarters of these men served three years or more here, and nearly half of them had civic court experience (many of them extensive) which pre-dated their term of office on the Marriage Court. The Marriage Court judges were thus clearly marked as men with legal abilities who knew how to operate the civic law code and were acquainted with the complex civic legal procedures.

The Discipline Lords had simple procedures and virtually no legal rigmarole, though it too developed its own rituals. Many of the Discipline Lords, by contrast, also worked on the *Einunger*, the comparatively informal court of arbitration which settled those small disputes that did not need to come to court (see Table 2.2). In the years before the institutionalization of the Reformation in 1537, the *Einunger* had increasingly concerned itself with the settlement of marital disputes, claims for compensation for loss of virginity and child support, and insult cases—all offences which now came under the purview of the Discipline Lords. The continuity between *Einunger* and Discipline Lords personnel must have fostered a certain consistency of approach, albeit under a rather different legal

---

[49] Sieh-Burens, *Oligarchie, Konfession und Politik*, pp. 171, 347 ff.; StadtAA, Reichsstadt, Ratsämterlisten 1536-48.

[50] See Köhler, *Zürcher Ehegericht und Genfer Konsistorium*, ii. 290. The full complement of judges was 21, plus 3 to 4 'chief judges': StadtAA, Reichsstadt, Ratsämterlisten 1536-48.

TABLE 2.1. *Offices held by Marriage Court judges appointed 1537-1546*

Office	Experience	% of known total	No experience	Unknown	Total
Civic court*	31	100	—	—	31
Executive office**	5	17	24	2	31
Small Council	17	59	12	2	31
Council	25	86	4	2	31
Einunger	13	49	16	2	31
Eisenherren	11	38	18	2	31
Other offices	16	55	13	2	31
Discipline Lords	15	52	14	2	31

Note: The following 3 individuals could not be definitively identified in the Ratsämterlisten: Georg Manasser, Hans Layman, Lienhart Mair (appointed 1548). Since their guild affiliation is given with their court position, however, we can determine civic court experience and guild membership in all cases. Eleven new Marriage Court judges were appointed in 1547-8, but the court does not appear to have been functioning in those years.

*Twenty-six men had a total of 3 years' experience or more on the civic court, and only 5 had less than 3 years'; while 14, nearly half, had civic court experience which predated their Marriage Court work.

**By executive office is meant any position which included the holder amongst the Thirteen, or a post as tax-master or wine-tax receiver. Here I follow the definition of 'höhere Ämter' used by K. Sieh-Burens in 'Die Augsburger Stadtverfassung um 1500', *ZHVSN* 77 (1983), 125-49, 138 f. None of the Marriage Court judges had consistent experience of such high office.

Source: StadtAA, Reichstadt, Ratsämterlisten 1520-35, 1536-48, and computer print-out of this source from the Tübingen Sonderforschungsbereich Projekt Z2, 'Stadt und Reformation'; and Ehegerichtsbuch 1537-46.

framework. For while the *Einunger* was in essence a court of arbitration, the Discipline Lords was an authority created to further discipline through punishment.[51]

---

[51] On the *Einunger*, see Liedl, *Gerichtsverfassung und Zivilprozess*, p. 30; and see StadtAA, Reichsstadt, Prot. der Einunger.

TABLE 2.2. *Offices held by Discipline Lords appointed 1537–1548*

Office	Experience	% of known total	No experience	Unknown	Total
Civic court*	36	61	23	8	67
Executive office**	15	25	44	8	67
Small Council	51	86	8	8	67
Council	67	100	—	—	67
Einunger	38	64	21	8	67
Eisenherren	37	63	22	8	67
Other offices	42	71	17	8	67
Marriage Court	16	27	43	8	67

Note: The following 7 individuals could not be definitively identified in the Ratsämterlisten: Jorg Hohenauer, Hans Layman, Conrad Mair, Hans Mair, Lienhart Mair, Georg Manasser, Lienhart Umbach, Ulrich Welser.

*Ten of the Discipline Lords had 3 years' or more of civic court experience; and another 10 had less than 3 years' experience.

**Taken to include membership of the Thirteen, or appointment to the position of tax-master or wine-tax receiver.

Source: StadtAA, Reichstadt, Ratsbücher, Ratsämterlisten, and computer print-out of this source from the Tübingen Sonderforschungsbereich Projekt Z2, 'Stadt und Reformation'.

Moreover, the Discipline Lords as a group could boast far longer political careers and much more developed political networks (see Table 2.3). All had been members of the Large Council, whereas only 86 per cent of Marriage Court judges were councillors. Membership of the Large Council, and the leading rank within the guild structure which was its prerequisite, was the absolute minimum foundation for any political influence within the city.[52] The political careers of twenty-five of the Discipline

[52] On the political institutions of Augsburg, see P. Dirr, 'Studien zur Geschichte der Augsburger Zunftverfassung', *ZHVS* 39 (1913), 144–243; H. Lutz, *Conrad Peutinger: Beiträge zu einer politischen Biographie* (Augsburg, 1958); O. Mörke, 'Die Fugger im 16. Jahrhundert: Städtische Elite oder Sonderstruktur?', *Archiv für Reformationsgeschichte*, 74 (1983), 141–62; I. Bátori, *Die Reichsstadt Augsburg im 18. Jahrhundert: Verfassung, Finanzen und Reformversuche* (Göttingen, 1969); and on the political establishment in the city, see especially Roth, *Augsburgs Reformationsgeschichte*, iii, iv; Sieh-Burens, *Oligarchie, Konfession und Politik*.

TABLE 2.3. *Length of political experience among Discipline Lords and Marriage Court judges, measured by membership of the Large Council*

	Marriage Court Judges		Discipline Lords	
	No.	%	No.	%
Councillor before 1530	12		25	
Councillor first elected between 1530 and 1533	6		15	
Pre-Reformation total	18	46	40	68
Councillor first elected between 1534 and 1539	8		13	
Councillor first elected between 1540 and 1548	6		6	
Post-Reformation total	14	36	19	32
New councillor	7	—	—	—
Total of those identified	39	—	59	—
Unknown	3	—	8	—
TOTAL	42	—	67	—

Lords dated back to before 1530 (over 40 per cent of those whose careers can be identified), while only twelve Marriage Court judges (just over a quarter) could claim this length of experience. Less than half the Marriage Court judges had become involved in civic politics before the first steps towards Reformation in 1534; the majority of the Discipline Lords had been members of the Council before the Reformation's official beginnings.

The comparative political inexperience of the Marriage Court judges is even more obvious at the higher levels of government. Most of the Discipline Lords had also served in some capacity on the Small Council, and a quarter had some experience in key governmental posts. But only about half of the Marriage Court judges had been members of the Small Council, and none of them could claim regular experience of high governmental office. Since the members of the Small Council were responsible for conducting criminal interrogations,[53] the close links between

[53] This is evident from the names of those present at interrogations. On occasion, the city notary might also observe interrogations—as Peutinger did during the trials of the Anabaptists, apparently formulating many of the questions

Discipline Lords and councillors were especially significant. Discipline Lords were thoroughly acquainted with the techniques of criminal interrogation and were well versed in dealing with those offenders who, as the interrogators saw it, required the discipline of severe punishment. When they imposed penalties on offenders, they did so with an awareness of the spectrum of disciplining methods available, and with an intimate knowledge of its harsher extremes. The overlap in membership of the Small Council and Discipline Lords also mirrors the essential coherence of the two authorities and their shared ethos. They both saw it as their duty to foster discipline and civic righteousness, by force if need be; and they worked from the same understanding of moral responsibilities—parental, husbandly, and civic.

Equally remarkable are the differences in social profiles of the Discipline Lords and the Marriage Court judges: ten of the forty-two Marriage Court judges, nearly a quarter, were patricians, seven of them men who had joined the patriciate in 1538. By contrast, only eleven, just over a sixth, of the sixty-seven Discipline Lords were patricians, and four of them were drawn from the new patriciate. The Discipline Lords were distributed fairly evenly among all the guilds: the Marriage Court judges, on the other hand, show a slight bias towards the more prestigious guilds, such as the merchants' guild, the salt-producers' guild, and the increasingly powerful furriers' guild. No Marriage Court judges came from guilds of such low prestige as the coopers', linen-weavers', fishers', or pedlars'.[54]

Striking, too, are the different patterns of service of Marriage Court judges and Discipline Lords. Marriage Court judges constituted something of a closed, coherent coterie, with only thirty-one judges appointed during the entire period 1537–46, most of whom officiated for three years or more. Discipline Lords, by contrast, almost never served two terms. Their continuity was achieved instead by a system of half-yearly rotation of offices, so that three 'old' Discipline Lords, as they were termed, always served with three 'new' ones. But the

---

as well. See Lutz, *Conrad Peutinger*, pp. 277–83, and cf. for Nuremberg, G. Strauss, *Nuremberg in the Sixteenth Century: City Politics and Life between Middle Ages and Modern Times* (Bloomington and London, 1966), pp. 225–7.

[54] L. Roper, 'Work, Marriage and Sexuality: Women in Reformation Augsburg', Ph.D. thesis (London, 1985), pp. 82–124.

differences in customary length of service illustrate the fundamental dissimilarities between the two authorities. Whereas a Marriage Court judge was a member of a defined group, with a good measure of civic court experience built up over consistent years of practice, Discipline Lords were, by comparison, almost faceless men. Any member of the governing élite might expect, in due course, to serve as a Discipline Lord, but only those with judicial experience and competence became Marriage Court judges. Aptly named 'Lords' (*Herren*), the Discipline Lords were closely identified with the broad governmental élite, the political 'lords' of the city. They were certainly not 'lords' (patricians) in the social sense of the word: their milieu was that of the guild élite, the leading political force in the town after 1537. Using the twin institutions for reforming the city—the harsh remedy of the criminal trial and the milder control of the discipline authority— this large group of men tried to create a godly community in Augsburg.

MORALS, GENDER, AND CRIME

Such a vast reorganization of the civic bureaucracy of punishment under the banner of creating the disciplined, godly Utopia had a marked impact on the citizenry. Its most remarkable effect was the increase in the proportion of women offenders coming before the Council for judgement. Throughout the 1530s and 1540s there was a steep rise in this percentage, accompanied by a spectacular jump in the absolute numbers of those offenders who confronted the Council: while twenty-one individuals came before it in 1521, 155 faced it twenty years later.[55]

The increased numbers of people interrogated, warned, and punished by the Council was accompanied by a change in the kind of offences presented to it; and this change, in turn, was linked to an increasingly rigid sexualization of certain kinds of crime, which gradually contributed to a further elaboration of male and female natures as inherently different. Men, both before and after the Reformation, were punished for fighting and rowdy behaviour on the streets: women rarely received penalties from

[55] Ibid. 114, table 2.9.

the Council for rough behaviour, though some were punished by the Discipline Lords. The threat which men, armed as a matter of course, were thought to pose to civic peace is evidenced not only by the numbers punished, but also in a provision of the 1537 Ordinance which forbade anyone to draw a weapon in the entire area surrounding the town hall or at any of the city gates or bridges—an interesting attempt to create a physically secure environment for the Council and its servants, safe from young men's random violence which the Council feared might rapidly turn to riot.

Women, by contrast, were called to answer for sexual offences. Indeed, the increased number of women offenders can be largely explained by the exclusion of the so-called 'Galli exiles' from the totals. These were a motley crew of prostitutes and procurers who were drummed out of town each year shortly before the new Council took office.[56] The new determined moralism of the Council allowed no such crude approach: instead, each offender was interrogated at length and punished not *en bloc*, but in a manner suited to the precise details of the crime. Sexual crime, which made up nearly half the crimes of which women were accused, accounted for only 14 per cent of male offences. On the other hand, more men than women came before the Council charged with adultery and fornication, chiefly because the Council of the late 1530s and early 1540s charged the clients of prostitutes with these offences. Crime-records alone, however, underestimate the extent to which women had become entangled with court and Council proceedings because of sexual crimes, for they were also well represented amongst those punished by the Discipline Lords.

Perhaps the most vivid manifestation of this shift in emphasis is the recategorization of the crime of rape. Whereas in the Civic Code of 1276 it had been classed as a crime of violence, the 1537 Ordinance marked its final incorporation into the range of sexual offences, grouping it as one extreme of immoral behaviour in a continuum passing through fornication and seduction. Immediately

---

[56] On the Galli banishments, see Chap. 3 below, and Buff, 'Verbrechen und Verbrecher zu Augsburg in der zweiten Hälfte des 14. Jahrhunderts', *ZHVS* 4 (1878), 160–232. By the sixteenth century the range of offenders appears to have narrowed until it comprised sexual offenders almost exclusively: see StadtAA, Reichsstadt, Strafbuch des Rats I, 1509–26; II, 1533–9, for lists of *Gallileute*.

following the warning of stern punishment for rape is a paragraph on seduction 'by word or deed' to a man's will. This provision ensured that men accused of rape would do best to argue that the woman had been seduced, or at least, that he had not seen signs of resistance—a strategy which focused the court's concern on the sexual behaviour of the woman, not that of the man.[57]

The comportment which increasingly began to be expected of women was modesty and chastity. The Council continued to take the few rape allegations which came before it extremely seriously, but these inevitably became the occasion for investigating not only the alleged rapist's behaviour, but the woman's chastity. Both before and after the Reformation, men had impugned women's sexual reputations to escape accusations of rape and seduction, but the 1537 Ordinance now explicitly supported this male plea. So, for example, Anna Peutinger, who explained that Wolf Rechlsperger had used 'threatening words' to make her submit to his will, found her narrative treated as an accusation of rape: a charge which Rechlsperger sought to escape by arguing that 'he did not think that he had taken her virginity, for she had long had an evil reputation for dishonourable things'.[58] To the Council, which, as we shall see in the next chapter, increasingly regarded a woman's chastity as central to virtue, this stain on her reputation counted against her, and made it disinclined to accept that she had been 'forced'. Because she was not a virgin, though she was a servant living with a relative, she was regarded as both more culpable for her sexual relationship with Rechlsperger than a young girl in her position would usually have been, and as more sexual.

[57] See C. Meyer (ed.), *Das Stadtbuch von Augsburg, insbesondere das Stadtrecht von 1276* (Augsburg, 1872), Art. XXXI, pp. 88–90; and cf. *Ains Erbern Rats | der Stat Augspurg | Zucht vnd Pollicey Ordnung*, fo. b/i^r. This may account for the low rate of reports of, and convictions for, rape. The provisions of the 1276 statute, which allowed for physical combat between woman and rapist, were no longer in use; and accused rapists had for some time been attempting to mitigate their crime by arguing that the woman had either not shown signs of resistance or had consented; or alternatively, that she was already 'of bad fame' and therefore must have consented. See e.g. StadtAA, Reichsstadt, Urg. Mittwoch vor Galli 1496, Conrad Scheyfelin; Urg. 11 Oct. 1496, Hans Rotklinger; Urg. 16 Mar. 1536 (stored Lit. 1536), Hans Landsperger; and note Urg. 5 Feb. 1534, Elisabeth Guterman, who made an allegation of rape against Baltas Eckenberger which she withdrew under threat of torture.

[58] 'Er acht auch nit das Er Jr die Junckfrauschafft genommen dann Si lange Zeit ain pos geschray vneerlicher sachen halb gehabt hab': StadtAA, Reichsstadt, Urg. 17 Jan. 1541, Wolf Rechlsperger, Segenschmid; and 17 Jan. 1541, Anna Peutinger.

Indeed, an even more important means by which female nature was defined and elaborated was the Council's interrogation procedure itself. The Council regularly put far more detailed sheets of questions to women than to men, demanding to be told the full details of women's sexual encounters. But female nature was sharply differentiated. Council methods revealed a pervasive distinction between sexually inexperienced virgins on the one hand, who might expect to meet with a milder paternalism from a Council which regretted their 'fall'; and the sexually experienced, and hence voracious and dangerous, women who led men astray. This was the principle which Anna Peutinger transgressed, and which cost her a sympathetic hearing. Women were either virgins or sexually experienced creatures of lust; a categorization which made it difficult for the Council to believe in wifely 'chastity', for underneath even the most pious wifely exterior there might be a lusting, power-hungry woman. Such a prospect lent a particular fascination to the interrogations of mature women.

The figure of the sexually hungry, masterful woman also made a frequent appearance in men's narratives as they were interrogated by the Council. In pleading which was often accepted by the Council, they would allege that they had been led on by women. As one man described it: 'she had sprung on him like a billygoat', an accusation which the Council cited verbatim in its condemnation of the woman to eternal exile.[59] This was a case of adultery by a man with a woman who was separated from her husband: yet while the man was sentenced to four weeks' imprisonment, the statutory punishment for single adultery, the woman's penalty was the customary punishment for prostitution.[60] The woman was the stronger party economically in this relationship. She had lent her lover money which he had not repaid, and it is possible that it was she who brought the case before the Council. The woman's assumption of the male position was perceived, by both Council and male opinion, as bestial and shocking. Yet it was also an acknowledgement

[59] 'vmb das Sie . . . an Jme, wie ain Bockh aufgesprungen ist': ibid., Strafbush des Rats II, fo. 158ᵛ, 13 Nov. 1539; and see Urg. 10 Nov. 1539, Margaret Aicheler.
[60] Ibid., Urg. 12 Nov. 1539, Hans Laminit; and Strafbuch des Rats II, fo. 159ᵛ, 13 Nov. 1539; Prot. der Zuchtherren II, fo. 64, 15 Nov. 1539.

of the power of women's sexuality. If it was a vocabulary of sexual relations which accorded recognition to women's active heterosexual desire, that language was also a domain of perpetual contest between men and women, where male mastery had constantly to be reauthenticated.

Despite their differences, Council and craftsmen shared common attitudes to sexual difference. Sexual relations could become the most potent area of expression of this kind of craft and civic patriarchalism, riven by contradictory beliefs about women's sexual natures and anxieties about embattled manhood. The language of daily speech and insult suggests what was at stake: one woman said of her husband that 'he is no man, neither at table nor bed', equating his sexual and economic incapacity.[61] Another accused a cowardly man of being 'slandering and hairless', an attack on his virility coupled with an accusation of what was thought to be the female fault *par excellence*—an evil tongue.[62] Men themselves could use such language to shame each other: one master told an apprentice who had been receiving advances from a fellow maidservant that he must sleep with her 'to save men's honour'; another told a woman he was trying to seduce that 'if I should lie with you and do nothing, I would be no man'.[63] Manhood was a status with a code of behaviour. To be a man was to have the power to take women; and male heterosexuality was thought to involve an active—though contested—exercise of mastery, a real 'fight for the trousers' as popular woodcuts depicted it.

Council interrogation and punishment policy concentrated on being educative, discovering the moment when 'discipline' had been lost. This concern led to a far more precise definition of the differences between women and men, and in the case of 'criminal' women above all, to an excavation of the individual's sexual and moral history, carried out in most detail, as we shall see in the next chapter, in the case of prostitutes. Interrogations

---

[61] Ibid., Urg. 5 Sept. 1532, Margaret Becz.
[62] Ibid., Urg. 14 Nov. 1528, Michel Scherpfstain.
[63] 'so sollt Er Mannseer rettenn': ibid., Urg. 28, 29 Jan. 1544, Hans Dempf and Anna Has; 'sollt ich ein nacht bei dir ligen vnd nichts mit dir Aussrichten wer ich doch kein man': words reported by Walpurga Frosch, ibid., Urg. 3–6 Mar. 1534, 6 Mar.

brought an unravelling of the household so as to reassert the proper household order. Marital disputes, as Chapter 5 will show, were consequently a field in which the Council was happy to intervene. Sin and guilt, though intensely personal, were seen to be shared, for not only the sinner, but those who gave them 'comfort, refuge or assistance' or who merely tolerated such goings-on were implicated. Brothel-keepers, innkeepers, householders, those who winked at adultery, and even those who encouraged marital disharmony were also believed to participate in the guilt. Similarly, the notions of sin and responsibility applied to the wider 'household', the city itself. Were it to tolerate sin and indiscipline or the abomination (*greuel*) of false belief, the city could justly expect divine retribution.[64] Seemingly trivial policing, such as banning dances or restricting pomp, began to be prefaced by long elaborate statements of the kind of order at which the Council aimed.[65] So linked were the convictions of civic righteousness and communal salvation that at the moment of greatest political danger, as the Schmalkaldic War loomed, the Council responded by publishing a mandate against spendthrifts (*Verschwender*) and increasing sexual discipline yet further.[66]

But though evangelicals made the language of moralism their own, absorbing and elaborating the sexual divisions which underpinned it, Protestants themselves were not always paragons of civic virtue. Sometimes even their champions spectacularly failed to measure up to evangelical standards, and were duly punished by the new institutions. Johannes Gebhart, schoolmaster of the new German school, had to admit to an affair with a 'compatriot' (*Landsmännin*) of his, a Bavarian servant-woman, and when his wife complained of his continuing 'unmarital' behaviour, and he himself showed disrespect to the Council, he was dismissed from the post.[67] As a semi-cleric and town official heading a Protestant-inspired institution, Gebhart's 'immorality' was serious enough; far more serious was the adultery committed by men who were the chief exponents of the Reformation in the town. Gereon Sailer, Dr Ulrich Jung, and Martin Haid, civic

---

[64] StadtAA, EWA, Akten 468.

[65] StadtAA, Reichsstadt, Schätze 16, fo. 54^r, 22 Dec. 1540; fo. 48^v, n.d.

[66] Ibid., Schätze 16, fo. 113^v, 26 June 1546.

[67] Ibid., Urg. 7 Mar. 1541, 26 Apr. 1541, Johannes Gebhart; Strafbuch des Rats III, fo. 30^r, 26 Apr. 1541.

notary, were all named, with some glee, by the Catholic monk and chronicler Clemens Sender as having committed adultery.[68] Yet if, by the late 1530s and 1540s, evangelicals could hardly lay exclusive claim to moral behaviour, and the moral world of the Reformation had become more complex, the power of moral rhetoric was not diminished. On the contrary, it remained a distinctive strand in civic rhetoric throughout the sixteenth century, and the notions of manhood and womanhood which the new interrogation procedures so powerfully reinforced lived on beyond the Reformation.

[68] *Chroniken der deutschen Städte*, xxiii, Sender, p. 404; see also StadtAA, Reichsstadt, Urg. 22 Dec. 1533, where Anna Lyndenmair names Gereon Sailer as a client when she worked as a prostitute; and note also RB 19./I, fo. 11^r, 22 Jan. 1545: Ludwig Jesske, preacher at St Moritz, was involved in a case at the Marriage Court because he had seduced a virgin, Sara Reisser, and promised her marriage. He fled to Friedberg and became a Catholic.

3
Prostitution and Moral Order *

'HERE at Augsburg the Council did away with the brothel at the prompting of the Lutheran preachers.'[1] This laconic sentence—a notation under the year 1532 by the Catholic monk Clemens Sender—is the only reference by any of the town's chroniclers to the closure of the city brothel, an event which they and subsequent historians seem to have thought of little consequence in the turbulent years of the Reformation. Augsburg was not the only city at this time to close a city brothel, an institution which had been an established part of civic life in most large towns for more than two centuries.[2] Such decisions marked a turning-point in the organization of prostitution, attitudes to it, and indeed, to sexuality. As the chronicler knew, these changes were connected with the new ethos of the Reformation.

But what was the system of tolerated prostitution which the reformers found so ungodly? Its most distinctive feature was the municipal character of the city-run brothel. The brothel-keeper was required, in most towns, to swear an annual oath of office to the Council just like other civic officials; and its terms might describe his duties as (to quote the Ulm oath) 'to further the interests and piety of the city and its folk, and to warn and keep

---

* This chapter is a revised version of 'Discipline and Respectability: Prostitution and The Reformation in Augsburg', which first appeared in *History Workshop Journal*, 19 (1985), 3–28.

[1] *Die Chroniken der deutschen Städte vom 14. bis ins 16. Jahrhundert*, 36 vols. (Leipzig, 1862–1931), xxiii. 337.

[2] On closures in other cities, see I. Bloch, *Die Prostitution*, 2 vols. (Berlin, 1912, 1925), ii. 260–2; and S. Karant-Nunn, 'Continuity and Change: Some Effects of the Reformation on the Women of Zwickau', *Sixteenth Century Journal*, 12/2 (1982), 16–42, here p. 23; and see also L. Otis, *Prostitution in Medieval Society: The History of an Urban Institution in Languedoc* (Chicago, 1985); M. Mazzi, 'Il mondo della prostituzione nella Firenze tardo medievale', *Ricerche storiche*, 14 (1984) 337–63; *Memoria* 17 (1986), special issue on prostitution.

it from harm'.[3] Though the brothel-keeper ran the business, and in some towns (as in Augsburg) owned the buildings, the civic authority might still be liable for repairs to the premises.[4] In return, the town made use of the brothel as a civic resource. During imperial visits, the Emperor and his retinue might be given a complimentary night at the brothel; and their evening was celebrated with torchlight processions and luxurious feasting.[5] At Würzburg, visits by town officials on St John's Day, and at Frankfurt, invitations to the prostitutes for the Council's annual venison feast, confirmed the brothel's role as part of the town's ceremonial resources, a means to demonstrate the power and hospitality of the commune.[6] The women, like other civic assets, were subject to inspection by other officials; the latter were usually midwives (though to the brothel-keeper's horror, the Ulm Council introduced inspection by male doctors, in the presence of the city employees responsible for patrolling beggars). The inspectors ensured that the brothel-keeper was fulfilling his obligation to provide the city with 'suitable, clean and healthy women'.[7] These three adjectives encapsulated the Council's

[3] Stadtarchiv Ulm, A 3988, Der frowen wiert ayd; and see StadtAA, Reichsstadt, RB 277, 'Aidbuch' of the fifteenth century, fo. 18ᵛ, frowen wirt aid. I am grateful to Rolf Kiessling for this reference. Since Augsburg has few records on the brothel before the Reformation, I have drawn on material relating to brothels in other cities. Surviving ordinances reveal that their organizations were broadly similar.

[4] See G. L. Kriegk, *Deutsches Bürgerthum im Mittelalter*, 2 vols. (Frankfurt, 1868–71), ii. 308; K. Obser, 'Zur Geschichte des Frauenhauses in Überlingen', *Zeitschrift für Geschichte des Oberrheins*, 70 (1916), 631–44; Dr. von Posern-Klett, 'Frauenhäuser und freie Frauen in Sachsen', *Archiv für die sächsische Geschichte*, 12 (1874), 63–89, here p. 67.

[5] C. Jäger, *Ulms Verfassungs- , bürgerliches und commercielles Leben im Mittelalter* (Heilbronn, 1831), p. 545; von Posern-Klett, 'Frauenhäuser und freie Frauen', p. 80; M. Bauer, *Liebesleben in deutscher Vergangenheit* (Berlin, 1924), p. 138; see also *Chroniken der deutschen Städte*, xi. 464; and W. Rudeck, *Geschichte der öffentlichen Sittlichkeit in Deutschland* (Jena, 1897), pp. 31–3.

[6] Kriegk, *Deutsches Bürgerthum*, iii. 327; Bauer, *Liebesleben*, p. 138. On the municipal nature of the brothel, see also, for France, J. Rossiaud, section 3 of J. Le Goff (ed.), *La ville médiévale des Carolingiens à la Renaissance* (Paris, 1980), p. 532; Otis, *Prostitution in Medieval Society*.

[7] Brothel-keeper's complaint: Staatsarchiv Ludwigsburg, B 207, Bü 68, no. 166. The doctor and the official in charge of beggars gave the woman an internal examination ('besechent sy einwertz Jrs leibs'), 'which no man has the right to do'. For clean women, see Stadtarchiv Ulm, A 3669 (Zweites Gsatzbuch), fos. 416 ff., Newe frawen wierts ordnung 1512. I have found no evidence that German prostitutes were organized in guilds, though this claim is even repeated in modern literature: the 'guild of prostitutes', however, is used ironically to refer to the women.

concerns: the women should be free from disease (syphilis was clearly one of its anxieties), should be of age, and should be sound specimens. In formulating such ordinances and in arranging annual inspections, the Council was declaring itself the special adjudicator in disputes between prostitutes and brothel-keeper, and adopting special responsibility for a trade which had no guild structure of its own.

It was therefore fully consistent with the brothel's place in civic society for the Council to speak of it as 'enhancing the good, piety and honour of the whole commune'.[8] But this language, and the manner in which the Council employed the brothel as a show-piece, clearly rested upon a male-defined understanding of whom the term 'commune' included. Just as only adult male citizens could enjoy full political rights and bear arms in defence of the commune, so here also, masculinity, virility, and membership of the polity were intimately connected. In theory, women too were supposed to benefit from the brothel because it made the city safe for 'respectable' women: yet here they were referred to protectively in terms of their relations to men, as the wives and daughters of citizens, even though they could be citizens in their own right.

Though a public institution, the city brothel was not officially open to all men. Theoretically, married men were forbidden to visit it; and all cities threatened punishment for any married man found within its walls.[9] Restrictions were placed on clerics using the brothel: Nuremberg banned them outright, while Nördlingen more realistically forbade them only to stay overnight.[10] But in

---

[8] Stadtarchiv Ulm, A 3988 (draft ordinance, 1510). On prostitutes as an integral part of their community, see M. Perry, '"Lost Women" in Early Modern Seville: The Politics of Prostitution', *Feminist Studies*, 4/1 (1978), 195–214; and R. Trexler, 'La prostitution florentine au xve siècle: Patronages et clientèles', *Annales*, 26/6 (1981), 983–1015.

[9] Bloch, *Die Prostitution*, i. 767. Note also StadtAA, Reichsstadt, Schätze 36/1, Zuchtordnung 1472. This refers to the woman 'who goes to a married man's house and does not spare the wife within'; and threatens her with banishment. It suggests both that there were 'home calls' for married men and that this, rather than the actual recourse to prostitutes by married men, was causing concern.

[10] Bauer, *Liebesleben*, p. 134 (Metz, 1332); J. Baader, *Nürnberger Polizeiordnungen aus dem 13. bis 15. Jahrhundert* (Stuttgart, 1861), p. 119; W. Reynizsch, *Uiber Truhten und Truhtensteine, Barden und Bardenlieder: Feste, Schmäuser . . . und Gerichte der Teutschen* (Gotha, 1802), p. 31 (Nördlingen, 1472).

Augsburg at least, in the early years of the sixteenth century, there are suspiciously few cases of married men being caught in brothels, and in other towns, cases usually multiply in the wake of mandates against concubinage and adultery.[11] One has only to compare the numerous convictions of married men found in the Zurich brothel during the Reformation years, when the Council was determined to translate principle into practice.[12] Travellers, a group which brought much of the brothel's custom, could easily deny being married; and such niceties were forgotten during the Emperor's visits or at imperial diets.

Brothels were designed for one particular group of men—journeymen and apprentices not yet married—and the 'free house', 'common house', or 'women's house' as it was variously known, was a central part of their cultural world. Richer men could afford the services of courtesans or retain a mistress, but the low prices of the city brothels ensured that ordinary apprentices and journeymen could afford to pay. A centre of popular entertainment of all kinds, brothels sold alcohol, board-games were played, and the brothel-keeper was supposed to watch out for professional cheats.[13] Its function, like that of taverns, as a focus of male entertainment explains why (as the Ulm Council complained) young lads of twelve or less were frequenting it.[14] For many, the excitement of going with a group of workmates, of looking, teasing, and fantasizing, comprised the amusement. The sale of food and alcohol was an important source of the brothel's profit, and in 1510 and 1512 the Ulm Council found it necessary to forbid the brothel-keeper to sell alcohol to take away, to hold drinking sprees, or to force prostitutes and clients to buy alcohol at inflated prices.[15] Brothels were a stage

[11] StadtAA, Reichsstadt, RB 13, fo. 83ᵛ, 1515; Strafbuch des Rats I, p. 185, 20 Sept. 1526; and for cases of married men punished for consorting with prostitutes, see e.g. pp. 19, 37, 46.

[12] W. Köhler, *Zürcher Ehegericht und Genfer Konsistorium*, 2 vols. (Leipzig, 1932, 1942), i. 145–7.

[13] Stadtarchiv Ulm, A 3988, Der frowen wiert ayd; A [6543], Aid- und Ordnungsbuch, fo. cccxvʳ; Bloch, *Die Prostitution*, i. 777. See also S. Schama, *The Embarrassment of Riches: An Interpretation of Dutch Culture in the Golden Age* (London, 1987), pp. 465–80.

[14] G. Geiger, *Die Reichsstadt Ulm vor der Reformation* (Ulm, 1971), pp. 173 f.

[15] Stadtarchiv Ulm, A 3988, Der frowen wiert ayd; Bloch, *Die Prostitution* i. 767–70.

for male bravado; and they were frequently the scene of fights, even though causing a disturbance in the brothel carried a double penalty.[16] The brothel's popularity exemplifies the distinctness of the leisure lives of young men and women: while men's entertainment involved spending money, drinking, or roaming the streets in bands at night to fight or perhaps to serenade the young women they fancied, women's social lives do not seem to have depended to the same extent on ready cash. They do not appear to have made much use of guild- or local drinking-rooms, and the indoor sewing-circle under the watchful eye of elders was more important to their leisure. Women who walked the streets alone at night risked being mistaken for prostitutes. Dances, fairs, and church ales were the occasions on which young men and women might meet, but sexual contact was not allowed.

Thus, through the institution of the brothel, the city was able to celebrate and encourage youthful male virility while at the same time insisting that these young men should not marry until their craft training was completed and they could support a wife and children. As they saw it, the brothel forestalled such relationships and helped to keep the town's 'respectable' women sexually inaccessible.[17]

The prostitutes on the other hand *were* sexually available, presented as objects of sexual fantasy and glamour, but they were not the social equals of their clients. When, in Nuremberg, the Council discovered that the prostitutes were preferring 'special beaux, whom they call their beloved men', to other customers, it was quick to order that this practice be stopped, and decreed that the women should be available to any man who paid.[18] As 'common women', they were not to develop disruptive preferences, relationships which might imperil the distinctions

---

[16] Stadtarchiv Ulm, A 3988, Der frowen wiert ayd; Bloch, *Die Prostitution,* i. 770; Reynizsch, *Uiber Truhten und Truhtensteine,* p. 31 (Nördlingen, 1472); for fights in and around the brothel, see StadtAA, Reichsstadt, Strafbuch des Rats I, p. 6, 30 Jan. 1510; p. 119, 10 Dec. 1521; Urg. 23 Sept. 1506; and for cautions against fighting, see Kreigk, *Deutsches Bürgerthum,* ii. 307.

[17] On the different social worlds of men and women, see R. Beck, 'Illegitimität und voreheliche Sexualität auf dem Land', in R. van Dülmen (ed.), *Kultur der einfachen Leute: Bayerisches Volksleben vom 16. bis zum 19. Jahrhundert* (Munich, 1983).

[18] Baader, *Nürnberger Polizeiordnungen,* p. 121; Reynizsch, *Uiber Truhten und Truhtensteine,* p. 31 (Nördlingen, 1472); G. Wustmann, *Aus Leipzigs Vergangenheit,* 3 vols. (Leipzig, 1885–1909), iii. 120.

between, on the one hand, respectable young women who could become wives, and on the other, the free, common women who, under Augsburg law, could not sue for paternity, and in some other towns could not even be raped, since they were owned by all men.[19] For youths, sexual experience with prostitutes was part of becoming a real man; but because its context was the milieu of young men's bands, and civic prostitutes were thought of as belonging to all men in common, it could also strengthen male bonding.[20]

From the prostitutes' point of view, the civic brothel might appear to be an institution which accorded them both respect and protection. Many measures served their interests: in Ulm, there was a separate bath for their use, and the food they were to receive was precisely prescribed; in Nördlingen a weekly bath was included in the rent. But if it seemed a beneficent regime, it placed the prostitutes firmly under the brothel-keeper's hand. In Ulm his control of the women's labour power was so complete that he could require them to spin yarn during the day or else reimburse him for lost earnings.[21] As we saw, the women did not have the right to refuse a client. From the brothel ordinances regulating the keeper's provision of food, alcohol, clothing, baths, and rent, it is obvious that there was little need for the woman to step outside the brothel to make any purchases. That this might account to a total *de facto* curfew is evident from the many regulations forbidding the brothel-keeper to prevent women leaving the brothel, even if their purpose was to go to church.[22]

---

[19] Stadtrecht 1276, Art s. xxxi, p. 88, and cxiii, p. 190. For prostitutes unable to bring accusations of rape, see H. Dillard, *Daughters of the Reconquest: Women in Castilian Town Society 1100–1300* (Cambridge, 1984), p. 196; and at Ems, von Posern-Klett, 'Frauenhäuser und freie Frauen', p. 75. Nor if a citizen 'disciplined' or beat a prostitute for her 'misdeeds' did this count as an insult: StadtAA, Reichsstadt, Schätze 36/1, Zuchtordnung 1472.

[20] See J. Rossiaud, 'Prostitution, Youth and Society in the Towns of South-Eastern France in the Fifteenth Century', in R. Forster and O. Ranum (eds.), *Deviants and the Abandoned in French Society: Selections from the Annales* (Baltimore, 1978).

[21] Bloch, *Die Prostitution*, i. 767–70; Stadtarchiv Ulm, A 3988 (draft ordinance); A 3669, fos. 416 ff.

[22] e.g. Baader, *Nürnberger Polizeiordnungen*, i. 119; J. Brucker, *Strassburger Zunft- und Polizei-Verordnungen des 14. und 15. Jahrhunderts* (Strasbourg, 1889), p. 469.

Economic pressures forced the women to keep working and made it hard for them to leave. In some towns, menstruating or sick women could choose not to work; while pregnant or seriously ill women were forbidden to do so.[23] On the eves of holy days and throughout Holy Week the brothel was shut.[24] On these days they earned nothing, yet they still had to meet the costs of food, rent, and clothing. Many fell into a cycle of debt, for the brothel-keepers would allow women to buy goods through them (at prices the keepers nominated) and would then deduct the money from their future wages. In Überlingen, for example, the keeper pocketed a third of each woman's earnings and then deducted debt repayments from the rest. In Ulm the money the women made was put into a box and distributed each week, one-third passing to the brothel-keeper, who also charged for rent and maintenance. Limits were imposed on how much he might lend the women or what he could sell them, though it is not clear whether these were effective. Though the women might scrutinize the pay-out, their control of their earnings was reduced to a minimum. In Überlingen, only gifts and what the woman earned from an 'overnight' customer were paid directly to her. This system made it hard for her to forgo a night customer and crucial that she should please the client so that she could command those extra gifts. A bout of sickness could be enough to put her behind in repayments, thus compelling her to chalk up yet another debt against her future earnings.[25]

[23] Baader, *Nürnberger Polizeiordnungen*, p. 120; Bauer, *Liebesleben*, pp. 128-9 (Würzburg). Both ordinances clearly allow the women to choose whether or not to work when menstruating; though intercourse with menstruating women is forbidden according to Christian precept and folklore. In Ulm in 1512 (Stadtarchiv Ulm, A 3669, fos. 416 ff.) and in Überlingen in 1524, menstruating women were banned from working (Obser, 'Zur Geschichte des Frauenhauses in Überlingen', p. 634). On attitudes to menstruation, see I. Maclean, *The Renaissance Notion of Woman: A Study in the Fortunes of Scholasticism and Medical Science in European Intellectual Life* (Cambridge, 1980), pp. 39-40; and P. Crawford, 'Attitudes to Menstruation in Seventeenth Century England', *Past and Present*, 91 (1981), 47-73.

[24] G. Schönfeldt, *Beiträge zur Geschichte des Pauperismus und der Prostitution in Hamburg* (Weimar, 1897), p. 109; Bloch, *Die Prostitution*, i. 767. But note StadtAA, Reichsstadt, RB 277, fo. 18ᵛ: the brothel-keeper was merely warned to 'permit no disturbance' at these times.

[25] Baader, *Nürnberger Polizeiordnungen*, pp. 118-19; Brucker, *Strassburger Zunft- und Polizei-Verordnungen*, p. 469; Obser, 'Zur Geschichte des Frauenhauses in Überlingen', p. 638; Stadtarchiv Ulm, A 3669, fos. 416 ff. It is difficult to see how the much-vaunted 'social security' system for prostitutes in

The vicious circle of indebtedness was aggravated by the practice of 'lending money' using women as security. The documents are vague on the point, but the inescapable conclusion is that women were in effect being sold into the trade and compelled to repay the capital 'lent' through their labour. It was rumoured that there were prostitute markets where women were bought or exchanged by brothels. If these tales have the ring of fancy, they do demonstrate that there was some concern about methods of procurement.[26] Yet this had its limits. The 1428 Ordinance of Augsburg, which accused the brothel-keeper of 'piling sin upon sin' by refusing to permit indebted prostitutes to leave the brothel, reveals that the 'sin' lay not so much in purchasing prostitutes, but in preventing women from reforming.[27] In Ulm, where it was, interestingly enough, the Church which raised this complaint, the Council decreed that women should be free to leave the brothel, whether or not their debts had been settled, on payment of 1 gulden—not an easy sum for a woman to raise. When she left, she could take only the clothes with which she had come to the brothel. For a known prostitute, without means of support and usually without accumulated capital, finding a position and making a new life outside the brothel would have been extremely hard. But if she once returned to prostitution, the brothel-keeper could reclaim her and demand payment of all debts.[28]

Ulm, to which each woman contributed 1 pence a week and the brothel-keeper 2 could ever have been sufficient for the women's needs, since pregnant, sick, and menstruating women were forbidden to work.

[26] For the rumour that the Ulm brothel-keepers were travelling to purchase prostitutes for 20 or 30 gulden, see Staatsarchiv Ludwigsburg, B 207, Bü 76; for the Augsburg brothel-keeper punished for exchanging a woman to the Ulm brothel because she had arranged a marriage, see StadtAA, Reichsstadt, Strafbuch des Rats I, p. 124, 10 Mar. 1522; and for complaints on buying and pawning women, see Baader, *Nürnberger Polizeiordnungen*, p. 117 (only those who were not previously prostitutes might be sold); Brucker, *Strassburger Zunft- und Polizei-Verordnungen*, p. 468; Reynizsch, *Uiber Truhten und Truhtensteine*, p. 31; and Kriegk, *Deutsches Bürgerthum*, p. 318 (1390), for 'whoreseller' as a profession.

[27] StadtAA, Reichsstadt, RB 3, fo. 109ʳ/p. 217, 1428.

[28] Ibid., fo. 109ᵛ/p. 218, 1428; Baader, *Nürnberger Polizeiverordnungen*, p. 120; Obser, 'Zur Geschichte des Frauenhauses in Überlingen', pp. 642 f. For a letter from the Ulm brothel-keeper objecting to even these provisions, see Staatsarchiv Ludwigsburg, B 207, Bü 68, no. 166.

The so-called 'free women' thus had little power over their lives or their earnings, and would have found it nearly impossible to leave a brothel whose regime they found intolerable for another. As a form of labour it was unlike any other within the town walls, where, as the boastful proverb had it, 'city air makes one free'. Though apprentices, servants, and journeymen too might be subject to restrictions on movement, might find it hard to leave an unpleasant master, and might also fall into debt with him, prostitutes faced a far severer discipline. They had little or no chance of ever becoming brothel-keepers themselves—in Augsburg the brothel seems to have been run only by men in this period—and they might become indentured labour, bound to work off debts which they had not even contracted. Ironically, the town brothel, used so often to represent the proud munificence of the free city, operated on a system which was the antithesis of the ideal of the free citizen controlling his own labour.

In addition to legal prostitution, however, there were networks of free prostitution, tolerated to some extent by civic authorities. Nuremberg on occasion allowed civic prostitutes to attack and 'discipline' free prostitutes who detracted from their trade.[29] In Augsburg a motley assortment of illegal prostitutes, their procurers, and small brothel-holders were banished each year just after St Gall's Day, the beginning of winter.[30] This fell a few weeks after St Michael's Day, when those who had been banished previously, travelling folk, and vagabonds might freely enter the city; and it coincided with the meeting of the Large Council, when the tax-rate for the coming year would be fixed.[31] A ritual of purification, a public spectacle where those on the Galli list were marched out of town to the sound of the storm-bell, it was hardly

[29] *Chroniken der deutschen Städte*, xi. 645 f.; Reynizsch, *Uiber Truhten und Truhtensteine*, pp. 32–6 (Nuremberg, 1492); and Stadtarchiv Ulm, A 3669, fos. 416 ff.

[30] The Strafbücher of Augsburg contain records of these lists. The last banishment took place in 1534. See also A. Buff, 'Verbrechen und Verbrecher zu Augsburg in der zweiten Hälfte des 14. Jahrhunderts', *ZHVS* 4 (1878), 160–232: though he states that petty thieves and vagabonds were also among those banished, by the sixteenth century the lists are almost exclusively of people connected with prostitution. For a similar annual round-up of prostitutes in Hamburg, see Schönfeldt, *Beiträge zur Geschichte des Pauperismus*, p. 99.

[31] StadtAA, Reichsstadt, Schätze 63, fo. 170^r; and fos. 8^v, 17^r; C. P. Clasen, *Die Augsburger Steuerbücher um 1600* (Augsburg, 1976), pp. 17 f.

a serious measure of policing. The guilty would soon secure an intercession from some dignitary and gain a pardon.[32] Indeed, the same women appear regularly on the lists of offenders: 'Margaret the Court Virgin behind St Stephen's' was listed nearly every year between 1515 and 1520.

Augsburg's policing, like that of other towns, concentrated instead on limiting the noise and public disturbance from prostitutes who solicited on the streets, and distinguishing prostitutes from 'respectable' women. Prostitutes were required a wear a broad green stripe on their veil, forbidden to wear wreaths like maidens, and were not allowed to wear silk cloth or rosaries.[33] They could not have a maid accompany them on the street. The distinguishing mark—whether a yellow stripe or a red beret as in other towns—classes prostitutes in a similar category to Jews, who were also compelled to wear some visible sign of difference. Both Jews and prostitutes were believed to perform essential services for the commune, yet both groups were excluded from full membership of the city, and Jews even from residence after the mid-fifteenth-century expulsions. Intercourse between Jew and Christian was theoretically punishable by death.[34] So also, ties with prostitutes were discouraged: women who befriended them might find themselves reputed prostitutes too; and a man who had too close a relationship with such women, who had one 'hanging about him' might be threatened with expulsion from his craft union.[35] Prostitutes were supposed to

[32] Thus in 1516 the banishments were delayed because of the Emperor's presence, so that 'my lords' should not be overwhelmed by petitioners: StadtAA, Reichsstadt, Strafbuch des Rats I, p. 64. But cf. *Chroniken der Deutschen Städte*, xxiii, Sender, p. 72, who says that in 1499 it was determined to banish offenders secretly. It is unclear whether this practice was continued or not.

[33] StadtAA, Reichsstadt, RB 3, fo. 406ᵛ/p. 464, fo. 232ᵛ; on prostitutes' clothing elsewhere, see Bloch, *Die Prostitution*, i. 814 f.; for clothes in the city colours, see Wustmann, *Aus Leipzigs Vergangenheit*, p. 122; and for prostitutes forbidden to wear wreaths, see von Posern-Klett, 'Frauenhäuser und freie Frauen', p. 84.

[34] Stadtrecht 1276, Art. xix, s. 11, p. 57; but see Buff, 'Verbrechen und Verbrecher'—the sentence was commuted. On distinguishing clothes for Jews, see A. Binterim, *Pragmatische Geschichte der deutschen National-, Provinzial- und vorzüglichsten Diöcesanconcilien, von dem vierten Jahrhundert bis auf das Concilium zu Trient*, 7 vols. (Mainz, 1835–48), vii. 468, Mainz, 1451; 481, Cologne, 1452.

[35] For an example, see StadtAA, Reichsstadt, Urg. 27 Feb. 1532, Kunigund Schwaier. On the threat prostitutes posed to honour, see von Posern-Klett, 'Frauenhäuser und freie Frauen', p. 71; and E. Maschke, 'Die Unterschichten der mittelalterlichen Städten Deutschlands', in E. Maschke and J. Sydow (eds.), *Gesellschaftliche Unterschichten in den südwestdeutschen Städten* (Stuttgart, 1967).

be foreign women, and brothels were forbidden to employ local girls—though many women from the town certainly worked as free prostitutes.[36] Like the Jews, prostitutes were conceived of as foreign in some sense; and just as Jews were buried outside the city walls, so also in Frankfurt the Council threatened the prostitutes with burial 'in the ditch', in unconsecrated earth.[37] Too intimate an association with either Jews or prostitutes could endanger the respectable citizen's civic existence.

Indeed, the symbolic position of the prostitute could be described as one of clearly defined marginality. Regulations made sure that 'the two species of the honourable and the dishonourable' were easily told apart.[38] Urban geography made the point: in Augsburg the brothel was strategically placed near a minor city gate, only just within the town borders yet conveniently close to the city centre. In Hamburg and Strasbourg the city Councils restricted free prostitution to a few streets.[39] None the less, prostitutes formed part of urban culture, participating in races at the shooting-carnivals and appearing at weddings and dances.[40] In Vienna they partnered the young men in the St John's Day fire-dances, and at carnival time in Leipzig they processed through the city to protect the town from the plague and preserve women's fertility, as it was said.[41] Prostitutes had particular saints—St Afra of Augsburg had herself

[36] Baader, *Nürnberger Polizeiordnungen*, p. 119; and for the punishment of a brothel-keeper for doing precisely this, see StadtAA, Reichsstadt, Strafbuch des Rats I, p. 214, 10 Mar. 1522.

[37] Kriegk, *Deutsches Bürgerthum*, ii. 329, 394 n. 256 (Frankfurt, 1546). Cf. Binterim, *Pragmatische Geschichte der deutschen Concilien*, vii. 469, Mainz, 1451; priests' concubines were threatened with refusal of church burial.

[38] H. Hoffmann (ed.), *Wurzburger Polizeisätze Gebote und Ordnungen des Mittelalters 1125–1495* (Würzburg, 1955), p. 203; and see also H. Deichert, *Geschichte des Medizinalwesens im Gebiet des ehemaligen Königreichs Hannover* (Hanover and Leipzig, 1908), p. 243.

[39] Schönfeldt, *Beiträge zur Geschichte des Pauperismus*, p. 99; Brucker, *Strassburger Zunft- und Polizei-Verordnungen*, pp. 459, 465 f.

[40] On shooting-carnivals, see Kriegk, *Deutsches Bürgerthum*, ii. 327; M. Radlkofer, 'Die Schützengesellschaften und Schützenfeste Augsburgs im 15. und 16. Jahrhundert', *ZHVS* 21 (1894), 87–138, here p. 103. For weddings, see Bauer, *Liebesleben*, p. 137 (Rothenburg); Kriegk, *Deutsches Bürgerthum*, ii. 327; and for dances, see Brucker, *Strassburger Zunft- und Polizei-Verordnungen*, p. 466 (prostitutes banned from attending weddings); J. Schrank, *Die Prostitution in Wien*, 2 vols. (Vienna, 1886), i. 105 (prostitutes banned *henceforth*).

[41] Schrank, *Die Prostitution in Wien* i. 105; Rudeck, *Geschichte der öffentlichen Sittlichkeit*, p. 35; Wustmann, *Aus Leipzigs Vergangenheit*, iii. 129.

been forced into prostitution by her mother—and in Ulm the prostitutes burnt a weekly candle in Our Lady's church, 'to the praise and honour of Mary, and as a comfort to all Christian souls'—a phrase which expresses the prostitutes' inclusion in the work of prayer and worship of the community.[42] But this public acceptance was double-edged, serving also to imprison the women in their identity as prostitutes, a separate species of woman. At the same time, the provision of brothels legitimated the social construction of male desire as a force which must have an outlet or cause chaos. The men who gained their first sexual experiences with prostitutes were distanced from them psychologically and socially. Prostitutes counted as dishonourable people who could pollute others. The extent of their dishonour was clearly manifested in the various systems devised to supervise the women. According to the 1276 Civic Code of Augsburg, prostitutes should be under the control of the hangman, the most dishonourable figure of the entire city.[43] In Regensburg, when the brothel-keeper died in 1532 he was buried under the gallows like a criminal, despite the considerable fortune he had amassed.[44] In Vienna the hangman and the beadle were paid from the revenues of the brothel. All these regulations aligned prostitutes with the social outcasts, polluters, and dishonourable members of the city.

Such a marginal position also gave prostitutes a paradoxical kind of symbolic freedom. According to the folk-customs of one area, prostitutes could attend weddings, where they chased the groom and staged a mock capture, demanding money to let him

[42] Though of course directing prostitutes to burn a candle to the Virgin may have an ironic point. I am grateful to Carol Willock for suggesting this, *Die Reichsstadt Ulm vor der Reformation*, pp. 173 f.; Stadtarchiv Ulm, A 3669, fos. 416 ff.

[43] Stadtrecht 1276, Art. xxvii, ss. 3, 8, pp. 71, 72. In Vienna the hangman and beadle were paid from the brothel's revenues: Kriegk, *Deutsches Bürgerthum*, ii. 298; in Leipzig the executioner was in charge of the brothel as late as 1519: J. Glenzdorf and F. Treichel, *Henker, Schinder und arme Sünder*, 2 vols. (Bad Münster, 1970), i. 92 f.; at Zwickau the brothel was next to the hangman's house on the city wall: Karant-Nunn, 'Continuity and Change', p. 21; and Bloch, *Die Prostitution*, i. 745.

[44] *Chroniken der deutschen Städte*, xv. 108, Leonhart Widmann. On the concept of honour and the class of the 'unehrlichen', see esp. K. Lorenzen-Schmidt, 'Beleidigungen in schleswig-holsteinischen Städten im 16. Jahrhundert, soziale Norm und soziale Kontrolle in Städtegesellschaften', *Kieler Blätter zur Volkskunde*, 10 (1978), 5–20.

go.[45] They could punish those who misbehaved sexually by ritually shaming them. Thus the Nuremberg Council permitted civic prostitutes to shame their free competitors; and on another occasion prostitutes paraded through the streets a woman found committing fornication with her lover in the brothel.[46] Free prostitutes had more freedom to walk the streets at night than did 'respectable' women; and though their dress was supposed to be restricted, its style did not fit the strict categories to which 'respectable' women were subject according to their class position.

The Church, too, gave prostitution considerable sanction. The tradition of toleration derived from Augustine, and Aquinas justified the need for prostitutes in vivid analogy as well, comparing them to a cesspit for a palace. Though dirty in themselves, it was their function to purify a town—without them it would soon become corrupt.[47] The image equated prostitutes with what was dirty and evil, while making men's sexuality appear an uncomplicated natural urge. These ideas could lead to the advocacy of prostitution by appeal to religious values. The ordinances of both Nördlingen and Nuremberg opened with prefaces defending the brothel's existence and noting that 'in Christendom common women are tolerated by the Holy Church in order to prevent worse evil'.[48] A Dominican preacher, Johannes Falkenberg, could even advise the city of Cracow to establish a brothel on precisely these grounds; and in some ecclesiastical towns the Church derived revenues from the local brothel.[49]

In confession manuals, visits to prostitutes by bachelors were ranked among the less serious sexual sins, and in one such manual they were classed in the second of eight ascending categories as 'whoring', worse only than fornication, and on a par with intercourse on several occasions while single. Another, published

---

[45] Sebastian Franck, *Weltbuch, spiegel und bildtniss des gantzen erdtbodens*, Tübingen, V. Morhart, 1534, fo. cxxviiiᵛ.

[46] *Chroniken der deutschen Städte*, xi. 645 f.

[47] J. Brundage, 'Prostitution in the Medieval Canon Law', *Signs*, 1/4 (1976), 825–45; Bloch, *Die Prostitution*, i. 645.

[48] Baader, *Nürnberger Polizeiordnungen*, p. 117; Reynizsch, *Uiber Truhten und Truhtensteine*, p. 29 (Nördlingen, 1472).

[49] Bloch, *Die Prostitution*, i. 646.

in Augsburg, ranked 'the common and public sinning women' in the second of the eight categories too, above single folk who committed fornication, but below adulterers, seducers, and masturbators. The author warned that fornication alone was 'sufficient for eternal damnation', but he noted that people thought little of it.[50] Though prostitutes might have a representative presence in the church—witness the prostitutes' candle at Ulm—it is more difficult to determine whether they attended church and mass. The brothel ordinances insisted that they be free to do so, but the need for such a ruling suggests that in practice they were hindered or chose not to attend. Some towns ordered the women to sit separately in church so that 'respectable' women should not be offended—or men distracted. At Ulm, prostitutes were allowed an annual confession, but they were to be directed to a particular church by the officials in charge of beggars, a humiliating provision. Even in church a prostitute was reminded that she was not like other women.[51]

PROSTITUTION AND THE REFORMATION

Augsburg had not permitted its prostitutes to attend church, so their appearance in 1520 in a special area of St Maurice's church to hear the sermon of Dr Speiser was a dramatic event.[52] By

---

[50] *Der spiegel des sünders*, Augsburg, A. Sorg, 1480; and *Beichtbuchlin*, Augsburg, 1491. See also T. Tentler, *Sin and Confession on the Eve of the Reformation* (Princeton, 1977), esp. p. 141; and note Binterim, *Pragmatische Geschichte der deutschen Concilien*, vi. 286, Constance, 1328; 306 f., Augsburg, 1355; 397, Trier, 1310: intercourse with prostitutes is not classed as a 'reserved sin'; and note also vii. 302, Eichstetten, 1453: 'some go so far as to say that simple fornication [*Hurerei*] is no serious sin', and advises confessional instruction to counteract this error.

[51] *Chroniken der deutschen Städte*, xxv, Wilhelm Rem, p. 123: on the first occasion when the women went to the sermon at St Moritz's, two escaped. For Ulm, see Stadtarchiv Ulm, A 3669, fos. 146 ff. For prostitutes sitting in separate parts of the church, see Brücker, *Strassburger Zunft- und Polizei-Verordnungen*, p. 406; and for being warned to do so, see Kriegk, *Deutsches Bürgerthum*, ii 325; prostitutes were not to take communion: Binterim, *Pragmatische Geschichte der deutschen Concilien*, v. 367; must go on the Friday after Easter to avoid offence: v. 367; and were no longer to go in pairs to church: J. Siebenkees, *Materialien zur nürnbergischen Geschichte*, 4 vols. (Nuremberg, 1792-4), iv. 592.

[52] For the prostitutes' first attendance at sermons, see *Chroniken der deutschen Städte*, xv. 123; and F. Roth, *Augsburgs Reformationsgeschichte*, 4 vols. (vol. i: 2nd edn., Munich, 1901; vols. ii-iv: Munich, 1904-11), i. 86 ff., on Speiser.

1522 at the latest, Speiser was clearly identified with the evangelical camp. So, when Easter approached in 1526, and Augsburg's Lutheran preacher Johannes Frosch heard the confessions of the prostitutes, what better proof could there have been of the power of the preaching of God's Word? We do not know what Frosch preached, but we can assume that he would have exhorted the prostitutes to leave their profession, not for the walls of a convent of Magdalenes, but to marry, just as the reformers were doing. In these early years of the Reformation the period before Easter was always especially charged. Easter, the occasion of the annual communion, was the festival on which the reformers focused their demands to celebrate the Last Supper in both kinds, giving the Cup to the laity—or else carried out liturgical experiments, even without the permission of the civic authority. The exhortations to prostitutes to repent thus took place at a moment of intense popular piety and expectation. Though the Council was not to declare for the Reformation until eight years later, and did not introduce a full Reformation until 1537, on this occasion it identified itself publicly with Frosch's campaign, and awarded him an honorarium of 1 gulden.[53] And in the following years, as small numbers of prostitutes left the brothel, the Council showed its support for the reintegration of the women into respectable life by presenting them with an outfit of clothes—a gift both practical and symbolic, for the mock noble attire of prostitutes branded them as such.[54] One of the women at least, married; but we do not know what became of the others.[55] In 1533, with the brothel shut, the turn against prostitution seemed complete when a former brothel-keeper's wife could write: 'and we both spouses daily give God Almighty thanks, praise and honour because [the Council] has helped the

[53] StadtAA, Reichsstadt, Baumeisterbuch 1526, fo. 67ᵛ; and Baumeisterbuch 1530, fo. 60ᵛ
[54] Ibid., Baumeisterbuch 1529, fo. 66ʳ; Baumeisterbuch 1530, fo. 60ʳ; Baumeisterbuch 1532, fos. 67ᵛ, 74ᵛ, 75ᵛ, 80ʳ. Most seem to have left just after Easter.
[55] Ibid., Baumeisterbuch 1529, fo. 67ʳ. Note an early redemption, Baumeisterbuch 1513, fo. 53ᵛ. When the brothel was closed in Nuremberg in 1562, however, the women were expelled from the city: Siebenkees, *Materialien zur nürnbergischen Geschichte*, iv. 595. Nuremberg is an interesting case—although very early a Protestant city, it did not close its town brothel, a fact which may be connected with the less Zwinglian-influenced, less moralistic theology in sway in that town.

above-mentioned my husband to leave this sinful state and condition'. Even the brothel-keeper appeared to have seen the error of his ways, an impression dented only by her shrewd assessment in the next line of this petition that 'my lords of the Council' would not, in any case, permit the brothel to reopen.[56] The evangelical preachers were closely associated with the campaign against prostitution which gained momentum in the 1520s and 1530s; but their rhetoric can be seen to pass through different stages and directions. At first, attacks on prostitution were part of a range of anticlerical salvoes. Taking up elements of a long tradition of hostility to monks and priests, they portrayed them as lecherous women-stealers.[57] In this propaganda, little distinction was made between allegations that monks frequently resorted to brothels, that they seduced married women and virgins, or that they kept concubines—all was 'whoring'. So Johannes Strauss, in a pamphlet on confession, urged men to be wary if their wives' sessions at confession lasted suspiciously long.[58] Unlike Protestant pastors, priests lacked

---

[56] StadtAA, Reichsstadt, SKUK 2.75, Schuldbriefe, supplication of Margaret Stegman. The brothel was eventually sold to the Council for debt. From the intricate series of documents surrounding the sale it emerges that the brothel-keeper usually paid off the purchase price through the brothel income, which was lucrative enough for one keeper to pay 2 gulden per week. The brothel itself was a valuable piece of property, worth 1,050 gulden in 1531. See StadtAA, Reichsstadt, SKUK 2.75, Schuldbriefe, 19 Oct. 1530; 6 Mar. 1531; after 18 Mar. 1533; 18 Mar. 1533; 26 Mar. 1533; Stadtgerichtsbuch 1533, fos. 32b, 39a, 45a, 77b, 80a; and RS, 16 June 1533, 16 Sept. 1533. The Imperial Ordinances of 1530 and 1548 have sometimes been credited with bringing about the closure of city brothels; but since their provisions are directed against fornication, adultery, and procuring alone, and at restricting prostitutes' clothing, this seems unlikely: *Aller dess Heiligen Romischen Reichss gehaltener Reichsstäg Ordnung . . . 1356 bis 1603*, Mainz, J. Albin, 1607, pp. 218, 374, 688; and *Die Peinliche Gerichtsordnung Kaiser Karls V von 1532* (Carolina), ed. A. Kaufman, 4th edn. (Stuttgart, 1975), pp. 80 f.

[57] e.g., Anton Firn, *Supplication des Pfarrers vnnd der Pfarrkinder zů sant Thoman*, [Augsburg, P. Ulhart], 1524; Johann Eberlein, *Die ander getrew vermanung an den Rath der stadt Vlm*, [Augsburg, M. Ramminger], 1523; Jakob Strauss, *Ein Sermon in der deutlich angezaiget*, [Augsburg, G. Nadler, 1523?]; id., *Ein neüw wunderbarlich Beycht büechlin*, [Augsburg, S. Grimm, 1523].

[58] Jakob Strauss, *Ein neüw wunderbarlich Beycht büechlin*, and see S. Ozment, *The Reformation in the Cities* (New Haven and London, 1975), pp. 51-3. But the pre-Reformation Church had also taken the problem seriously: Binterim, *Pragmatische Geschichte der deutschen Concilien*, vi. 412, Trier, 1310: 'The confessions of women should be heard in a public, not a covered place; also one should not look in their faces, but either the headcloth should be held before the eyes or one should look away.'

3. Leonhard Beck, *The Monk and the Maiden*. (Geisberg no. 140, Kupferstichkabinett SMPK, Berlin).

wives and therefore they endangered other men's women. Urbanus Rhegius, an evangelical preacher at Augsburg, went so far as to declare that 'every monk is a whorer, either in secret or in public'.[59]

These themes find pointed illustration in a woodcut of 1523 (see Plate 3). At one level the picture is a typical Reformation

[59] Urbanus Rhegius, *Ernstliche erbietung der Euangelischē Prediger*, [Augsburg, P. Ulhart, 1524], and see also Jacob Fuchs, *Ain schöner Sendbrieff an Bischof vō Wirtzburg darinn Priester Ee beschirmbt wirdt*, [Augsburg, H. Steiner, 1523]. For examples of hostile invective directed against the priests' concubines themselves, see *Concubinarij: Vnderricht ob ein Priester ein beyschläfferin haben mög*, [Strasbourg, J. Cammerlander], 1545, fo. D^r; *Dialogus von Zweyen pfaffen Kochin*, [Erfurt, M. Buchfürher, 1523]; Hans Kolb, *(Ein) Reformation notdurftig in der Christenheit mit den Pfaffen | und ihren Mägden* (n.d., n.p.; *Die Flugschriften des frühen 16. Jahrhunderts*, Microfiche series, ed. H. Köhler (Zug, 1978–   ), no. 328/924); *Von dem Pfründmarkt der Curtisanen und Tempelknechten*, n.p., 1521 (*Flugschriften Microfiche*, 279/796).

indictment of the lustful monk. The trusty peasant stands for the common man, supporter of the Reformation. He is the actor in the picture, and his discovery of the priest's seduction of his daughter is the drama. Yet at another level the woodcut can be interpreted as a satire on prostitution, directed as much against the women characters as against the clergy. The mother who turns away from the scene is smiling as she holds her hand to her face, and the viewer is struck by her large, bulging purse. Her daughter seems captivated by the monk, despite her professed repentance of her loss of virginity. The mother's feet lead away from the monk, as if, unlike her husband, she is departing: has she been paid off by the monk just as he is now attempting to bribe the peasant? Drawing on a stock myth about prostitution, the artist implies that the women are in league for the monk's money.[60]

The linking of anticlericalism and prostitution was not restricted to the level of a literary and pictorial device. By 1537 the Council was ordering all men to separate from concubines and commanding the women to leave town.[61] Such edicts had been repeatedly promulgated throughout the fifteenth and sixteenth centuries,[62] but now the Council set about enforcing them, paying spies to report on 'suspicious persons' and fining heavily those men whom it found guilty. Particular concern was expressed about the 'whoring' of the priests as the Council made its first tentative steps to introduce the Reformation in 1534.[63] At the same time, a dramatic series of trials of prostitutes who confessed their dealings with clergy, and told how one young virgin had been hawked around to various clerics, fuelled the tendency to identify priests as the polluters and women-stealers of the town.[64]

Anticlerical feeling of this type, however, rapidly shaded into attacks on prostitutes themselves. They came to be classed with

---

[60] This woodcut is also described in R. Scribner, *For the Sake of Simple Folk* (Cambridge, 1981), pp. 38-40.

[61] *Ains Erbern Rats | der Stat Augspurg | Zucht und Pollicey Ordnung*, Augsburg, 1537.

[62] StadtAA, Reichsstadt, Schätze 36/1, Zuchtordnung 1471.

[63] Ibid., Lit. 1534, Nachtrag I, no. 24, fo. 29r; and Nachtrag II, no. 29 (Kötzler), fos. 1r-4v; and see also K. Wolfart, *Die Augsburger Reformation in den Jahren 1533-1534* (Leipzig, 1901).

[64] StadtAA, Reichsstadt, Urg. 27 Feb. 1532, Kunigund Schwaiher; and see also 9 Sept. 1532, Ulrich Diether and Barbara Diether.

the Catholic priests; and the concubines were the people exiled following the trials. As early as 1520 Luther had explicitly argued that there should be no brothels in a Christian society:

Finally, is it not a lamentable thing that we Christians should openly tolerate in our midst common houses of ill-fame, though we all took the oath of chastity at our baptism? I am well aware of the frequent reply, that it is a custom not confined to any one people, that it would be difficult to stop, and that it is better to have such houses than that married women, or maidens, or others held in greater respect, should be dishonoured. Nevertheless, ought not the secular but Christian government to consider that that is not the way to get rid of a heathen custom?[65]

Luther was engaging (albeit tentatively) with the time-honoured defence of brothels here: that they protected the honour of respectable women. This argument became more sophisticated as reformers began to claim that brothels actually caused the ill they were supposed to contain. As Johannes Brenz wrote: 'Some say one must have public brothels to prevent greater evil—but what if these brothels are schools in which one learns more wickedness than before?' Here the reformers were questioning the corner-stone of the theory of male desire which justified prostitution because men's lust was an anarchic, uncontrollable force which could only be channelled in specific, less socially disruptive directions. At times the reformers even seem to be grappling with the paradoxes of their society's sexual paradigms: 'If the authorities have the power to allow a brothel and do not sin in this, where not only single men (who sin heavily) but also married men may go, and say this does no harm . . . Why do they not also permit a women's brothel, where women who are old and weak and have no husbands may go?'[66] If women are

---

[65] *Martin Luther: Selections from his Writings*, ed. J. Dillenberger (New York, 1961), p. 483; *D. Martin Luthers Werke* (Weimar, 1883–), vi. 404–69, An den christlichen Adel deutscher Nation, here p. 467, ll. 17–26.

[66] Johannes Brenz, as cited in Melchior Ambach, *Von Ehbruch vnd Hurerey*, Frankfurt, C. Iacob, 1543, fo. H/4ᵛ; and ibid., fo. A/3ᵛ and *passim*. See also S. Ozment, *When Fathers Ruled: Family Life in Reformation Europe* (Cambridge, Mass., 1983), pp. 55 f.

are indeed the more sensual sex, as sixteenth-century society held them to be, and if men, as more rational beings, are better able to control their lusts than women, why should women not be allowed brothels? The writer, Melchior Ambach, pushed the argument to this *reductio ad absurdum* to show the fallacious reasoning of those who supported brothels; but as he did so, he laid bare the contradictions in the sexual natures ascribed to women and men. Implicitly he was suggesting that men, too, could be regarded as sexually responsible subjects.

However, the belief that sex was a force to be denied at society's peril returned in the demands that men and women ought to marry young. Indeed, in the passages cited earlier, the writers usually proceeded to praise marriage, the 'better way' instituted by God. Marriage was classed as the only possible context for sex for the Christian. But if the reformers rejected chastity as an ideal, binding on all clerics, they did advocate chastity for those men and women who were not of an age to marry. Certainly, the pre-Reformation Church did not sanction sexual experience for youths, but it did not assume that young men would be virgins when they married. Yet this was exactly what the new Church held up as the ideal for all men—an interesting example of the ways in which the preoccupations of the reformers themselves, so heavily determined by the monastic experiences many had rebelled against, could lead them to advocate a monastic ideal for all. Even so, they did not believe that men or women could be expected to maintain this chastity for any length of time, and their consequent recommendation of early marriage to avoid the perils of unsatisfied lust led them into open conflict with secular tradition. The latter favoured late marriage and discouraged matches until the man had completed his craft training.

As the reformers' ethic was elaborated, prostitutes themselves began to be perceived as evil temptresses, objects of hate in their own right rather than as the satellites of the old priests. Worse than merely vain, selfish, and luxurious, prostitutes came to be regarded as evil. It is interesting that the reformers were drawn to the symbol of the Whore of Babylon as well as that of the Beast of Revelation to represent the papacy (see

Plate 4).[67] The polemical images of the richly attired prostitute, dressed like a noble woman and riding the seven-headed Beast, which adorned the Lutheran Bible and appeared as pamphlet illustrations were also visions of the powerful woman flaunting her sexuality and the riches it has brought her. Perhaps the viewer was reminded of the depictions of women riding men not animals—for example, Phyllis astride Aristotle, made foolish by his love of a woman (see Plate 5).[68] And the rhetoric which surrounded the theme of the Pope as Babylonian Whore was deeply imbued with the sense that these were the Last Days, the Prostitute-Pope a sign of the impending apocalypse. The prostitute was a menacing as well as a sinful character.

The various levels of the demonization of prostitutes can be seen coalescing in Luther's denunciation to his students of a group of prostitutes who had recently arrived near Wittenberg. He asked them to believe that 'the evil spirit sent these whores here', and called them 'dreadful, shabby, stinking, loathsome and syphilitic'. These women, Luther says, are murderers, worse even than poisoners, for 'such a syphilitic whore can give her disease to ten, twenty, thirty, and more good people', and he goes on to say that, were he a judge, he should have them 'broken on the wheel and flayed'.[69]

There is no sympathy for the prostitute here, and it is she, not the men who are her customers, who is named as the source of sin. Disease is a metaphor of her nature, and she, not her clients, is the origin of the illness. Her infection is of little consequence: it is the transmission of the sickness to 'good people' which calls forth Luther's invective.

---

[67] See also on views of prostitutes, M. Wiesner, 'Luther and Women: The Death of Two Marys', in J. Obelkevich *et al.* (eds.), *Disciplines of Faith* (London, 1987); and on Luther's attitude to sexuality, see H. Oberman, *Luther: Mensch zwischen Gott und Teufel* (Berlin, 1982).

[68] For a literary equation of the prostitute, the 'free women', with the powerful female, see Johannes Diepolt, *Ein Sermon an Sankt Mariae Magdlenae Tag . . .*, n.p., 1523 (*Flugschriften Microfiche*, 456/1233.

[69] Martin Luther in *Luther: Letters of Spiritual Counsel*, ed. G. Tappert (London and Philadelphia, 1955), pp. 292–4; *D. Martin Luthers Werke*, iv, Tischreden 4857 n.

4. *The Babylonian Whore astride the Seven-Headed Beast* (Luther's German Bible, Revelations 17, Wittenberg 1547 edn., by kind permission of the British Library.)

5. Peter Flötner, *The Power of Womanhood.* (detail, *Aristoteles and Phyllis*, Geisberg no. 818, Inv. No. XV/1, 168–171, Kunstsammlungen der Veste Coburg).

Disciplining Prostitutes

When the Augsburg Council came to close the brothel, pronouncements about the dangers to health that it caused were notably absent;[70] and when, in the 1530s and 1540s, it campaigned to abolish free prostitution and punish those involved in it, no mention was made of venereal disease. Rather, it developed a new language to define sexual sin which was a fusion of elements of both civic moralism and religious rhetoric, all the more powerful for its ambiguity.

[70]On the abolition of prostitution and the spectre of venereal disease, see, for further detail, my 'Prostitution and the Reformation in Augsburg', *History Workshop Journal*, 19 (1985), 3–28. Cf. Karant-Nunn, 'Continuity and Change', pp. 23–4—the Council mentioned the danger of syphilis when it closed the brothel. But note her comment, p. 24: 'Venereal disease itself did not drive them to close the brothel. The Reformation did.'

The Discipline Ordinance of 1537 was the principal marker of change here, as it was in the organization of human relationships in general, now to be ordered in accordance with the principles of civic righteousness. But the manner in which it deals with prostitution is distinct. The ordinance does not mention prostitution by name, but speaks instead of those who commit fornication and adultery. No longer a clearly identifiable trade, prostitution was subsumed under these sins; and the prostitute was not addressed as a separate class of woman. The sexual discipline which the whole citizenry was to adopt was both more all-embracing and less well defined than it had been before the Reformation. Now any sexual relationship outside marriage was counted sinful and any occasion on which the sexes mingled, such as dances, might lead to sin. So absolute were the demands of the ideal that the Council was drawn inevitably to define marriage and the relations which ought to hold between husband and wife, parents and children, masters and servants as it articulated the concept of discipline. Indeed, the ordinance amounted to an attempt to order the household, to emphasize the distances which ought to exist between its members, and to define the rights and duties of each. The same ordinance also included an admonition to all citizens to wear clothing appropriate to their social position, so that each may 'be recognized for whom he or she is'.[71]

Prostitution had previously been regarded as the cure for the dangers of male lust, protecting (as all who favoured its existence insisted) the honour of women within the household. The wives, daughters, and maids for whom they feared were their own; and the sexual threat derived from the young men of the house. Once the brothel was abolished, and prostitutes were considered either as fornicators or adulteresses like other women, it is not surprising that such care should have been devoted to redrawing the boundaries within the household. Nor is it difficult to see why one of the Reformation's major concerns should have been the reworking of the concept of incest, making it both a narrower but a far more strictly held set of rules.[72]

---

[71] *Ains Erbarn Rats | der Stat Augspurg | Zucht vnd Pollicey Ordnung*; and note the very lengthy edition of 1552, StadtAA, Reichsstadt, Fasz. Zuchtordnungen.

[72] See Köhler, *Zücher Ehegericht und Genfer Konsistorium*; and J. Goody, *The Development of Family and Marriage in Europe* (Cambridge, 1983), esp. pp. 172–81 on the Reformation's redefinition of incest.

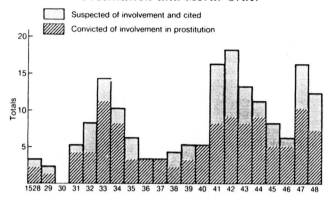

GRAPH 3.1. Prostitution in Augsburg 1528–1548

Source: Figures have been compiled from StadtAA, Reichsstadt, Urg. 1528–48; RB 15, 16, 17, 18, 19, 20, 21, 22; Strafbuch des Rats I, II, III, IV; Prot. der Zuchtherren I, II, III, IV, V, VI, VII, VIII.

But it was as it was put into practice in the investigations and interrogations of wrongdoers that the meaning of the new ideal of discipline was worked out. The trials of prostitutes gave the opportunity for its fullest expression. The last of the Galli banishments took place in 1534, and from then on, instead of merely warning or banishing prostitutes, the Council began to subject them to systematic interrogation. The questioning increased in length and detail, and by the 1540s it frequently extended over more than one session, and more often involved the use of torture.[73] Less concerned with travelling prostitutes, who in any case were probably better able to escape the Council's net, the Council showed especial interest in women domiciled in the town, particularly those of the lower guild strata. But prosecutions during the period 1528–48 do not follow a steady pattern. Three main crises may be discerned: the years 1532–4; 1541–4; and 1547–8, when the Council not only convicted a larger number of people, but questioned a greater number of suspects (see Table 3.1 and Graph 3.1). The first crisis marks the period when the civic brothel was dissolved and evangelical

---

[73] Whereas in interrogations of all those involved in prostitution between 1529 and 1534 torture was used in 6 out of 30 cases (about 1 in 5), in the 5-year period 1539–44 its use was authorized in 11 out of 39 cases (approaching a third): StadtAA, Reichsstadt, Urg. 1529–34; 1539–44.

TABLE 3.1. *Prosecutions   and   convictions   for prostitution and involvement in the trade 1528-1548*

Type of Offence	Men	Women	Total
Convicted			
Prostitutes	1	66	67
Procurers	7	28	35
Brothel-keepers	2	15	17
'Permitted sinful deeds'	3	15	18
TOTAL			137*
Suspected			
Prostitutes	—	20	20
Procurers	6	19	25
Brothel-keepers	3	5	8
'Permitted sinful deeds'	4	9	13
TOTAL			66**

Note: * The total number of charges was 110: 6 women worked as procurers and prostitutes; 4 as brothel-keepers and prostitutes; 10 as procurers and brothel-keepers; and 3 prostitutes were convicted of allowing 'sinful deeds', as were 4 procurers.

** The total number of charges was 58: 3 suspected procurers were also suspected of prostitution; 3 suspected brothel-keepers were suspected of being procurers; 1 of those suspected of allowing 'sinful deeds' was also suspected of procuring, and 1 other of brothel-keeping.

Source: Figures have been compiled from StadtAA, Reichsstadt, Urg. 1528–48; RB 15, 16, 17, 18, 19, 20, 21, 22; Strafbuch des Rats I, II, III, IV; Prot. der Zuchtherren I, II, III, IV, V, VI, VII, VIII. None of these sources is a complete record of prosecutions.

fervour was at its height. The following years saw a significant drop in convictions; and 1537, the year of the formal completion of the Reformation legislation in Augsburg, saw little action against prostitutes. Numbers rose comparatively sharply in 1541–4, the heyday of the strongly evangelical, guild-dominated Councils which also took most radical action against dancing, gaming, and popular festivals. Prosecutions remained at a reasonably high level, and a final peak was reached in 1547-8, the years of pessimism after the defeat of the Schmalkaldic League which also saw the holding of another imperial diet in Augsburg, always a magnet for women working as prostitutes.

Above all, the prostitution trials of the second quarter of the sixteenth century reveal an obsession with the parental background of the accused woman. Thus, when Appolonia Strobel was suspected of prostitution, both her parents were summoned by the Council and interrogated. Her father was asked 'whether he had not noticed and known that his daughter went after dishonourable things'; 'why he had allowed her to leave his house and be outside it day and night'; 'why he had not punished her indiscipline in a fitting manner'.[74] These were not ingenuous questions, but accusations designed to impress upon him his failure as a father. The following day he was interrogated again under threat of torture, and he was told that the Council refused to believe that he had not known all about his daughter's misdeeds. The questions put to Appolonia's mother were different. She was informed that it was well known that her daughter 'leads an unchristian dishonourable life', and asked 'why she had permitted and not interfered with this for some time past'.[75] The Council tried to bring her to confess that she had been party to her daughter's prostitution and profited from it. At her second questioning she was told that 'it is not to be believed that she knew nothing of her daughter's affairs', and admonished that 'if she were an honourable mother she could well have prevented such things'.[76]

Showing a genuine fascination with prostitution and its causes as an almost pathological condition, the Council was locating the reasons for Appolonia's disgrace in her parents' failure to behave

[74] 'Ob er nit gemerckht vnd gewisst hab das sein dochter vnerlichen sachen nachganngen sei'; 'Warumb er Jr gestatt hab, aus seinem hauss zughon, vnd darauss bei tag vnd nacht zesein'; 'Warumb er sein dochter nit gebuerlicher weiss vmb Jr vnzucht gestrafft hab': ibid., Urg. 28 July 1542, Lienhart Strobel.

[75] 'ain vncristlich vnerbar lebenn füre warumb Sy solchs ain Zeythere gestattet vnd zugesehen hab': ibid., Urg. 25 July 1542, Appolonia Strobel d. Ä.

[76] 'Das sie Jnn irer ersten vrgiecht anzaig sie hab nit gewisst dz dauid Baumgartner mit Jrem dochter sündtliche Werckh getrieben oder sie Jrer Junckfrawschafft beraubt hab. dz sei nit glaublich dann sie Jne vor vnd nach dem sie mitteinander zuschaffen gehapt Jnn Jrem hauss gesehen. Vnd wa sie ain erliche Mutter gewest het sie solliche ding wol furkomen mogen . . .': ibid., Urg. 28 July 1542, Appolonia Strobel d. Ä.

as a true mother and father. Parents' duties were seen to involve religious duty, and the roles accorded father and mother were sharply differentiated. Lienhart Strobel, as befitted a household head, was to observe his daughter's style of life and punish her for any moral lapses; while the mother's authority was conceived of as more personal and immediate. Maternal influence over the daughter was supposed to relate directly to sexual matters—the mother, rather than the father, was chided for the loss of her daughter's virginity, and the Council pressed her to admit that she had acted as her daughter's procuress. Behind this accusation we might detect the belief which seemed to emerge in Leonhard Beck's woodcut—that mothers are only too eager to entice their daughters into prostitution, and that mother and daughter collude to profit from the business.

This was an essentially bourgeois conception of parental responsibility. Lienhart Strobel was not a craftsman but a day-labourer, and he spent his working day in the fields or in town, not in a workshop based in the house where he lived. His wife took in washing and did needlework, while Appolonia also earned money sewing on contract. Each family member had to work independently for the household to survive. Lienhart Strobel explained that he could not know what went on in his house during the day, and he saw nothing unusual in his daughter staying out overnight or leaving home for a period while she was on a sewing engagement. Strobel could not be an ever-present patriarch, noting his daughter's activities and guarding her virginity, for his work was structured differently. Yet he had his own conception of good fatherhood—as his perplexed account of how he saw his duty puts it: 'He had always directed his daughter to the good', and 'if she had done something dishonourable despite this, he did not know about it.'[77] His words lack the conviction of paternal authority, confident of its power to punish. His view of what was 'dishonourable' was

---

[77] 'Er hab sein Tochter allweg Zum guten gewisenn vnnd gehalltten. hab Sy darüber etwas vneerlichs gehandelt das wiss er nit'; and to the accusation that young and married men were coming to the house and buying him drinks (i.e. bribing him to turn a blind eye to his daughter's prostitution), he said: 'Es seyn wol vil Eerlicher Leut Zu Jme ganngen vnnd mit Jme Zecht Er hab aber allweg sein gebürliche Zech bezalt', and insisted at the next interrogation that he had never earned a dishonest penny: ibid., Urg. 28 and 29 July 1542, Lienhart Strobel.

inherently practical and related to meeting general social obligations rather than focusing on sexual behaviour. Repudiating suggestions that he had lived off his daughter's earnings, he maintained that 'he had always paid his round' and never profited from immoral earnings. 'Paying one's round', his practical metaphor for right living, was far removed from the Council's religious terminology: two rather different moral worlds were brought into collision here.

Appolonia's mother also defended her behaviour as a parent, but her replies betray contradictory attitudes. She insisted that she did not know of her daughter's relationship with the patrician David Baumgartner at first, and so could not be held responsible; and she added that nothing dishonourable had ever taken place in her house. Yet she also admitted that once she discovered the situation she had warned Baumgartner that he ought to keep the promise he had made to compensate her daughter financially, and she threatened to write to his father. Her careful distinctions reveal her sense of discomfort—while she claimed not to be involved, she was determined that her daughter should receive financial compensation. Similarly, Anna Stockler's mother, a widow, asserted under interrogation that, like a dutiful parent and acting in her father's place, she had admonished and beaten her daughter as soon as she discovered her involvement in prostitution. But, she explained, she was dependent on her daughter's earnings. If she were too strict, she feared Anna would desert her. In a casuistical argument, she claimed never to have touched a penny of her daughter's dishonest earnings but only what she was paid for her sewing; and if she had permitted her to go to the house of a client, that had been for the sole purpose of sewing, nothing more. Else Stockler placed trust in the man's promise not to leave her daughter in the lurch.[78] What she saw as maternal responsibility was ensuring her daughter a good match; and both women knew that their daughters could only hope to escape from the treadmill of poorly paid sewing by offering their clients 'extra services' and saving a dowry.

Yet however much parents could be blamed for the prostitution of their daughters, the real culprits in the Council's eyes were the procurers.[79] It was they whom the Council took most

[78] Ibid., Urg. 27 Apr. 1541, Els Stockler.
[79] For further detail, see my 'Madri di depravazione: Le mezzane nel Cinquecento', *Memoria*, 17/2 (1986), 7–23.

trouble to trace and punished most severely. This approach found
dramatic expression in the case of Agnes Veiheler, who was
discovered to have been involved in a network of about six
women, arranging parties and clients for them. Only a few years
previously she would almost certainly have been sent packing
at the Galli banishments. But in 1533 she was interrogated three
times and held for two full weeks, condemned, branded on both
cheeks, publicly whipped, a statement of her crimes was read out
over her at the market-place, and she was banished for ever.[80]
The prostitutes with whom she worked were merely expelled.
Veiheler's celebrated case thus functioned to cast her as the villain
of the piece, and to represent women like her as the root cause
of the immorality of the times. To do so required crediting
Veiheler with considerable cunning and ruthless calculation, yet
she emerges from the interrogation as extremely naïve, unable,
even under interrogation, entirely to conceal her pride in her
contacts with such élite names as the Welser, Fugger, and Meuting
families.

The image of the procuress was further heightened by a case
in 1542, in which it was alleged that a procuress named
Hailigenmair had forcibly kidnapped a young girl and let her out
only to work as a prostitute.[81] Such an allegation touched on
deep fears about the predatory nature of women and about child-
stealing; and it was a most vivid representation of the most
abhorrent kind of 'procuring'—a crime which, as the 1537
Ordinance put it, took so many forms that it was impossible to
describe them all or to stipulate fitting punishment.[82] Yet under
interrogation the allegedly kidnapped girl claimed that she had
gone to Hailigenmair of her own volition because her parents
were trying to force her into a marriage with a carpenter and
refusing to permit her to marry a weaver journeyman with whom
she had exchanged promises of marriage. She averred that she
was still a virgin, and denied that pressure had been put on her

---

[80] StadtAA, Reichsstadt, Urg. 14–27 Aug. 1533, Agnes Veiheler; punished 30
Aug. 1533 (Strafbuch des Rats II, fo. 9ʳ), and branding carried out 2 Sept. 1533
(notation on Urg).

[81] Ibid., Urg. 28 Sept. 1542, Anna Haylgenmayr, including extracts from
protocols transcribed at the Zuchtherren, 18 Sept. 1542; Urg. 29 Sept. 1542,
Margret, Stachius Prunnenmair's daughter.

[82] *Ains Erbern Rats | der Stat Augspurg | Zucht vnd Pollicey Ordnung.*

to work as a prostitute. The interrogation of Hailigenmair concentrated on the fact that she had usurped the role of the girl's parents, asking her: 'How dare she take a child around the country without her parent's knowledge'; 'how she came to take the Prunnenmair daughter to Gablingen?',[83] and accusing her of having acted as the girl's procuress. The close connection between the defence of parental authority, particularly as it related to the choice of marriage partner, and the creation of an image of the procuress as the rival, evil parent disposing of the daughter to other men is evident here. In this case, the Council's authority was deployed unequivocally in defence of the parental right to control a daughter's marriage. A year later, Margaret Prunnenmair and Hans Hurlacher appeared before the Marriage Court; their marriage promise to one another was declared void at both parties' request because Margaret's parents had refused permission for the match. Now Hurlacher had married elsewhere.[84]

Indeed, anxieties became directed towards the very relationship between procuress and prostitute, a kind of emotionally intense, evil inversion of the mother–daughter union. In 1541 another suspected procuress, Ursula Lemplin, was asked: 'Since Catharina Ziegler complains that she cannot be without her, Lemplin, she should say what she did to her, and whether she had not bewitched [*verzaubert*] her.'[85] In this case it was alleged that Lemplin had imprisoned the girl and taken her to a nobleman; yet the Council was also confronted with a relationship between the two women which was not based on compulsion alone. Interestingly, the allegation of sorcery derived from Ziegler's mother; according to Ziegler, when she returned to her mother after eight days with Lemplin, 'Lemplin had said she will do you no good and will not stay with you; upon which her mother replied: If she does not stay with me then she [Lemplin] must

---

[83] 'Wie sie dorff ain dochter auss vnd auff dz lannd fuern on Jrer eltern wissen. Wie sie der Prunnenmairin dochter gen Gablingen gefuert hab': StadtAA, Reichsstadt, Urg. 28 Sept. 1542. The conclusion of the case is uncertain.

[84] Ibid., Ehegerichtsbuch 1537–46, fo. 126ʳ, 18 June 1543.

[85] 'Dhweil sich die Catherina Ziglerin beclagt sie konne on sie die lemplin nit pleiben, soll sie anzaigen, was sie Jr gethon, vnnd ob sies nit bezaubert hab': ibid., Urg. 9 Aug. 1541, Ursula Lemplin, also called Mairin and Reyschnerin. She was exhibited in the *Pranger*, led out of the town, and banished: Strafbuch III, fo. 38ᵛ, 13 Aug. 1541.

6. Heinrich Vogtherr the Younger, *The Procuress* (Geisberg no. 1469, Berlin).

have enchanted [*verzaubert*] her, which in her, Catharina's, view, was the case.'[86] The parallels with the allegations about sorcery which men occasionally made when they were entangled in love affairs or emotions they could not understand or control are striking.[87] Just as men could minimize the disruption of such affairs to their lives by repudiating any willed emotional involvement and alleging witchcraft, so Ziegler effected a reunion with her mother by casting Lemplin as a sorceress. But her implied association of the procuress with the witch was an equation which is an important, though submerged, element of the image of the evil procuress.

This image of the procuress is reflected in the patterns of conviction and interrogation. Of the forty-one people convicted of procuring between 1528 and 1548, thirty-five were women; of the twenty-five suspected of procuring but later exonerated, nineteen were women; and almost all the men convicted or suspected were the husbands of women suspected of procuring.[88] Further, of those whose marital status was known, by far the largest number suspected or convicted of procuring or of involvement with brothel-keeping were married. By contrast, the vast majority of those convicted or suspected of prostitution alone were single (see Table 3.2). Such figures supported the Council's view of prostitution as a trade in which single, inexperienced (if not quite innocent) 'daughters', the word the fifteenth century had so often used to refer to the civic, professional prostitutes, were corrupted by evil, bewitching mother-figures.

The procurers themselves, however, repudiated this view of their work. They were self-assured women, one even going so far as categorically to refuse to leave town as a punishment for procuring. She said 'she thought because it was young single girls it didn't matter', and argued that she had only used 'single girls who weren't any use before'.[89] Many of the women also worked

---

[86] 'da hab die lemplin zu Jrer muter gesagt, Sy wurd Jr kain gut thon vnnd nit bey Jr pleiben, Daruff jr muter geanntwurt, Wann Sy bey Jr nit plibe So must Sy sie etwan verzaubert haben, Das sey auch Jr der Katharina achtenns geschehen': ibid., Urg. 8–11 Aug. 1541, Catharina Ziegler.

[87] See Chap. 5 below.

[88] 7 men suspected of involvement in prostitution, and 7 others convicted out of the 13 men suspected and 13 men convicted were married to convicted or suspected women.

[89] 'Hab gemaint die weil es Jungenn ledige madlin seien gewesenn es schade nit'; 'allein was ledigs maidlen die zuuor Auch on nucz gewesen seien': StadtAA, Reichsstadt, Urg. 16 Dec. 1532, Margaret Rupfenvogel.

TABLE 3.2. *Marital status of those involved in prostitution 1528-1548*

	Unknown	Single	Married	Deserted	Widowed	Total
Prostitute only	8	32	7	9	2	58
Suspected of prostitution only	3	5	4	3	1	16
TOTAL	11	37	11	12	3	74
Percentage	15	50	15	16	4	100
Procurers etc.	17	4	22	6	3	52
Suspected of procuring etc.	14	1	20	4	3	42
TOTAL	31	5	42	10	6	94
Percentage	33	5	45	11	6	100

Source: Figures have been compiled from StadtAA, Reichsstadt, Urg. 1528-48; RB 15, 16, 17, 18, 19, 20, 21, 22; Strafbuch des Rats, I, II, III, IV; Prot. der Zuchtherren I, II, III, IV, V, VI, VII, VIII.

Note: Since 3.2 is classified by individual not offence its totals differ from 3.1.

as employment agents for maidservants, and saw procurement merely as finding a particular type of employment for a woman. Several justified their work as procurers by the need to earn money. Thus Juliana Godler confessed to working as a procurer, but explained: 'she was poor and had nothing and so helped herself by this'.[90] Margaret Rupfenvogel, attempting to excuse her work as a procurer as an aberration, insisted that she had only worked while her husband was away and she had no money. Their self-justifications may have drawn on a tradition of tolerance for those who worked as procurers to make ends meet: the evangelical chronicler Jörg Preu described the notorious case of Agnes Veiheler, commenting with some sympathy that poverty was to blame.[91] But procurers' most common strategy for escaping punishment by the Council was to argue that their girls were already corrupt, and that they had merely found them work.

[90] Ibid., Urg. 26 Aug. 1502, Juliana Godler.
[91] *Chroniken der deutschen Städte*, xxix, Jörg Preu, p. 55.

So Agnes Veiheler alleged that another procuress had already led her prostitutes into sin;[92] and Veronica Haug told the Council that the girl she was accused of leading astray had never been 'pious', for six years ago she herself had seen her go into a stable behind an inn with one of the guests while a boy stood on guard outside.[93] Their tangled justifications reveal the extent to which they shared the Council's assessment of the prostitutes as fallen women, women who were 'no use'—they differed from the Council simply in attributing the prostitutes with more responsibility for their actions. To them, prostitution was an option which a woman might reasonably choose, not a path determined by parental irresponsibility, male seduction, or procurers' scheming. But they felt there to be certain moral codes of procuring: all were anxious to argue that their girls were unmarried and non-virgins. Ironically, their values coincided with those of the Council here, for both Council and procurers were, in the end, far more interested in the moral peril and marital status of the prostitutes than in the morals of the clients.

But it was in the interrogations of the prostitutes themselves that the Council most explicitly developed its language of sexuality, crime, and sin. Using the religious rhetoric of sin, it attempted to arouse a sense of guilt in the women, while at the same time robbing them of their own words to define what happened. Let us return to the interrogation of Appolonia Strobel. The first question she was asked was prefaced with: 'Since it is well known that for some time past she has led an undisciplined and ungodly life . . .', and asked her to name who had first involved her.[94] These words were new: until the 1530s a neutral word like 'trade', or the term *Buberei*, villainy, a word so broad as to cover any sort of misbehaviour and lacking religious connotations, would have been used to refer to prostitution.[95] The force of the word *unzuchtig* can hardly be caught in the English word 'undisciplined'. In essence a civil, moral term—the

---

[92] StadtAA, Reichsstadt, Urg. 14–27 Aug. 1533, Agnes Veiheler.

[93] Ibid., Urg. 14 July 1528, Veronica Haug.

[94] 'Nachdem kuntlich sey das Sy ain zeitlanng ain vnzuchtig gotlos lebenn gefürt': ibid., Urg. 25 July 1542, Appolonia Strobel d. Ä.

[95] For examples of this language, see ibid., Strafbuch des Rats I. I am not arguing that 'sin' had never been used by the Council in relation to prostitution before the Reformation. But it was used infrequently, and without the consistency, clarity, and association with the concepts of honour and discipline.

series of ordinances regulating citizens' moral behaviour were *Zuchtordnungen—unzuchtig* carried implications of disorder as well as of sexual misbehaviour, and it represented the antithesis of the *Zucht*, the moral order, which the Council wished to inculcate. The word 'ungodly' added an explicitly religious dimension, echoing the injunction that no fornicator shall enter the Kingdom of Heaven.

The questioning centred on the occasion on which she had lost her virginity. 'Who was the first?', the interrogators asked Appolonia Strobel; and, doubting her answer, they tried to shake her statement at the second interrogation. The very expressions they used to refer to this first intercourse—'robbed her of honour', 'brought her to fall', 'felled her', 'weakened her'—imply corruption and the destruction of her integrity. By extracting a response to the question 'Who had first brought her to fall?', the woman was made to participate in her own condemnation.

'Because she is robbed of her virginity,' the Council told Catharina Ziegler, 'it is not to be supposed that she has remained pious since.'[96] Once fallen, promiscuity was inevitable, the Council believed. Prostitution was described as 'unchaste acts', 'sinful acts', 'the undisciplined life', 'dishonourable doings'. The central words from which these expressions derive are honour, discipline, and sin. Good women were 'honourable', 'disciplined', 'chaste', or 'pious', *fromm*. *Fromm*, as the Council used the word, meant right living, obeying the sexual code; but it also meant pious, right believing. Piety began to merge with sexually orthodox behaviour.

The techniques involved derived from those of the confessional; but now it was the Council who required details of the events. The object of the interrogation was a complete revelation of the woman's sexual history, a kind of verbal undressing of the prostitute, leading to an acknowledgement, from her, of her sinfulness.[97] The new moralism made a very sharp distinction between married women and single women working as prostitutes. Married women were found guilty and punished for 'having committed adultery many times', as the

---

[96] 'Dhweil sie der Junckfrauschafft beraubt, ist zuuermuten sie sei seithere nit frumme bliben': ibid., Urg. 8 Aug. 1541, Catharina Ziegler.

[97] Cf. A. Dross, *Die erste Walpurgisnacht* (Hamburg, 1981), on the interrogation of witches.

placard read out and displayed at their punishment put it.[98] Single women were accused of multiple fornication. The moralization of the offence had the effect of denying the existence of prostitution as a trade—instead, two quite separate types of immorality were distinguished. And, conversely, there was now no clear distinction between prostitutes and adulteresses or fornicators.

The logical consequence of this redefinition was that the women's clients were equally sinners; and indeed, the Council did begin to take note of the names of all customers. In the 1540s it proceeded to punish a number of men, including some quite prominent civic figures. It even maintained, consistently, that men who knowingly visited married prostitutes were guilty of adultery even if they were bachelors.[99]

Yet though there are reports that prominent evangelicals such as Martin Haid (civic notary), Gereon Sailer (humanist and civic doctor), and Ulrich Jung (doctor and patrician) were found guilty of resort to prostitutes, all appear to have been fined and cautioned privately.[100] The group of about a dozen men found guilty in the 1540s, and treated with what appears to have been exemplary firmness, turn out, however, to have been connected with three men—Hans Gunzburger, Hans Eggenberger, and Anthoni Baumgartner.[101] The last two were members of the new patriciate, while Gunzburger, a friend of the Baumgartner clan, was able to secure the intercession of Charles V's secretary on his behalf. The Baumgartners were a prominent Catholic family, so one may suspect that motives other than the pursuit of sexual equity led the now firmly evangelical Council to act against them. Moreover, both Eggenberger and Baumgartner were known to have squandered their fortunes; and in 1544 Anthoni Baumgartner

[98] e.g. StadtAA, Reichsstadt, Strafbuch des Rats IV, fo. 112ʳ, 20 Sept. 1547, Ursula Niclin; Urg. 14, 18 Aug. 1533, Agnes Veiheler; Strafbuch des Rats IV, fo. 103ʳ, 2 Apr. 1547, Anna Beckh; Strafbuch des Rats IV, fo. 113ᵛ, 1 Sept. 1547, Kunigund Geiger.
[99] Ibid., Prot. der Zuchtherren III, fo. 72, 21 Sept. 1541, Hans Eggenberger, Endris Degen; fo. 73, Philip Bloss; fo. 77, 7 Oct. 1541, three men; fo. 103, 11 Feb. 1542, Georg Beckh; fo. 104, 13 Feb. 1542, Jacob Ruff, Jacob Breising.
[100] *Chroniken der deutschen Städte*, xiii, Sender, p. 404.
[101] See the *Urgichten* of Barbara Scherer (StadtAA, Reichsstadt, Urg. 9 July 1541); Barbara Riedhauser/Mair (Urg. 16 Sept. 1541); and Emerenciana Hefeler (Urg. 9 Feb. 1542): they implicated some men who were not, as far as we can tell, punished. See n. 99 above.

was to forfeit personal control of his assets.[102] Of the three, only Eggenberger faced the rigours of an interrogation, though torture was not used. The questions he faced had more to do with his financial mismanagement than with his sexual exploits.[103]

Though all these men faced very heavy fines, and though the Council was determined that even when patricians were found guilty 'it should be done this time as it is done to others in such cases', men were not in fact as severely punished as women. Men were more often able to convert imprisonment terms into fines;[104] and they found it easier to have their offence treated as an aberration rather than as the occasion for a full investigation of all the details of their 'sinful life'. Many men whom the Council listed as clients do not appear to have been summoned; and those it chose to proceed against follow a pattern. Where priests had first been identified as the source of the evil, now suspected Catholics, renegade patricians, and spendthrifts were its targets. But the fact that it chose to prosecute clients at all did mark a major change in civic attitudes to prostitution.[105]

Sin in the Reformed City

Prostitution, of course, was abolished neither by the closure of the brothel nor by the campaign against prostitutes and clients, riven as it was by contradictory attitudes to sexuality. Demographic pressures, low wages, and a declining job market for women ensured that there was no shortage of women willing to work as prostitutes. Imperial diets, when rich visitors and their retinues crowded the city, had always been magnets for prostitutes, foreign and local; yet though prosecutions increased in 1547 and 1548, when the diet again met in Augsburg, the

---

[102] StadtAA, Reichsstadt, US 30 Jan. 1544.

[103] Ibid., Urg. 26, 27, 28 Apr. 1541, Hans Eggenberger.

[104] e.g. ibid., RB 17/I, fo. 102ᵛ, 13 May 1543, David Baumgartner; Prot. der Zuchtherren III, fo. 77, 7 Oct. 1541, Max Hartman, Hans Fockher; fo. 73, Endris Degen; RB 17/I, fo. 47ᵛ, 15 Mar. 1543 (Anthoni Baumgartner was fined the colossal sum of 400 gulden for the third offence).

[105] This raises the fascinating question of the Counter-Reformation's distinctive moralism and its attitude to prostitution—which cannot be discussed here. But see Bloch, *Die Prostitution*, ii.

Council did not attempt a mass expulsion, intervening only in what it felt to be troublesome cases.[106]

Ironically, the closure of the city brothel encouraged the growth of small-scale brothel prostitution and free street-walking. It gave women greater control of their trade, and the records' confirmation of the dominance of women working as procurers, prostitutes, and brothel-keepers stands in marked contrast to the long operation of the city brothel by men. Women certainly lost the protection of the civic institution, where brothel-keeper and city guards were soon on hand to deal with rowdy young men; and the private brothels could exploit the women who worked in them even more mercilessly than the city enterprise. The chances of discovery were greater, and the punishments were more severe. Despite the reformed Council's classification of prostitution as either fornication or adultery, in practice, prostitutes were most often banished from town, just as they had always been.[107] Under the provisions of the new Discipline Ordinance, adulteresses and fornicators were sentenced instead to four weeks' imprisonment, a punishment which literally retained them within the city walls. And now the banishments of procurers and prostitutes were often accompanied by shaming rituals, public exhibitions, whippings, and the rigours of interrogation with torture and imprisonment. Procurers were consistently punished more severely than prostitutes, enduring additional humiliations and receiving fewer pardons.[108] Considered to be hardened criminals and sinners rather than victims led astray, neither the educative punishments nor the exhortatory homilies which the Council delivered to prostitutes

---

[106] A higher number than average (12) were convicted of involvement in prostitution, and a further 18 were suspected in 1547; while in 1548, 9 were convicted and 14 suspected. But this was insignificant in relation to the number of prostitutes working. Cf. estimates of 1,500 prostitutes at the Diet of Regensburg, 1471, and 700 'public' and at least as many more 'secret' prostitutes at the Council of Constance: Bloch, *Die Prostitution* i. 710–11; and on sexual indulgence at the Diet in 1547–8, see Barthomomäus Sastrow's comments in U. Brosthaus (ed.), *Bürgerleben im 16. Jahrhundert: Die Autobiographie des Stralsunder Bürgermeisters Barthomomäus Sastrow als kulturgeschichtliche Quelle* (Vienna, 1972), p. 57.

[107] The unprinted Execution Ordinance which amplified the provisions of the 1537 Ordinance stipulated banishment for prostitutes: Köhler, *Zürcher Ehegericht und Genfer Konsistorium*, ii. 311.

[108] For figures, see my 'Work, Marriage and Sexuality', p. 173.

as part of their interrogation were felt to have any effect on procurers.

Those prostitutes interrogated, however, did not seem to regard what they were doing as a form of sexual delinquency, but as work. It is hard to distinguish what may be the scribe's bowdlerizations in a text which has already been transposed into the third person, but it is noticeable that the women never employed the moral terms of the Council, choosing instead such neutral words as 'had to do with him', 'the matter', 'the business' to describe the sexual transaction.[109] This contrasts with the familiar affection with which men spoke of prostitutes, calling them 'the pretty ones', 'daughters', 'common women', and using their nicknames—language which denied that prostitution was work.[110]

If prostitution is indeed a transaction, then we need to place it in the context of the other exchanges of sex and money which took place in Augsburg if we are to understand its meaning. A clearly related exchange is the money which a seduced virgin could claim not only for childbed and child support, but also for 'her honour', a price which she determined.[111] Here there is the same conceptualization of the woman's honour as a material asset which could be sold; and which is distinct from the seller. This custom in turn derived its meaning from the institution of the morning gift, paid to the bride on the morning after the wedding-night.[112] The seduced woman is thus a virgin who has sold her reputation once; and what she receives is calculated so that she may marry within her class, thus partially healing the wound to her honour. The wife's virginity is also 'sold', but she has a new honour as a wife which now rests upon her continued fidelity. In prostitution the woman is classed as 'dishonourable': she has severed the link between money and fidelity to one man; but the bond between money and sexual ownership remains, for she is owned by all men.

---

[109] See StadtAA, Reichsstadt, Urgichten throughout: 'mit ihm zu tun haben'; 'mit ihm zu schaffen haben'; 'die Sache'; 'Hanndel', etc.

[110] These are expressions which occur in the Augsburg documents. For a list of all known expressions, see Bloch, *Die Prostitution*, i. 732 ff.

[111] For cases of compensation, see Ordinariatsarchiv Augsburg, Prot. des bischöflichen Konsistoriums (the vols. 1535-6 survive), and for the post-Reformation period, see StadtAA, Reichsstadt, Ehegerichtsbuch 1537-46.

[112] See Chap. 4 below.

The parallel forms of the construction of prostitution and marriage are striking—one derives its meaning from the other, but each also infects the other with its inversion. Perhaps some of the fire of the Hailigenmair case, where two mother-figures proposed rival futures for the daughter—the natural mother insisting on marriage to a carpenter, the supposed procurer thought to be inducting the daughter into prostitution—arose from a contemporary apprehension that marriage and prostitution were indeed parallel deployments of women to men, exchanges of sexual ownership and cash.

The Meaning of Prostitution

The most distinctive characteristic of late medieval prostitution was that it was understood and sanctioned as a phase in a young man's life, part of his induction into manhood and marriage.[113] Older men who frequented brothels might be described as behaving 'like youths'. It reinforced male bonding and defined sexual virility as the essential male characteristic. The practices of prostitution, interestingly enough, seem to echo those of marriage: men could sleep overnight with civic prostitutes; and a man might say he was 'wedded to a prostitute for the night'. For youths, prostitution was understood through the prism of marriage, and it allowed them to learn and act out the 'masculinity' of married men.

Virginity, too, appears to have been a shared obsession for both prostitute and client—hardly surprising, given its central role in the systems of marriage and the notions of paternal and maternal responsibility. Women charged more for their first times, and procurers demanded a high price for virgins. In Augsburg the brothel had been known as the 'Virgin's Court', and one prostitute was nicknamed 'Margaret the Court Virgin behind St Stephen's'. But the heavy-handed irony of the slang perhaps suggests another element in prostitution. Just as the Council demanded of prostitutes: 'Who was the first?', so the taking of a woman's virginity confirmed the man's masculinity, his ability to destroy her sexual intactness and determine her reputation. This was the ultimate confirmation of manhood, something of which men

[113] See Rossiaud, 'Prostitution, Youth and Society'.

might dream, even though an experienced prostitute could not fulfil it.[114]

The closure of the town brothel represented a recognition that men's sexual natures were not uncontrollable, and a faith that male lust could be educated and directed towards marriage. Prostitutes were no longer regarded as a separate category of dishonourable women to be tolerated and regulated: indeed, in the new moral language of the Council, prostitution was not even a term. But, conversely, the implementation of the new ideal required far greater powers of surveillance. Between 1528 and 1548 there were at least 110 convictions for offences relating to prostitution, while in over half as many cases again, people were suspected of involvement and questioned. The number of visitors a woman had, what kind of men, and when they came became indices of suspicious behaviour. The boundary between prostitute and non-prostitute became blurred. No longer a group of dishonourable women, clearly defined by where they lived and what they wore, there was little difference between prostitutes, fornicators, or adulteresses—indeed, any woman might be a prostitute. And if the prostitute were not always to blame for her misdeeds, the procurer who led her on the path to sin was increasingly seen as a kind of evil mother. When older women had so much to gain from prostituting 'daughters', how could one distinguish good matrons from evil? Or how, even, could one be sure of a natural mother's motives? The campaign against prostitution rapidly fed suspicion of all women, regardless of status.

But these shifts in attitude were always disputed and never achieved total acceptance. By 1562 Augsburg was responding to Nuremberg's plea for advice on whether or not to close their brothel by admitting that some regretted the closure of Augsburg's brothel.[115] The familiar defence of prostitution as protection for the wives and daughters of 'respectable folk' was resurrected. Yet what does appear to have been an abiding legacy of the Reformation was the obsession with women's sexual experience. Whereas the new Church weakened or abolished individual

---

[114] On the meaning of virginity, see L. Accati, 'Il furto del desiderio', *Memoria*, 7 (1983), 7-16.

[115] Siebenkees, *Materialien zur nürnbergischen Geschichte*, iv. 593-6. I am grateful to Merry Wiesner for drawing my attention to this.

confession, the Council now demanded a full and true account of the woman's sins. The whore had become a moral category, not a professional prostitute; and she stood for the lust of all women. If we might identify a more lasting transformation in sexual attitudes, it is located in the strengthening of the belief that women's lusts were to be feared as unbridled and demonic. The Reformation, which seemed at first to offer a sexual ethic identical for men and women, and appeared to bestow a new dignity on the married wife, suspected all women, single or married, of being ever ready to surrender themselves to their lust for debauchery.

4

Weddings and the Control
of Marriage*

THE moralism of reformed Augsburg placed marriage at the heart
of economic, moral, and social ordering it wished to establish.
For both sexes, independence within the household workshop
was tied to marriage. For men, the nexus between marriage and
masterhood was a deeply rooted moral principle, and its
transgression could touch off anger and violence, even as
Augsburg folk perceived that their imagined old certainties of civic
and domestic order were crumbling. So, Georg Roll's attempt in
1562 to set himself up as a master watchmaker, employing
journeymen who, like himself, were unmarried, sparked off a
major dispute within the trade which culminated in a violent
fracas at, fittingly enough, a wedding dance to which Roll, as a
dishonourable, upstart 'master', had not been invited.[1]

This incident suggests how important weddings and their
attendant ritual and festivity might be as theatres for the
conflicting definitions of masterhood and the place of marriage.
Indeed, the forms of wedding celebration provide a complex echo
of some of the shifts in belief and the effects of the moral reformist
movement in Augsburg; complex, because the power of ritual to
the actors engaged in it derives partly from what they feel to be
its ancient, traditional qualities, the continuity it is felt to create
with past generations. Yet this lineage is also illusory, for ritual
is sensitive to change and can be explicitly remade to express new

---

* This is a revised version of 'Going to Church and Street: weddings in Reformation
Augsburg', which was first published in *Past and Present*, 106 (Feb. 1985), 62–101.
(World copyright: The Past and Present Society, 175 Banbury Road, Oxford.)

[1] On this case, see StadtAA, Reichsstadt, HWA Uhrmacher 1544–1602,
fos. 87ʳ ff., 11 July 1566, 19 Mar. 1566; and HWA Schmiede 1530–69,
fos. 659ʳ ff., 8 Nov. 1566; 667ʳ ff., 1567; 675ʳ ff. (undated); 683ʳ ff. (undated);
695ʳ ff. (undated); and throughout both Fasz. See also M. Bobinger,
Kunstuhrmacher in Alt-Augsburg (Augsburg, 1969), pp. 29–30, 68.

beliefs and aspirations. The changes that wedding ritual and festivity underwent in reformed Augsburg provide a window on to some of the transformations accomplished by the Reformation, and the web of forces involved. At one level these were institutional, and concerned the new Church, the Council, the guilds, and the control these bodies wished to exert over a social institution which had different significances for each; at another, the conflicts at play revolved around sexual relations, what it ought to mean to be a man or a woman, and how the social divisions between rich, poor, and middling folk should be expressed—or challenged.

MARRIAGE AND MASTERSHIP

Weddings were an enactment of a human exchange: the gift of bride and groom to each other. This mutual giving was made manifest in both popular ritual and religious rite. Husband and wife drank from the same cup, ate from the same bowl, or joined hands to symbolize their union. Its clearest enunciation was found in the exchange of rings and vows at the church door. Though the ring was not the item on which patricians lavished most money, its symbolic centrality was acknowledged. Johann Surgant's *Manuale* for priests includes a homily to be read to the congregation on the meaning of the ring. It was worn on the fourth finger of the left hand because a vein led from there direct to the heart, mirroring the sexual and emotional union of the couple. Made of gold, the most precious of metals, it stood for offspring, the greatest benefit of marriage. As an unending circle, it represented the indissolubility of marriage.[2]

Yet while the exchange of rings was reciprocal, the roles that husbands and wives agreed to fulfil for each other in marriage were fundamentally dissimilar. Sometimes these surfaced in words. Hans Amman, a weaver, explained that since his wife Margaret had recently died, leaving him with two small children,

---

[2] Johannes Surgant, *Manuale curatorum predicandi prebens modū*, [Basle, M. Furter] 1503, fo xcviiiᵛ. On wedding ritual before the Reformation, see M. Schröter, *'Wo Zwei zusammenkommen in rechter Ehe': Sozio- und psychogenetische Studien über Eheschliessungsvorgänge vom 12. bis 15. Jahrhundert* (Frankfurt, 1985).

one just 19 weeks old, he wished to marry an elderly servant woman: 'Because I am of the comfortable hope that she will faithfully help me bring up my children for me, will profit my nourishment, and help in my craft.' Another petitioner, writing at about the same time on a widow's behalf, noted that she had decided 'for the sake of her creditors and in order to repay her debts, to take a husband'.[3]

The language conveys the actors' intuitive view of marriage as a trading of complementary roles.[4] The widower needed a wife to cook for him, to help prepare the yarn, and to finish the cloth he wove; the widow required a husband to furnish her with material support. At core, marriage was a bargain in which a man agreed to provide for a woman financially, while she undertook to bring up his children, keep house, and provide some assistance in the work of his craft.

Throughout the wedding ritual the mutually complete but distinct offices of husband and wife found non-verbal expression in gifts, clothes, and action. Oscillating between single-sex celebrations and parties for men and women together, wedding festivities constantly created and reflected on sexual difference. So important was sexual definition that, according to an ordinance of 1571, male bankrupts could be made to suffer the indignity of sitting among the womenfolk at weddings, a powerful denigration of their manhood at a moment when ritual rejoiced in the dissimilarity of the sexes.[5] So also a patrician bridegroom might present his betrothed with the conventional gifts of rings, a golden chain, a pair of ornamental tankards, and a wedding-dress—gifts which, though they became the bride's personal property, represented his munificence. Some of the jewellery might be made to order for the occasion or specially bought for her in another town; some might be ancestral property from the groom's family. It was both emblematic of the man's personal wealth, status, and history and a pledge of his willingness to keep her in a manner befitting his rank.[6] Her gifts to him, on the other

³ StadtAA, Reichsstadt, Fasz. Hochzeitsamt, Hochzeitsherren 1562–1806, before 20 Apr. 1563; HWA Schuhmacher 1548–69, 14 Jan. 1555, Hartprunner and Steidlin

⁴ Cf. M. Segalen, *Love and Power in the Peasant Family* (Oxford, 1983).

⁵ F. Hellmann, *Das Konkursrecht der Stadt Augsburg* (Breslau, 1905), p. 98.

⁶ On wedding gifts, see StadtAA, Reichsstadt, Hochzeitsordnung 1575, fo. 4ʳ'ᵛ'; and for examples of wedding gifts given, see B. Greiff (ed.), 'Tagebuch des Lucas

hand, were fewer, and their monetary value was negligible: two shirts, two towels, and six handkerchiefs was the total allowed her in the 1550 Ordinance at Augsburg. In theory if not always in practice, the bride herself embroidered the shirt and sewed its ornamental collars. They represented her skill as a seamstress and housekeeper worthy of the control of the household stocks of linen, and prefigured the emotional investment of time and care that she would make in household tasks.[7]

The material contributions made by bride and groom to the new household also differed. The man brought his tools of trade, while the woman was responsible for providing household goods 'according to her honour', as the contracts put it, whether they amounted merely to a cow, a bed, and a few old tin pans—all Burkhart Zinck's first wife could scrape together—or the household goods worth over 100 gulden which Maria Schechner, daughter of the mayor of Munich, brought to her husband.[8]

But how did the young man and woman come to assume the positions of master and mistress of a household? First marriage for both men and women marked the transition from childhood and dependence within a household to adulthood and the formation of a new household unit. For young men, marriage was the moment at which they achieved economic independence, took out citizenship and guild membership, became full political members of the urban community, and, after a year's respite, became liable to taxation.[9] The merchant Lucas Rem did not marry until in his 30s when he was able to embark on his own family-based business,[10] and Hieronymus Fröschel timed his marriage to coincide with his return to Augsburg to set up an independent legal practice.[11] For professionals and merchants as for guildsfolk, full male sexual maturity was synchronized with

Rem aus den Jahren 1494-1541', *Jahresbericht des historischen Kreisvereins im Regierungsbezirke von Schwaben und Neuburg für das Jahr 1860*, 26 (1861), 1-110, here pp. 43 ff.

[7] StadtAA, Reichsstadt, HWA Goldschmiede 1532-80, 1552, Felicity de Taxis.

[8] *Die Chroniken der deutschen Städte vom 14. bis ins 16. Jahrhundert*, 36 vols. (Leipzig, 1862-1931), v, Zink, p. 128; StadtAA, Reichsstadt, Fasz. Hochzeiten 1463-1729, Schechner = Scheierlin, 1567.

[9] C. P. Clasen, *Die Augsburger Steuerbücher um 1600* (Augsburg, 1976).

[10] Greiff, 'Tagebuch des Lucas Rem', pp. 31, 43.

[11] F. Roth, 'Der Augsburger Jurist Dr. Hieronymus Fröschel und seine Hauschronik', *ZHVS* 38 (1912), 1-83, here pp. 20 f.

social, financial, and political adulthood; and it was attained conclusively by acquiring a wife.

Let us plot the course through marriage for members of that social group which the authorities in Reformation Augsburg viewed as the backbone of the city's moral and productive economy, the craftsmen. If all passed smoothly, the young journeyman should become engaged, then (having completed the statutory number of years' work-experience) pass the examinations for masterhood, marry his bride within a few months of the engagement, and establish a workshop of his own where he, in turn, would employ unmarried journeymen and apprentices. Marriage marked the boundary between the guild of masters, who had to have wives, and the journeymen, who ought not to, and weddings enacted the rites of passage between these two states. At the *Undertrunk*, the carousing which confirmed the conclusion of the engagement, an all-male group celebrated with the groom. Eight of them were journeymen from the peer group the groom was now leaving, and twenty-three were masters, the groom making the twenty-fourth at their tables. Effectively the engagement might become a festival of admission to the guild, for the drinking-party could be held in the guild's own rooms, and masters of the guild might act as witnesses to the engagement.[12] On its conclusion the young men would go to the bride's house in a noisy procession to serenade her and her female guests.[13] Young men formed a distinct group in the wedding procession and sat at separate tables from the masters at the wedding feast. The wedding dance, open to anyone the couple chose to invite, was a celebration of the guild's corporate identity. Dances acted out the disparity between the bridegroom, who now had a permanent partner, and the other journeymen, who vied with each other for the attentions of young women at the wedding.[14]

---

[12] StadtAA, Reichsstadt, Hochzeitsordnung 1540, fos. a/ii^v–a/ii^v. Guild servants naturally received payments at weddings: see Zünfte 160, Ledererhandwerksordnung, fo. 2^r; Zünfte 245, Zunftbuch der Schlosser, Schmiede und Schleifer, fo. 7^r.

[13] For attempts to restrain this, see ibid., Hochzeitsordnung 1540, fo. a/ii^v; 1550, fo. a/ii^v.

[14] Sometimes young men resorted to inviting the women to the dance themselves: ibid., Fasz. Hochzeitsordnungen, before 30 Aug. 1563; Fasz. Hochzeitslader und -laderinen, Leichensager und -sagerinen 1550–1629, I, before 27 July 1564.

But if ideally the transition to social and sexual adulthood should coincide, the two did not always merge so smoothly. As the century wore on, and an increasing population competed for work in a declining economy, it became more difficult for journeymen to become masters. The period a journeyman had to work before qualifying as a master was lengthened, and masters began to insist that only bachelors might attempt the masterpiece.[15] Many trades even became closed shops, open only to masters' sons and sons-in-law.[16] Such regulations, imposed in different trades for various periods of time, were designed to limit competition and protect the workshop as a form of production. But their result was the creation of a group of men who were forced to delay marriage perhaps indefinitely or face serious financial hardship if they took a wife. For a woman who lacked the guild rights which stood her guild-sisters in such good stead as a kind of dowry of status and connections, attractive to any non-guildsman seeking entry to the trade, such regulations must have made sexual and emotional relationships extremely perilous. A couple without citizenship or trade rights who married in the Augsburg of the 1560s faced immediate exile from town. As the examinations and conditions of entry to the trades became more stringent, more men failed, thus extending the period between engagement and marriage beyond the customary few months.[17] Some couples found themselves obliged to postpone their weddings for several years as they waited for the young man to qualify as a master.[18] The many petitions from engaged couples, 'married' in the sense that property arrangements had been concluded yet unable to cohabit or hold the wedding, show the suffering this caused. As one petitioner finally pleaded: 'that they will allow the above-mentioned my son-in-law to hold his wedding now, and following this . . . present the masterpiece, for because of weighty reasons the marriage can no longer be

---

[15] See e.g. ibid., HWA Schmiede 1530–69, fo. 575ʳ; and HWA Uhrmacher 1544–1602, fos. 111ʳ ff.; and provisions of trade regulations in HWO/B and HWO/C.

[16] R. Wissell, *Des alten Handwerks Recht und Gewohnheit*, 2 vols. (Berlin, 1929), i. 192–5; and see Chap. 1 above.

[17] StadtAA, Reichsstadt, HWA Sattler 1548–1600, 1553: the saddlers complained of the tensions which this caused between the families of engaged couples.

[18] For examples of petitions from those caught by the rules, see ibid., HWA.

delayed'.[19] Presumably the woman was pregnant. In effect, a ritual which had once been a prelude to a wedding had become a separate celebration, one phase in a tense and uncertain passage towards marriage and masterhood.

Such a development, however, was diametrically opposed to the reformers' understanding of matrimony. They advocated that young men should marry early to avoid the perils of unsatisfied lust. In his imaginary ideal state of Wolfaria, Eberlin von Günzburg envisaged girls marrying at 15 and boys at 18.[20] (By contrast, some of the trade ordinances from the 1550s and 1560s speak of a minimum age requirement of 20, 22 even for masters' sons, for mastership in a trade; and others established training periods of four or even up to ten years, with an additional requirement of a stated term of work-experience in the trade.[21]) Sexual maturity, these reformers believed, not financial security, was the point at which one should commence the search for a wife. Perhaps it is significant that in 1568 a pamphlet by Leonhard Culmann was reprinted in Augsburg.[22] One of its principal targets of criticism was the belief that marriage ought not to be embarked upon until the man was financially independent: real Christians, Culmann averred, ought to marry as soon as they felt sexually ready, trusting in God to provide, and welcoming financial hardship as a cross sent to try them. Men's sexual natures, he believed, made it impossible for them not to fall into sin unless they took a wife.

These arguments spoke directly to the Augsburg of the 1560s and 1570s, where the Council had introduced regulations against what it had described in 1543 as 'the dissolute, ill-considered and forward marriages of foreign servants and incoming folk'[23] who were unable to support themselves and had to rely on Council

---

[19] Ibid., HWA Schmiede 1530–69, fos. 243ʳ ff. 153ʳ ff.

[20] S. Ozment, *The Reformation in the Cities* (New Haven and London, 1975), p. 100.

[21] See e.g. StadtAA, Reichsstadt, HWO/C, fos. 412ʳ–418ᵛ, 11 Feb. 1555, Messerschmiede *et al.*; HWO/B, fos. 150ʳ ff., 1 July 1549, Goldschmiede; HWO/B, fos. 233ʳ ff., 2 Mar. 1549, Tuchscherer; HWO/B, fos. 333ʳ–335ᵛ, 23 July 1549, Maler *et al.*

[22] Leonhard Culman, *Iunge gesellen Iungkfrawen vnd Witwen so ehelich wöllen werden zu nutz ein vnterrichtung*, Augsburg, 1568 (1st edn., Nuremberg, 1531).

[23] StadtAA, EWA, Akten 147, Berueffe 13 Oct. 1543; and similar rhetoric, StadtAA, Reichsstadt, Schätze 16, fo. 60ᵛ, 7 May 1541.

poor-relief. But though the policy of discouraging early marriage reached its fullest development in the final quarter of the sixteenth century, its roots lay in the years of the Reformation. So in 1529 the Council had decreed that those who took out citizenship must also purchase guild rights,[24] and in 1535 new citizens had to prove assets of 50 gulden (30 for weavers).[25] By 1543 those without assets, or who had not served at least ten years in the city, were not to receive citizenship or set up house in the city,[26] and in 1563 the Council began to demand guarantors.[27] In the same year the Council's officials began to conduct examinations of all those intending to marry who were not members of the city élite of merchants and patricians, ascertaining whether the couple could support themselves and whether the man had fulfilled his trade's requirements. If neither was from Augsburg, or if they lacked sufficient means, the couple were refused permission to establish a household and made to leave town.[28] Over the five-year period from 1564 to 1568, 209 such couples were only allowed to celebrate their weddings in the city on condition that they left town immediately afterwards to start married life elsewhere; that is, a ratio of one couple banished for every ten accepted.[29] These people had close enough links with the city to make them want to hold their festivities in Augsburg— there must have been many more who left both town and employment on marriage without even applying for this dispensation.

Thus the Council was able to attempt some kind of population control by enforcing a kind of reverse migration of ex-country folk back to the country at the point of marriage. This policy served the labour needs of the town by providing a pool of cheap, short-term servants and journeymen who, it was thought, could

---

[24] Ibid., Fasz. Bürgerrecht, Ordnung Bürger aufzunehmen.

[25] C. P. Clasen, *Die Augsburger Weber: Leistungen und Krisen des Textilgewerbes um 1600* (Augsburg, 1981), p. 17; and StadtAA, Reichsstadt, Schätze 16, fo. 147ᵛ, 26 July 1562; and Hochzeitsprotokolle I, 1563–9.

[26] StadtAA, EWA, Akten 147, Beruffe 13 Oct. 1543.

[27] StadtAA, Reichsstadt, Schätze 16, fo. 143ᵛ, 26 July 1562; and Hochzeitsprotokolle from 1563 onwards.

[28] See ibid., Schätze 16, fo. 147ᵛ, 21 Mar. 1563; and note also a list of questions from 1576 which has survived: Fasz. Hochzeitsamt Generalia 1552–1777 und Verordnungen.

[29] Total calculated from ibid., Hochzeitsprotokolle I, 1563–9.

TABLE 4.1. *Citizenship and marriage patterns 1564–1568*

	Citizens								
	Women	%	Men	%	Both	%	Neither	%	Total
1564	150	31	137	29	193	40	—	—	480
1565	138	29	148	32	181	39	1	0	468
1566	139	38	109	30	109	30	8	2	365
1567	118	35	98	29	115	34	9	2	340
1568	123	32	116	30	136	35	11	3	386
TOTAL	668	33	608	30	734	36	29	1	2039

Source: StadtAA, Reichsstadt, Hochzeitsprotokolle I, 1563–69.

easily be incorporated into the workshops of their employers. For the trades, who feared a surplus of masters, and for the Council, who blamed new households of young, unskilled, and improvident couples for what it felt to be the growing poverty in the town and the over-burdening of the city's poor-relief system, marriage and migration controls were a convenient solution to civic crisis. Its effect on marriage patterns was apparently further to entrench the notion of marriage as a trading of resources, so that the number of citizens marrying non-citizens was consistently high, amounting to almost two-thirds of total marriages between 1564 and 1568 (see Table 4.1).

The Council's response to continued crisis was to try to draw the limits on migration yet more tightly. It even pleaded with widows and citizens' daughters to practise a sort of civic endogamy, blaming their marriages to 'foreign craft journeymen' for the town's economic misery and over-population, 'when they [women] could easily get honourable citizens' sons'.[30] Indeed, there was a very slight preponderance of female-citizen marriage to non-citizens, so that women's marriage patterns could be argued, albeit with slender justification, to be allowing male immigration to the city. But this the Council could hardly have known, and the effect of the Council's rhetoric was thus to stigmatize women's marriage choices as disruptive to the urban economy, while—ironically—attributing to them an independence in marriage choice which contradicted its own

[30 Ibid., Schätze 16, fo. 143ᵛ, 26 July 1562.]

beliefs about feminine conduct. At the same time, it presented sexuality itself, through the medium of marriage, as the real site of danger to the communal economy. The threat to the commune could only be averted through the civic control of marriage.

Indeed, the Council's exhortation to its womenfolk to choose local marriage partners can be seen as a reflection of the patrician-merchant élite's own priorities in matchmaking, an élite which by the 1560s had become the dominant political force in the town. This élite had long practised a connubium between its members, and the vast majority of the marriages its members had concluded had been endogamous. Marriage was the principal means by which membership of the *Mehrer*, the prestigious élite society of Augsburg which mingled with the patricians, could be perpetually re-recruited from amongst the merchants.[31] Thus, for Augsburg's families of rank, endogamous marriage ensured the optimal exchanges of status and financial power. By contrast, for Augsburg's guildsfolk, whose marriage patterns show a marked exogamous bias, the social and economic assets of guild or trade membership and citizenship had most value for the foreigners who lacked these qualifications, not for locals. Both élite and 'commoners' might concur in perceiving marriage as a means of social and economic exchange; but the exchanges involved were of different 'assets'. Grounded in a marriage-game played with different counters, the Augsburg élite Council's admonitions to endogamy can have found little resonance amongst tradesfolk.

Conversely, the policy of civic control of marriage itself, and of immigration controls on those foreigners who did not marry local people, was one which could unite Council and trades—

[31] See K. Sieh-Burens, *Oligarchie, Konfession und Politik im 16. Jahrhundert* (Munich, 1986); P. Dirr, 'Kaufleutezunft und Kaufleutestube in Augsburg' *ZHVS* 35 (1909), 133–51; O. Mörke and K. Sieh, 'Gesellschaftliche Führungsgruppen', in G. Gottlieb *et al.* (eds.), *Geschichte der Stadt Augsburg* 2nd edn. (Stuttgart, 1985); K. Sieh, 'Bügermeisteramt, soziale Verflechtung und Reformation in der freien Reichsstadt Augsburg 1518–1539', unpubl. MA thesis (Augsburg, 1981). On Augsburg's élite, see also P. von Stetten d. J., *Geschichte der adelichen Geschlechter in der freien Reichsstadt Augsburg* (Augsburg, 1762); J. Strieder, Zur Genesis des modernen Kapitalismus (Munich, 1935); and id., *Das reiche Augsburg* (Munich, 1938); entries by P. Geffcken in W. Baer (ed.), *Augsburger Stadtlexikon* (Augsburg, 1985), and the forthcoming work by P. Geffecken, *Soziale Schichtung in Augsburg 1396 bis 1521*.

who, after 1555, increasingly represented divergent, even irreconcilable, religious and social interests—in an essentially conservative evocation of the household-workshop ideal. So, in the few cases where two non-citizens were permitted to take up residence in the city after marriage, the rider would sometimes be added that they 'should not have their own smoke' (i.e. establish their own household unit), or that they might remain 'so long as they served'.[32] But the ideal of the harmonious household workshop had been most fully articulated by the guild-dominated Councils of the 1530s and 1540s, and it was the language of lay, civic evangelicalism which still echoed in the thunderings from the 1562 Council against those who

had not even finished learning their trade, or straight after their learning years, and before they have wandered a time in their trade, pledge themselves and marry, and what is even more troublesome and insufferable, without the counsel, knowledge and permission of their fathers, mothers, guardians or relations, they get married themselves, and thereby, without any timidity or shame, they publicly let it be known that an honourable Council must support them in the hospital or out of the civic alms, with their wife and children.[33]

On this issue the clerical Protestant view of marriage threatened directly to contradict that of secular authority. Yet the irony was that, having handed over jurisdiction in matrimonial matters to secular authority, reformers strengthened the tendency of Council and trade to use marriage as an instrument of social and demographic policy. There was little the restored Catholic Church could do to reverse this trend after 1548 either, for the pressures to marry as the craft dictated were developed within internal civic politics, beyond the reach of the Church.

---

[32] See e.g. StadtAA, Reichsstadt, Hochzeitsprotokolle I, 1563-9, fos. 120ᵛ, 131ᵛ.

[33] 'Jtem Die Junge Vnerfahrne, vnd die Jr hanndtwerch. etwo noch nit gar ausgelernet, oder gleich nach den Ler Jaren. vnd Ee sie zuuor ob Jrem hanndtwerck ain Zeitlanng gewanndert. sich zusamen verpflichten vnd vereelichen. vnd das noch beschwerlicher vnd unleidenlicher, one Vatter, Muetter. Jrer vormunder oder freundt. Rat. wissen vnd willen, liederlich vnd leichtferttigclichen. selbst verheurathen, sich dabey vermessenlich one alle scheu oder scham. offenlich vernemen vnd hören lassen, ain E. Rat muesse Sy, im Spital oder Allmuesen seckhen, mit weib vnd khindern fueren, vnd erhalten': ibid., Schätze 16, fos. 143ᵛ-144ᵛ, 26 July 1562.

MARRIAGE AND MATRONHOOD

For women of guild rank, however, the route from girlhood to mistress of a household did not parallel men's path to adulthood. Like her husband, she moved from the society of unmarried members of her sex into a new peer group of married women; but unlike him, her marriage did not bring financial independence. In a sense, she did not obtain full social maturity on marriage. Widowhood was the closest she came to it, and even that status did not confer political rights.

Throughout the wedding festivities the bride's role was passive. During the courtship, when the young man might serenade her at night, she was expected to remain indoors, for while the streets were the theatre for young men's night-life, a young woman out of doors alone at night would be taken for a prostitute. When the young man came to her house to ask formally for her hand in marriage, the young woman might not even be in the room.[34] Only when the matter had been agreed between her parents and the suitor would she join them and be taken by the hand. In the wedding procession itself, the bride was led to church by two men, and even in the bedchamber she might be handed over to the groom by her father or a group of kinsfolk. Her ritual roles stress her passivity, contrasting it with the aggressive sexuality of young men.

The symbolic object most associated with the bride was the wreath. Denoting triumph and festivity, it was also linked with her virginity. In Augsburg, at the engagement and again at the wedding, the bride presented the groom with a wreath. During the procession to the church she wore her hair loose or uncovered save for the bridal wreath or crown. Her peer group of unmarried women distributed wreaths to all the guests. It is hard to determine whether the wreath had always symbolized the offering of the bride's virginity to the groom, or whether this was a later development as the Church, continuing its pre-Reformation campaigns, tried to prevent the couple celebrating their sexual union until after the wedding. Certainly by the late sixteenth century, in both Protestant and Catholic regions, women who had slept with their men before the wedding were being

[34] See ibid., HWA Buchbinder 1528-1642, 1564, Maria Neckass.

compelled to wear a mock wreath of straw through the streets, or a wreath open at the back, in a public exhibition of their 'shame'.[35] In the 1590s a Protestant preacher expounded the wreath as a sign of the woman's chastity, given to the groom; worn by the groom, it was no more than a reminder of his obligation to live chastely.[36] And in the popular custom Sebastian Franck describes in his *Weltbuch* there does indeed seem to be a symbolic equation of the wreath with virginity: when she has entered the bridal chamber the bride's wreath is removed, and 'then she must cry for shame, for if she does not, she is no virgin'.[37] The wimple, head-dress of the respectably married woman, was now to replace the wreath.

If we can view the wreath-giving as symbolic of the man's complete sexual ownership of the woman, his payment of the *Morgengabe* would seem to be its counterpart. Though the custom was extremely ancient, and the *Morgengabe*'s value no longer constituted such a large proportion of the marriage good, it appears to have retained its symbolic importance in Augsburg— and not only amongst the élite. Several couples who did not have a large marriage good, and who came from the ranks of guild families, still provided a morning gift. Though its value normally stood at a substantial level of between 10 and 20 per cent of the value of the 'matching' (the sum, usually equal to the dowry, which a man supplied on marrying), there was no entirely consistent pattern to its worth, and it might even equal the value of the matching itself.[38]

Paid on the morning after the wedding-night, the morning gift seems to be payment for the bride's virginity. Conversely, women whose 'flowers', 'honour', or maidenhead was 'stolen' by a seducer might claim damages for the loss of the asset. Like a material resource, virginity had a price: not because it was a piece

---

[35] See my 'Going to Church and Street: Weddings in Reformation Augsburg', *Past and Present*, 106 (1985), 62–101, for further references on the wreath and associated customs.

[36] Michael Sachs, *Nutzer Bericht von der bedeutung der Schnur vnd Crantze*, Mulhausen, A. Hantzsch, 1589.

[37] Sebastian Franck, *Weltbüch, spiegel vnd bildtniss des gantzen erdtbodens*, Tübingen, V. Morhart, 1534, fo. cxxviii^v.

[38] See D. O. Hughes, 'From Brideprice to Dowry in Mediterranean Europe', *Journal of Family History*, 3 (1978), 262–96. No widow received a morning gift in Augsburg, though Mediterranean widows did.

of property in itself, but because it stood for the complete sexual rights a man might obtain in a woman. Once married, the 'honour' she had bestowed on him on the wedding-night was transformed into her honour as his wife, and the morning gift might be seen to represent her standing as mistress of the house. But its retention was conditional on her sexual loyalty: if the couple should be separated by the ecclesiastical court, then Augsburg's civic law code decreed that the wife must forfeit her morning gift if she were to blame for the marriage breakdown.[39]

Yet if the imagery of popular ritual appeared to focus on the bride's passivity and the groom's aggressive masculinity, it also illustrated the vulnerability of male potency. The wedding-night was an occasion loaded with danger, for this was the juncture at which a jealous lover might take revenge, either through the public medium of 'rough music', or else by stealth, by casting 'knot' spells to render the man impotent.[40] Moreover, according to the terms of the marriage contract, sexual union had to be completed before the inheritance relationships might come into force, and impotence was sufficient ground for dissolving a marriage under both Protestant and Catholic marriage law.

The sexuality of the bride herself may have been perceived as threatening to men. The sexual union occurred on feminine territory, in the bed which the bride brought as the central item of her trousseau. Beds were often handed down from mother to daughter. Its large frame might be painted or carved with individual motifs, and it was layered with mattresses, feather quilts, pillows, and bolsters covered with the linen she had supplied.[41] In the room where it stood she would give birth and rest for several days after labour. To complete the union of marriage, the man had to enter female space, risking both physically and symbolically the loss of his own virility and identity.

Before the Reformation the Church's aid could be invoked to protect against evil influences from without; and in censing the

---

[39] Stadtrecht 1276, Art. LXXXIV, pp. 163-5.

[40] See A. Franz, *Die kirchlichen Benediktionen im Mittelalter*, 2 vols. (Freiburg, 1909), i. 178-84.

[41] See Stadtarchiv Ulm, [6662], Kauf- und Heiratsvertragsbuch; and for beds in Augsburg marriage contracts and property settlements, see StadtAA, Reichsstadt, Fasz. Hochzeiten 1463-1729, and SKUK 14.1.

chamber and scattering holy water and salt, the priest may also have helped to neutralize the powers within the room.[42] The guests themselves provided sympathetic support. When the couple retired, the guests would celebrate the *Ansingwein*, encouraging the bride and groom with song. At this noisy drinking-session, for which the couple provided the alcohol, ribald jokes were made and obscene songs sung, and these can be interpreted as a means of frightening away evil spirits. Laughing about the opposite sex was also a way of reducing sexual anxiety. The reformers abolished the blessing of the bridal chamber as yet another papal abuse, and the reformed town Council forbade the *Ansingwein* as an unseemly, riotous custom. Yet it proved enormously difficult to eradicate, and by 1550 those who held weddings at their own expense—usually members of the élite— were once again permitted to offer the *Ansingwein* to their guests.[43] The Catholic Church reintroduced the blessings of bed and chamber for its members.[44]

A series of competitive sexual games played at weddings betray contradictory attitudes to male and female sexuality. Young men might run spoon races to the bride, acting out the competitive, active elements of masculinity so prominent elsewhere in festivity, as we shall see below. But in some regions, according to Sebastian Franck, prostitutes would steal the groom, demanding a ransom from the bride. This custom might embody the groom's leave-taking from the sexual promiscuity tolerated in young men, and his entry to monogamy: instead of having sexual access to a group of women, he was to have rights to only one. Yet the game also suggestively represents male enslavement to female sexual power. And in other regions, Franck notes, it was the bride herself and the young women who would hold the young men to ransom—a fascinating reversal of the carnival custom in Nuremberg, known in Augsburg too, where nubile women who

[42] The blessing of bed and chamber does not appear in the written liturgical texts at Augsburg until 1656: F. Hoeynck, *Geschichte der kirchlichen Liturgie des Bistums Augsburg* (Augsburg, 1889), p. 170, but this does not mean it was not practised before that date. Cf. H. Reifenberg, *Sakramente, Sakramentalien und Ritualien im Bistum Mainz seit dem Spätmittelalter*, 2 vols. (Münster, 1971), ii. 468 nn. 2546, 2547, who shows that although the blessings are not incorporated in the Mainz rituals either, contemporary sources refer to them.

[43] StadtAA, Reichsstadt, Hochzeitsordnung 1550, fo. b/iiiᵛ.

[44] Hoeynck, *Geschichte der kirchlichen Liturgie*, p. 170.

had not married that year were forced to 'pull the plough' (*Eggenziehen*) through the streets.[45]

Even the supposedly clearly defined roles of husband and wife might be a terrain of contention within the very marriage service which purported to sanctify those roles. In the readings from the story of the Creation and of the Fall, or in the frequently selected Pauline passages on the proper relation between husband and wife—which Reformation liturgies could so easily adapt to the household model of their own day—masculinity was associated with authority, femininity with obedience. The wedding sermons, which replaced the bridal mass as the most important feature of reformed wedding services, made the message explicit: 'The man should know that it is God's will and ordinance that he should rule her and the whole house in Christian earnest and by good example, raise them in all discipline and respectability, and keep wife and child.' The woman, however, 'should always consider that God the Lord has placed her under the man's authority'.[46] Yet at the most intense moment of the sacred drama, the exchange of marriage vows, a popular custom was enacted which conveyed quite a different vision of married life: the woman who managed to stand on her husband's foot or to place her hand uppermost would be the ruler in the house.[47] And it was a foolish woman who did not try to be first into bed or to put some mustard and dill in her shoe during the wedding. As the north German rhyme put it: 'I've got mustard and dill; man, when I speak, keep still.'[48]

---

[45] Franck, *Weltbūch*, fo. cxxviiiᵛ. For *Eggenziehen*, see H. Bächtold-Staübli, *Handwörterbuch des deutschen Aberglaubens*, 10 vols. (Berlin and Leipzig, 1927–42), ii. 563; and for the practice in Augsburg, see StadtAA, Reichsstadt, Schätze 16, fo. 38ʳ, 26 Jan. 1539—the Council found it necessary to forbid the practice.

[46] Konrad Sam, *Handtbuchlin darĩ begriffen ist die Ordnung vnd weiss, wie die Sacrament vnnd Ceremonien der kirchen zů Vlm gebraucht vnd gehalten werden*, Ulm, 1531, fos. a/viiᵛ, b/iᵛ.

[47] Bächtold-Staübli, *Handwörterbuch*, iv. 160; H. Weinhold, *Die deutschen Frauen in dem Mittelalter*, 2 vols. (3rd edn.; Vienna, 1897), i. 360 f.; H. Reincke, *Die Bilderhandschrift des hamburgischen Stadtrechts von 1497* (Hamburg, 1917), p. 190 and pl. 13.

[48] Bächtold-Staübli, *Handwörterbuch*, ii. 296; for the custom of climbing into bed first, see A. Birlinger, *Aus Schwaben: Sagen, Legenden, Aberglauben, Sitten, Rechtsbräuche, Ortsneckereien, Lieder, Kinderreime* (Wiesbaden, 1874), p. 415.

MARRIAGE AND PROPERTY

Marriage involved the movement of property, and wedding rituals dramatized the transfers which took place. Though women had rights in property, the trading of goods at marriage was not symmetrical. Traditionally, the bride's parents provided the trousseau (*Fertigung*) and dowry (*Heiratsgut*) which were transferred to the administration of the groom. Among the rich, the parents or the groom himself would provide the 'matching' (*Widerlegung*). This property, however, did not pass directly to the woman or to her family. Together with the dowry, it remained under the husband's administration, and he was obliged to protect that property as the portion which would pass to the woman in the event of his death without children. Only the morning gift passed under the woman's control. The property transactions, unlike the exchange of consent between man and woman, were thus acted out primarily between men.[49]

The levels of dowry and matching were acutely sensitive to social and economic standing. The fifty-nine wedding contracts I have been able to trace of couples who married between 1520 and 1559 show a marked pattern, as Tables 4.2 and 4.3 reveal. A large group of guildsfolk provided dowries of less than 100 gulden, while a second distinct level of spending lay between 100 and 1,000 gulden. There were no patricians in these groups, which consisted of wealthy guildsfolk in the main; and 1,000 gulden appears to have constituted a definite social boundary: no patrician, either those who were admitted to the patriciate in 1538 or those of the 'old' patriciate, gave or received less than this level of dowry. Yet several merchants and upper guildsfolk (usually those who held office within their guild) are also to be found in this group, most—but not all—marrying patricians. Nearly all of those whose dowries exceeded 1,000 gulden could boast the ultimate symbol of social arrival in the Augsburg élite:

---

[49] Thus the dowry or indirect dowry cannot be analysed as basically a form of ante-mortem inheritance for the bride. See U. Sharma, 'Dowry in North India: Its Consequences for Women', in R. Hirschon (ed.), *Women and Property: Women as Property* (Oxford, 1984); and cf. J. Goody and S. J. Tambiah, *Bridewealth and Dowry* (Cambridge, 1973); and J. Goody, *The Development of the Family and Marriage in Europe* (Cambridge, 1983), pp. 240–61. See also my 'Gender and Property in Sixteenth Century Augsburg', forthcoming.

TABLE 4.2. *Dowry level in Augsburg 1520-1559* (in gulden)

Under 100	18
100-499	9
500-999	4
1,000-4,999	18
5,000-8,000	5
TOTAL	54*

Note: *Five further contracts do not use the dowry/matching system.

Source: StadtAA, Reichsstadt, Fasz. Hochzeiten 1463-1729; SKUK 14.1; US Lit. Personenselekt.

TABLE 4.3. *Social status of couples receiving dowries of 1,000 gulden and over 1520-1559*

	Groom	Bride
Patriciate	3	7
Joined patriciate 1538/9	5	5
Member of the *Mehrer*	4	2
Not from Augsburg	3	2
Merchant	3	1
Guild or trade member*	5	6
TOTAL	23**	23

Note: *Five each of the brides and grooms who received dowries of 1,000 gulden only were guildsfolk; and each of them either married another guildsperson or a foreigner.

**Of these 23 marriages, 16 were noted in the *Hochzeitsbücher* of the *Bürgerstube*.

Source: StadtAA, Reichsstadt, Fasz. Hochzeiten 1463-1729; SKUK 14.1; US Lit. Personenselekt.

their unions were listed in the marriage books of the *Bürgerstube*, proof that they had the right to mingle in the social world of the patricians.[50]

---

[50] See A. Haemmerle, *Die Hochzeitsbücher der Augsburger Bürgerstube und Kaufleutestube bis zum Ende der Reichsfreiheit* (Munich, 1936).

Not all Augsburgers had enough property to make formal marriage contracts of this sort: as Franz Kötzler, a civic secretary, described their custom, they put their goods together,[51] whereupon, though jointly owned, the man as household head administered them. Even when the bride's parents were too poor to provide a dowry, they aimed at least to provide a bed. The civic dowry fund, established to enable deserving couples to marry, awarded the chosen couple with 10 gulden, enough to buy a good bed with a little to spare.[52]

The engagement, which followed a week or so after the property negotiations, celebrated these exchanges. In some cities it was held on church ground, and in Augsburg a priest might attend the exchange of promises, though he was not to wear his cope or stole.[53] There the woman's father promised his daughter to the bridegroom (or his parents). The previously agreed written settlement of marriage which specified dowry, 'matching', morning gift, and trousseau was contracted between the bride's parents and the groom.[54] On the publication of the contract and the exchange of marriage promises between bride and groom, a festive drink was shared as a pledge to the agreement and the parties shook hands, just as people did when they completed a deed of sale. At this point a groom of the upper classes would honour his future wife with presents of jewellery, sometimes representing a greater material investment than the wedding-ring itself.[55] From the engagement onwards, the couple were known as bride and groom and could refer to each other's families in terms of kinship.[56]

---

[51] StadtAA, Reichsstadt, Fasz. Sammlung von Ordnungen, Statuten und Privilegien.

[52] On Augsburg's dowry foundations, see R. Kiessling, *Bürgerliche Gesellschaft und Kirche in Augsburg* (Augsburg, 1971), p. 224; A. Werner, *Die örtlichen Stiftungen für die Zwecke des Unterrichts und der Wohltätigkeit in der Stadt Augsburg*, 2 vols. (Augsburg, 1899-1912), ii. 23, 32. By the sixteenth century, Augsburg's Baumeisterbücher show dowry payments of 10 gulden to deserving couples; and property settlements of the same period normally value a good bed at around 5 to 10 gulden. see OlfUIf 0.1, Verträge und Vergleiche, and 9.1, 9.3, Teilbriefe.

[53] Hoeynck, *Geschichte der kirchlichen Liturgie*, p. 162.

[54] Previously married brides might form an exception. If the groom had not reached majority, his parents might represent him in the contract.

[55] As Lucas Rem's wedding accounts make clear: Greiff, 'Tagebuch des Lucas Rem', p. 45.

[56] See e.g. StadtAA, Reichsstadt, HWA Buckbinder 1528-1642, fos. 6ʳ ff., 7 Dec. 1563; HWA Schuhmacher 1548-69, 1557, supplication of Marx Speth.

Engagement did not yet finally establish the marriage, but the obligations of the contract were deep. The reformed theologian Martin Bucer's clash with the Ulm city Council over the issue of engagements gives a glimpse of the seriousness with which the Council regarded them. Appraising engagement from the standpoint of the churchman, Bucer argued that it should be seen as no more than a financial contract which, if either party felt 'serious regret and disinclination' and if no sexual union had taken place, they should be free to dissolve before the Marriage Court. This suggested reform of marriage law, one among a list of proposals by Bucer, immediately met with criticism from the Council's legal adviser. Expressing incomprehension, he tactfully suggested that Bucer must be referring to grounds for dissolving the contract which would be serious enough to justify the annulment or divorce of a marriage. The Council, not surprisingly, followed the advice of its own official. The financial arrangements, far from being a mere formality, were binding because the union of property was such a fundamental element of marriage.[57]

At the wedding the couple laid claim to the social prestige which the marriage contract and dowry level had already set out, by displaying their wealth—in giving, in dressing, and in feasting. Among merchants and patricians, weddings were the most expensive celebrations an individual was likely to hold, far exceeding the amounts spent on burial or at the parties in honour of the birth of children. Felicitas de Taxis, a bride in 1552, spent over 200 gulden on her wedding-clothes and presents;[58] Raphael Sättelin von Haldenburg paid over 600 gulden when he married the patrician Elisabeth Herwart in 1523;[59] and Lucas Rem, for a wedding of which he was justly proud, spent nearly 1,000 gulden

[57] Stadtarchiv Ulm, [8983] I, fo. 252^r. Bucer's unsigned memorial is to be found at fos. 242^r-259^v; the reply at [8983] II, fos. 311^r-326^v. The memorials have previously been erroneously attributed to the Ulm preachers, but clearly contain editorial remarks in Bucer's hand. I am grateful to Dr Jean Rott and Prof. Martin Greschat for confirmation. Canon law would have allowed dissolution of an engagement if both parties agreed: see B. Gottlieb, 'The Meaning of Clandestine Marriage', in R. Wheaton and T. Hareven (eds.), *Family and Sexuality in French History* (Philadelphia, 1980); and her 'Getting Married in Pre-Reformation Europe: The Doctrine of Clandestine Marriage and Court Cases in Fifteenth-Century Champagne', Ph.D. thesis (Columbia, 1974).

[58] StadtAA, Reichsstadt, HWA Goldschmiede 1532-80, 1552.

[59] Ibid., Personenselekt Raphael Sättelin von Haldenburg.

in 1517, almost a quarter of which was spent on food alone. By comparison, although the bride's parents met half the wedding expenses, Rem received a dowry of only 3,000 gulden.[60]

The weddings about which we know most are those of the rich. Though the Council of 1532 introduced what was felt to be the most severe legislation ever known in Augsburg restricting wedding festivity, and though those ordinances drafted at the height of the Reformation (especially that of 1540, with its marked guild tone) continued to admonish Augsburgers to celebrate their weddings in sober fashion, members of the Augsburg élite increasingly escaped the stricter provisions. Council ordinances, as well as financial constraints, ensured that the weddings of the rich were longer, more sumptuous, and larger celebrations than those of poorer folk. Foreigners and church dignitaries had never been included in the totals of permitted numbers of guests—a statute which favoured richer citizens, merchants, and patricians who had large networks of kin and friendship outside the city. The arrival of the foreign guests was itself an impressive spectacle: in Nuremberg the bridegroom would ride out with a posse of young men to welcome them into town. By 1540 the Augsburg regulations permitted special small banquets to be held in their honour.[61] In any case, simply by applying to the Council, richer citizens could gain exemption from the harsh sumptuary regulations. When the patrician Honold and Vetter families petitioned for an extra table of guests they were allowed it, while two ordinary citizens making the same request were sharply told to abide by the Council's ordinance.[62]

There was always an abundance of food and a variety of dishes at the proper wedding. There should be enough left over to send gifts of food to those who could not attend the wedding and to provide charity to poor people, pregnant women, and neighbours. Both Church and Council repeatedly tried to channel such excess into almsgiving—hardly with much success[63]—for

---

[60] Greiff, 'Tagebuch des Lucas Rem', p. 49.

[61] StadtAA, Reichsstadt, Hochzeitsordnung 1540, fos. a/iii[r], b/iv[r]

[62] Ibid., RB 17/I, fo. 8[r], 18 Jan. 1543; fo. 47[v], 15 Mar. 1543.

[63] The custom was banned completely in the very harsh Ordinance of 1532 but revived in 1536. In 1540 food could be given to the tradespeople who worked at the wedding, and by 1550 foreign guests were allowed to take food away. The kind of food provided indicated status: thus Rem was proud to provide game at his wedding, and his guests brought gifts of venison to the feast: Greiff, 'Tagebuch des Lucas Rem', p. 48.

even almsgiving became pageantry designed for maximum display rather than charitable effectiveness. The church plea to remember poor, respectable householders at the time one entered on marriage oneself went unheard. How much more dramatic to provide food for the entire crowd of onlookers, as Hans Baumgartner did, dishing out a curious porridge of sweet and sour left-overs, than to leave a discreet contribution to the worthy poor-relief fund as Church and Council advocated.[64]

The weddings of poorer folk, where no formal dowry, morning gift, or matching figured, could not approach the luxury of those of the merchants or patricians. Even so, lavish spending on weddings seems to have been customary among most townspeople. The Ulm Council found it necessary to prevent people pawning their goods to pay for a wedding,[65] and in Augsburg, where those of smaller means could hold weddings in taverns and have the guests pay for their own meals, the Council had to forbid people bribing the innkeeper to provide better and more expensive fare than the ordinance allowed.[66]

Such visible consumption of wealth was of course in pointed contradiction to the civic authority's policy of careful housekeeping and preventing the wastage of city and individual resources. It responded by printing ordinances against lavish weddings, drafting eleven new sets during the century and reprinting several editions. Not relying on the printed word alone, it had them proclaimed annually in guild-houses and at the patrician club.[67] A special body of Council members patrolled the ordinances, interviewing guests and hosts to ensure that not too much had been spent on presents, that the guest-limits had not been exceeded, nor extra parties held.[68] The ordinances themselves, progressively longer and more elaborately produced

---

[64] *Chroniken der deutschen Städte*, xxix, Preu, p. 51; E. Sehling *et al.* (eds.), *Die evangelischen Kirchenordnungen des 16. Jahrhunderts*, 15 vols. (Leipzig, 1902-11), xii, Bayern II, p. 83.

[65] Stadtarchiv Ulm, 3669, Zweites Gsatzbuch, fo. 197^r (1449). Note also Sehling, *Evangelische Kirchenordnungen*, xv, Würtemberg I, pp. 142-3, for people unable to pay for their weddings.

[66] StadtAA, Reichsstadt, Hochzeitsordnung 1550, fo. b/i^r; 1562, fo. 6^r; 1575, fo. 10^r.

[67] Ibid., Schätze 16, fo. 52^r.

[68] Ibid., Hochzeitsexecutionsordnung 1542; and note Hochzeitsordnung 1575, fo. 15^r: those who informed received a portion of the fine.

as the century wore on, were a paradoxically exuberant monument to the virtues of simplicity and restraint. For despite its apparent disapproval of the extravagance, the Council accepted that its own members could break the limits and pay the fines. The ordinances provided a framework which sanctioned social distinctions, and within which rule-breaking was itself a sign of social standing.

By 1575, as Augsburg society became yet more stratified, wedding ordinances prescribed different restrictions and even distinct customs for the patricians, merchants, and commoners. A patrician might spend up to 150 gulden on rings for his bride, merchants might spend only half that, and members of the commune no more than 3 gulden. The rich, who held weddings at their own cost, were permitted more guests than those where guests paid for the food they ate.[69] The order in which people walked to the church, took up their places at the dance, or even sat around the dinner-table began to be determined by Council decree. Weddings were becoming pageants of the town's social structure, where each individual might read off his or her place in that society.[70]

PARENTS, KIN, AND PERMISSION TO MARRY

Marriages represented the joining together of two sets of kin as well as of two individuals. In a society in which marriages were frequently arranged by the couple's parents, considerations of the prestige, property, or business connections which would be formed by the marriage played an important part in the choice of partner. The new kinship network created by the marriage was made visible in the wedding festivities as the celebrations moved between two audiences: that of the kin, and that of work associates, peers, and neighbours.

---

[69] Ibid., Hochzeitsordnung 1550 and in following years.

[70] For order in processions and seating, see ibid., Hochzeitsordnung 1599 (complete copy, Anschläge und Dekrete 1522–1682, I, nos. 1–100); and cf. the very strict social classification of the Kleiderordnung of 1582 and the Hochzeitsordnung 1575, fo. 4^{r-v}; and see also L. Lenk, *Augsburger Bürgertum im Späthumanismus und Frühbarock (1580–1700)* (Augsburg, 1968), p. 30.

By tradition, the engagement itself, the wedding procession, and the dance were played out before a wider audience, for the couple could invite whomever they chose, whether or not they were related. The festive *Undertrunk* was an occasion for the bride and groom's peers to meet together, as was the drinks party held by single-sex groups after the bride and groom's separate ceremonial baths.[71] But the celebrations on which most money was spent and most food provided—the evening meal and dance after the engagement, the wedding feasts—were primarily celebrations for the couple's kinsfolk.

Surprisingly, the Council's wedding ordinances supply no consistent definition of this kin group. They oscillate in apparently random fashion over the sixteenth century, narrowing the range of relations who might be invited in an attempt to limit numbers at the feasts, or widening the category, presumably in response to popular demand. The nadir of the wedding feast was reached in 1532,[72] when, in the most severe regulations against extravagant weddings, it was stated that only the couple's parents, grandparents, brothers and sisters, and their spouses might receive invitations. But a mere four years later the Council relented and permitted aunts, uncles, nieces and nephews, and first and second cousins to attend.[73]

However defined, the kin group was neither equally extensive nor equally important for all Augsburgers. Its significance was not entirely unrelated to social rank: servants, at the lower end of the social scale and mostly recruited from the countryside around Augsburg, and foreign journeymen were unlikely to have a circle of relatives within the city. Recognizing this explicitly, the Council granted them permission to invite non-related guests so that their lack of kin resources would not condemn them to too meagre a wedding. Guild members usually elected to hold an *Undertrunk* for fellow-guildsfolk rather than a party for

---

[71] StadtAA, Reichsstadt, Hochzeitsordnung 1540, fo. a/ii^v^; for the bride and groom's baths, see RB 3, 1392–1441, fo. 74^v^ p. 148; and Hochzeitsordnung 1575, fo. 6^r^.

[72] Ibid., Hochzeitsordnung 1532.

[73] See Goody, *Development of the Family and Marriage in Europe*, pp. 103–82, 262–78. It would be instructive to link the changes made by the reformers to the 'forbidden' degrees of marriage with the groups of people allowed to attend wedding feasts, but I have been unable to uncover any precise correlations.

kinsfolk on the night of an engagement.[74] Yet, increasingly by the later half of the sixteenth century, guild and kin networks would have tended to coincide for many of those who reached master status. Thus, in the brewers' trade between 1562 and 1570 only ten purchased their trade rights; twenty-eight inherited them from their parents, and thirty married into the trade.[75] The smiths' trade presents a similar picture: between 1532 and 1547 only 28 per cent of those who had trade rights had purchased them, a proportion which fell to 23 per cent in the years 1552–60, and to 13 per cent between 1561 and 1569. All the rest either had parents with trade rights or had married in.[76]

Just as the importance of the kin group varied within Augsburg society, so also did the weight of parental involvement in matchmaking. At one end of the spectrum, parents and close kinsfolk might arrange a marriage quite independently of the couple's wishes. Felix Platter returned home to Basle to find his marriage negotiations well advanced, and recollected his confused feelings after his first formal meeting with his bride-to-be: 'So for my part I went to bed with the strangest thoughts.'[77] In some cases the parents' role might amount to little more than formal assent to a match which had already been agreed by the couple themselves. Elisas Stegherr informed his parents in writing that he wished to marry 'an honourable girl', and they had to take his word for it that she was a suitable match.[78] At the other extreme, a couple might arrange to marry without any consideration of parental wishes, or might even contradict them.

Might we then posit a correlation between wealth and social status and the extent of the participation of parents and kin in selecting a partner? No simple connection will suffice. Barbara Kupfereisen's mother took no less trouble in arranging a match with a piper, although the family could not even afford to give her a bed.[79] Children, whether rich or poor, did not always concur in the parental choice. While Augsburgers of all social

[74] StadtAA, Reichsstadt, Hochzeitsordnung 1540, fos. a/iiʳ–a/iiiʳ.
[75] Ibid., Zünfte 50, Zunftbuch der Bierbräuer 1560–1723.
[76] Ibid., Schätze 46b, Schmiedezunftbuch.
[77] T. Platter, *Tagebuch: Lebensbeschreibung, 1536–1567*, ed. V. Lötscher (Basle, 1967), p. 298.
[78] StadtAA, Reichsstadt, HWA Schleiffer 1548–1662, 12 June 1570.
[79] Ibid., Urg. 7 July 1544, Affra Schmid; and Urg. 4, 5 July 1544, Barbara Kupfereisen.

groups might be conscious that marriage was often the best—or only—route to social status, this did not preclude warm courtships, sometimes between couples whose matches would have been socially approved, but sometimes where mutual attraction could lead to social disaster.

None the less, parental settlements were not the only socially recognized method of contracting a marriage. Though the formal procedures of proposal and engagement respected the power of parents and kin to dispose of their children in marriage, there was a series of traditional rituals through which people could court the opposite sex.

As the Augsburg preachers complained: 'in corners', when they were drunk, 'behind their parents' backs',[80] young people were liable to court and propose marriage to one another. Most often, but not always, the man was the initiator, using forms of words such as: 'Will you take me in marriage?'; 'If you will take me in marriage, shake my hand on it'; 'Will you take me in the holy sacrament of marriage?'[81] Though no one verbal form was prescribed, the proposals follow recognized patterns, reminiscent of the words used in the Church's own wedding ceremony. These clandestine marriage promises might be made in fields, houses, or even in bed as a condition of sexual union. The man might give a pledge of the promise, such as a coin, a ribbon, or a hairpin, or the couple might symbolize their union by drinking from a common cup. Usually they shook hands on the contract, as the parties did at engagements; and sometimes a drinking-celebration with the couple's friends would be held.

The doctrine of the pre-Reformation Church had given some support to marriages contracted in this fashion, concluded without parental consent. Since the sacrament consisted in the free exchange of promises, parental permission for the match was not technically necessary; and, as we saw, while the Church declared such marriages illegal and threatened those who embarked on them with excommunication, the unions were still counted valid. In practice, to judge by the cases which the pre-Reformation Augsburg diocesan court decided in 1535 and

<hr />

[80] Ibid., Lit. 1534, Nachtrag 30. The original is in poor condition.
[81] Ordinariatsarchiv Augsburg, Prot. des bischöflichen Konsistoriums 1535, 1536.

TABLE 4.4. *Categories of case heard at the ecclesiastical and reformed civic Marriage Courts*

	Pre-Reformation ecclesiastical court 1535–6		Reformed civic Marriage Court 1537–46	
	No.	%	No.	%
Disputed marriage contract	315	69	74	25.0
Impediment	67	15	1	0.5
Divorce	45	10	86	29.0
Virginity or childbed compensation without allegation of marriage	22	5	58	20.0
Impotence	6	1	1	0.5
Bigamy	—	—	4	1.0
Remarriage sought	—	—	12	4.0
Miscellaneous and unclear	—	—	59	20.0
TOTAL	455	100	295	100

Source: Ordinariatsarchiv Augsburg, Prot. des bischöflichen Konsistoriums; and StadtAA, Reichsstadt, Ehegerichtsbuch 1537–46.

1536—the only pre-Reformation years for which records have survived from the sixteenth century, and which include almost no cases from the city—disputed marriage promises (for whatever ground) made up the bulk of the business,[82] and it rejected the vast majority of these petitions. But the reason they were declared invalid was the lack of the mandatory two witnesses to attest the promise. By contrast, as Table 4.4 shows, in the civic Marriage Court established in Augsburg after the Reformation, disputed marriage promises were not the largest category of cases dealt with over the years 1537–46, and the civic court in fact showed a greater tendency to recognize disputed marriage promises.

[82] Cf. T. Safley, *Let No Man Put Asunder* (Kirksville, 1984), p. 184, who shows a similar lower proportion of marriage contract disputes in Protestant Basle than in Catholic Freiburg or Constance.

But if the reformed Marriage Court could employ a more flexible approach to decisions concerning allegations of marriage promise, it was determined to uphold the principle that no marriage which was not approved by the couple's parents should be recognized. Secular law had long favoured the right of parents to determine their children's marriages, and under Augsburg civic law (as in many other towns) parents could disinherit children who flouted their wishes.[83] Social ostracism could result: Anna Pfister, who married far beneath her station, was refused admission to patrician functions thereafter.[84] While the Church's ambivalence towards clandestine marriages probably did little to impair parental influence over the vast majority of children— parental objections may lie behind many of the cases of disputed marriage promise brought before the church courts[85]—it did at least increase the bargaining power of couples who determined to marry, hoping that their parents might relent and supply a dowry.

The reformers made parental consent a pre-condition of a valid marriage. Deriving the duty to follow one's parents' wishes from the practice of the early Church, the words of St Paul, and the commandment to honour father and mother, the Augsburg reformers elevated respect for parents to the status of a religious value and regarded the Reformation as having restored it. To the objection that 'nearly half the city had got married without permission of parents or guardians', they answered that this had been 'in the time of ignorance', before the days of the Christian magistracy 'which has restored obedience to parents'.[86] The reformers did recognize reciprocal obligations: parents should not force their children into marriages for which they had 'neither will nor heart',[87] nor should they prevent them from marrying. In post-Reformation Augsburg, where the Council's Discipline

---

[83] Stadtrecht 1276, Art. LXXVI, Zusätze, pp. 154 f.

[84] *Chroniken der deutschen Städte*, xxv. 57-61.

[85] Cf. R. Houlbrooke, *Church Courts and the People during the English Reformation 1520-1570* (Oxford, 1979), pp. 62 f. On the practices of the Augsburg diocesan ecclesiastical court before the Reformation, see F. Frensdorff, 'Ein Urtheilsbuch des geistlichen Gerichts zu Augsburg aus dem 14. Jahrhundert', *Zeitschrift für Kirchenrecht*, 10 (1871), 1-37.

[86] StadtAA, Reichsstadt, Lit. 1534, Nachtrag 30, fo. 10ʳ⁻ᵛ; they also appealed to natural and Roman law.

[87] Ibid., fos. 10ᵛ-11ʳ.

TABLE 4.5. *Marriage promise suits in the ecclesiastical and reformed civic Marriage Courts*

	Ecclesiastical court 1535-6		Reformed civic Marriage Court 1537-46	
	No.	%	No.	%
Woman brings suit	176	56	42	57
Man brings suit	139	44	7	9
Parental refusal	—	—	16	22
Unclear	—	—	9	12
Judgements				
Marriage promise declared void	263	83	57	77
No decision/unclear	40	13	2	3
Marriage promise declared binding	12	4	15	20
TOTAL	315	100	74	100

Source: Ordinariatsarchiv, Augsburg, Prot. des bishöflichen Konsistoriums 1535-6; StadtAA, Reichsstadt, Ehegerichtsbuch 1537-46.

Ordinance put into words the duty of children to show 'all due obedience, in subjection' to their parents, couples had to prove that they had their parents' approval before they could get married.[88] If parents objected to the match, they could try to have the union dissolved by the reformed Marriage Court, and in fourteen of the sixteen cases brought before the Marriage Court between 1537 and 1546 (see Table 4.5), the court declared the promise void, even though the parties admitted having vowed marriage to one another. Indeed, so much latitude was given to the court's discretion in determining the validity of a marriage that it was even able to dissolve consummated unions.[89]

[88] *Ains Erbern Rats | der Stat Augspurg | Zucht vnd Pollicey Ordnung*, Augsburg, 1537, fo. b/ii'.

[89] Luther in fact considered even a secret engagement to be binding if it were followed by intercourse: H. Dieterich, *Das protestantische Eherecht in Deutschland bis zur Mitte des 17. Jahrhunderts* (Munich, 1970), pp. 56-9; for other reformers, see pp. 94-6. Some mention an age-limit, some do not. For examples of the court's willingness to dissolve even consummated unions and cases where promise was admitted, see StadtAA, Reichsstadt, Ehegerichstbuch 1537-46, fo. 70', 7 June 1540; fo. 71', 23 June 1540; fo. 78', 3 Nov. 1540; and fo. 60', 30 Nov. 1539; fo. 66', 3 Feb. 1540.

TABLE 4.6. *Compensation cases brought by women in the ecclesiastical and civic Marriage Courts*

	Ecclesiastical court 1535-6		Reformed civic Marriage Court 1537-46	
	No.	%	No.	%
Marriage promise only	86	43	21	21
Marriage promise and virginity compensation	35	18	10	10
Marriage promise, virginity compensation, and childbed support	55	28	10	10
Marriage promise and childbed support	—	0	1	1
Total number of marriage promise suits	176	89	42	42
Virginity compensation only	2	1	19	19
Virginity compensation and childbed support	16	8	13	13
Childbed support only	4	2	23	23
Total number of compensation suits without marriage promise	22	11	58	58
TOTAL	198	100	100	100

Source: Ordinariatsarchiv, Augsburg, Prot. des bishöflichen Konsistoriums 1535-6; StadtAA, Reichsstadt, Ehegerichstbuch 1537-46.

In consequence of this more socially utilitarian approach to the recognition of marriage, the Council was also readier to order compensation for women who had lost their virginity or needed child support. Nearly all the women who brought suits for compensation to the civic court were awarded damages, whereas little more than half of those who approached the ecclesiastical

TABLE 4.7. *Judgements in compensation cases in the ecclesiastical and reformed civic Marriage Courts*

	Pre-Reformation court 1535-6		Civic Marriage Court 1537-46	
	Granted	Refused	Granted	Refused
Virginity alone	21	16	24	5
Virginity and childbed support	33	38	23	—
Childbed support alone	4	—	21	6
Reason for payment unclear	—	—	3	—
TOTAL	58	54	71	11

Source: Ordinariatsarchiv, Augsburg, Prot. des bishöflichen Konsistoriums 1535-6; StadtAA, Reichsstadt, Ehegerichtsbuch 1537-46.

court were successful (see Tables 4.6 and 4.7). In effect, the reformed civic Marriage Court had abolished the legal claim which sexual consummation of a marriage promise made on marriage; and the implications of the severing of the link between sexual relationship and marriage obligation can perhaps be discerned in the strikingly larger proportion of women using the reformed civic Marriage Court instead of the ecclesiastical court to bring compensation claims which did not allege that a promise of marriage had been made.[90] Here the effect of the Council's policy was in full accord with the tendencies of its approaches to marriage, household order, and the control of sexuality: it entrenched civic authority's involvement in the control of marriage, while insulating the stable marriage relationships the Council wished to foster from the intricate claims and counter-claims of private, disputed marriage promises and illicit sexual relationships.

In fact, the rhetoric about the need for parental permission for marriages was merely the focus of a far broader campaign to subject the institution of marriage to the needs of civic society.

[90] Cf., however, Safley, *Let No Man Put Asunder*, p. 142, who finds a far lower number of compensation disputes in reformed Basle later in the century— only 94, compared to 431 marriage contract disputes.

By use of the analogy between parental and civic authority, the move could readily be made from the appeal to the need for children to be obedient when they chose a partner to the argument that people ought to have their marriage choices vetted by civic authority. It was symptomatic of this slide that in 1562 the Council should have followed an indictment of disorderly, ill-considered youthful marriages as responsible for the city's economic and social misery with an attack on 'what is even more troublesome and insufferable, [they marry] without the counsel, knowledge and permission of their fathers, mothers, guardians or relatives'. It was these people, the Council went on, who 'without any timidity or shame . . . publicly let it be known that an honourable Council must support them in the hospital or out of the civic alms, with their wife and children'.[91] In this way, an equation was made between those who married without permission and those who refused to work, scrounged off poor-relief, and disturbed the common good. When a lengthy interrogation for 'commoners' who wished to marry in Augsburg was devised, it contained questions not only about the couple's economic resources and abilities, but also about whether or not they had their parents' permission for the match.[92] Thus, before the publication of the Council of Trent's provisions on marriage, but well after the reintroduction of Catholicism into the town, a Council policy on the recognition of marriage was in operation which completely contradicted Catholic dogma. It drew its strength from a conception of marriage which had been given its fullest articulation in the years of the reform, when, despite the differences of emphasis in religious and civic rhetoric, Protestantism had worked to sanctify the effective control of marriage by secular authority.

But this policy was not simply imposed by the Council on an unwilling populace. The attractions of such a vision were very deep, for it touched on longings for an imagined, orderly urban world, where the differences between men and women's roles and duties were clearly defined. In such a world, the securing of each household's sustenance (*Nahrung*) simply rested on every

[91] StadtAA, Reichsstadt, Schätze 16, fos. 143ᵛ–144ᵛ 26 July 1562.
[92] See the list of questions which has survived from 1576, ibid., Fasz. Hochzeitsamt Generalia 1552–1777 und Verordnungen, and some notations in the Hochzeitsprotokolle I, 1563–9.

member of the household fulfilling their duties correctly—the man's, to carry out the work of his craft, the woman's, to assist him, obey him, and care for their comfort. That subsisting in daily life was hard, and that correct living did not ensure economic security, by no means lessened the seductions of the myth. And though, for women, the ritual of weddings did not disguise the fact that marriage involved obedience and was often difficult, painful, and harsh, it held out the promise that it would bring protection and security. The words which the wedding homilies and Council exhortations alike intoned—peace, friendship, ordered obedience—invoked feelings of warmth and safety. Sexual divisions could be felt to be the guarantor of personal and social harmony. This invocation of order could appeal not only to the Council or to those established craftspeople whose interests it apparently served, but to those shut out who desired to be incorporated into an imagined community, a perfect city.

5
Discipline and Marital Disharmony

MARRIAGE was at the heart of the new reformed order; yet it was marriage which proved the most troubling human relationship and married spouses who often seemed to the Council to behave in the most disorderly fashion. It was within marriage that the Council most sought to inscribe the natural, complementary hierarchy of masculinity and femininity—in the Pauline words of the Discipline Ordinance: 'a married couple live together in the fear of God, in deepest love and unity, yea, are one person, so that the man should love his wife as himself, and the woman fear the husband, and have him before her eyes, and consider him to be her head'.[1] Yet, central as marriage was to the Council's conception of order, and symbolic though it was of the morals of evangelicalism, the Council's policy on marriage was fractured, contradictory, and even administratively confused.

Because marriage was so closely tied to social status and hierarchy within a workshop-based culture, distinguishing master from journeyman and wife from servant, orderly marriage was crucial to social order in a wider sense. But when the Council adjudicated the endless stream of marital disputes where husbands attacked wives, wives insulted their husbands, or men would not 'share their earnings', its daily experience contradicted—and worse, the punishments it meted out actually undermined—the vision of natural patriarchal authority and female subservience which it held so dear.

[1] 'Vnd nach dem die Eegemahel beyainander in der forcht Gottes | höchster liebe vnd ainigkait leben | Ja ain Mensch sein | also | das der Man das Weib | wie sich selbs | lieben | Vnd herwiderumb | das Weib den Man | als jr haupt | voraugen haben | vnd förchten sollen | So vermanet vnd will auch ain Erber Rat | das solche Eeliche höchste Trew vnd Liebe | hilff vnd dienst | getrewlich gelaist werde . . .': *Ains Erbern Rats | der Stat Augspurg | Zucht vnd Pollicey Ordnung*, Augsburg, 1537, fo. a/vi[v].

The implications of this contradiction touched on central political dilemmas in the Augsburg of the 1530s and 1540s. This was a period when the Council's own political self-image hovered uneasily between an authoritarian and a communitarian understanding of its power. As it took on the role of punishing disorderly spouses, and in particular when it began to discipline husbands and masters, its intervention in the sphere of the household threatened to prise apart the uneasy coalition of brotherhood between Council and guildsmen. Marriage, supposedly the shared value of Council and guild, was also the issue which exposed the most acute differences between them.

COUNCIL MARRIAGE POLICY

The confusion of the reformed Council's marriage policy derived partly from the different, even incompatible traditions on which it drew. Settling marriage disputes was an issue which had originally concerned Church and guilds as well as Council, while neighbours or prominent councillors had sometimes acted as informal arbiters. In 1537 the Augsburg Council tried to reorganize the control of marriage in the wake of its take-over of jurisdiction from the church courts, just as it had done in other areas of sexual and social life. Like other evangelically minded town Councils throughout southern Germany and the Swiss confederation, Augsburg instituted a Marriage Court and permitted divorce in certain circumstances.[2] However, control was not so easily accomplished in the case of marriage disputes. Council policy on marriage hesitated uncomfortably between three different perceptions of marriage: the religious heritage which placed emphasis on marriage as a sexual union; the guild-influenced views of marriage in terms of labour partnerships, honour, and work relations; and its own pragmatic tradition of settling marital and property disputes, where practical considerations sometimes dictated the toleration of 'separations' of marriages which had simply broken down.

---

[2] On the working of these courts elsewhere, see A. Staehelin, *Die Einführung der Ehescheidung in Basel zur Zeit der Reformation* (Basle, 1957); W. Köhler, *Zürcher Ehegericht und Genfer Konsistorium*, 2 vols. (Leipzig, 1932, 1942); and T. Safley, *Let No Man Put Asunder* (Kirksville, 1984).

This confusion is evident in the legislation on marriage disputes. As all agreed, the chief sin against marriage was adultery, and as such it was execrated in the 1537 Ordinance as a 'godless evil', to be punished by four weeks' imprisonment, three of which could be commuted to a heavy fine. This was a provision which reflected the older, craft view of adultery as a public sin which must be punished because it disrupted household relations. Once expiated, the couple would return to living and working together. Evangelical theology, however, had a slightly different view. For evangelicals like Martin Bucer who influenced the Council as it drew up the new legislation, the sexual union was basic to marriage, and adultery sundered that union, even though an injured spouse should be encouraged to forgive. This view was adopted in the new civic marriage law, where adultery was not merely grounds for separation as it had been under the pre-Reformation church courts, but cause for divorce—a possibility which the Discipline Ordinance was careful not to mention, however.

But if adultery was a sin alongside fornication and blasphemy, the Discipline Ordinance could not be so definite about the other ways in which a marriage might become disorderly. However the Council defined it, infringement of 'the position and duties of married people' was not a crime nor quite yet a sin. Whereas a cuckolded spouse could in theory gain a divorce and the chance of remarriage, the spouse whose partner was 'disobedient', violent, or 'behaved unfittingly' had no grounds whatsoever for bringing a case for divorce. In part this grew out of the Council's inheritance of the basic principles of canon law, which did not recognize 'normal' domestic violence, still less behaviour at odds with the principles of married life, as reason for separation. Instead, using such secular notions as 'right', 'fairness', and 'justice', the Council proclaimed its intention not only to adjudicate between warring couples (a capacity which it had exercised hitherto), but to punish those who should be found wanting. Unlike adultery, prostitution, or blasphemy, where sin and penalty were clear, there were no universal laws in disorderly marriages, and judgements could only be made according to the particular circumstances of the case and in the light of the behaviour of each individual husband and wife.

As the Council viewed it, what caused marital disharmony was wilful, perverse misbehaviour on the part of one or other spouse. Just as it catechized prostitutes, their parents, and procurers on the moment of their going astray, and then required them to confess all the occasions on which they had committed crimes or sins, so also in marriage disputes the Council worked from the assumption that particular failings, individual blameworthy deeds, were responsible for disorderly marriages. So, in its 1537 Ordinance it termed such behaviour 'unjust' (*ungerecht*, an interesting word, legal rather than full-bloodedly moral in its resonances), warned its subjects against committing any of those acts which, it believed, led to undisciplined marriages, and threatened all marital delinquents with 'appropriate punishment'. It was a notion of human wrongdoing which would not square with Lutheran understandings of the inherent evil of all human beings, but it found much support both from older traditions of civic righteousness and from Bucerian moralism—translated, of course, from a church discipline model to a mode of control securely in the hands of secular authority.[3] Indeed, the Ordinance of 1537 propounded a secular theory of marriage disturbance and its causes which did not sit easily with the legal categorizations with which its own Marriage Court actually operated. The range of marital misconduct which it outlined was far wider: for husbands, desertion of one's wife, 'or keeping her otherwise in an unchristian, unfitting manner, or treating her in such a way', were condemned. For wives, the following were enumerated: 'where a wife will not be subject to her husband in all obedience and love, and help him nourish her offspring and bring them up devoutly, if she leaves her husband, or undertakes something against her husband's person, property, honour or life, or otherwise acts in an unsuitable or punishable

---

[3] Augsburg was unusual in the degree of control retained by secular authority, and the Council never sought advice from the clergy. On the involvement of clergy in other reformed Marriage Courts, see Staehelin on Basle, *Die Einführung der Ehescheidung in Basel*, and Köhler, *Zürcher Ehegericht und Genfer Konsistorium*. Bucer tried and failed to implement congregational discipline in Strasbourg, a programme he apparently bruited in Augsburg too. See W. Bellardi, *Die Geschichte der 'Christlichen Gemeinschaft' in Strassburg 1546–1550* (Leipzig, 1934).

manner'. Many more prohibitions attached to female behaviour, elaborating the central duty of wifely subordination in sweeping terms—even the husband's property was sacrosanct, while no protection was afforded her own possessions.

But though disorderly marriages were caused by identifiable failings, these failings were not crimes. Aside from adulterers, marital criminals were harder to identify than prostitutes or thieves, and they could not be exhibited in the stocks in quite the same way as exemplars of wickedness, satisfyingly expelled from the city. Most misbehaving couples were merely cautioned and 'spoken together' again in a kind of secular re-enactment of the original marriage ceremony, where a priest 'spoke the couple together'. Those whose marital behaviour was so intolerable that they were eventually exhibited and exiled, such as the violent Gregori Frei Weisser, were disturbing figures, men whose extreme violence was an uncomfortably close parody of patriarchal behaviour rather than the behaviour of straightforward, psychologically distinct types of miscreant. Though a chronicler like Jörg Preu regularly spiced his writings with the names and histories of adulterers, prostitutes, and procuresses expelled from town, he does not mention violent husbands. Their banishment discomfited rather than purified the city, and their stories did not make piquant material for a chronicle.

Consequently, contrary to the drift of Council policy in every other aspect of order, the control of disorderly marriage was actually rendered far more confused by the Discipline Ordinance. Aggrieved parties could go to the *Einunger* (a court which resolved petty disputes) as they had previously, to the new Marriage Court, to the Discipline Lords, or to the Council itself [5]—a lack of system which reflected the Council's own indecision about the nature of unmarital behaviour as sin, crime, matter for rebuke, or subject of adjudication. Even so, busy city

---

[4] 'oder Sy sunst in annder weg | vnchristlich | vngebürlich halten | oder mit jr handeln wurd. Hingegen | Wa ain Weib jrem Man nit wolt in aller gehorsame vnd liebe vnnderthänig sein | jr Haussgesind vnd kind | helffen Gotselig ernören vnd ziehen | sich von jrem Man thůn | oder etwas wider jres Mans Person Gůt | Ere | oder leib fürnemen | oder sich sunst vngebürlich vnd sträflich halten wurde . . .': *Ains Erbern Rats | der Stat Augspurg | Zucht vnd Pollicey Ordnung*, fo. a/vi^v.

[5] The 1537 Ordinance, drawn up before the Marriage Court was in operation, mentions only the *Einunger*, the Punishment Lords, and the civic court.

mayors continued regularly to draw up agreements and settle
fights between unhappy couples on a less formal basis, so that
the settlement of marriage disputes became an ongoing concern
of a wide range of civic authorities, occupying the skills and time
of the most important civic officials.

This administrative confusion is also reflected in the different
ways men and women used the courts and authorities available.
Though many spouses did see their wives or husbands brought
before the Council and punished for adultery, only a handful took
their guilty spouses to the Marriage Court and secured the
dissolution of the union—which evangelical marriage theology
and secular marriage law in Augsburg assured them that they
could. Most rested content with the punishment their spouses
received, took them food and drink during the period of
imprisonment, and continued to run a workshop with them. On
the other hand, a steady stream of couples took their spouses to
the Marriage Court and sued for divorce although they could only
allege violence and general misbehaviour, grounds which were
simply not recognized by the Marriage Court. Apart from adultery,
only the plea of desertion was admissible, and even then the
period of absence required was at least several years. Such use
of the available remedies does not so much suggest that people
obstinately misunderstood the divorce legislation, as that they
were seeking something else—a redrawing of their relationship
with their spouses, backed with the sanction of Council authority.

The entire issue of disorderly marriages took up so much
Council time—involving even the city mayors—and caused so
much dispute because it exposed how marriage, far from forming
the guarantee of harmonious relations in household and
production alike, was inherently unstable. It brought to the
surface the unequal status of male and female interests and the
fragility of what the Council claimed to be a natural,
complementary hierarchy of man to woman. Even when the
Council chose biblical language to speak of man and woman as
one flesh, in the next breath it chose another biblical phrase to
imagine them as head and body, entirely different parts.
Elsewhere the Council spoke of the essentially shared nature of
the married couple's property (albeit under the control of the
husband) and labour, in which the inherently ill-defined separate
tasks of woman and man were brought together by the concept

of *Nahrung*, or sustenance, a word which refused to distinguish between male and female work. Yet by intervening in the relations between disorderly husbands and wives, the Council was bound to unmask the differences between them. The more it sought to instruct the woman on precisely how she should help to secure the sustenance of the workshop, the more it defined her work as distinct; the more it ordered the husband to 'share his earnings' fairly with his wife, the more apparent it became that women did not have the same control over money and material goods as men did.

Indeed, when the 1537 Ordinance explicitly justified the Council's role in feudal terms as a duty to 'protect' its subjects, this conception was bound to cut across its alliance with the brotherhood of guildsmen. Instead of understanding its own authority as arising from a confederation of guildsmen-electors, the Council saw itself as an authority which, like the other feudal powers beyond the city, had a duty to protect the weak. In marriage the weaker power was all too often the wife, so Council intervention entailed the interposition of its authority between that of master and wife—an intervention which guildsmen did not welcome. The household, which should have been the sacrosanct unit, became a field for Council investigation; the natural hierarchy of patriarchal relations was exposed as contingent and, in some cases, unjust; and the 'one flesh' of marriage was revealed as a veneer covering unequal relations between men and women.

Yet despite the Council's unwillingness to specify and categorize the varieties of marital disorder, the flood of cases which came before it were almost formulaic in the kinds of accusation they made. These revolved chiefly around work relationships, the control of money, sexual behaviour, adultery, and violence. These issues were at the nub of the differences in power between men and women.

Drink, Work, and Money

Picking up a board with a nail in it, Bernhart Hartman 'gave his wife a couple of blows with it', and without stopping to see whether she was wounded, left her bleeding, jumped on his horse, and rode out of town. Called before the Council to defend his failure to report this blood-spilling, just as he would have been obliged to report any fight in which blood was spilt, Hartman gave his version of the fight and of the series of arguments which preceded it. He had picked up the board because she had insulted him as a knave, a thief, and a rascal and had smashed a pot on his head. Presenting his retaliation partly as punishment, he also argued that he had wounded her in 'self-defence' when she caught him, pulled him into a corner, 'kicked him in his shame that is still swollen', and 'held him so tightly that a neighbour had had to separate them'. Asked by the Council whether he had not tried to kill her, since he had run off without checking her wounds, and whether he had not said that he wanted to beat her quite to death, he denied the intention but did not know what he had said. He had had a fair bit to drink at his wife's table, he admitted; but he demanded that witnesses should be heard who would support his side of the story. He added that on a previous occasion he had come home, found his wife gone, and the beds and almost all the household goods sold, and insisted that he had given her money to purchase meat and bread but she had let him buy the provisions. He concluded his interrogation robustly, saying that he no longer wished to stay with his wife because she led such a bad life.[6]

For Hartman, who stoutly defended his extreme brutality (though even he hesitated to present it solely as part of his patriarchal duty to punish his wife's evil tongue), what lay behind his anger was his wife's verbal and physical violence, and an ongoing quarrel about money and property. Though their quarrel issued in Hartman's spectacular violence, the themes of the argument were commonplace enough, and despite the extreme nature of the violence, his account of the fight has an almost banal similarity with the kinds of marital argument which regularly came before the Council. As usual, the fight began—and the Council's questioning assumed that it was caused—by drinking. As Hartman insisted that the Council should remember, the background to the fight was that she had once removed and sold the household goods, a destruction of the community of goods which still rankled with him. His wife's insults of him as a thief, rascal, and knave were an imputation against his standing as a

---

[6] StadtAA, Reichsstadt, Urg. 26 July 1544, Bernhart Hartman.

loyal citizen and a working craftsman in an honourable trade. What counted in Hartman's favour was that, as a witness on his behalf stated, he was a 'coarse pious man who had improved his house, who neither gambled nor drank away his money', and who 'had left his wife in no lack that he, witness, could see'.[7] This defence was a firm statement of what guildsfolk and Council alike held to be the duties of a married man.

Yet though Hartman and his wife—no strangers to the courts because of their 'wild marriage'—were told once more how they should live in marital union, the interrogation of witnesses and the reiteration of homilies did less to confirm the positive vision of married household life than to reveal the deep and often irresolvable conflicts between men and women which had led to this bloody fracas. Hartman had been refusing to give his wife money to buy 'meat and bread', a refusal which touched the niggling ambiguity in marital property relations, for while in theory the goods of a married couple belonged to both, it was the husband who administered them. This ambiguity could lead to crass conflicts of right if one of the couple had been married before, as may have been the case with Hartman's wife. As one of her witnesses complained: 'he sits in her goods, takes the rent, and gives her nothing'. According to Hartman's wife, the quarrel had begun not with her insults, but with Hartman's demand that she should give him money when she had none. Money and who controlled it were issues of contention between men and women, and could not be solved by the ambiguous formula of joint sharing of goods under the husband's authority.

As had happened in the Hartman case, these contested assumptions were sometimes acted out in a literal destruction of the shared property of marriage. The man or woman might start to remove all the valuables from the house, a dramatic declaration of loss of confidence in the other's ability to provide and manage resources. Women above all had recourse to this tactic, and would denude the household as Bernhart Hartman's wife had done, taking beds, bedclothes, pots and pans, crockery, and anything

[7] Ibid., testimony of Christoff Sprenng, weaver: 'dann sprenng [scribe's mistake for Hartman] sey ain grober fromer Mennsch. der sein heislin bisheer gepessert das sein weder verspillt Noch verdrunckhen. Er zeug auch khain mangl gesehen. den er seiner hausfrawen gelassen.'

else that could be pawned.[8] These objects, however, might often constitute that portion of the couple's material goods provided by the woman as part of her dowry; and they also clearly stood for women's work in the household. These rituals of separation thus suggest that beneath the ideology of joint property there was a resilient tacit understanding of some property belonging to men and some to women, even in the craft milieu where no contracts reserved separate property and all was supposedly held in common.

To the Council, always alarmed at spendthrift ways which might undermine the city's economy and what it saw as its limited resources, the question of men's control of joint property became most vexed when men frittered away their goods. Cautious about limiting male authority, however, the Council was chary of removing control of finances from men who showed themselves incapable of managing their financial affairs. Even where the wife's own property was being misspent by an unscrupulous husband, and even when her family was powerful enough to appeal for Council intervention against the husband, the Council was reluctant to act. It would usually patiently caution the couple not to live beyond their means, and if the woman's family was blocking the man's access to the dowry, the Council would normally attempt a settlement whereby the husband gained control of the money but promised to spend it wisely.[9]

Yet on occasion the Council's abhorrence of spendthrift men, the social pariahs whom—with the work-shy—it held to be largely responsible for city poverty, overcame its support of patriarchal authority in the household. Husbands like Bernhart Hartman were actually ordered to pay their wives a stipulated sum for housekeeping, a dramatic restriction of their previously untrammelled control of household earnings. No less a personage

---

[8] See e.g. ibid., Urg. 15 Feb. 1502, Sebastian Probst; Urg. 11 May 1527, Franz Riem; Urg. 21 May 1532, Georg Liebhart; Urg. 27 Jan. 1533, Narcis Regitzer; Urg. 21 July 1539, Bartholome Stierpaur; Prot. der Zuchtherren VI, fo. 49, 10 June 1545, Hans Vb and wife.

[9] e.g. Lienhart Klain was given full control of the couple's goods but warned not to be a spendthrift (ibid., Prot. der Zuchtherren II, fo. 110, 14 June 1540); and Georg Erdinger was to be paid the full dowry when he supplied security for his wife's morning gift and matching, despite his work-shy habits and the debts he had contracted (SKUK 8.1, Verträge und Vergleiche, 4 June 1535).

than the miserly patrician Ambrosi Jung, a doctor, was ordered to pay his wife 2 gulden per week for the purchase of 'bread, meat and fish and the maintenance of the house kitchen'.[10] In other cases the punishment imposed by the Council on a hopeless husband might effectively award financial control of the couple's assets to the wife. By exiling a ne'er-do-well, the Council was in fact limiting his ability to destroy altogether the household's material existence—a consequence which was evident to both people and Council. Jorg Pawhof was finally exiled by the Council in a bid to protect what remained of the property he was frittering away.[11] Gregori Frei Weisser, whose wife the Council described approvingly as a 'pious, hardworking and simple woman', was finally exiled for his blasphemy, spendthrift ways, and general misbehaviour, effectively ending the marriage and leaving her in control of what little property was left. But this was a drastic—and rare—solution, and the Council was careful to muster its support in this case by reiterating that eight honourable men had testified against Frei Weisser.[12]

More usually, however, the Council's pious admonitions availed little: Bartholome Stierpaur, who had been ordered by the court and then by the Council to pay his wife housekeeping money, was still demanding money from her. She claimed that he 'gave not more than a penny for the house' and sometimes bought her only half a pound of dripping for a whole fortnight, and even that she could barely drag out of him; and she pleaded with the Marriage Court that he was selling all their goods and giving her no say in the transactions, which he was not legally entitled to do. He was extremely violent, she claimed, beating, kicking, and insulting her, 'so that it is insufferable for a beast (whom one previously hadn't given anything to eat), let alone a human being'.[13] She concluded by begging the court 'to help

[10] Ibid., Strafbuch des Rats IV, fos. 68ᵛ, 69ᵛ-70ʳ, 23 Feb. 1546.
[11] Ibid., Strafbuch des Rats III, fo. 33ᵛ, 25 June 1541; and Prot. der Dreizehn VI, fo. 153ʳ, 25 June 1541.
[12] Ibid., Urg. 17 June 1539, Gregori Frei Weisser; Strafbuch des Rats II, fos. 151ʳ, 152ʳ, 16 and 18 June 1539.
[13] Ibid., Urg. 15 Mar. 1539; Urg. 21 July 1539, Bartholome Stierpaur; Strafbuch des Rats II, fo. 141ᵛ, 18 Mar. 1539; Strafbuch des Rats II, fo. 154ᵛ, 24 July 1539; 'das Es ainem Vich (dem man Zuuor nichts zuessen geben will) geschweigen ainem menschen vnleydenlich ist': complaint of Stierpaur, Urg. 21 July 1539, Bartholome Stierpaur.

her graciously, as a Christian authority', so that 'she might be released from such misery and wretchedness'. In this case the Council refused divorce and did nothing to secure her property or to protect her. Once again it threatened exile, but took no action, repeating its 'good text' of advice to the couple—homilies which by this time had worn thin.

Irresponsibility with money was not, however, a purely male vice. In comments which owed much to the long association of women, lust, and luxury in both lay and religious tradition, men and Council complained of women's spendthrift ways and failure to work. Here women's contraction of debts without their husbands' permission could be a flashpoint, though men were not required to gain their wives' approval if they borrowed money.[14] For the Council this was an extreme form of disobedience, flouting both the principles of wifely subordination and the careful stewardship of resources; and it was willing to respond by ordering one such woman to remain indoors as a sort of household prisoner, depriving her completely of the freedom of movement which it believed her to have abused by contracting debts. What made such attitudes doubly contradictory was that women's economy required them to spend time outside the household, and depended upon a system of credit where women pawned goods for short periods of time, stored goods for sale, and even lent out or pawned clothes as surety for small expenses and raw materials. The Council was prepared to recognize this on occasion in relation to men, so that even those under house curfew might be released from it on the grounds that their work demanded travel.[15] If, on the issue of women's debts, guildsmen and council were at one therefore, that agreement was often at odds with the realities of life in craft households.

The second major plank of the unity of marriage was the shared nature of labour, naturally divided between men and women in accordance with their sex. In abstract this was clear enough: the woman's primary domain was *haushalten*, understood in the broad sense; men's duty was to provide for the family. At one

[14] On debt law in Augsburg, see F. Hellmann, *Das Konkursrecht der Reichsstadt Augsburg* (Berlin, 1905).
[15] StadtAA, Reichsstadt, Urg. 17 Jan. 1541, Wolf Rechlsperger, Segenschmid, whose punishment was modified so that he could travel on business: Strafbuch des Rats III, fo. 26ʳ, 26 Feb. 1541; fo. 31ʳ, 28 May 1541.

level, marriage quarrels acted out these expectations in orthodox fashion. Bartholome Seiz complained that his wife refused to cook for his friends and, on occasion, for him as well, and averred that 'it was not endurable for him that his wife should refuse him his food';[16] another husband beat his wife and deserted her 'until she learnt to keep house';[17] and a third justified his ill-treatment of his wife with the telling allegation that she never gave him new sheets.[18] These complaints were raised because they were understood by the husbands as derelictions of wifely duty, and they expected the Council to believe the same. Women, by contrast, might refuse domestic services if they felt their husbands were failing to provide: Margaret Schnitzer tried to justify her bigamy on the ground that her first marriage no longer existed: 'for he sold the wimple from her head, thereto, if it were not for pious people, he would have left her and her children to die of hunger'.[19] The sale of the wimple, symbol of honest wifehood, was a metaphor of the destruction of mutual obligation. The same woman refused her husband food and locked the bread away because she and the children were on poor-relief on their own account and owed the errant husband nothing. Yet these litanies of complaint did not simply cement the 'naturalness' of what was expected of men and women in marriage. Sexually stereotyped allegations like these supported a view of the duties of the married estate not so much as natural consequences of the different natures of men and women, but rather, a kind of sexual bargain which, when broken, freed the other of obligations. Indeed, the Council's own behaviour in this case lent weight to such a view, for though it prosecuted Schnitzer for her bigamy, it was the Council which had banished her husband in the first place, after a long series of offences and failed marital reconciliations, thus effectively terminating the marriage.

The bitter marital disputes over the division of labour could even question the gendered nature of labour itself. In a long and

[16] Ibid., Urg. 14 Mar. 1541, Bartholome Seiz: 'dann es sej Jm Je nit leidlich. das Jne sein weib sin Essen vorhalten wolte.'

[17] Ibid., Urg. 3 Mar. 1539, Sixt Schaller.

[18] Ibid., Urg. 17 June 1539, Gregori Frei Weisser.

[19] 'dann er Jr dem schlair ob dem kopff verthann. darzu Sy vnd Jre Khinder wo fromb leuth nit gewesen, hungers sterben lassen': ibid., Urg. 29 Feb. 1544, Jorg Claiber; extract from Discipline Lords interrogation dated 13 Feb. 1544 filed with this case.

acrimonious quarrel over several issues with his wife, Simon
Streib appears to have been angered by her failure to 'work'—
that is, to assist him in his work of weaving by preparing the
flax—hence retarding his work rhythms. As he put it: 'his wife
does not want to work, or help him in the house, and goes round
saying openly that she only took him so that she could do as she
pleased'. So that he could 'shock her, and bring her to work',
he pretended to sell a garment of hers, a tactic which symbolically
destroyed the community of goods in retaliation for what he
perceived as her failure to share the burden of labour. But, as
emerges from the interrogations and reports of witnesses, Anna
Streib was in fact caring for a brood of children from a previous
marriage and organizing a household which included at least five
adults, as well as assisting Streib. Because of the invisibility of
this 'work', Streib could perceive his wife as lazy; while the
inherent vaguenesses of 'housekeeping and assisting in *Nahrung*'
could create confusion over how husband and wife thought tasks
should be organized. The children, competitors for her love and
distractions from the 'real' work, thus became the target of
Streib's rage: the fight was sparked off when he roughly snatched
the 'special' soup that had been made for an invalid child and
ate it himself, insisting on the best love and food because he was
the bread-winner.[20] Martin Horner beat his wife because, he
said, she was a 'bad housekeeper . . . for she was always going
out with her sewing-bees and wanted to have money to buy
drinks, that was more her thing than housekeeping'.[21] Though
property was the major issue in the fight between Bernhart
Hartman and his wife, the submerged issue of the division of
labour figured as well. The arguments about who should have
cash were also a dispute about whose responsibility it was to
buy food. It was to Hartman's role as a model, non-gambling
worker that his witness appealed, and this was precisely
what he claimed his wife had impugned by insulting him
as a dishonourable 'thief and rascal', a 'traitor' deserving
death who had no right to a political role as citizen or
elector.

---

[20] Ibid., Urg. 17 Apr. 1544, Simon Streib. See also on this case, L. Roper,
'Housework and Livelihood: Towards the *Alltagsgeschichte* of Women', *German
History*, 2 (1985), 3–9.

[21] StadtAA, Reichsstadt, Urg. 2 Mar. 1541, Martin Horner.

The very ill-defined nature of women's tasks within the household, the intermingling of work and leisure, is perhaps most graphically illustrated in the sewing-bee: at once housework, in that it involved the work of garment repair and the sewing of objects for household or people's uses, it could also constitute a woman's social circle; and, like the male use of the tavern, it became the site for male fantasies about what women did together. Not surprisingly, it was often imagined sexually, as a place where indescribable orgies took place; and *Gunkelstube* was ambiguous in meaning between sewing-room and brothel.[22] When the Council showed some sympathy for the overburdening of a woman like Anna Streib, telling Streib roundly that his complaint 'that his wife is lazy . . . has not been discovered to be the case, therefore it is pure malice on his part', it implicitly questioned the craft-defined notion of labour which gave Streib such self-confidence in his own fulfilment of his marital duty to provide. The extent of this revision of guild-based notions of labour was, however, limited: the Council was less inclined to regard Martin Horner's wife's sewing-bees as labour, and appears to have accepted his litany of complaints.

So intense might this suspicion of women's work and female cliques become that men often focused their anger on where their wives had spent the day, resenting either a wife's absence from the house without permission, or her admission of visitors to the house, particularly male visitors, when the husband was not present. These disputes are connected with the control of space and movement—as the husbands explained their attitudes, they objected to a woman opening the house without her husband's approval, or else to her independent life outside the house. Her pursuits were always imagined to be frivolous, idle, or—worse—sexual, the inevitable consequence of idleness. At times this could result in a direct expression of jealousy both for and of the other sex: Steffan Karg said that it was the sight of his wife's red beret which triggered off his beating of her, for it symbolized her carefree, sexual life and reminded him of his own enslavement to the hard work he hated.[23] Lucas Muller beat his wife because

---

[22] On sewing-circles, see H. Medick, 'Village Spinning Bees: Sexual Culture and Free Time among Rural Youths in Early Modern Germany', in H. Medick and D. Sabean (eds.), *Interest and Emotion: Essays on the Study of Family and Kinship* (Cambridge, 1984).

[23] StadtAA, Reichsstadt, Urg. 6 Sept. 1527, Steffan Karg.

she spent time outside the house and, in his view, would not work. On one occasion, when she had taken some gold buttons with her to do some sewing at Dr Marschalk's house, Muller interpreted her absence 'without his knowledge or permission', her pretty looks, and especially the gold buttons as proof that she was on an assignation, and refused to believe that she had been teaching Marschalk's daughter embroidery and beat her so hard that 'her face ran over with blood'.[24] Sexual possessiveness merged with fear that his wife was roaming outside the confines of the household, a freedom which he, chained to his belt-making business, perceived as wanton pleasure-seeking: when he was interrogated by the Council he angrily demanded that she be forced to work. Yet while men found it hard not to think of their wives as sexually vulnerable and lustful, the very patterns of the craft-workshop life made it impossible for women to remain secluded in the house or lodgings with children and servants, and required them to arrange sales or personal work-deals with visitors. In a culture which placed such emphasis on wifely chastity but also viewed all women as fickle, which delighted in stories, images, and songs about what wives got up to in the absence of their husbands,[25] the twin pressures of a female work life which could not be insulated and a concept of unguarded women as dangerous could lead men to try to impose a beleaguered patriarchal authority by force.

The endless series of disputes about work and money all show a firm understanding of men's and women's labour and culture as inherently different—so different that men's anger often took the form of an attack on the object which, like Steffan Karg's wife's red beret or Lucas Muller's wife's gold buttons, symbolized both womanhood and all they hated about their own lives. Though the Council responded to the endless series of marital fights which came before it by reiterating its pieties about married life, based on an essentially bourgeois conception of the imaginary household in which the master directed the labour of wife, servants, and journeymen, what Council intervention uncovered was the constant potential for disharmony between men and

---

[24] Ibid., Urg. 6 Dec. 1534, Lucas Muller.
[25] See also D. Wuttke (ed.), *Fastnachtspiele des 15. und 16. Jahrhunderts* (Stuttgart, 1978): Hans Sachs, 'Das Teufelbannen'; Jakob Ayrer, 'Der abhanden gekommen Jann'; and Hans Sachs's mockery of male jealousy, 'Der Eifersüchtige'.

7. Georg Pencz (?), *Adultery* (Geisberg no. 827). The husband, dressed in fool's costume, is deceived by his wife and shuts his eyes to what is going on. Like the cat under the table, women, once having got a taste for men, are insatiable. The image is accompanied by a long poem.

8. Erhard Schoen, *Allegory of the Faithlessness of Women* (Geisberg no. 1155).

women. When the Council specified men's and women's labour or ordered men to share their sustenance with women, their understanding of work and money undermined the concept of an inevitable unity of male and female interests in marriage, and potentially threatened to part company from the guild notion of work as craft labour.

Chief among these issues was drinking, a matter which placed the Council, with its perennial concern about the disorder caused by excessive drinking, at odds with guildsmen, for whom alcohol was an essential part of social life. In an almost ritual fashion, complainants would narrate the quarrels of husband and wife as beginning when the husband returned from the tavern. For women, drinking crystallized arguments over the control of labour and money because it made visible the question of who had control of the household budget. To women who perceived their role as securing the household sustenance, making sure that household resources stretched to cover essentials and were fairly divided, men's drinking at the tavern provided a focus for their anger at the difficulty of making ends meet.

Moreover, the inn constituted a rival social group to that of the household. It provided a space for male gossip, for the exchange of news about craft-related matters, consignments of raw materials, and the like; it was the place where day-labourers might expect to hear of work, and where men might discuss political matters and religious ideas. It is no coincidence that guilds had their own guild-rooms where the otherwise rather atomized work patterns of individual craft shops could be mitigated and corporate loyalty fostered. Men nearly always drank together without their womenfolk, and the bonds created between drinking-mates could be strong indeed, overlapping as they often did with guild networks or the shared trade interests which kindred crafts, such as baking and brewing, butchery and tanning, might bring. As women saw it, this was the environment in which men discussed their wives, egging each other on to treat them roughly: Hans Griss was accused of plotting with his drinking-mates to beat his wife, while another group of bakers boasted to each other as they drank in the guild-rooms about how they would deal with adulterous wives.[26] Perceiving tavern-

---

[26] StadtAA, Reichsstadt, Urg. 30 Aug. 1526, Hans Griss; Urg. 29 Apr. 1527, Martin Scheffler.

going as entertainment, spending on oneself, women often complained of their men wasting time and money 'behind the wine', complaints which merged with a general hostility to male tavern culture, the collective extra-marital identity which it offered men, and their own continued 'labour' in the house.

The Council, too, was hostile to tavern culture and had long wished to control men's drinking, which it saw as one of the chief causes of vice. It found itself aligned with women's view of the causes of marital disorder here, and increasingly began to view the cultures of men and women as separate and hostile rather than harmoniously conjoined in the household. In Ulm the campaign against excessive drinking reached such a pitch that the sale of alcohol after the night-bell was prohibited;[27] and in Strasbourg it was decreed that being under the influence of liquor no longer constituted a valid reason for failing to remember what one had done, but was to bring an additional penalty.[28] Drunkenness, the Augsburg Council maintained, led to 'deformation of the noble reason into animal-like insensibility, ruin of souls, bodies, lives, honour and goods'.[29] Taverns were also the places where murmuring against the authorities was most likely to commence, a view strengthened by the discovery that the plot to overthrow the Council in 1524 had been planned during carousing-sessions.[30] Drinking, the Council maintained, must inevitably threaten the household's economic subsistence and increase the numbers dependent on poor-relief. Thus the Council frequently found itself in the position of supporting angry wives against drunkard husbands, accusing the men of improvidence, trying to limit the consumption of alcohol, forbidding those men on poor-relief even to enter a tavern, and attempting to isolate men from those circles of male friends of which the Council remained abidingly suspicious. It would frequently impose a tavern ban on a delinquent male in the belief that this would make him docile and disciplined.

[27] G. Geiger, *Die Reichsstadt Ulm vor der Reformation* (Ulm, 1971), pp. 175 f.
[28] Strasbourg Ordinance of 1529 in Stadtarchiv Ulm, A 3971.
[29] 'was jamers vnd vnrats | als verstellung der Edlen Vernunfft | in vihische vnsinnigkait | verderbung der Selen | leibs | lebens | Eren vnd Guts | augenscheinlich darauss eruolgt': *Ains Erbern Rats | der Stat Augspurg | Zucht vnd Pollicey Ordnung*, fo. a/iv^r^.
[30] StadtAA, Reichsstadt, Urg. 11 Sept. 1524, Pauli Kissinger; Urg. 1523, Hans Bogenschutz; Urg. 6–21 Oct. 1524, Lienhart Knoringer.

Women were seldom accused of drunkenness; but when they were, the social patterns of their drinking were different. Anna Krug, accused of habitual drunkenness, drank at home alone rather than in inns.[31] Whereas, however seriously the Council regarded it, men's excess drinking was popularly viewed as a male peccadillo, women's drunkenness was considered to be extreme delinquent behaviour. None of Anna Krug's neighbours testified in her support, for her drinking created no bonds of loyalty; and she gave a self-description which glorified the ostracism she experienced: 'one could say nothing of her but shame and fault; she was full of this, and she was not ashamed of this at all'.[32] Her 'fullness', playing both with the meaning of 'full' as drunk and with the Council's moral cadences, was the complete inverse of Council ideas. At the same time she insisted that she only spent on drink the money which she earned herself through making playing-cards, and that she never touched her husband's earnings or the money he left around the house. Men did not feel called upon to make such justifications, for they were convinced that the money they spent on drink was theirs, earned by the sweat of their brows, despite the Council's attempts to convince them to the contrary.

Above all, however, drunkenness was imagined as a male vice. Consequently, when the Council seriously attempted to control drinking, it described drunkenness in the Ordinance of 1537 as that public sin which robbed man of his reason and made him like the animals; that is, abolished that faculty which made a man capable of being 'head' of his wife. The campaign against drink brought together several themes of its wider hostility against disorderly men: men who could not be trusted to act as disciplining patriarchs; who spent money recklessly; and who might be a cause of political disorder. However, as it interrogated drunkards, seeking to educate them into a realization of the evil of their ways, it became clear that many men were unable to carry out what the Council saw as their manly responsibilities; and not only those good-for-nothings on poor-relief whom the Council

---

[31] Ibid., Urg. 10 June 1541, Anna Krug.
[32] 'man kondte annders nichts dann schannd vnnd lasster von Jr sagen. des were sie voll. vnnd schem sich desselben nichts.' Clerical moralists, too, abhorred drunken women: S. Ozment, *When Fathers Ruled: Family Life in Reformation Europe* (Cambridge, Mass., 1983), p. 68.

forbade to even enter a tavern, but guildsmen too. What was the Council to make of Hans Eisenprecht, a weaver, who after getting himself 'full of wine', treated his wife 'inhumanly evilly', and caused a general fracas in the neighbourhood so severe that not one of his neighbours would testify in his favour?[33] Or of Steffan Enngelmair, another weaver, who chased his wife down the street when he was 'overburdened with wine', cursing the night-watchmen when they stopped him, and on the following day showed contempt for lawful authority by simply failing to turn up before the Discipline Court?[34] Those who cocked a snook at authority and let animal passions rule their actions through drink were hardly model patriarchs, and the Council castigated them for their failings. But drunkenness, and especially the addiction to brandy, was so widespread that the Council began to be more censorious of the tavern culture so central to work rituals, demanding to know, for instance, exactly who Eisenprecht's drinking-companions had been so that it could track them down as accomplices. Moreover, the Council's abiding suspicion of the fitness of some guildsmen to be 'heads' in their houses increasingly weaned the Council away from its alignment with guild politics, making it yet more concerned to take over from the guilds the right to punish drunkards. By 1538 it had restricted the guilds to punishing only minor acts of drunkenness on its own premises, and reserved the right to intervene even in guild affairs should the guilds prove 'lax' in administering appropriate punishment.[35]

Violence

But it was in its attitudes to violence between husband and wife that the contradictions in the Council's idealization of married life became most evident. Ostensibly, the Council adamantly supported the right of the husband to chastise his wife, servants, and children. In an extension of its own hierarchical self-image, the Council could compare the husband's relation to his house with that between Council and city: as the divinely instituted

[33] StadtAA, Reichsstadt, Urg. 7 Feb. 1541, Hans Eisenprecht.
[34] Ibid., Urg. 2 Nov. 1541 (under 1542), Steffan Enngelmair.
[35] Ibid., Fasz. Ordnungen 54 (Zuchtordnungen), 'Straf vff den Stuben vnnd Zunnfftheusern belangend'; HWA Fischer, 1429–1551, 3 July 1538.

authority, both were also responsible for their subjects' sins. The father, the Council maintained, had a positive duty to punish his children for their wickedness—as we saw, it was precisely the failure to do so which constituted Lienhart Strobel's guilt in relation to his errant, 'unchaste' daughter Appollonia.[36] Similarly, the husband had a duty to punish his wife for adultery. If he did not, he was an accessory, not merely because it was presumed that he must be receiving payment for his 'toleration', but because failure to punish and restore order amounted to participation in the crime of indiscipline. By contrast, the Council seldom accused a wife of being an accessory to a husband's affair with another woman, even in cases of the seduction/rape of servants, where the wife must have been aware of what was happening. Though she had authority over her daughters, she lacked both power and responsibility over her husband in the Council's version of the domestic scenario.

The Council well knew the intimate connection between the maintenance of discipline (*Zucht*) and the use of force. For try as it might to instil a sense of pious living in the offenders who came before the courts, the Council was aware that its ultimate sanction was physical violence, whether that meant systematic torture in order to get the offender to provide a full confession, or public physical punishment: whipping, maiming, or, as a last resort, execution. In the case of husbands, therefore, the Council was fully prepared to support men's use of force in order to buttress discipline within the household. Such an attitude was widely shared. As a satirical woodcut of the 'tamed lion' depicted it, men who let themselves be flattered and manipulated by female wiles were at risk of allowing themselves to be ridden by women, a fearful sexual humiliation. The King of the Beasts had to use his claws.[37]

At the same time, however, the Council's deep-rooted suspicion of poorer craftsmen—above all of day-labourers—as violent, work-shy, and hardly possessing the virtues of discipline, made it wary of these men and willing to champion their wives against them. Just as it tried to stamp out fighting and boisterous

---

[36] See Chap. 3 above on prostitution.
[37] For a different interpretation of this image, see Ozment, *When Fathers Ruled*, pp. 51, 70-1.

9. German school,
sixteenth century, *The
Taming of the Lion*
(Geisberg no. 1431,
Kupferstichkabinett
SMPK, Berlin).

10. Hans Leonhard
Schäufelein, *The
Nappy Washer*, Inv.
No. I 86, 222,
Kunstsammlungen der
Veste Coburg. In this
role-reversal, the man
is forced to wash the
nappies while the
well-dressed woman
with her large purse
holds the stick over
him.

disturbances between men and impose order on the city's violent street life, limiting the disorder caused by the behaviour of what it saw as unrespectable louts of the lower orders, so also it identified this group of males as the source of violence in marriage. (Men of the élite, by contrast, might engage in similar behaviour without touching off such fears: Simon Manlich, a member of an established merchant, non-patrician family, married to Marina Herbrot, daughter of the redoubtable, wealthy guild politician Jakob Herbrot, was never punished for drunkenness, spendthrift behaviour, or insulting his wife, although all these faults were mentioned in the private contract they agreed before the Council in 1545.[38])

Ironically, despite its idealization of marriage and the productive and emotional relations within the ordered craft household, the Council remained deeply pessimistic about married life, convinced of the inevitability of violence in marriage. At least seventy men came before the Council or Discipline Lords accused of wife-beating and were sent straight back to their wives; but only five cases of divorce on grounds of cruelty ever reached the Marriage Court and none of the pleas was granted.[39] Often, wife-beating was not the cause of arrest but emerged as a minor accusation in the course of interrogation, a fact which suggests that by no means all cases of even quite serious violence were prosecuted. As we shall see, the Council's repeated homilies to fighting couples effectively treated violence as a regrettable fact of life.

The Council's conception of household discipline (*Zucht*) coloured its rhetoric of marital relations. Thus it cautioned men to discipline their wives fairly.[40] *Strafen*, to punish, the word both the Council and many of the men it interrogated chose to use here, was also the verb the Council used for its own attempts

---

[38] StadtAA, Reichsstadt, RB 19, fos. 97ʳ–98ᵛ, 16 June 1545.

[39] For figures and categories of cases, see L. Roper, 'Work, Marriage and Sexuality: Women in Reformation Augsburg', Ph.D. thesis (London, 1985), pp. 226 ff., esp. tables 5.4, 5.5, 5.6.

[40] The Council certainly did not take the view that wives should never be physically chastised. Ozment, who argues that physical chastisement was frowned upon, has to use Puritan theologians to support this view: the German Protestants from whom he quotes are objecting to the abuse of authority and the punishment of the innocent, not casting doubt on the husband's right to discipline, by force if need be (Ozment, *When Fathers Ruled*, pp. 54 f.).

to impose discipline, a verb which can range from verbal correction to physical chastisement and carries with it the notion that the punishment is just. Consequently, there must be a 'reason', or, as it urged many husbands, 'he should not punish her without reason'.[41] On the other hand, women who 'answered back' to their menfolk, or who taunted them verbally, were never described by the Council as engaged in *strafen*, even though the Council might share their criticism of their men as drunken and lazy. Their subordinated position within the household ruled such an intervention illegitimate; and few women sought to describe their actions in this way. Rather, in both the Council's and the men's language, women's insubordinate speech was presented as a kind of verbal violence to which male physical violence was an inevitable response.[42] Men, too, did not seek to deny that they had beaten their wives, but affirmed their actions, describing them as 'punishment' and setting them in the context of husbandly authority.

Yet the reality of the marital disputes with which the Council dealt bore little relation to the model of dispassionate exercise of just authority which the Council proposed. If the Council pictured women as the verbal and men as the physical aggressors, the accounts of quarrels showed both women and men to be using physical violence. Further, as the Council's own near equation of insult and blow implicitly conceded, men's 'chastisement' of their wives did not proceed in measured, orderly fashion. In the cases which came before the Council, there was no special instrument set aside for administering correction: rather, both men and women grabbed whatever objects—often domestic tools, kitchen knives, jugs, and so forth—were nearest to hand. In these cases, men used their entire bodies, their capacity for greater physical force, without employing disciplined, distanced restraint, but kicked, beat, punched, and even bit their wives. Their narratives of punishment often disintegrate at this point:

[41] e.g. StadtAA, Reichsstadt, Prot. der Zuchtherren VI, fo. 110, 2 Sept. 1545, Veit Hainlin; Prot. der Zuchtherren II, fo. 166, 29 Nov. 1540, Clas Hort.

[42] e.g. Paul Scheifelhut's wife was told not to give him 'evil words', even though the Council agreed he was violent and work-shy (ibid., Prot. der Zuchtherren III, fos. 130, 139, 167, 170, 1 June, 5 July, 25 Sept., and 7 Oct. 1542); Hans Kreidenweiss's wife was told not to insult him when he did not have work, though the Council held him to be a violent, gambling drunkard (ibid., fo. 39, 21 May 1541).

under interrogation they usually did not deny the blows they had struck, but rather disputed the force or the instrument.

Indeed, sixteenth-century urban society bolstered male 'natural' strength with a cultural tool: urban males were entitled to wear a weapon. Frequently, men resorted to their weapons in such fights, using their swords not to cut, but rather to bruise and beat their wives. To the Council this was a serious abuse, and even more serious when the weapon was unsheathed; yet the existence of the weapon entrenched the cultural inequality between men and women, an inequality which the Council was not willing to alter. More than a symbol, the weapon was a cultural phallic force. Weapons were traditionally passed down from father to son, and the richly patterned decorations on the swords of noblemen show how the weapon could be stamped with its owner's personality.[43] For the defence of the city, all male inhabitants were required to own some weapon, and the capacity to bear arms was in turn linked to the right to a political voice in the city's affairs, to maleness, and to adulthood.[44] Conversely, as part of the punishment of a disorderly man, the Council might prescribe that he be forbidden to wear a weapon, a shameful punishment which was a cultural castration.

The interaction of Council expectations and men's and women's assumptions about male and female behaviour could thus serve to intensify the differences between their physicality as described in the interrogations. Partly because of the strength of the alignment of men with the sword, and with a more physically direct form of expression, the very narratives of the men and women who came before the Council tended to become stylized, so that women, who had no right to punish, may not have been able to describe or even carry out their physical retaliation so readily. This reluctance emerges in the way they presented themselves as passive sufferers, enduring their husbands' blows. Simon Streib's wife, who found a kindly ear in the Council, admitted that her husband was sometimes 'wild',

---

[43] See J. Hayward, 'Blank- und Feuerwaffen und sonstige Arbeiten aus unedlen Metallen', in *Welt im Umbruch: Augsburg zwischen Renaissance und Barock*, 3 vols. (Augsburg, 1980, Munich, 1981), ii; B. Thomas, 'Augsburger Harnische und Stangenwaffen', in *Welt im Umbruch*, ii, and catalogue, pp. 487–537.

[44] J. Kraus, *Das Militärwesen der Reichsstadt Augsburg 1548–1806* (Augsburg, 1980), pp. 74–104.

but omitting any reference to his beating of her, pleaded only that 'he might have sympathy with the children, for then she would happily suffer for God's sake'.[45] Only comporting themselves as victims could assure women of the Council's 'protection', promised to the weak in the 1537 Ordinance.

All this might have confirmed the natural order of subjection of woman to man except that the extravagant sufferings of women and the brutality of the 'disciplining' which the men described were too uncomfortably extreme, and were indeed a disturbing, exaggerated reflection of tendencies within the Council's own exercise of power. The degree of force needed to impose patriarchal discipline on women who presented themselves as victims was a testimony to the contestedness of that sexual order. Worse, by intervening to protect the weak, the Council was bound both to undermine the authority of the master of the house and, by implication, to ally itself with the wife rather than with the man, who believed his political interests to be embodied in the Council. By invading the household, the consequences of the Council's gradual understanding of itself as an authority and not as a voice of the communal jurisdiction of guildsmen became manifest—to the rage of guildsmen.

The Council's attempts to determine the limits of acceptable force led it into interesting contradictions. For while it defended the duty of husbands to discipline wives, children, and servants, it also held certain types of violence to be intolerable; and the new Discipline Courts established in the wake of the Reformation allowed women to bring such cases to court far more readily. Frequently, the Council proceeded by declaring a 'peace' between the two parties, which tacitly recognized that husband and wife were at war and converted a repetition of the offence into a transgression against Council authority, not merely against the spouse. For this offence, men could be punished with short sentences of imprisonment, with banishment, or—as in the case of Gregori Frei Weisser, who had been reconciled with his wife no fewer than five times, was guilty of 'great blasphemy', and had ignored warnings from all civic authorities—their general insubordination might be considered so extreme that their

---

[45] 'vnnd wo Er mit den khinden ain mitleid hett, wolt sie noch gern ain gotleid tragen': StadtAA, Reichsstadt, Urg. 17 Apr. 1544, Simon Streib.

tongues were cut out.[46] The Council began to require a husband who wounded his wife to report to the mayor the following day, just as men involved in street fights were obliged to do. How easily an angry husband, convinced he had the right to discipline his wife, could fall into insubordinate language is revealed in the case of Bernhart Hartman, who shouted that he would 'beat his wife, even if four mayors and Council members were watching'— language which did his cause no good with the Council.[47]

However, the Council's admonitions to 'live peacefully', and its careful contracts which, in a kind of remarriage ritual, 'spoke the couple together' once more, lost force with repetition. When Paul Scheiffelhut appeared for the fourth time in a year for quarrelling, or Hans Kranich and his wife came to court for the fifth time in as many years, raising the same grievances, the Council's piously phrased homilies rang hollow.[48] Its firm conviction that problems were the result of 'wicked behaviour' of one or other spouse, and could be corrected by punishment, gave way to a kind of working assumption that faults were likely to lie on both sides, as the list of conditions routinely imposed on both spouses show. This approach, however, veered towards assuming that the fragility of marital harmony lay in the nature of the institution itself rather than in individuals' 'punishable faults', and left the Council vaguely pleading with the offenders to 'live peaceably and well, and hold each other as honourable wives and husbands'. Some spouses, impatient with this approach, called the Council's bluff: Magdalena Dirrenberger, threatened with banishment if she did not reach accommodation with her husband, happily chose exile rather than live with him![49] This effective divorce was certainly not what the Council had in mind.

[46] Ibid., Urg. 17 June 1539, Gregori Frei Weisser; and Prot. der Dreizehn V, fo. 79ʳ, 19 June 1539.

[47] Ibid., Urg. 26 July 1544, Bernhart Hartman.

[48] Paul Scheifelhut: ibid., Prot. der Zuchtherren III, fos. 130, 139, 167, 170, 1 June, 5 Sept., 7 Oct. 1542; Hans and Elisabeth Kranich: Strafbuch des Rats III, fo. 33ʳ, 21 June 1541; fo. 69ʳ, 24 Aug. 1541; Prot. der Dreizehn VI, fo. 150, 21 June 1540; Prot. der Zuchtherren V, fo. 90, 4 Aug. 1544; fo. 61, 26 May 1544 and 2 Mar. 1545; Prot. der Zuchtherren VI, fo. 44, 7 June 1545; Ehegerichtsbuch 1537-46, fo. 137ʳ, 15 Oct. 1543, divorce refused; fo. 140ʳ, 7 July 1544, divorce refused again; Urg. 2 Oct. 1545.

[49] Ibid., Strafbuch des Rats III, fo. 33ᵛ, 25 June 1541, Magdalena Dirrenberger and Jorg Liebhart.

Nor did Council policy eliminate violence in marriage. Council intervention was selective, and its own pronouncements gave robust confirmation of men's right and duty to discipline. Bernhart Hartman's wife was reduced finally to a desperate plea to the Council: 'she asks therefore most humbly to separate her from her husband, for she did not know how to stay with him. If she should be forced to return to him, she would be caused to leave home and hearth and to wander in misery.'[50] When cautions failed, as they usually did, to have an effect on the behaviour of warring couples, the Council's only sanction was banishment, a penalty which disrupted the household, destroyed the economic existence of innocent and guilty spouse alike, made remarriage impossible, and made a mockery of Council pieties about marital harmony. Short of this, the Council could issue yet another paper 'reconciliation', tacitly accepting that marital faults were likely to continue rather than constituting crimes to be named, isolated, and punished once and for all.

Moreover, by intervening in the private relationship of husband and wife, the authorities were also undermining the values they wished to uphold. At one level they were merely assuming the role of mediator which neighbours or notables had traditionally performed. But as they attempted to extend their good policing (*gute Polizei*) into marriage, some husbands and wives began to be made accountable to the authorities for their actions rather than to each other.[51] The household became a sphere of public-official concern; quarrels were breaches of the civic peace; and husbands had to justify their beatings of their wives, explaining their exercise of authority. Indeed, the Council's intervention was seen as an assault on male prerogative. Gregori Frei Weisser told the Council that his wife's constant complaints to the authorities

---

[50] 'Bitt derhalben zum vnnderthenigsten Sy von dem Mann zu schaffen dann sy wiss nit bei Jme zubeleiben Solt sy aber Widerumben zu Jme geschafft werden, wurde sy verursacht, von hauss vnd hof Jn das Ellendt zu geen': ibid., Urg. 26 July 1544, Bernhart Hartman.
[51] Cf. G. Strauss, *Luther's House of Learning: Indoctrination of the Young in the German Reformation* (Baltimore and London, 1978), pp. 118 ff., who argues that the period saw a general shift away from family to state power. Safley, too, has argued that the Protestant magistracy 'used the judicial establishment to obtain a more penetrating control of it [marriage]', and that marriage and communal identity had become more important; a process which had very ambivalent and distinct effects on men and women, however.

about his violence were just a ploy to get him banished—she had said publicly 'that she would run him out of town'.[52] As Narcis Muller urged the Council in an enraged appeal to shared male interest: 'If a man crosses them [women] and hurts them, they can well get them put in irons; and they count on this, and plague the men so badly, as happened to him with his wife; and he thought it good, that one should not give the women so much free rein.'[53] This was a view of male and female relations as a state of permanently anarchic warfare in which a male Council ought to defend its brothers. Just how far the Council had moved from that conception of brotherhood with guildsmen was apparent in its ongoing, though hesitant, attempts to discipline men.

Adultery

Guild, Council, preachers, and citizens concurred in viewing adultery, that 'godless evil' as the 1537 Ordinance called it, as a serious sin and a punishable crime. Punishment of adultery had long been a matter of concern to guilds because it disrupted the unity between sexual and productive relations. The understanding of adultery with which craftspeople, preachers, and Council operated turned out, however, to be differently accented in practice. For the preachers, for whom sexual fidelity was the prime constituent of marriage, adultery by either spouse was equally serious. Martin Bucer, whose views carried great weight and who visited Augsburg during the introduction of the institutionalized Reformation, saw sexual relations as so integral to human nature that he not only regarded marriages as sundered by adultery, but even proposed that both guilty and innocent party should be able to remarry in order to prevent further sin.[54]

---

[52] StadtAA, Reichsstadt, Urg. 17 June 1539, Gregori Frei Weisser.

[53] Ibid., Urg. 6 Apr. 1541, Narcis Muller.

[54] H. Dieterich, *Das protestantische Eherecht in Deutschland bis zur Mitte des 17. Jahrhunderts* (Munich, 1970). Although Bucer certainly influenced the Reformation settlement in Augsburg, there is no evidence that his idiosyncratic views on the remarriage of guilty divorced spouses found a sympathetic hearing in Augsburg, and we know they had been decisively rejected at Ulm. See Köhler, *Zürcher Ehegericht und Genfer Konstistorium*, ii. 281-9, however, who argues that although the actual Marriage Court did not reflect Bucer's principles, Bucer had written his *Scriptum maius vom eegericht* for Augsburg. The original is in

Few evangelicals were prepared to go so far. But the drift of their teaching was inherently opposed to the older, guild understanding of marriage and household.

For guildsmen, by contrast, marriage was seen in terms of its relation to the household workshop as both a productive and sexual relationship. In the words of the Nuremberg poet Hans Sachs, the recipe for happy marriage ran thus:

> Therefore a young man should not neglect
> To firstly keep his wife in bounds,
> Raise her to be careful and sensible,
> So that in his work in future
> She won't uselessly consume his goods,
> But help to faithfully nourish him
> With work, which is a woman's duty!
> Thereby he may then better
> Come to rest and good income.[55]

Sometimes the priorities of the work relationship in marriage won out. As one husband put it, pleading for his adulterous wife to be let off punishment, he needed her 'so that she can attend to her small children and to me, for this business [the adultery accusation] has brought me into great mishap and disadvantage in my craft'.[56] Here again the legacy of the older notion of public sins is evident, a notion which regarded open, public adultery (especially if the couple lived together) as a sin, but 'secret' liaisons as an essentially non-punishable matter to be dealt with by confessional discipline. By 'public' was meant a state of

Strasbourg, Archives Municipales, Archives du Chapitre de Saint-Thomas, Varia Ecclesiastica II/167, fos. 133ʳ–171ʳ. Köhler's ascriptions of Bucer's material are not reliable (he mistakenly attributes Stadtarchiv Ulm, [8983]/II, fos. 242ʳ–259ᵛ, to two different local Ulm preachers, when both are clearly in the handwriting of Bucer's secretary and annotated in Bucer's hand); and here he offers no conclusive grounds for believing that the work was written for Augsburg. I have found no evidence to support his view at Augsburg or in the original at Strasbourg.

[55] 'Derhalb ein jung man sich nit saum, | Behalt erstlich sein weib im zaum, | Ziech sie fürsichtig und vernünfftig, | Das sie im sein arbeyt zukünfftig, | Nicht thu unützlich verzeren, | Sonder helff in getrewlich nehren | Mit arbeyt, die eym weib zustehe! | Darmit mag er dann dester ehe | Kummen zu rhu und guter narung.' Cited in M. E. Müller, *Der Poet der Moralität: Untersuchungen zu Hans Sachs* (Bern, 1985), p. 255.

[56] 'damit sy Jrem kleynen kindlein vnnd mir auswarten moge dann dise hanndlung mich sonnst Jnn grossen vnfal vnd nachtail pracht hatt meines hanntwercks halb': StadtAA, Reichsstadt, Urg. 3 Mar. 1534, Walpurg Frosch.

affairs in which the sexual and productive relations of the workshop were disrupted, a situation which was thought to lead to public disorder. The persistence of such attitudes was evident even as late as 1544, when the Discipline Lords contemplated not interrogating Gregori Bair about his adultery with the wife of Hans Schweiker, since, as she pleaded, 'otherwise no one knows of the business'. She begged the authorities 'to find ways and means so that she could remain in her domestic honour, for her cousin was Guild Master Veneberger's brother'.[57]

This notion of public sinning could lead to very different attitudes to adultery, depending on the status of the man and woman involved. When, before the Reformation, guilds had demanded the punishment of their adulterous members and had held them to be dishonourable, the men they had in mind were those whose adultery affronted work relations, so that the master's wife was not truly mistress of the house, not secret relations between master and servant. Such affairs, which did not break the chains of social and sexual subordination within the household, were not regarded seriously by guildsmen. Once the affection cooled or the woman became pregnant, there was a recognized code of respectable behaviour for ending the affair and 'doing the right thing' by the woman. If she had been a virgin, she was paid compensation, her lying-in and childbirth expenses were paid for by the man, financial support for the child was arranged, and the woman was paid for her part in child care. These arrangements, sometimes drawn up in contract form, offered a minimum of protection for the woman, but for the man they furnished a method of concluding the affair by contractually discharging the relationship's emotional and material obligations, just as the conclusion of a contract of service would have done.[58] With the man in the role of restitutor and disburser of

---

[57] 'Vmb Gotzwillen Bittende, dieweill sonst niemanndt der sachen wissen, mitl vnd weg furzunemen damit sj bej heislicher Ern erhalten werden möcht dann Jr vätter sej Zunfftmaister Venebergers Eeleiplicher bruder gewesen': ibid., Urg. 5 June 1544, Gerog Bayr. The Council was not impressed and proceeded to interrogate.

[58] Ordinariatsarchiv Augsburg, Prot. des bishöflichen Konsistoriums 1535, 1536; and StadtAA, Reichsstadt, Ehegerichtsbuch 1537–46, for examples of such contracts. It is likely that the adulterous cases are amongst those in which no promise of marriage is alleged to have been made.

money, the woman as recipient, these settlements restored the harmonies of gender and class differences.

The Council's ambiguous heritage of guild and evangelical notions of adultery produced a persistent lack of clarity about what precisely counted as that 'godless evil'. Whereas the pre-Reformation secular ordinance had banished those who lived together without being married,[59] the new Discipline Ordinance of 1537 offered a far more sweeping definition of the sin, covering liaisons where the couple did not live together or even kept the affair secret. Previously, those few shocking cases denounced as 'adultery' had, when punished, resulted in exile and the immediate loss of honour which brought exclusion from a man's workmates or a woman's associates.[60] Now, according to the letter of the ordinance, even 'secret' relations were to be punished with a period of imprisonment, so that the Council, workmates, and spouse all had to acknowledge such cases as adulterous, reintegrate the damaged honour of the adulterer into the guild, and learn to live with the offender again. The Council steered a somewhat hesitant path between these radically distinct notions of adultery, by turns ignoring and punishing married men who 'persuaded their maids to their wills' or visited prostitutes. Underlying this ambiguity was a deeper uncertainty about the definition of marital fidelity and the place of sexual relations within marriage. Pre-Reformation clerics had held that spouses had an obligation to fulfil the marital debt for each other, though in practice the long list of unsuitable occasions—holy eves, menstruation, after a birth, during the period of nursing—created a discipline through the confessional which could give considerable support to wives who refused their husbands.[61] Evangelicals, by contrast, with their affirming attitude towards sexual relations, upheld the marital duty even more firmly. Popular evangelicalism, with its themes of anticlericalism, made much capital out of insinuating that women who went to lengthy

[59] Ibid., Schätze 36/1, Zuchtordnung 1472.
[60] See e.g. ibid., Strafbuch des Rats I, p. 46, Montag nach Joh. Bapt. 1514 (exile); p. 111, Aftermon. n. Reminiscere 1521 (exile). Such cases were rare, however.
[61] T. Tentler, *Sin and Confession on the Eve of the Reformation* (Princeton, 1977); M. Weber, *Ehefrau und Mutter in der Rechtsentwicklung* (Tübingen, 1907); L. Roper, 'Luther: Sex, Marriage and Motherhood', *History Today*, 33 (Dec. 1983), 33-8.

confession sessions were up to no good with the priest; or that the women were undermining male authority by criticizing their husbands' sexual performance to the eagerly listening confessor. But when confronted by angry husbands who claimed that their wives 'would not perform marital work', that 'she positions herself strangely', or that 'when he wanted to go on her, she kicked him away',[62] the Council tended to pass over their complaints in silence. It would not uphold the claim that guildsmen had an enforceable right to their wives' sexual services.

In practice, the civic Marriage Court continued to do as the ecclesiastical courts and local tradition had done, dealing with illicit liaisons by asking the woman to state an appropriate figure as her compensation claim, and forcing reluctant men to meet their obligations. Though technically guilty of adultery, men continued not to regard this as adultery in the full, serious, public sense, since they did not consider it as an affront to domestic and work relations. Sometimes, but not necessarily, married men would be punished by the Council for their adultery. Similarly, hardly any wives sued for divorce on these grounds,[63] though several cases did come before the Council where a wife found herself living in the same house as her husband's mistress. In a situation such as this, where jealousies and arguments about precedence between wife and servant could cause ructions, the men left the disputes to the womenfolk, and it is significant that women in these cases usually resorted to the tactics of shame and ridicule, carrying out nocturnal mock serenades or securing indirect revenge by encouraging the menfolk to beat their rivals, rather than taking the matter directly to the Council. Hans Geisselmair's servant employed the strategy of leaping up on his wedding cart and refusing to get off until he paid for their affair;[64] while Matheis Dietl's maid threw something at his wall the day before his wedding and, continuing to work for him,

---

[62] StadtAA, Reichsstadt, Urg. 17 June 1542, Caspar Muelich; Urg. 7 Sept. 1532, Matheis Dietl; 12 June 1533, Hans Karrer.

[63] In cases between 1537 and 1546, only 6 women sued for divorce on the grounds of their husbands' adultery, though 15 husbands cited their wives' unfaithfulness. For figures, see Roper, 'Work, Marriage and Sexuality', pp. 226 ff. (and table 5.3).

[64] StadtAA, Reichsstadt, Urg. 6 June 1548, Hans Geisselmair.

watched the marriage disintegrate.[65] But a powerful master could dissuade a servant from taking any action whatsoever: Laux Ravenspurger, a patrician, had only to threaten court action to persuade his servant to drop her allegations.[66]

However, if the mistress of the house had an affair with a man of lower social status within the household, or with an equal outside it, the effects were usually cataclysmic for both household and lovers. These relationships undermined the master's authority and honour, shaming him and—by implication if it were unpunished—his guild. The allegation that 'he was not the first over his wife' was understood as an insult to the man not to his wife; and to guildsmen, female adultery was theft, 'the abduction of wife and honour'. In a sense which men could do very little about, their honour depended at least in part on the sexual fidelity of their wives. This was a fundamental point of insecurity which may illuminate why men's fantasies about controlling their wives so often took the form of trying to contain them physically within the household—a fantasy in which the Council colluded when, on occasion, it put adulterous wives under house arrest. Such a collective sexual double standard could draw on powerful reserves of support amongst evangelical guildsmen, and it is interesting that one of the demands of the pro-Reformation men who assembled by the Perlach tower in the abortive rebellion of 1524 was that 'the furrier' should be released—a man who had been imprisoned because he murdered his wife, supposedly for her infidelity.[67] To evangelical guildsmen he was not a criminal but a man who had justly punished the woman who had impugned his honour.

Unable to discharge and end an affair by contract, women found it hard to keep affairs casual or to impose a shape on the relationship's development. Often they chose to elope, destroying the household. Since a woman's honour and social position

---

[65] Ibid., Urg. 7 Sept. 1532, Matheis Dietl.

[66] Ibid., Ehegerichtsbuch 1537–46, fo. 52^r, 23 June 1539: in the case of Hilaria Bachmair, servant of Laux Ravenspurger, against Laux Ravenspurger, Ravenspurger gives authority to Wilheml Schoffl, notary, but no further action is taken. But in Sept. of the following year he was fined 100 gulden and put in irons on suspicion of having attempted to rape one of his servants: Strafbuch des Rats III, fo. 17^r, 4 Sept. 1540.

[67] P. Broadhead, 'Internal Politics and Civic Society in Augsburg during the Era of the Early Reformation 1518–1537', Ph.D. thesis (Kent, 1981), p. 151.

turned even more crucially on her wifehood than on her work, an elopement could cast her as a whore and force both illicit partners into a life of vagabondage. Hans Deylhoffer, who had been a tailor and whose sister was married to a goldsmith, one of the city's most prestigious crafts, was described as a beggar when he returned to Augsburg in 1532: refusing to be parted from his mistress, he had been forced to leave town and was now a broken man.[68] Women with children faced agonizing tensions, for though they might attempt to take the children with them, the rigours of life on the road often made this impossible. One couple, carrying a child in swaddling clothes, had to leave him with an innkeeper; another child, so its father alleged, had died because of the freezing cold when it travelled with its eloping mother; and misery at being parted from their children may have driven many women back to the city.[69] The trials of those who returned—despite certain punishment—reveal the nature of these tensions, so severe that many couples could bear only a few months away from the town.

Though the Council ostensibly (in good evangelical fashion) considered male and female adultery equally seriously, in fact it showed far more interest in those cases where a married woman was involved. Interrogating both men and women, it sought to uncover the nature of the disorderly force behind the adultery, trying to elicit from the women why and how they had 'fallen' and then bringing them to confess their sin. In one of the rare extant letters by women, Agnes Axt petitioned the Council in 1542 in words she knew would appeal to its members. In a flowing, practised hand which was almost certainly not her own, the script confessed that 'I, poor captured woman, have unfortunately forgotten the female honour and sinned against God, your Graces as a just authority, my pious husband, and my old father and mother, and my whole kin, out of simpleness and falling from the grace of God.'[70] The order of her accusations,

[68] StadtAA, Reichsstadt, Urg. 4 Nov. 1532, Hans Deylhofer.

[69] StadtAA, Reichsstadt, Urg. 29 May 1526, Christian Hefelin; Urg. 21 May 1532, Georig Liebhart; Urg. 22-9 May 1539, Anna Sommer.

[70] 'Wiewol Jch Arms gefanngens weibspild wider Gott, Euer gnadenn, als ain gerechte Oberkhait, Meinen frumen hausswirth, vnnd Allte Vatter vnnd Muetter, vnnd ain gannze fraindschafft, aus blödigkhait vnnd verlassung der gnaden Gottes mich laider wider die Weiplich Erberkhait vergessen vnd gesündet hab . . .': ibid., Urg. 26 May 1542, Agnes Axt.

which the translation cannot convey, places God, secular authority, the husband, her parents, and kin, in a descending scale of authority, all of whom have been offended by her infringement of female honour or chastity. The letter is an affirmation of that secular and divine order, and of her subjection within it. This is the 'female honour' which she has forgotten. Yet though she admits her own evil will and intentional sin, the language also presents her as a passive creature, 'simple' rather than intelligently wicked, a woman who has fallen from grace rather than one who jumped; and it tries to seek mercy on the grounds of her feminine weakness. Now, it would seem, Axt had reclothed herself in the garb of appropriate womanly behaviour—a conversion which might have seemed like true contrition were it not for its utter reversal of Axt's previously forthright insubordinate behaviour to Council and husband alike. (Earlier, this same woman had admitted that she quite fancied the patrician Anthoni Baumgartner, and would have slept with him if she had not been disturbed; and had countered accusations about her previous indiscretions by immediately complaining of her husband's rough treatment of her.) Her puzzled husband, handed this petition for his comments, had to ask the Council for advice on whether to accept this supposedly reformed wife back! Surely neither was duped by this pantomime. In a case such as this, interrogation procedures designed to educate an individual back into wifely behaviour threatened to topple over into farce.

Indeed, in part the problem lay in the Council's perception of sexually experienced married women as sexually voracious rather than chastely submissive. Unlike young prostitutes, the Council was less likely to view such women as innocent victims corrupted by debauched older women or by the wiles of male seducers, but as temptresses in their own right. The married woman Anna Sommer, seduced by 'young Gunzburger', a notorious philanderer, was interrogated three times, with torture, about 'many men or bachelors, with whom she had committed adultery', despite her hot denials that anyone but Gunzburger had been involved. The Council refused to see her as a victim of Gunzburger's wiles and cast her as a libertine.[71]

---

[71] Ibid., Urg. 22 May 1539, Anna Sommer.

Men, too, saw sexually experienced women as embodying powerful desires, and the lusty wife was a commonplace of popular culture. What is striking about the language men in particular used to express their emotions when describing an adulterous liaison is their sense of powerlessness. Often, men accused women of having bewitched them, describing their emotions as a force external to themselves, or even quite contrary to their volitions. Stoffel Burckhart told his lover that he could not keep away from her, despite knowing that this was an act of disobedience to authority as well as an immoral act;[72] Hans Gabler told how he had gone to Venice to escape his relationship with his mistress but had been unable to remain there: 'the cause being, Gablerin [his lover] did it to him, that following the previous time she had bodily work with him . . .' he could not remain away.[73] One woman, desperate to keep her adulterous husband, consulted a wise woman who told her: 'your husband does not leave gladly, he leaves with his heart bleeding in his body; but he must do it, and she [his mistress] gave it to him to eat three times'. In the rhythm of folk-song or folk-tale the same woman recounted his tragic farewell speech as he eloped: 'My dearest wife, it must be, I would rather let my head be cut off than that I should leave you and the children, but it can never be, I must leave you, I must give my life for it, I must make the parting.'[74] Christian Hefelin explained: 'he could not stay away from . . . the cobbler's wife, similarly she could not stay away from him, he did not know how . . . it was just a thing'.[75] All these women were sexually experienced, and their desires were

---

[72] Ibid., Urg. 13 Mar. 1531, Stoffel Burckhart and Anna Paur.

[73] 'hab er nit beleiben mogen der vrsach. der gablerin hab Jme es gethann, das er auff vorgeend handlung so er leiplicher werck dieweil er Jr knecht gewesen mit Jr gepflogen Also wider heraus': ibid., 26 Mar. 1533, Hans Gabler.

[74] 'Euer Man zeucht nicht gern, er zeucht das Im sein hertz im leib Pluettet, Er muess aber thun, vnnd sy hab Ims drey mall zuessen geben . . .'; 'Mein hertzliebs weib, Es muess sein, Ich wollt mir lieber das haupt lassen abschlagen, dann das Ich von dir vnnd meinen khinden soll ziechen, Es khan aber laider nimer sein, Ich muess von dir, Ich muess mein leben darumb geben, vnnd muess den zug thon': ibid., Urg. 18 Feb. 1545, Anna Harrer. The Council repeated the accusation of sorcery against Harrer without making it clear whether it accepted it: Strafbuch des Rats IV, fo. 43ʳ, 21 Feb. 1545.

[75] 'Er hab des Schuchsters weib . . . nit muessig konnden geen, dessgleichen sy sein auch nit, er wiss nit wie es nur ain ding [sic]': ibid., Urg. 20 May 1528, Christian Hefelin.

imagined as a powerful, irresistible force which could be conjured up to command men.

This view of married women as potential sexual viragos was common currency. If, as Ozment has argued, Reformation morality did not cast a wife as the 'maid or common servant of her husband', its leading tone was hardly that which Ozment characterizes as invoking 'the mother of the house', who enjoyed 'a position of high authority and equal respect'.[76] Indeed, the rhetoric of motherhood is noticeably absent, and married women were addressed in terms of their wifehood and its concomitant obedience, not in terms of their motherhood. The Council's growing obsession with policing disorderly male behaviour did lead it to create a system which offered women far more recourse against violent husbands; but it did so in terms of the Council's duty to the weak, offering protection on the grounds of wifely subordination. That protection, however, depended on properly modest wifely behaviour.

Finally, adultery, like all the bones of contention between men and women, raised the issue of the extent of Council jurisdiction and the integrity of the household; but it did so in a peculiarly dramatic form. So, for example, the weaver Martin Frosch attempted to deal with his wife's adultery himself. As he recounted events, he first formally warned Numenbeck to stay clear of his wife, 'for words were going round which gave him no pleasure'.[77] Numenbeck replied to this verbal admonition by threatening to take Frosch before the Council to clear his name of this imputation, or to meet Frosch on the Lechfeld to settle the matter by a duel. Frosch's description insinuates that the aggression came only from Numenbeck, and makes his own reaction to the affair seem somewhat passive, an impression not contradicted by Numenbeck's account of events.

In a petition to the Council, Frosch continued to minimize both the impact of the adultery and the extent of his wife's involvement, insisting (in a near allegation of rape) that his wife was 'outsmarted and half forced'[78] into the affair—a strange formulation, for all the other interrogations suggest that she was

[76] Ozment, *When Fathers Ruled*, pp. 54, 202 n. 12.
[77] 'dan es gienge reden Vmb darab er kein gefallen het': StadtAA, Reichsstadt, Urg. 3 Mar. 1534, Lienhart Numenbeck and Walpurg Frosch.
[78] 'yberlistiget vnd woll halb benottiget': ibid.

a willing partner! He goes on to explain that he has forgiven her, and asks that she be let out 'so that she can attend to her small children and to me, for this business has brought me into great mishap and disadvantage in my craft'.[79] This is a very explicit statement of the priority of household economics over moral vengeance. Now that he had forgiven his wife, he frankly did not see what further role the Council had in this 'domestic' matter.

The Council's involvement in this affair remains interestingly ambivalent. It had removed the liaison from the domestic sphere and, by relentless questioning, had sought to uncover all the details of the Numenbeck–Frosch relationship. Yet it stopped short of interrogating the couple until their statements became consistent, and it only sentenced them to a week's imprisonment, a leniency it would be less willing to display in the years after 1537. Numenbeck lost all honour, was denied admission to all honourable occasions, banned from participation in elections, excluded from inns, banned from wearing a weapon, and ordered to keep away from Frosch. She, too, lost all honour and was ordered to stay indoors for six months, except to go to sermons.[80] The Council thus instituted a sort of internal exile, constraining the two in their separate households. Whereas at this time the statutory punishment for adultery could have been banishment, the Council chose conservation of the household instead of strict punishment. Yet even the Discipline Ordinance of 1537 did not remove such conflicts: in 1539 Anna Sommer, who committed repeated adultery with Hans Gunzburger, and whose husband pleaded for her, was only punished as if for a single offence, and was condemned to six months' 'internal exile'.[81] Preservation of the household could win out over strict execution of the prescribed punishment for the sin the Council condemned most strongly.

What Frosch and Sommer both wished to avoid was a thorough investigation of the household, for this would inevitably (despite the Council's avowed aim of protecting honour) destroy not only

---

[79] 'damit sy Irem kleynnen kindlein vnnd mir ausswarten moge dann dise hanndlung mich sonnst Jnn grossen vnfal vnd nachtail pracht hatt meines hanntwercks halb': ibid.

[80] StadtAA, Reichsstadt, Strafbuch des Rats II, fos. 22ᵛ-23ʳ, 10 Mar. 1534.

[81] Ibid., Urg. 22 May 1539, Anna Sommer; Strafbuch des Rats II, fo. 153ʳ, 21 June 1539.

the honour of the adulterers, but also the honour and authority of the master and the integrity of the household. Even in the case of the greatest sin against marriage, Council policy walked a tightrope between a guild-influenced pragmatism which sought to sustain the domestic unit, and a vision of itself as an avenging instrument, entering the household and prying suspiciously into its workings. When the Council entered the supposedly private boundaries of the house with its agents, the night-watchmen, theirs was a curiosity far less trammelled than that of the anxious neighbours who hesitated to cross the threshold, and it disturbed the 'peace' within forever.

Although the Council's policy on marriage seemed to allow it to celebrate the natural roles of men and women, its articulation in fact served to focus on the discontents of marriage and to underline the potential disharmony of interests between men and women. Patriarchal authority turned out to be fragile, and patriarchs themselves were often feckless, violent men who could not be trusted with the burdens of authority. Despite the Council's investment in a guild-influenced ideal of marriage and household, its policing policies worked to strengthen its mistrust of craftspeople and guilds, and to expose a disorder for which it had neither secular nor spiritual remedy.

6

The Reformation of Convents

THE female religious life was understood through a metaphor at once social and sexual: the nun was the bride of Christ. This was more than a casual simile, for the nuns' living conditions, clothing, way of life, devotional style, and the imaginative space they occupied in sixteenth-century people's minds were determined by their paradoxical status. The nun was married, yet her 'spouse' brought her no integration into a husband's family. She was bound to a group of women by a vow which made them co-spouses and fellow-sisters. Yet while the convent used the language of kinship, it created a series of relationships which were at odds with civic kin structures. At the same time, a woman's choice of convent and the offices she held in it were very much determined by family connections, and her worldly family drew comfort, status, and support from her vocation. Finally, she was simultaneously wedded and virginal, an ambiguous sexual status which was central to her social and symbolic position.

It has often been argued that convent life offered women an alternative to marriage, an option which ensured that wifehood was not the only socially valued role for women.[1] Whatever the extent of a girl's actual decision-making power, it created at least a theoretical choice for young girls. Yet the viability of such a choice was crucially determined by the girl's social status. In

[1] S. M. Wyntjes, 'Women in the Reformation Era', in R. Bridenthal and C. Koonz (eds.), *Becoming Visible: Women in European History* (Boston, 1977); N. Z. Davis, 'City Women and Religious Change', in id., *Society and Culture in Early Modern France* (London, 1975). For an empirical study based on a prosopography of 250 nuns in Upper Hesse, see C. Vanja, 'Klosterleben und Gesellschaft: Lebensläufe von Nonnen und Stiftsfrauen in spätmittelalterlichen hessischen Konventen', in W. Schröder (ed.), *Lebenslauf und Gesellschaft: Zum Einsatz von kollektiven Biographien in der historischen Sozialforschung* (Historisch-Sozialwissenschaftliche Forschungen, 18; Stuttgart, 1985).

Augsburg, a city of seven convents and one religious foundation, there was room for only between 150 and 200 nuns. Ten or so of these positions would have been unavailable to local women: St Stephen's, a noble foundation, was populated by women of high birth from beyond the city.[2] Of the remaining places, at least seventy, and probably more, were held by women whose families made up the town's élite: the old patricians, those who joined the patriciate after 1538, and the members of the *Mehrer*. Figures from the admittedly patchy records of the membership of convents in the city between 1517 and 1548 bear this out (see Table 6.1). Of the 136 women for whom we have information, sixty-seven, about half, came from the old and expanded patriciate, *Mehrer*, merchant, and upper guild families. If we compare this number with the total of 319 marriages and remarriages amongst this broad élite between 1517 and 1548 we can see that the number, though small, is proportionally significant.[3]

The élite's domination of the civic convents was even greater than it appears, since there were many more 'foreign' nuns than the nine of good family whom we know were not natives of Augsburg. In all, only about fifty nuns at the very most could have been drawn from the ranks of small-scale merchants, craftspeople,

---

[2] These figures have been arrived at by compiling all references to nuns. Sources include archival references: *Die Chroniken der deutschen Städte vom 14. bis ins 16. Jahrhundert*, 36 vols. (Leipzig, 1862-1931); L. Hörmann, 'Erinnerungen an das ehemalige Frauenkloster Katharina in Augsburg', *ZHVS* 9 (1882), 357-86; 10 (1883), 301-54; 11 (1884), 1-10; *Ad Sanctum Stephanum 969-1969: Festgabe zur 1000 Jahr-Feier von St. Stephan in Augsburg* (Augsburg, 1969); L. Juhnke, 'Bausteine zur Geschichte des Dominikanerinnenklosters St. Katharina', *Jahresbericht der Oberrealschule Augsburg 1957-8* (Augsburg, 1958), 60-110; A. Haemmerle, *Das Necrologium des Dominikanerinnenklosters St. Margareth in Augsburg* (Munich, 1955); id., *Das Necrologium des Benediktinerinnenklosters St. Nicolaus in Augsburg* (Munich, 1955); Primbs, 'Das Stift von St. Stephan in Augsburg', *ZHVS* 7 (1880), 109-56; P. Siemer, *Geschichte des Dominikanerklosters Sankt Magdalena in Augsburg (1225-1808)* (Vechta, 1936); I. Baumann, *Geschichte des Stern-Klosters Maria Stern in Augsburg 1258-1828* (Munich, 1958). These totals were compared with Kiessling's estimates of numbers in the fifteenth century: R. Kiessling, *Bürgerliche Gesellschaft und Kirche in Augsburg im 14. und 15. Jahrhundert* (Augsburg, 1971), p. 40. On St Stephen's, see *Ad Sanctum Stephanum 969-1969*.

[3] A. Haemmerle, *Die Hochzeitsbücher der Augsburger Bürgerstube und Kaufleutestube bis zum Ende der Reichsfreiheit* (Munich, 1936), pp. 14-38. By contrast, the total numbers of marriages per annum in Augsburg between 1539 and 1546 ranged between 370 and 768: StadtAA, Reichsstadt, BMB 1540-7.

TABLE 6.1. *Convents and social status 1517–1550*

	St Martin's	St Margaret's	Horbruck	St Ursula's	St Stephen's	Maria Stern's	St Nicholas's	St Katherine's	Total
Old patriciate 1538/9	1	—	1	1	—	2	3	7	15
patriciate	—	—	—	—	—	4	6	12	22
Mehrer	1	3	2	—	—	2	1	9	18
Merchant guild	—	—	—	—	—	—	—	6	6
Other guilds	—	—	2	—	—	—	2	2	6*
Non-Augsburg nobility	—	—	—	—	6	—	—	—	6
Non-Augsburg Other/	—	4	—	—	—	1	—	—	5
Unknown	6	8	10	1	2	8	1	22	58
TOTAL	8	15	15	2	8	17	13	58	136

Note: Two of these women belonged to élite families who opted to transfer to the guilds in 1368.

and below, despite their far greater representation in the city population.

Such a class profile contrasts with that of men. Secular clergy ranged socially from the nobles of the Cathedral chapter, on a par with the women of St Stephen's, through the canons of St Maurice, St George, and Holy Cross, who sometimes came from local élite families, to the vicars and chaplains of very modest social origins;[4] while in the city's monastic institutions, particularly amongst the mendicant orders, Augsburg origins and social standing were not so vital for admission. Nuns presented a rather more homogeneous group, drawn from fairly comparable social backgrounds. There were, none the less, clear sociological distinctions between convents: the Franciscan convents tended by the sixteenth century to recruit mainly from rather poorer families, though prioresses were on the whole of a higher social standing, while almost the entire population of the Benedictine convent of St Nicholas appears to have been drawn from the élite. The city's largest, most emphatically civic convent remained St Katherine's, a Dominican foundation. A microcosm of the city élite, almost all of the leading families of the city were represented in it.

Indeed, recruitment reproduced the divisions within the élite itself. Of the 136 women for whom we have records, fifteen were drawn from the old patrician families of the city; a further twenty-two can be identified as coming from those families who were co-opted into the patriciate in 1538; eighteen women belonged to families of the *Mehrer*, the extended élite, including many merchants, which both intermarried and mixed socially with the patriciate; two came from the families of what might broadly be identified as the élite, but who had none the less opted to transfer to the guilds rather than remain in the patriciate in 1368. Below these is a group of families who might be identified as upper middle class: merchant families not included amongst the *Mehrer*, and upper guildspeople. This strata is harder to identify, but six of the women are known to have come from merchant families. Since the merchants' guild itself tried to restrict membership to inheritance and intermarriage only, it had shrunk to a select group of thirty-six families. Political activity can be taken to be some

---

[4] Kiessling, *Bürgerliche Gesellschaft*, pp. 31–41.

index of the other upper guild families, and four women came from families such as these.[5]

Convent women thus constituted a particular kind of élite. With fifteen women members, the old patriciate of seven families was proportionately much better represented in the convents than either the group of thirty-eight families who joined the patriciate in 1538, or the much larger, fluctuating group of between fifty and a hundred *Mehrer* families. With only around ten convent sisters, the upper guild and merchant families were barely present.

Yet this élite was also deeply divided by the Reformation into those who had become evangelical (whether Zwinglian, Lutheran, spiritualist, or Anabaptist) and those who remained loyal to the old faith. As Protestant sympathizers left the convent, the remaining women were increasingly drawn from the group most under threat after 1537—the families least attracted to the Reformation, whose loyalty to the city was regarded with some suspicion. Their alienation from civic life was enacted dramatically when several of these families left Augsburg in 1546, at the moment of greatest danger to the city.[6] Yet the wider élite also constituted the group which, under the imperially imposed constitution of 1548, was to dominate civic politics as a coherent ruling class for several centuries.[7]

The strength of the convents' resistance to the Reformation dramatized and focused the divisions within the élite. On occasion, families themselves were split, as when Bernhart Rem, for example, called on his sisters to leave the convent; or when Felicitas Peutinger left the convent of St Katherine's despite her parents' firm adherence to the old faith.[8]

[5] On the structure of Augsburg's élite, cf. O. Mörke and K. Sieh, 'Gesellschaftliche Führungsgruppen', in G. Gottlieb *et al.* (eds.), *Geschichte der Stadt Augsburg*, 2nd edn. (Stuttgart, 1985). On the convents' histories, attachments to orders, and beguine origins, see Kiessling, *Bürgerliche Gesellschaft*, pp. 31–42; W. Liebhart, 'Stifte, Klöster und Konvente in Augsburg' in Gottlieb, *Geschichte der Stadt Augsburg*.

[6] F. Roth, *Augsburgs Reformationsgeschichte*, 4 vols. (vol. i: 2nd edn., Munich, 1901; vols. ii–iv: Munich, 1904–11), iii. 362–3.

[7] I. Bátori, *Die Reichsstadt Augsburg im 18. Jahrhundert: Verfassung, Finanzen und Reformversuche* (Göttingen, 1969).

[8] Bernhart Rem, *Ain Christlich schreiben | so ain Euangelischer brüder seiner schwestern | ainer closter iunckfrawen zugeschickt*, Augsburg, n.d.; id., *Ain Sendtbrieff an ettlich Closterfrawen zu sant katherina vnd zu sant niclas in Augsburg*, [Augsburg, P. Ulhart], 1523; and see *Antwurt zwayer Closter frauwen*

For the citizenry, therefore, the campaign to abolish the convents and reincorporate the women into the life of the city had some strange and contradictory undertones. In the early years of the Reformation the nuns who rejoined the worldly life of the town could be welcomed, and the reabsorption of all convent women seemed inevitable. But the continued existence of the convents was the most obvious and persistent reminder, throughout the 1530s and 1540s, of the town's divisions—religious, social, and political. Convents focused several grudges at once. To the evangelical craftsman, they stood for class privilege, the power of the 'lords' (*Herren*), as Jörg Preu's chronicle described them, for the old religion and its unchristian doctrines of works-righteousness, and for the power of women. It is not surprising that one of the main emphases of the politics of the post-1537 Councils was to tackle the convent issue.

Closing Convents

By the late 1530s and 1540s, Council policy had developed into an attempt to close convents, reaching agreements on the nuns' future and incorporating the institution's assets into civic charitable funds. Where this was not possible, it aimed to isolate the women from the support of male members of the order, and to encourage the gradual decline of the institution—or at least, its control by lay civic authority. The hallmark of the policy was 'integrationism', the incorporation of the nuns into the city community and the elimination of monastic institutions as alternative focuses of power in the commune. Because the women's convents demonstrated least receptivity to the Reformation, they became the main target of this campaign to rid the city of popery. As we shall see, it was a policy which was coloured by class and gender presumptions as well.

im Katheriner Closter zŭ Augspurg | an Bernhart Remen | Vnd hernach seyn gegen Antwurt, [Augsburg, P. Ulhart, 1523]; *Chroniken der deutschen Städte*, xxiii, Sender, p. 179. Felicitas Peutinger made her evangelical sympathies clear when she attended the wedding of the reformer Urbanus Rhegius. Despite the presence of several other members of the élite, Konrad Peutinger did not attend. See H. Lutz, *Conrad Peutinger: Beiträge zu einer politischen Biographie* (Augsburg, 1958), pp. 118, 265, 396.

Such a policy was not solely a product of the Reformation, however. Its roots lay in the fourteenth- and fifteenth-century Councils' attempts to incorporate the religious institutions into the community, to subject them to taxation, and to increase lay control over them.[9] At that time the Council had pressed for the appointment of lay guardians to oversee the institutions' investments and administration of property, and had urged those in orders to become citizens. The attempt to impose citizenship had largely failed, but guardianship had proved more successful, particularly among convents, perhaps partly because the city's links with the women's convents had always been closer than those with the monasteries.[10] The extent of the guardians' influence varied, but it was centred on representations in relation to property, extending in some convents to a degree of control over disciplinary matters.[11]

A hundred years later, the Council's procedure followed similar lines. In 1537, as part of its more energetic reforming policy, it extended the scope of guardianship in all convents to include control over the appointment of prioresses, increased the power of the parish guardians over the parish church and eventually the foundation at St Stephen's, and appointed 'solicitors and real guardians' for Maria Stern's, St Martin's, and St Margaret's.[12] Guardians were gradually to take over not only those duties which women could not carry out for technical reasons (as in, for example, some feudal contracts), but to begin to fulfil the wider role which the male members of the orders had once played for the convent women. In the state of disintegration of the monasteries brought about by the Reformation, this extension of Council involvement could be justified by analogy with the 'emergency bishop' function which evangelicals had urged it to exercise over parish churches.[13] Yet ironically, the very extension of its protection over convents made it far more difficult for the Council to deal with the nuns once the full Reformation was

---

[9] Kiessling, *Bürgerliche Gesellschaft*, pp. 145, 70–98.

[10] Ibid. 132–45.

[11] See e.g. StadtAA, KWA G47, 7 Sept. 1473; 17 Jan. 1490. The Council also attempted to get convents to contribute to guard expenses: StadtAA, Reichsstadt, Prot. der Dreizehn II, fo. 363ʳ, 14 Oct. 1529.

[12] Ibid., Prot. der Dreizehn III, fo. 256ʳ, 12 July 1537.

[13] See I. Iserloh, *Geschichte und Theologie der Reformation im Grundriss* (Paderborn, 1980), pp. 76 f.

imposed in 1537. Though it could exile the Catholic clerics and the women of St Stephen's who would not take on citizenship, the convent women could not be dealt with in this way.[14]

The ideals of civic righteousness and evangelical moralism also required that all members of the civic community should share one faith and worship in a uniform manner, at least publicly. The first moves towards this ideal were made in 1534, when the Council closed a number of churches and forbade the nuns to receive spiritual advice from male members of their orders.[15] In 1537 it issued a new Church Ordinance, prescribing identical forms of public worship for all Augsburg churches and forbidding nuns to hear mass, go to confession, or receive the sacrament.[16] No element of popery was to be retained in the newly evangelical city, purified of the spiritual fornication of false religion just as it was to be cleansed of sexual sin. What were considered to be redundant churches were shut and chained,[17] or, as in the most complete conversion, that of the convent church of St Martin's, it was flattened to the ground 'and a square was made out of it, where now green vegetables and salad and such things are sold'.[18]

All nuns were now to be led to hear the one Word of God, just as the erring Anabaptists had been forced to do a decade before.[19] Obedience to civic authority was fused with religious orthodoxy. It was on the orders of a Council official that the women of St Katherine's assembled to hear Musculus, the Council preacher, and the city's mayor and retinue attended the sermon

---

[14] Roth, *Augsburgs Reformationsgeschichte*, ii. 320. Thus in 1534 the mere threat of permanent exile was enough to dissuade the non-citizen women of St Stephen's from leaving town for a period: *Chroniken der deutschen Städte*, xxix, Preu, p. 61.

[15] e.g. ibid. xxiii, Sender, pp. 387 f. (St Katherine's, St Nicholas's, St Margaret's).

[16] E. Sehling. *et al.* (eds.), *Die evangelischen Kirchenordnungen des 16. Jahrhunderts* (Leipzig, 1902-11), Bayern II, pp. 50-84; and see Roth, *Augsburgs Reformationsgeschichte*, ii. 361 ff.

[17] Ibid. ii, chap. 7; K. Wolfart, *Die Augsburger Reformation in den Jahren 1533-1534* (Leipzig, 1901), p. 109.

[18] Roth, *Augsburgs Reformationsgeschichte*, ii. 319, 345 n. 37: 'und machet ain platz daraus, darauff man das gren kraut und sallat und solich ding fail hat'.

[19] See F. Uhland, *Täufertum und Obrigkeit in Augsburg im 16. Jahrhundert* (Tübingen, 1972); and F. Roth, 'Zur Geschichte der Wiedertäufer in Oberschwaben', *ZHVS* 28 (1901), 1-154.

with them.[20] In 1537 the Council was commanding that 'the Word of God should also be proclaimed' to the women at St Nicholas's.[21] Even at this date the Council appears to have trusted in the Word's power to convert the nuns to the evangelical faith, in the same way that in the early years of the Reformation, Luther had expected the conversion of the Jews. When the women did not convert, unorthodoxy in belief became equated with civil insubordination, a development which had also been prefigured in the trials of the Anabaptists. The Council rapidly began to speak of the nuns of St Nicholas's and St Katherine's as 'refractory' (*widerspenstig*), or to employ the more loaded term, 'disobedient' (*ungehorsam*), with its overtones of insurrection.[22] It would describe some nuns as 'goodhearted', others as 'the stiff-necked ones'—a pair of oppositions which nicely confused the feminine attributes of pride and gentleness with hostility or amenability towards the Council's policies.[23]

Indeed, the Council was not without reason for fearing that doctrinal heterodoxy might be allied with alienation from the civic body and, ultimately, with rebellion. The most telling demonstration came as the Council met to discuss the reforms of 1537. It was rumoured that St Nicholas's, a convent outside the city walls, had appealed to the Dukes of Bavaria for protection.[24] This convent was one of the few remaining buildings of an unfortified suburb just beyond the Red gate, demolished in the fourteenth century because of the strategic threat it posed should an enemy gain control of it.[25] Whether

---

[20] *Chroniken der deutschen Städte*, xxix, Preu, p. 80. The Council also planned that each nun should be individually interrogated by the *Kirchenprobst* once a month about her beliefs: Roth, *Augsburgs Reformationsgeschichte*, ii. 361–2.

[21] 'das Inen, das wort gottes auch verkundt werden solle': StadtAA, Reichsstadt, Prot. der Dreizehn III, fo. 252^r, 30 June 1537.

[22] Roth, *Augsburgs Reformationsgeschichte*, ii. 361, Beilage I. So far as the women of St Katherine's were concerned, the Council ordered impatiently: 'soll Jnen nochmals zu ainem vberflus erzaigt werden, welche mangeln hete. solt Ir, nochmals aus der schrift, gnugsam freuntlich vnd schlecht bericht beschehen': StadtAA, Reichsstadt, Prot. der Dreizehn III, fo. 244^r, 5 June 1537.

[23] Ibid., Prot. der Dreizehn III, fo. 252^r, 30 June 1537.

[24] Roth, *Augsburgs Reformationsgeschichte*, ii. 320.

[25] D. Schröder, *Augsburg* (Historischer Atlas von Bayern, x, *Schwaben*; Munich, 1975), p. 141. An attack on the site was repulsed in 1462: *Chroniken der deutschen Städte*, xxv, Franks Annalen, pp. 328–9; and again in 1492–3: ibid. xxiii, Sender, p. 61.

the rumour was true or not, it realized the Council's worst fears. The Council responded by loading the women ignominiously into a cart and leading them into the city, where they were forcibly relocated in St Katherine's, a convent of a different order. Such treatment was a telling enactment of what the policy of 'integration' of convents into the walled city could mean.[26] But this was only the most notable such incident. Ironically, any effort which the women made to bolster their independence in the town by seeking outside support, whether from their order, from Catholic rulers, from Rome, or from imperial authority, was bound to be perceived as a hostile act which alienated them yet further from the city community. When St Katherine's secured a papal confirmation in 1526, an imperial letter of protection of 1530, and then threatened in 1534 to exchange Council for imperial protection, the convent's manœuvres only served to entrench the Council's suspicion of the convent's loyalty. Just how intense such apprehension could become was shown a few years later, when the Council ordered that the nuns of St Katherine's and St Nicholas's should only be allowed visitors with the guardians' permission, 'to prevent evil plots against an honourable Council'.[27]

As the billeting of the Benedictine nuns of St Nicholas's in the Dominican convent of St Katherine's showed, the policy of civic religious uniformity amounted to a direct assault on the distinctiveness of orders and the monastic ideal itself.[28] Of this the Council was fully aware: in 1534 its adviser commented: 'and though one might say in the popish fashion, that they are not of the same order and don't belong together, yet it is certainly true that neither the identity nor the difference of clothing makes

[26] See Preu's unsympathetic account, ibid. xxix, p. 75; and Roth, *Augsburgs Reformationsgeschichte*, ii. 362, Beilage I; and StadtAA, EWA, Akten 468, for expression of fears that Catholics would form an alliance. Note also A. Gasser, *Annales de vetustate originis, amoenitate situs . . .* (*Scriptores Rerum Germanicarum*, ed. G. Menck, 3 vols.; Leipzig, 1728-30: vol. i, no. xvii), p. 1803—the nuns of St Katherine's attempted to put themselves under the protection of King Ferdinand.

[27] Roth, *Augsburgs Reformationsgeschichte*, i. 345; ii. 362.

[28] Even after the re-Catholicization of the convent, the Council persisted in billeting women from St Nicholas's at St Katherine's temporarily. See the complaint (undated) of Susanna Ehinger, Staatsarchiv Neuburg, Kl. Augsburg, St. Katherine, Akt 81: again her chief complaint was the disruption caused by mixing two orders. Ehinger took office in 1552: StadtAA, Reichsstadt, RS, 11 Apr. 1552.

Christians'.[29] This disingenuous remark tacitly recognized the centrality of the habit and the order it symbolized to the convent's sense of identity. With its systems of authority and support which extended beyond the city, the order was felt to be incompatible with the city-wide, shared version of the 'Christian life', here presented as universal. Indeed, this antagonism might occasionally be presented as a simple clash of jurisdictions. Thus the memorial commissioned from Dr Franciscus Frosch of Strasbourg exhorted the Council to proceed against St Katherine's and the Dominicans because they were infringing the authority, government, and guardianship powers of the Council.[30] Truth in the convents and in the rest of the city had to be the same.[31]

Suspicion of monastic administration was also tinged with a sense of impropriety at the notion of women controlling property and resources.[32] In 1534 one writer thought it inappropriate that a woman should head a convent. In correspondence with Martin Bucer about convents, Gereon Sailer averred that 'a woman is far weaker in spirit and body and therefore more easily persuaded and led astray'.[33] Views about women's unfitness to exercise authority of any kind gave added impetus to the appointment of guardians, and they appeared to be vindicated when, in 1533, the nuns of the convent of St Clare on the Horbruck had to declare before the civic court that 'due to our mistakes and weakness, we can no longer provide nor maintain [our convent]'; and handed over all their property, income, rents, and debts to the civic foundling house.[34] No representatives of the Franciscan order were present, and the transaction, agreed between the women and the convent, marked the apogee of civic control of the convents.

[29] Quoted in Roth, *Augsburgs Reformationsgeschichte*, ii. 362, Beilage I: 'Und wiewol man sagen möcht auff babstische art, sie weren nit ains ordens und fuegten nit zusamen, so ist doch gewisslich ware, dass weder die gleicheit noch ungleicheit der claider christen macht.'
[30] StadtAA, Reichsstadt, Lit. 1534, June–Sept., 28 July 1534.
[31] For a similar statement of the dangers of conflicting sermons, see ibid., Lit. 1534, Nachtrag II/29, Franz Kötzler, fo. 25ʳ.
[32] e.g. ibid., Lit. 1534, Nachtrag I/24, fos. 26ʳ ff.
[33] Roth, *Augsburgs Reformationsgeschichte*, ii. 189: 'Eine Weibsperson ist von Gemut und Leib viel schwacher, verfuhrlicher und beweglicher.'
[34] 'aus etlichen vnnsern mannglen, vnnd geprechen, nit mer mugen fursehen noch vnnderhallten'; StadtAA, Reichsstadt, RS 22 Dec. 1533.

In fact, what survives of the convent's records does not demonstrate incapacity, but an active, capitalistic system of investment-generating income rather than a secure, low-yield programme: 1,600 gulden was invested with Raimond, Anthony, and Hieronymus Fugger, and a 35-gulden annual interest-due was paid from the monastery of St Ulric and St Afra. A further nine dues contracted with country dwellers were sizeable and redeemable, apparently recently contracted commercial loans.[35] These debtors were drawn from the region surrounding Augsburg, but not from the areas where the convent owned land, suggesting a wide and adventurous commercial network. In all, the value of these bonds approached 2,950 gulden, and might be expected to generate income of at least 100–150 gulden per year—a considerable sum when compared with the 400 gulden which was the total annual income in 1551 of the socially more exclusive St Martin's.[36] In addition to its bonds, the convent also possessed a modest amount of land, listing thirteen farming properties at Göggingen, Hirblingen, Herbertshofen, Mertingen, Ried, Kleinkitzighofen, and Maingründel which could also be expected to contribute to the convent's income.[37] Even though it had sold one property at Erlingen, not far from Herbertshofen, it retained substantial scattered interests to the north, west, and south-west of Augsburg. The convent itself, nestling beside the inner wall of the city, close to the Lech and in a craft area (in 1533 its neighbours were a smith and a dyer[38]), must also have been moderately valuable. The chronicler Clemens Sender estimated that it had 2,500 gulden in cash alone.[39] All these resources were required to support a convent of only nine women, well below

[35] Resources detailed ibid., RS 22 Dec. 1533, before the Stadtgericht; and see US 22 Dec. 1533. One rent at least is definitely known to have been contracted in the 1530s: Lit. 1533, undated letter, a rent of 6 gulden had been purchased by Anna Kollerin, mistress of the house.

[36] Haemmerle, *Das Necrologium des Benediktinerinnenklosters St. Nicolaus*, p. 2.

[37] J. Jahn, *Augsburg Land* (Historischer Atlas von Bayern, xi, *Schwaben*; Munich, 1984), pp. 531–3, for details of the holdings of the foundling house, which incorporated some of the original Horbruck properties. Unfortunately, Jahn does not attempt to reconstruct the Horbruck convent's holdings. For the convent's sale of 'Ellingen', probably Erlingen near Herbertshofen and Mertingen, see StadtAA, Reichsstadt, Lit. 1533, undated letter, Anna Kollerin.

[38] Ibid., RS 22 Dec. 1533.

[39] *Chroniken der deutschen Städte*, xxiii, Sender, p. 358.

its full strength.[40] The evidence hardly paints a picture of a poor
or mismanaged convent: indeed, since Horbruck was the convent
in which lay involvement in convent administration had made
most headway, this would have been the ultimate irony.[41]

The price the Council paid for acquiring these assets for its
foundling house was not especially high. Each woman was given
an annuity of 50 gulden, which amounted to a total projected

[40] For records of the departure of 4 women in 1524, see StadtAA, KWA G47,
10–12, 9 Jan. 1524, Agatha Pregizerin; 27 Jan. 1524, Anna Kestelerin; 21 Apr.
1524, Madlena Millerin and Anna Sunderin. Kiessling estimates the convent's
numbers at 10; 9 women are known to have left in 1524, but there were 9 nuns
and 3 lay sisters when the convent closed in 1533. The numbers could conceivably
have been made up in new recruits since that date, but this seems unlikely as
most of the nuns are known to have been quite elderly—by 1540, only 5 were
still alive (StadtAA, Reichsstadt, BMB 1540). Kiessling's estimate would therefore
have to be revised upwards for the sixteenth century.

[41] On past civic involvement in the convent's administration, see Kiessling,
Bürgerliche Gesellschaft, p. 142. On the convent's financial situation, see StadtAA,
Reichsstadt, Lit. 1533, undated letter, Anna Koller, '1533' pencilled in by archival
hand. In this letter, Anna Koller accuses the convent women of luxurious living,
and appeals to the Council, claiming that only her careful administration has saved
the convent from ruin. She says she owes her post to the Council and will not
act without their permission. Roth cites this source without criticism as proof
of the convent's decline due to the 'Misswirtschaft'of its mistresses (*Augsburgs
Reformationsgeschichte*, ii. 190). However, Koller notes at least one Council figure,
the 'guild master Drechsel', who is opposed to her. This man is presumably Hans
Drechsel, repeatedly guild master of the butchers' guild in the early 1530s, and
member of the Small Council in 1531, 1532, and 1533 (StadtAA, Reichsstadt,
Ratsämterlisten, computer print-out by the Tübingen Sonderforschungsbereich
Projekt 22, Stadt und Reformation of this source). Koller was no longer mistress
when the convent was closed, but had been replaced by Walpurg Burckhart. Thus
either the Council proved unable to support Koller, their appointee ('Von Jn
[convent women] vnd von ainen Ersamen Rat gesetzt worden bin': Koller, Lit.
1533)—a possibility which, given the Council's tradition of involvement in the
convent, virtually unchallenged by this date, is unlikely—or else the Council itself
eventually withdrew its support. Burckhart had held the post previously (StadtAA,
KWA G47, 26 Mar. 1521). Whatever the truth of the matter, Koller's protestations
make it plain that most sisters did not accept her analysis of the convent's financial
position—indeed, they suspected Koller herself of purloining convent funds.
Moreover, Koller claimed that despite the sale of the farm at Ellingen, the convent's
affairs were now in order and no financial emergency existed. Finally, her
indebtedness to the Council, and the decidedly hostile tone of her diatribe against
the 'allten geprauchs mit Reychlichem wolleben vnd teglicher wirdschaft halten'—
accusations which perfectly fitted the tone of Council anti-monastic rhetoric—
suggest that Koller was not an objective judge of affairs at the Horbruck. Contrary
to Roth's argument, the document does not prove the convent to have been
financially mismanaged—if anything, it suggests that it was financially sound; and
hints that the divisions within the convent may have been used by the Council
to persuade the nuns to sell up.

outlay of 4,500 gulden for the Council. For the women, a pension of this size was probably worth more than the assets which many of the nuns in this largely non-élite convent would have brought with them, and it assured them a moderately comfortable life.[42] For the Council, however, the settlement was a dramatic success: it had acquired, through the convent's holdings, the rural influence which was an increasingly strong motif of its policy in these years; it had removed a convent; and the enterprise had not required much of an immediate financial outlay.[43]

This successful outcome set the seal on the Council's future approach to convents and monasteries alike. From then on the Council proceeded by trying to incorporate the institution's assets into a civic charity, and by settling pensions on the nuns or monks. But the cost turned out to be far higher in the case of female monastic institutions.[44] Firstly, fewer women left convents of their own accord, and pensions were thus more costly; secondly, convent women proved to be shrewd negotiators; and finally, women's perceived inability to earn a living made it necessary to assure them an income which would at least preserve their class position. Men could always learn a trade or become preachers elsewhere. So, in the late 1530s, when the Council suggested such an arrangement to the rebellious nuns of St Nicholas's, it met with no success.[45] It did succeed, though at vastly greater cost, in disbanding the richer, more powerful Dominican convent of St Margaret's and transferring its assets to its neighbour, the civic hospital of the Holy Spirit: a nice example

---

[42] For Agatha Pregizer, Anna Kesteler, Madlena Miller, and Anna Sunder, the amounts they received on leaving the convent are known. They ranged from 22 to 30 gulden, probably about a half to two-thirds of the total dowry the women had brought with them. The value of the *Leibgeding* given by the Council was thus substantially greater: see StadtAA, Reichsstadt, US 22 Dec. 1533, Felicitas Hailpronner; and US 22 Dec. 1533, Anna Kellner, for examples of the contract.

[43] Since 4 of the women are known to have been dead by 1540 (ibid., BMB 1540), the remaining 5 would have had to have lived for at least a further 14 years each on average before the Council's total expenditure would have reached 4,500 gulden.

[44] Cf. the donation of the male Franciscan monastery to the Council (ibid., US 18 May 1535)—no pension arrangements for the men are mentioned. But note Roth, *Augsburgs Reformationsgeschichte*, ii. 188—the monks of the Carmelite monastery received pensions of between 15 and 45 gulden.

[45] This is clear from the interesting 'Verträge ca. 1538', Barbara Langenmentlin, in StadtAA, Reichsstadt, im Kasten, 'Archivalien zur Zurückstellung in die Bestände, (Blendinger)' [*sic*].

of integrationism, since the convent had itself been engaged in nursing work.[46] And as late as 1546 it finally persuaded the last surviving nun at St Martin's to take a pension and hand over the convent keys.[47]

The cost of this policy in St Margaret's case was enormous, and the outlay demonstrates the priority the Council placed on its resolution. In accordance with their higher social status, the sisters of St Margaret's were able to secure a more generous annuity from the Council: 100 gulden each per year, in addition to a yearly feast, perpetual use of the convent's garden, a share of the convent's moveable goods, and a lump-sum payment of 30 gulden each.[48] The ten annuities would have been worth 10,000 gulden at commercial rates, but because of the nuns' longevity, 28,000 was eventually paid out. The hospital also pledged to provide the nuns with substantial goods in kind during their lifetimes: due to inflation, the costs of this rose and were estimated at 9,904 gulden by 1574.[49] Thus, for a total outlay of nearly 40,000 gulden, the city gained only some rural holdings, centred on the villages of Eppisburg and Riedsend where the convent had the local jurisdiction, and property scattered in villages in a strip of land in the northern part of the Augsburg–Dillingen–Donauwörth triangle.[50] In addition to its fairly substantial premises in the city, the convent had some land and property rights within the town, but practically no interest-bearing deposits.[51] Even the convent

---

[46] StadtAA, Reichsstadt, US 23 Sept. 1538; Lit. 1538, July–Dec., 23 Sept. 1538; Roth, *Augsburgs Reformationsgeschichte*, ii. 322; Lit. 1538, July–Dec., undated letter.

[47] Roth, *Augsburgs Reformationsgeschichte*, iii. 139, 173 n. 71.

[48] See Kiessling, *Bürgerliche Gesellschaft*, p. 38, for an assessment of the convent's position in the fifteenth century. The two lay sisters were to receive a half settlement. For full details, see StadtAA, Bestand Kirchen und Klöster, Salbuch St. Margareth, 23 Sept. 1538; Lit. 1538, July–Dec., 23 Sept. 1538, draft and parchment copy and collection of further documents.

[49] 'Was den frawen St. Margareten Closters für Leibgeding 36 Jarlanng geben worden', and 1574 supplication: StadtAA, Reichsstadt, Lit. 1538, July–Dec.; and 1574 reckoning, same collection. The women found the annuities insufficient: see letter, same collection, 22 Oct. 1551.

[50] StadtAA, Bestand Kirchen und Klöster, Salbuch St. Margaret, for details. Places identified from Jahn, *Augsburg Land*. He does not provide any details of the extent of the convent's land-holdings, however, but only a list of the hospital's holdings (pp. 510–30) which omits this property. It may have been sold.

[51] 1574 reckoning: StadtAA, Reichsstadt, Lit. 1538, July–Dec., 22 Sept. 1538.

buildings proved of limited value to the hospital: in 1574 the hospital representatives complained: 'From it, the poor get no benefit, but rather have many costs and damages in maintaining the large buildings.' But the benefits for the Council were twofold: it had gained further control over the rural hinterland which it had been trying to establish—it is possible that the particular site of the holdings, just a short distance from Dillingen, the bishop's residence, may have made the area especially attractive as a point from which to exercise pressure against the bishop—and it had got rid of a powerful convent, its assets now incorporated into the civic hospital.[52]

But even where integration was not carried out to such a degree, the issue of control of resources rapidly became a flashpoint between the Council—or its representatives, the guardians—and the women. The entire convent archives of both Maria Stern's and St Nicholas's were seized and deposited in the town hall in 1537; two years later the Council demanded that St Stephen's hand over all its property deeds together with a list of its assets, and threatened to count them void if it did not do so.[53]

The second issue to crystallize both notions of women's incapacity to hold authority and the desire to incorporate convents into the city administration was that of convent offices. Here, the very idea that women might hold positions of power could be viewed as unchristian, contrary to the right order of subjection which ought to exist between women and men. An anonymous memorial to the Council of 1534 provides a particularly clear articulation of these beliefs. The writer describes how God 'has made the woman . . . subject to the man as her head' because of her weaker nature. Consequently: 'How should it come to any good, when women join themselves in a separate

---

[52] Eppisburg was also part of Imperial Marshal Pappenheim-Biberach's complex of territory, with which the Council was often involved: Jahn, *Augsburg Land*, pp. 77, 90, 178. Note also, on the convent's property at Täfertingen, pp. 114, 117, 519; and at Gersthofen, p. 297.

[53] Baumann, *Maria Stern*, p. 6; Roth, *Augsburgs Reformationsgeschichte*, ii. 362; StadtAA, Reichsstadt, Prot. der Dreizehn III, fo. 231ᵛ, 27 Mar. 1537; Roth, *Augsburgs Reformationsgeschichte*, ii. 362. St Nicholas's was refused the return of 'truchen, Silbergeschirr Sigel brief Register', etc., and given only a copy of the register in 1539: StadtAA, Reichsstadt, Prot. der Dreizehn V, fo. 74ʳ, 12 June 1539. For the demand to St Stephen's, see ibid., RB 16, fo. 160ᵛ, 22 May 1539.

life, so that, contrary to the ordinance of God, yes, against nature, they give themselves into obedience to a woman, who has neither the reason nor the understanding to govern whether in spiritual or temporal matters, who ought not to govern, but to be governed.'[54] Intensely 'lay' views about the proper Christian life inform the writer's critique of monasticism and allow a very determined attack on the fitness of women to exercise any power in any sphere. Natural and godly law, the Protestant family writ large, forbade women all authority and denied them any role not contained within the household.

Ideas of this stamp were increasingly echoed in Council policies. As early as 1528 the Council had taken it upon itself to 'confirm' prioresses in their position.[55] After 1537, however, it felt able to intervene directly, summarily deposing Felicitas Endorfer in 1539 and replacing her with Anna Ravenspurger, and threatening to depose the prioress at St Nicholas's as well.[56] In 1543 the Council noted that the guardians of St Katherine's needed to choose a new prioress, but added: 'but the Council considers the Reihingin to be the most capable', clear evidence of its direct involvement in the selection.[57] Convents who elected their own prioresses were reprimanded.[58] The Council was canny in its selection, however: Anna Ravenspurger came from a patrician family, her sister was a senior member of the

---

[54] 'Etlich Artickel belanngendt ein Cristenliche Reformacion so von ainer Christenliche Oberkait, von ampts wegen, soll bedacht und notig furgenomen werden': ibid., Lit. 1534, Nachtrag 24: 'Wie soll nun das gut thun, das weyber sich zusamen thunt, in ein besonnders lebenn, also, das sie sich, wider gottes ordnung, Ja wider die nattur, in ein gehorsam eins weybs begeben die da weder vernunfft noch verstanndt hat zuRegieren, es sey auch in göttlichen, oder weltlichen sachen, die nit solte Regieren sonnder geregiert werden.'

[55] e.g. (Stern) ibid., Prot. der Dreizehn II, fo. 213ʳ, 10 Mar. 1528; note also the formulation used by Anna Koller, Horbruck: see n. 42 above.

[56] StadtAA, KWA ad B26 III, St. Katharina, Nachtrag 22 Aug. 1539; Roth, *Augsburgs Reformationsgeschichte*, ii. 322. It was careful to insist none the less that Endorfer had also been appointed by the Council: 'Wie dann ain Erber Rat verschynner Zeit Fraw Felicitas Endorfferin, den anndern allen zu ainer priorin furgesetzt vnd verordnet gehapt . . .'. On St Nicholas's, see Roth, *Augsburgs Reformationsgeschichte*, ii. 362 ff., Beilage 1537.

[57] StadtAA, Reichsstadt, RB 17 II, fo. 34ʳ, 30 Aug. 1543; RB 17/II, fo. 38ʳ, 11 Sept. 1543: 'Doch acht ain Ersamer Rate die Reihingin fur die tuglichst'. She had previously been *Schaffnerin*: see StadtAA, KWA ad B26/III, St Katharina, Nachtrag 22 Aug. 1539.

[58] e.g. Roth, *Augsburgs Reformationsgeschichte* ii. 362 ff., Beilage 1537; iii. 139.

convent.[59] In the case of less powerful convents it showed a similar mixture of crass interventionism and shrewdness: the superior of Maria Stern's was deposed by the Council in 1537; while in 1543 the old and new mayors were commissioned to persuade the nuns at St Ursula's, one of the city's least prestigious convents, to accept a woman of the patrician Ilsung family as their superior.[60]

Even so, the convents were loath to accept either the Council's or the guardians' right to nominate officials. In 1541 the nuns of St Nicholas's had to be warned not to elect a prioress without Council involvement, even though the Council had made plain its wish to be involved in the selection of 1536.[61] For the Council, a sympathetic prioress was crucial to the co-option of those convents which could not be persuaded to disband. Further, the measures placed the convent and its head under the direct protection of the city, and rendered the prioress a kind of civic official responsible to the Council. For the women, on the other hand, the election of a superior was a convent matter for which in principle they alone were responsible. In the Dominican convents, for example, it was clearly understood by the monks that *electio tamen Priorissae libere pertinet an conventum*.[62] The Council was doing far more than merely ratifying the

---

[59] Her sister Barbara is placed third in the list of 1526, suggesting she held important office.

[60] Baumann, *Maria Stern*, p. 29; StadtAA, Reichsstadt, RB 17/I, fo. 75, 12 Apr. 1543. There is some ambiguity here: according to some sources, the convent of St Ursula simply relocated to Dillingen. However, the 'nuns at St Ursula' are repeatedly referred to in Council sources, in addition to those of St Nicholas's. They may possibly be identical with those of St Nicholas's, now living at St Ursula's—the question cannot be conclusively answered by the existent documents. There was an 'Ilsung woman' 'at St Ursula's' (Prot. der Dreizehn VI, fo. 70ʳ, 22 Jan. 1541); and, as it happens, a member of that family is also listed among the sisters of St Nicholas's in 1536 (US 17 Feb. 1536). However, she is referred to as a 'Pfründnerin' not as a sister; and it is thus most unlikely that the Ilsung woman at St Nicholas's was also the prioress at St Ursula's.

[61] StadtAA, Reichsstadt, Prot. der Dreizehn VI, fo. 99ʳ, 26 Apr. 1541 (St Nicholas's). Regarding the election of 1536, it is significant that all the documents pertaining to the election of Margaret Herwart are in the city archive, presumably confiscated (ibid., US 1534-8, 'oath', n.d.; US 17 Feb. 1536; US 8 June 1536; US '1536'). In the notarial accounts of the cost of the election, the full correspondence to Rome and to other prelates is listed, but there is no mention of a letter informing the Council. Most probably the convent was called to account for its refusal to recognize the jurisdiction of the Council.

[62] Siemer, *Geschichte des Dominikanerklosters St. Magdalena in Augsburg*, p. 52.

convent's choice here, and its action could not be construed as the assumption of duties previously carried out by Dominican monks. After the death of the Ilsung woman, the Council even determined that St Ursula's nuns should not have any more prioresses; and in 1539 the Council restricted the number of offices at St Katherine's to prioress, counter-notary, and *Schaffnerin*—a powerful attack on the convent's systems of discipline and hierarchy.[63]

There may have been a further element in the Council's determination to secure the right to appoint prioresses and control other offices while remaining apparently uninterested in intervening in the monastic elections. Within the civic political community, office-holding was fundamentally based on a system of election. This was symbolically crucial, no matter how predetermined the results by relations of seniority and deference. To be a politically active citizen-guildsman was to have the capacity to elect one's guild representative to the Council. Masculinity and political ability were linked and expressed in the active ritual of voting, carried on in each guild-chamber, doors locked against outsiders and womenfolk. At each level of the political pyramid, a smaller group of electors were responsible for appointing to office, so that the most politically powerful men were also those who participated in the most elections.[64]

Women were entirely excluded from this form of political activity, and no office they held within the community appears to have been allocated by vote.[65] Convents were the only institutions in the city where women elected to office. Even in the soul-houses (*Seelhäuser*), lay charitable institutions composed entirely of women, both the admission of new members and the appointment of a 'mistress' were matters which concerned the *Seelhaus* patron alone, not its inmates. A semi-laicized, urbanized convent in which women could none the less elect and appoint to office was a political and conceptual contradiction. Convents

[63] StadtAA, Reichsstadt, RB 19, fo. 76', 30 Apr. 1545, for St Ursula; StadtAA, KWA ad B26/III, St. Katharina, Nachtrag 22 Aug. 1539.
[64] See P. Dirr, 'Studien zur Geschichte der Augsburger Zunftverfassung', *ZHVS* 39 (1913), 144–243; and Mörke and Sieh, 'Gesellschaftliche Führungsgruppen'.
[65] See StadtAA, Reichsstadt, Ratsämterlisten 1520–35; 1536–48. I have developed the argument of this paragraph in my ' "The Common Man", "the Common Good", "Common Women": Gender and Language in the German Reformation Commune', *Social History*, 12/1 (1987), 1–22.

could not be subsumed into a civic political framework as a kind of sub-guild. Their mode of decision-making breached the equations of masculinity, political capacity, and election. The incorporation of convents into the city could thus invoke and activate different civic notions of the appropriate male and female spheres. Indeed, in civic terms the idea of the single woman was itself problematic. Single women were in theory forbidden to have 'aigen Rauch', to have, that is, their own independent households, unless they became citizens. They must either take a position as a servant within a household, marry, lodge within a household, or leave town.[66] Of course, class, though unspoken, was the crucial proviso: to become a citizen one needed to have assets of at least 50 gulden, together with membership of a guild. It was the proliferation of independent households of women of craft class and below which the Council wished to discourage.[67] Convent women constituted a serious anomaly once they were to be integrated into this framework. A group of unmarried women, they had their collective 'own smoke'. Yet they were not quite citizens, and clearly not part of a household. The only comparable civic social unit was the town brothel, an early casualty of the Reformation.[68]

Restricting single women's opportunities to be householders was another means by which the city buttressed the inaccessibility of workshop enterprise to spinsters. In any case, if a woman had not inherited guild membership from her father or through a husband, she could not acquire this prerequisite of citizenship. The nuns' substantial role in economic production thus further affronted beliefs about what was fitting for women. We know

[66] See also the complaints about many 'ledige Töchter', who 'under dem schein streichens, Spuelens, Spinnens, und Antreens' had 'aigne gemach und rauch'. This was to be banned: C. P. Clasen, 'Armenfürsorge in Augsburg vor dem Dreissigjährigen Krieg', *ZHVS* 78 (1984), 65–115, here p. 74.

[67] See e.g. StadtAA, Reichsstadt, RB 17/II, fo. 31', 30 Aug. 1543, Appolonia Schusterin von Auerbach, who was refused citizenship but permitted to live in Augsburg so long as she has a 'dienst' there; RB 17/II, fo. 21', 11 Aug. 1543, Anna Mairin, who was allowed to remain 'so lanng sie zudienen willens, wo sie aber aigen Rauch halten wolt, soll sie Burgerrecht kauffen . . .'; see also Fasz. Bürgerrecht, undated, Peutinger's hand, note on citizenship for women: those women who worked as maids were not to have 'aigen rauch' unless they were citizens; restrictions on women who worked as wet-nurses, seamstresses, and *Kindbettkellerinnen*.

[68] On the other comparable social institution, soul-houses, see below.

that St Katherine's had its own weaving industry, and that it and St Margaret's had substantial enough bakeries to be called upon to bake bread for distribution to the poor.[69] In 1517 Wilhelm Rem had expressly commissioned these two convents and the hospital to use the corn he had donated to bake bread for cheap distribution to the poor, because 'the bakers were baking poor and badly baked bread' and overcharging for it.[70] In this case, the convent women's enterprise could be seen to be directly undercutting the town's master bakers, impugning their skill and taking their business. Perhaps it was not coincidental that it should have been a baker's boy who interrupted a sermon in St Margaret's in 1523, sparking off a minor riot.[71]

If convents were anomalous, nuns who could be persuaded to leave the convent constituted a yet graver anomaly. In theory, the aim of reformers and Council alike was to find them husbands, a solution which would reinsert the women into households. But the Council was able to recognize that for many of the women, especially those who did not choose to leave in the early Reformation years, marriage was simply not possible. Some, including several who left of their own accord, continued to live in female households: two convent women who left Maria Stern's in 1537 are known to have lived unmarried in the same house in St Jacob's suburb until 1553.[72] Of the twenty-two named women who are known to have left convents independently, seven are known to have married, but a further five are known not to have taken husbands. The dowries which convent women brought with them were forfeit to the convent should they marry. Several women attempted to sue for their return, however, and were supported by the Council in doing so: as early as 1535 the Council lent 15 gulden to Katherina von Fridingen, who married Paul Phrygius, and it supported her claim for compensation against the foundation.[73] But the convents regularly refused such

[69] Kiessling, *Bürgerliche Gesellschaft*, p. 181; *Chroniken der deutschen Städte*, xxv, Rem, pp. 74, 77.
[70] *Chroniken der deutschen Städte*, xxv, Rem, p. 77.
[71] Ibid. 199.   [72] Baumann, *Maria Stern*, p. 26.
[73] StadtAA, Reichsstadt, BMB 1535, fo. 70ᵛ; see also BMB 1524, fo. 77ᵛ, for the cryptic statement: '15 fl der closterfrauen vom S. Steffan geben'. In supporting such claims the Council was continuing a long tradition, as can be seen from its stance revealed in a collection of documents concerned with departures from the Horbruck convent in the fifteenth century: StadtAA, KWA G47, 6 July 1500; 7 Sept. 1473; 12 Oct. 1473; 3 Sept. 1498; 8 June 1496, 17 Jan. 1490.

requests, and it frequently took decades to secure any money. Even when it was paid, the initial dowry was often substantially less than their worldly blood-sisters might have expected. In 1538, and again in 1539, the Council commanded the convent of St Nicholas to pay women of the Ulstett and Rem families the 100 gulden which each had brought the convent—and this was over ten years since they had left the convent. Yet both came from families which were co-opted into the patriciate in 1538, and dowries for women of their class regularly reached 3,000 gulden or more.[74] This disparity was compounded by the fact that families often disposed of all available income as dowries for their children, and could not later increase a dowry for a child whom they had not anticipated would inherit. Similarly, members of monastic institutions often relinquished their rights to inherit, or took a smaller share—settlements which it was hard to reverse if they later left orders. For ex-convent women, marriage to a social equal was therefore difficult. Interestingly enough, the prospect of bitter familial property disputes was one of the considerations which weighed most heavily with Johannes Rehlinger in 1534, when he advised the Council not to release people from monastic vows.[75]

Even evangelicals might recognize that convent women turned out into the world as a result of closure were unlikely to marry. Many of the women at the Horbruck convent, for example, were elderly, and the more unwilling to adapt to married life, even if partners had been available. The Council tacitly admitted as much when it bestowed annuities on convent women instead of granting cash settlements, thereby providing them with an ongoing means of support. Despite the strong civic tendency to perceive widows and single women as objects of charity, ex-nuns at least secured themselves independent incomes.

---

[74] *Chroniken der deutschen Städte*, xxiii, Sender, p. 180, implies the women left in 1526; see Prot. der Dreizehn IV, fo. 230^r, 23 Dec. 1538; and V, fo. 74^r, 12 June 1539, for attempts to regain the 100 gulden. Two members of the Rem family had marriage settlements of 3,000 gulden apiece. Brigitte Rehlinger, who left St Katherine's in 1526, received only 400 gulden (*Chroniken der deutschen Städte*, xxiii, Sender, p. 180), whereas dowries paid to members of the Rehlinger family regularly stood at 3,000 or 4,000 gulden.

[75] StadtAA, Reichsstadt, Lit. 1534, Nachtrag 21. He also argues that convent women and ex-monks do not marry their social equals, and that this shows the unsuitability of such arrangements.

One final dimension of the convent's anomalous nature can be noted. Women were notably absent from urban public ceremonial. They were not included in the annual swearing of the civic oath although they were citizens. Nor, to judge by the descriptions of the events, were they present as a group in the ceremonies of public welcome to the Emperor.[76] Though journeymen and apprentices might celebrate their festival, the *Dänzeltag*, and male citizens might hold 'civic processions', women had no comparable collective rituals.[77] This is not to say that women were absent from ritual altogether: they took prominent roles in wedding celebrations, they did much of the work of mourning, and childbirth was primarily celebrated amongst the circle of womenfolk. But these rituals were not civic. They did not incorporate women into the *polis*, or give them a role within the commune. The ceremonial activity of the nuns— their distinctive dress, the choral singing upon which the women at St Katherine's placed such emphasis, their appearance as a known group at public worship—was thus at odds with a major and ancient strain of civic public ritual. The consequent difficulty for the Council of even conceiving of a group of women acting together as a cohesive unit is betrayed in a phrase in its draft ordinance for St Katherine's, where it speaks of the difficulty of 'preventing anger, jealousy, hatred and disunity among so many women'.[78]

The Logic of Enclosure

But it was perception of the nuns' sexuality which was the key factor in the reformed Council's policy and popular hostility towards convents. This expressed itself in two contradictory impulses. The first, based on a conviction of the fragility of the nuns' virginity, permanently under threat from lascivious clerics, led to calls for convent security to be intensified. At St Katherine's the 'drunken guards' were to be sacked and replaced by 'capable

[76] Ibid., Schätze 63, P. H. Mair, fos. 93ʳ–94ᵛ; fo. 190ᵛ.

[77] On the Dänzeltag, see C. P. Clasen, *Die Augsburger Weber: Leistungen und Krisen des Textilgewerbes um 1600* (Augsburg, 1981), pp. 116–18.

[78] StadtAA, KWA ad B26, St. Katharina, Nachtrag: 'zu erhaltung Zucht, Erberkait friede Christliche Liebe vnnd ainikait, vnnd verhutung, Zorn Neidt hass vnnd vnainikait vnnter so viel frawen pilden'.

ones'; and by 1539 no visitors were to be allowed except with Council permission.[79] The Council gradually took upon itself the responsibility for policing the enclosures of such convents as St Ursula's: in January 1541 and again in March of that year it granted permission for Frau Schellenberger and Frau Ilsung to visit women in the convent.[80] Such anxieties were especially directed against monks, who were perceived as the most licentious of the clergy. As early as 1526 the Council determined that Dominicans should not be present in the convents when the accounts or other secular matters were dealt with. In 1531 the Council forbade the Dominicans to visit St Katherine's apart from reading mass, giving communion, and hearing confession. And in 1537, when it replaced the convent's guards, it also ordered the maids and servants to swear an oath of loyalty—a manœuvre designed to wean their allegiance away from the convent women.[81] In a society in which gossip about liaisons between monks and nuns frequently featured convent servants as go-betweens, the underlying imputation of this measure was clear. Such speculations were fuelled by a series of scandals involving monks, particularly the Dominicans. In 1538 the women at St Nicholas's were forbidden all visitors and the convent was locked—a far stricter enclosure than this non-observant convent had ever experienced.[82] In such decisions the Council was presenting itself in the guise of a male protector, guarding the virginity of its 'daughters'. Ironically, this concern could achieve far stricter enclosure than the observant reforms of the mid-fifteenth century. It finds its fullest expression in the Ulm Council's ordinance for the *Sammlung* in Ulm, transformed from a Franciscan convent

[79] Ibid., Prot. der Dreizehn III, fo. 231ᵛ, 27 Mar. 1537; Ordinance of 1539: StadtAA, KWA ad B26/III, St. Katharina.

[80] Ibid., Prot. der Dreizehn VI, fo. 70ʳ, 22 Jan. 1541; VI, fo. 91ʳ, 10 Mar. 1541.

[81] Ibid., RB 15, fo. 113ᵛ, 8 Oct. 1526; for 1531, see Roth, *Augsburgs Reformationsgeschichte*, ii. 191, 208 n. 72, for a scandal involving the Dominican Johann Lichtenberger, exiled from the city for committing adultery with the wife of one of his 'Beichtkinder'; and Herr Simprecht (?Tayber), accused of enacting a mock confession for his girlfriend. Roth thinks these events explain the Council's decision to restrict the monks' access to the convent of St Katherine's, which he dates to 1532; it occurred, however, in 1531, a few months prior to these scandals: StadtAA, Reichsstadt, Prot. der Dreizehn III, fo. 56ᵛ, 14 Feb. 1531; Roth, *Augsburgs Reformationsgeschichte*, ii. 190, 207-8 n. 71. For 1537, see StadtAA, Reichsstadt, Prot. der Dreizehn III, fo. 231ᵛ, 27 Mar. 1537.

[82] StadtAA, Reichsstadt, Prot. der Dreizehn IV, fo. 176, 22 Oct. 1538.

to a civic foundation in 1536. No one was to leave the convent without permission; and women who did not go to the evangelical sermons were not to be permitted to leave the convent even to visit relatives.[83]

Protectiveness of this kind had a long tradition. In 1441 the Council had fully supported the attempts of the Dominicans to impose a stricter enclosure on the nuns of St Katherine's, and Council workmen had carried out the labour of bricking in the iron grilles and raising the surrounding walls. This had met with spirited resistance from the nuns themselves, who reputedly attacked the workmen with spits, forcing them to retreat, and then appealed to the bishop.[84] Over a hundred years later, in 1563, strict enclosure and a rule of silence were reintroduced by the prioress Susanna Ehinger, with the support of the Counter-Reformation theologian Peter Canisius, once again with the Council's tacit agreement.[85] Both episodes illustrate how solicitude for the convent women's virginity issued in regulations which controlled and restricted their activities—and aroused their fierce opposition. Male virginity, by contrast, viewed neither as a civic resource nor as an attribute imperilled by forces outside the monastery, did not call forth a similar response of protection, and no comparable enclosure was attempted.

Comparison with the civic brothel is illuminating. Prostitutes' sexual availability was viewed as a civic resource, and the brothel was seen as a theatre of civic ceremonial as well as a place of release for what would otherwise have been dangerously disruptive young male lust. Here, too, the question of enclosure was a vexed one. The Council had repeatedly ordered the brothel-keeper not to forbid his women to leave the brothel to go to church or to force them to remain in the brothel against their will, but though the Council claimed not to approve of this enclosure, it clearly aimed only to mitigate its strictness, not to abolish it. Convent women's virginity, on the other hand, could be seen as constituting a civic resource too; for the women's holy lives, chastity, and prayerfulness benefited the entire commune.

[83] Stadtarchiv Ulm, U 5307 and [8989], Wednesday after Ulrici 1536; and cf. StadtAA, KWA ad B26/III, St. Katharina, Nachtrag 22 Aug. 1539.

[84] *Chroniken der deutschen Städte*, v, Zink, pp. 103 f.

[85] Ibid. xxxii, Mühlich, pp. 394 f. The Council was involved in the visitation leading up to the reform.

Some convents, of course, elicited this response more than others: St Katherine's, most closely associated with the city patriciate and the élite, was also the convent about whose purity the Council evinced most concern; while St Stephen's, a foundation of noble women from beyond the city, continued to follow undisturbed a far less rigid convent life.

The second contradictory strain in Council and popular attitudes to nuns was to see the women themselves as intensely and actively sexual. Virginal women, forever poised at the moment of transition from daughterhood to wifehood, yet brides of Christ, their sexual status made them compelling. A convent full of such women compounded the ambiguities between wifehood, sisterhood, and daughterhood, and was therefore a magnet for male sexual imagination. For evangelicals, who rejected the belief that nuns were the brides of Christ, the women's uncertain status made them a sure target of sexual gossip and innuendo. Franciscus Frosch advised the Council to reform the convents as part of its duty to ensure 'discipline' among the citizenry, 'for what sort of christian discipline the monks have been imposing in the convents is unfortunately so evident that it requires no further proof'.[86] Similarly, in an anonymous memorial, one writer stressed women's far greater weakness and susceptibility to temptation, and moved on to speculate upon 'what misery, terrible deeds must occur in women's cloisters, in erring consciences, in secret burnings, secret swearing, blasphemy, evils which may not be spoken of, for it cannot be denied that a woman is far more easily persuaded, easily misled and more cunning than a man'.[87] The image of the lascivious monk is turned on its head here: it is the women who are the sexual predators, and the female cloisters which are 'a thousand times worse' than male monasteries.

Even the opponents of the evangelicals might share this assessment of 'cloister folk' (*Closterleut*). Johannes Rehlinger

[86] StadtAA, Reichsstadt, Lit. 1534, June–Sept., 28 July 1534: 'dann was christenlicher zucht, bisher durch verstehung der munchen, bey den frawen Clostern gespürt vnnd befunden worden sey, das ist laider, so offenbar, das es kain verrern beweisens bedarff'.

[87] Ibid., Lit. 1537, Nachtrag 24: 'was Ellenden, Jamers sich muss in frawen clostern Zutragen Jn Jrrigen gewissen in haimliche Brennen haimlichen schweren, Lästern dauon nit zureden ist, dann ye vnleugbar das ain weybsbild, vil beweglicher, verfurlicher vnnd furwiziger jst, dann mans personen'.

strongly advised the Council not to relieve monastics of their vows and 'encourage them to leave, and to follow the luxury of the world (to which nature is in any case inclined), also to fall . . . into dishonourable, wicked things, such as forbidden unseemly unchastenesses and other sins . . .', and argued that the only way to prevent such evils was for the Council to enforce the enclosure of the monastic institutions.[88]

Nuns who left their convents were consequently viewed as being in intense sexual danger, both from their own lusts and those of others. In the early years of the Reformation, as the first nuns left convents, Luther's immediate preoccupation was to find husbands for them—a concern he did not have when monks began to leave monasteries. Indeed, he himself was not persuaded of the need to marry at this time. A description of the nuns' arrival by one of Luther's students captures the mixture of excitement and apprehension: 'A wagon load of vestal virgins has just come to town all more eager for marriage than for life. May God give them husbands lest worse befall.'[89]

In Augsburg also, Bernhard Rem argued that the only way in which a nun who left a convent could resolve her natural sexual lustfulness was to become a wife and mother. In a series of open letters published in pamphlet form, advising his sisters to leave the convent and embark on a truly godly life, the note of sexual suspicion is seldom distant. Rem perceived the women as idle, and their lack of employment gave scope to the Devil. In an equation of lack of evangelical fervour with sexual licentiousness, he claimed that the sisters refused to read the Bible, though 'the reading of the Holy Scriptures dampens the lusts of the flesh'. He went on to argue that the women's second enemy was their 'own flesh', and that if a sister lacked the rare gift of chastity, she must 'burn with desire'. The convent was perceived as a kind

---

[88] Ibid., Lit. 1534, Nachtrag 21: 'zu raitsen, heraus zugien, vnd den wollust der welt (zu dem allem dann, on das die natur genaigt ist) destermer zuprauchen, auch sich ettwann nit allain in vnerlich lasterliche sachen, als in verpottne vnzimliche vnkeuschaiten, vnd andere sunde zugeben . . .'.

[89] Quoted in R. H. Bainton, *Women of the Reformation in Germany and Italy* (Minneapolis, 1971), p. 36. See also S. Ozment, *When Fathers Ruled: Family Life in Reformation Europe* (Cambridge, Mass., 1983), for an exposition of these fears.

of sexual hothouse, where all the women's religious exercises must become tainted with sexuality.[90]

In place of the convent, he proposed the ideal of Christian wifehood: 'A wife who washes her children's nappies each day, who feeds them pap, gives her husband food to eat, and nourishes her children in the sweat of her brow', who believes truly and prays a simple Our Father, will reach Heaven before a nun will. Rem is unable to envisage any destiny other than marriage for women. The married estate is described solely in terms of women's domestic work, so that service to others, and not, for example, the independent study of God's Word, is women's only means of fulfilling their spiritual duties. Behind his admonitions lies the unspoken assumption that unless women are married, their lusts will make them unable to resist the Devil's snares.[91]

This language was adopted by the Council itself in the reformed ordinance for St Katherine's, instituted by Council decree in 1539. It cites the women's idleness (*Muessgang*) as a cause of the 'evil', and recommends the reading of the Scriptures 'in order to dampen human desires and to subject the inheritance of Adam to the spirit of truth'.[92]

A similar conjunction of attitudes finds expression in the words spoken during a riot at St Margaret's in 1523. Sparked off by an argument about whether women ought to pray to St Margaret for help during pregnancy, it rapidly became an exchange of sexual

---

[90] 'Der ander feynd | ist euwer aygen flaisch | da hilfft kain Closter | kain wüste | kain hohe maur . . .'; 'Nu gedenck | in was geferlichait stande alle die | die sich mit gelubdte verknupft haben zůr junckfrawschaft | vnd befinden das sy die genad nitt haben | sy brinnen in begird | da ists hertz schon abgefallen | vnd wellt gott | das nit noch bosers geschech': Rem, *Ain Sendtbrieff an ettlich Closterfrawen*, fos. a/iv^r, a/iv^v.

[91] 'Ain eefraw | die jrem kindlin altag seine windelen weschet | den brey einstreicht | jre hausswurt zů essen gibt | die kinder im schwayss irs angesichts ernört | die würt euch vor lauffen | sy vertrawt allain auff Christum | ist nit hochfertig vermaint durch jr arbayt nit frum zů werden sonder durch glauben in Christum. vnnd jre werck thůt sy jrem nechsten zů gůtt | bekennt jr sünd | vertrauwt der barmhertzigkait gottes vnd last got in allen dingen | sein eer | bettet ain Pater noster | mit verstandt vnnd hertzen . . .': ibid., fo. b^v. Rem's slightly defensive tone as he writes about the 'works' of a good wife, 'which are not done out of a spirit of pride or that she might become saved through her works', suggest the ideological tensions here—Rem is in fact advocating a lay holy life in which a woman's behaviour is crucial to her salvation; but he is also aware that this looks dangerously like works-righteousness, anathema to a good evangelical.

[92] StadtAA, KWA ad B26/III, St. Katharina, 22 Aug. 1539.

insult. One nun reversed the allegations of lasciviousness, arguing that when the citizens invited Rhegius and the other evangelical preachers, 'they seduced their wives for them'—a form of words which represented the alleged adultery as an offence to the male citizens, and women as the vehicles of the insult.[93] In retaliation, a lay woman remarked that the nun would not be averse to being seduced but no one would have her—an insult which mixed beliefs about the sexual rapaciousness of nuns with taunts about their unattractiveness.

The Catholic Church had assured a special spiritual position to the woman who resigned her sexuality in favour of the monastic life. Her sexual sacrifice could be considered yet more worthy because female virginity was considered socially more precious than male virginity. As a convent woman, she might become a bride of Christ, removed from social kinship into a separate, holy role. Yet her sexuality might be not so much resigned as transmuted into a passion for Christ, one which might allow an intensely sexual and maternal language of devotion. She could imagine herself as Christ's lover, or, in a vision which allowed her to express power and protectiveness, she could identify herself with Marian motherhood. Because of her womanhood and Christ's masculinity, such a relationship could be expressed in language which was much more direct, less purely metaphorical than it remained for men, for whom it was mediated through a social experience of maleness.[94]

The Reformation abolished the requirement that priests should be unmarried and sexually inactive, and severed the link between sexual purity and cultic eligibility. For the reformers there was, at one level, no distinction between Christians—all could serve equally, regardless of sexual status. But the reformers also recognized the office of preaching the Word. Not all Christians were fitted to perform this office, and those who were called to it continued to be set apart. For women, however, the severing

---

[93] *Chroniken der deutschen Städte*, xxiii, Sender p. 199: 'minnten den burgern ire weiber'.

[94] I am not, of course, claiming that only virgins could become convent sisters; but I am arguing that it was this symbolic constellation which coloured all women's understanding of the monastic life. On passion imagery, see S. Beckwith's unpublished paper on Margery Kempe; C. Bynum, *Jesus as Mother: Studies in the Spirituality of the High Middle Ages* (London, 1982).

of the connection between virginity and holiness demolished the particular devotional space which the pre-Reformation Church had allowed them. Once the nexus between virginity and holiness had been removed, so also the power of sexually direct religious language was weakened. Protestant women rarely imagined Christ as a child, while Luther cautioned that Mary was just like any other humble Christian soul, a comment which denied that her femininity had any particular significance.[95] On the other hand, earthly women were understood to be inescapably sexual, unable to ignore the imperative of lust, and able only to channel it into marriage.

Convents after the Reformation

Of the convents which had existed before the Reformation, only four—St Margaret's, Horbruck, St Nicholas's, and St Martin's—failed to survive until the reintroduction of Catholicism. St Katherine's and Maria Stern's continued an unbroken settlement in the city throughout the period; and St Nicholas's and St Martin's lasted until the eve of the city's defeat in the Schmalkaldic War. Even in the early 1550s, women who identified themselves as nuns of the Benedictine convent of St Nicholas were being billeted at St Katherine's.[96] Not one of the male monasteries remained in the city through these years. The reasons for this startling asymmetry must be sought in two directions: first, in the sense of female community a convent might provide, no matter how divided by class or personality; and second, in the wider divisions of gender and labour in the society in which the convent was set.

How many nuns left their convents in the 1520s, 1530s, and 1540s? It is hard to arrive at accurate figures. In 1526 St Katherine's numbered fifty-six women, but a few years later it had sunk to twenty-four, and was eventually to fall to less than

---

[95] See Luther on the Magnificat: *D. Martin Luthers Werke* (Weimar, 1883–). vii. 544–604. On the very different role of the Madonna in Counter-Reformation Europe, see L. Accati, 'The Larceny of Desire', *Memoria*, 7 (1983), 7–16; and see also M. Wiesner, 'Luther and Women: The Death of Two Marys', in J. Obelkevich *et al.* (eds.), *Disciplines of Faith* (London, 1987).

[96] Letter of Susanna Ehinger, Staatsarchiv Neuburg, Kl. Augsburg, St. Katharina, Akten 81.

a dozen.[97] Early in 1524, nine women left the Horbruck convent: only the same number remained to hand over the convent in 1533.[98] St Martin's had shrunk to one woman by 1546; and there were only two women at St Ursula's in 1547.[99] The records I have compiled of individual nuns show there to have been at least fifty-five nuns still in convents in the 1530s, a figure which excludes women from the largest convent, St Katherine's. Comparing this figure with the 150-200 nuns whom Kiessling estimates as living in the fifteenth-century city, and subtracting from it the fifty nuns of St Katherine's, we find a survival rate of at least 50 per cent. The major exodus of nuns did not begin until the late 1530s; and even by the very late 1540s, there must have been at least twenty to thirty nuns still living in Augsburg.[100]

As we saw, not all nuns who left convents got married: some were supported by pensions; others continued a semi-monastic life in the houses of relatives, as the papal dispensation of 1539 permitted the nuns of St Katherine's to do.[101] Some convents were clearly populated by elderly sisters. Nearly half the women who left the Horbruck convent died within six years, and the chronicler Clemens Sender described a woman at St Nicholas's as 'an old one'.[102] But the burial dates which Bauman provides for the women of Maria Stern's indicate that they were most likely middle-aged at the time of the Reformation; while all the women who left St Margaret's in 1538 were still alive some twenty years later.[103] Many of the women were still well able to work once they left the convent, therefore, and had many years ahead of them 'in the world'.

[97] See Juhnke, 'Geschichte der Dominikanerinnenkloster St. Katharina', for a copy of 1526 list; for the estimate of 24, see the *Remsche Chronik*, cited in Roth, *Augsburgs Reformationsgeschichte*, ii. 348 n. 56; and for the estimate of 10-11, see Juhnke, 'Geschichte der Dominikanerinnenkloster St. Katharina', p. 71. However, only 13 women who had left the convent as a result of the Reformation and re-Catholicization were demanding pensions in 1552.

[98] StadtAA, Reichsstadt, BMB 1524, fo. 63ᵛ, 23 Jan. 1524; RS 22 Dec. 1533.

[99] Roth, *Augsburgs Reformationsgeschichte*, iii. 173 n. 71; 172 n. 69.

[100] Kiessling, *Bürgerliche Gesellschaft*, p. 40 and n. 40; and during the 1540s there were at least 11 at St Katherine's, 2 at St Martin's, and at least 2 at St Nicholas's, and 6 at Maria Stern's.

[101] StadtAA, Reichsstadt, US 29 July 1539.

[102] Ibid., BMB 1540; *Chroniken der deutschen Städte*, xxiii, Sender, p. 358.

[103] Baumann, *Maria Stern*, p. 26; StadtAA, Reichsstadt, Lit. 1538, July–Dec., documents on St Margaret's.

For monks who left monasteries, there were opportunities to learn a trade or simply to transfer their training and become evangelical preachers. A similar vocational transition was not available for women. The works for which convent life would have trained them included the administration of charity, weaving, simple notarial skills, nursing, and needlework.[104] Some branches of weaving and needlework, exempted from guild control, would not have been closed to ex-nuns; but the distribution of charity and the policing of the Poor Law were firmly in the hands of the civic, male administration, even if Catholic notions of almsgiving had been compatible with civic poor-relief. Civic employment as notaries was not open to women, of course; and though it may have been possible for ex-nuns to earn odd bits of cash as occasional independent scribes for the illiterate, notarial work in general was not available to them. The closure of convents thus entailed a narrowing of the types of work which women might perform.

But it was in nursing, the main ministry of convents such as St Margaret's, that the most profound professional effects of the closure of convents could be seen. Nursing had been a task performed by lower-class lay workers and religious women of mixed class who regarded it as a work of religious devotion. But it became a low-status employment, too menial and ill paid to have been a possible option for an ex-nun. Something of the disruption which this occupational transformation caused to nurses can be glimpsed in a long, meandering statement of defence by a lay woman who worked as an official in St Margaret's before and after secularization. The hand is not a known notarial one, and the script, though flowing, is laboured.[105] She expressed a strong sense of the importance and skills of her work, and she was far from viewing it as just another servant position.

In her description of the convent women's work, nursing and charitable administration are inseparable. The nuns ensured that those without means of support were given alms from the goods

---

[104] Siemer, *Geschichte des Dominikanerklosters Sankt Magdalena*, pp. 60, 61; Kiessling, *Bürgerliche Gesellschaft*, p. 181; StadtAA, Reichsstadt, Prot. der Dreizehn V, fo. 216ʳ, 29 May 1540.

[105] StadtAA, Reichsstadt, Lit. 1538, July–Dec., with documents on St Margaret's, undated. On nursing, see also B. C. Hacker, 'Women and Military Institutions in Early Modern Europe: A Reconnaissance', *Signs*, 6 (1981), 643–71.

of inmates who died, they distributed necessaries, kept everything in good order, and cooked for the very ill. Continuity, in her view, is imperative, for only then do women understand the customs (*Brauch*)—an interesting term which has something of the flavour of craft training, yet draws on the idiom of ritual, custom, and order. She justifies her intervention as being 'purely for the sake of the poor and for the *allten breych*'—the principles which, she says, were once written up on boards outside the hospital of the Holy Ghost. Young nuns used to be taken on probation before they were accepted, and the loss of the old custom has led to the employment of mere 'maids', variable in quality, highly mobile, and lacking the commitment which—she implies but stops just short of saying—religious profession gave to the nuns. But she is equally explicit about the economic reasons for the decline: including food, she estimates that nuns received 100 gulden annually, whereas servants are paid at service rates. All the same, she argues against 'the maids' being paid similar wages, 'because previously as much good was done to the poor by one convent woman as now by two or three maids'. Her words blend the concepts of charity and service skill in a careful attempt to express the nuns' devotion in secular terms.

As she describes it, the hospital was an institution in which the kinds of work performed, the responsibilities, and the authority attached were assigned by sex. Consequently, the replacement of 'trained' convent women, who commanded a certain respect by virtue of class and religious position, with serving-maids who could draw on neither, meant a more profound shift in the balance of power between men and women in the control of nursing—or, as the petitioner experienced it, her complete subordination to the male officials.

But it was not only secular labour patterns which were disrupted by the Reformation. The division of devotional labour was transformed as well. For evangelicals, prayer for others was not something which could further their salvation, and nuns were no longer seen as providing a community resource of prayer. Thus, one of the early objects of attack were the monastic-run perpetual masses for the dead, organized by female religious institutions as well as by monasteries. The chapel of St Gall, where the women of St Stephen's held many of their votive masses, was

demolished in 1534[106] and the women were forbidden by their
guardians to hold any further anniversaries. But convent women's
especial religious talent was for prayer and singing: St Katherine's
in particular was proud of its choral abilities, and even conducted
a dawn rehearsal in 1517 to make sure that the planned vaulting
of its new church would not impair the sound quality.
(Significantly enough, the chronicler Wilhelm Rem interpreted
this, perhaps wilfully, as an example of convent loose morals.[107])
Yet while the evangelicals were renowned for their love of psalm-
singing, the choral tradition does not appear to have included
a place for exclusively female choirs as opposed to congregational
and male-choir singing. Instead, the pupils of the German school
appear to have played the chief role, with the congregation
singing occasional psalms.[108] After 1537, when the nuns of St
Katherine's were deprived of their choice of spiritual advisers,
it was through singing the office that they maintained the ritual
occasion.[109]

Nuns could express their devotional calling through the
ordering of time, ritual acts, and distinctive clothing—orderings
which also expressed a strong communal sense. As a result, it was
around the apparently trivial issues of clothing and rights over
bell-ringing and church furniture that some of the most bitter
battles between Council and convent were fought. By 1534, only
St Katherine's and St Nicholas's were still permitted to ring their
bells, but since St Nicholas's was situated outside the city, this
concession can have had only limited significance.[110] For St
Katherine's, however, bells represented the ordering of time
according to Catholic principles for both the nuns themselves and
for the townsfolk in the shadow of the church. Its bells chimed
the offices and marked the elevation of the Host instead of
announcing evangelical sermons. Because church bells were
credited with special powers to protect against harm, the question
of their control had special significance. By 1537, however, as
uniformity of worship was established, this control was
transferred to the convent guardians, who used the bells to

[106] Roth, *Augsburgs Reformationsgeschichte*, ii. 191.
[107] *Chroniken der deutschen Städte*, xxv, Rem, p. 54.
[108] Sehling, *Die evangelischen Kirchenordnungen*, Bayern II, p. 64.
[109] *Chroniken der deutschen Städte*, xxiii, Sender, p. 388.
[110] Ibid. 387.

announce the evangelical sermons which the nuns were required
to attend.

One of the first demands that any reformed Council made of
its Catholic convents was always that the women resign their
convent habits in favour of 'honourable worldly clothing'; and
it was this intervention which frequently met with intense
opposition from the nuns. In 1537 the nuns were forbidden to
wear what the Council minute-takers contemptuously referred
to as their 'kutten', and clothes for the women at St Katherine's
were made at the town's expense. In response, the women
secured a privilege advising them to wear their habits underneath
the new garments.[111] While evangelicals might maintain that
'clothing does not make Christians', the right to wear the habit
was important to these women because it remained a uniquely
feminine religious uniform, a badge of their order and their
particular estate. Evangelical men who resigned the monk's garb
could retain the preacher's vestments. The convent habit
desexualized the women in a society in which marital and social
status were coded in clothing—it expressed the women's
fellowship with one another and was the most vivid
demonstration that they belonged to an order, a wider fellowship
beyond the town. City-supplied 'honourable clothing' was thus
an intensely personal demonstration of the nuns' 'integration' and
enforced secularization.

The Reformation also ruptured a form of religiosity which both
bestowed a certain status on holy women and gave women some
stewardship of supernatural power. In a religious world in which
objects could be invested with certain kinds of supernatural
power, women might negotiate some of that sacral power even
without the immediate presence of the male priesthood. At Maria
Stern's there was a miraculous image of the Virgin, and there may
have been some cults attached to the church of St Margaret, helper
in childbirth: over fifty years after its suppression, the memory
of the convent's saint was still vivid enough for Catholics to
petition for its reopening.[112] Control of the furniture of convent
churches might raise similar questions of women's religious

---

[111] StadtAA, Reichsstadt, Prot. der Dreizehn III, fo. 244ʳ, 5 June 1537; Roth,
Augsburgs Reformationsgeschichte, ii. 327.
[112] Baumann, *Maria Stern*, p. 22; StadtAA, Reichsstadt, Lit. 1538, July–Dec.
(St Margaret's), petition 1594.

authority and allegiance. In 1534 the women at St Stephen's were at loggerheads with their guardians, who had seized the church's chalices and monstrances, including a silver monstrance which was carried in the Corpus Christi procession. St Stephen's was a parish church, so the dispute raised the question of to what extent the Catholic women should be able to determine the kind of worship carried out in the parish—the confiscated bowls, chalices, and monstrances all symbolized the centrality of the Host to Catholic devotion.[113] But the incident which most dramatically illustrated both the limitations and the importance of women's sacral roles occurred at St Katherine's, shortly after the Dominican monks had been forbidden to say mass in the convent and the nuns had been ordered to replace the chaplains which they themselves had traditionally appointed with a Council-approved evangelical preacher. Denied spiritual care, the nuns staged a 'dry mass', with neither Host nor wine. According to Sender, some of the nuns were so anguished at the absence of the Host that they fainted.[114] This remarkable liturgy reveals the women's determination to do all within their power, even to the point of almost adopting the priestly functions reserved to men, in order to maintain their form of cultic experience. But it also reveals the scope of their devotional roles, which, in a Host-centred devotion, could not extend to stewardship of the most holy object itself.

It has often been argued that the monastic life placed women's devotions under male control just as surely as did the Protestant model.[115] While it may be true that monks were responsible for directing and supervising women's spiritual development, this can also be viewed as a kind of guarantee of attention from the male religious. Such a system valued and nurtured a specifically feminine style of devotion. Convent women were assured of special pastoral attention, of regular confession and communion,

---

[113] Ibid., Lit. 1534, Nachtrag II/49.
[114] *Chroniken der deutschen Städte*, xxiii, Sender, p. 388. On the dry mass, the *missa sicca*, see A. Franz, *Die Messe im deutschen Mittelalter: Beiträge zur Geschichte der Liturgie und des religiösen Volkslebens*, 2 vols. (Freiburg, 1902), i. 79–84: the dry mass was recognized by theologians but not condoned by the Church. On the importance of the Host in late medieval religion, see C. Zika, 'Hosts, Processions and Pilgrimages in Fifteenth-Century Germany', *Past and Present*, 118 (1988), 25–64.
[115] Davis, 'City Women and Religious Change'.

and, in theory, of a kind of devotional tuition which was not available to their more numerous lay sisters. Intense bonds of attraction and respect—perhaps love—could be established between confessor and holy woman. It is not apparent that evangelical preachers were interested—even in theory—in cultivating women's devotional lives: their object, when preaching to convent women, was to persuade them to join the world, the mixed-sex civic congregation. The failure, despite some plans, to appoint a preacher with specific responsibility for the large group of nuns at St Katherine's perhaps indicates the low priority evangelicals placed on women's spiritual development.[116] Congregationally directed rather than concerned with the spiritual élite, no ongoing group of women had an especial call on the preachers' time—indeed, in the atmosphere of the early Reformation, charged with sexual gossip, this would have been unwise. Perhaps this may go some way towards explaining the dynamic of Caspar Schwenckfeld's intense pastoral relationships with Augsburg women. His correspondence provided the kind of serious attention to women's spiritual development which the Catholic clergy had formerly given.[117]

After 1537, there followed the most curious chapter in the history of the Augsburg convents. To the delight of chroniclers like the fiercely evangelical Jörg Preu, the proud women of St Katherine's were forced to hear the Council's preachers. As Preu recounts it, the women were hostile at first, but on the second occasion 'the Word pleased them a little better'.[118] Preu's mocking tone springs in part from his hostility to the 'big Jacks', whose relatives the convent women were, yet even he apparently welcomed what he saw as the women's gradual conversion and integration.

Yet the narrative disguises the profound paradox of this development. Effectively, the Augsburg Council was sanctioning the continued existence of the convent by simply 'evangelicizing' the institution. It was verring close towards defending a contradiction in terms: the Protestant convent, a possibility it

---

[116] Roth, *Augsburgs Reformationsgeschichte*, ii. 327.
[117] *Corpus Schwenckfeldianorum*, ed. C. Hartranft *et al.*, *passim*. See also G. Boanas and L. Roper, 'Feminine Piety in Fifteenth Century Rome: Santa Francesca Romana', in Obelkevich, *Disciplines of Faith*.
[118] *Chroniken der deutschen Städte*, xxix, Preu, p. 80.

never entertained in the case of male monasteries. Thus, women whom the reformers thought ought to marry and be incorporated into households, and who, they had argued, ought never to have been placed in all-female institutions, were now to remain in the convents with the full backing of the town's evangelical authorities. And such developments proved durable: in neighbouring Ulm, which remained Protestant, the evangelicized civic convent endured until secularization in 1808.[119]

Protestantization in Augsburg was successful, but only partially so. In St Katherine's (still by far the city's largest convent, its architecture a visible echo of the church of its Dominican brothers) an evangelical prioress took office and was succeeded by a second, evangelical prioress without the convent being either hopelessly split or destroyed. Evangelical sermons were preached for over a decade, but while some of the sisters attended, others simply avoided them. In some convents, women remained but lived an evangelical life or devised their own compromises—thus Helena Fugger remained in the convent of Maria Stern and continued to hold convent office, but gave up her professed vows and did not attend confession.[120] The wheel came full circle when, in 1547, Dominican visitors inspected St Katherine's, deposed the prioress, and demanded the reinstitution of the habit; and a few years later, Catholicism was forcibly restored to the convent of Maria Stern.[121] This time the defeated Council was powerless to help, and though the prioress of St Katherine's told the visitors that she was not answerable to officials who had not even appointed her, resistance was useless. She and six other nuns left the convent.[122]

What is remarkable about the process of re-Catholicization is, firstly, the time-lapse between the return of the Catholic clergy and the actual implementation of Catholicism in the convents. It was some time before either convent became orthodox again, and only the hierarchy of the order, not forces within the

---

[119] K. Frank, 'Die Franziskanerterziarinnen in der Ulmer Sammlung', in H. Specker and H. Tüchle (eds.), *Kirchen und Klöster in Ulm* (Ulm, 1979).

[120] See complaints on the new Ordinance of 1539: StadtAA, KWA ad B26/III, St. Katharina, 22 Aug. 1539; Baumann, *Maria Stern*, p. 26.

[121] Roth, *Augsburgs Reformationsgeschichte*, iv. 203–6 (St Katherine's); iii. 485–6, 516 n. 170; iv. 203–4; iii 486 (Maria Stern's).

[122] Ibid. iii. 516 n. 170.

convents, could bring about the change. Secondly, the departure of the ex-prioress of St Katherine's and seven others accounted for at least a third, and perhaps even a majority, of the membership during the 1540s. It follows that either the convent had continued as nominally Protestant during the Reformation with less than majority support—which would have meant coexistence of a sizeable, but powerful Protestant faction alongside a Catholic majority during those years—or else numbers of the women had quietly changed sides. In either case, it is clear that different confessions could exist together in a convent for long periods of time. And it suggests, too, that for both Catholic and evangelical women alike, confessional allegiance may even have been less important than the maintenance of a collective, devotional possibility.

SOUL-WOMEN

Soul-houses were lay charitable institutions where deserving poor might be accommodated in return for prayer for the soul of the founder. At first sight they appear simply to have been monastic institutions for those women without the means to provide the dowries usually demanded by convents. But their strikingly different fates during the Reformation, and the startling absence of any serious polemical attack on these houses, show that their positions in civic life were quite distinct.[123] If nuns embodied a form of life which was inevitably at odds with the secular world, soul-houses represented an institutional mixture which was far closer to lay life, combining charitable work, religious paid labour, and poor-relief. If there are close parallels with the beguine houses of lay religious sisterhoods or with women of the third Franciscan order, there are striking differences too. Soul-women could leave the house to marry or simply for good reason; they could be expelled for misbehaviour. Far more closely tied to the benefaction of a particular individual or family, they had no definite position within a wider religious hierarchy; while their own sense of community appears often to have been limited by

---

[123] My analysis thus differs slightly from Kiessling, *Bürgerliche Gesellschaft*, pp. 225–30, 238–40.

the institution's hierarchical rather than communitarian structure—important decisions usually rested in the hands of the benefactor and guardians. The social class from which soul-women were drawn was far lower: of the fifty-six women listed in the tax-books as *Seelfrauen* between 1534 and 1542, only four owned enough to raise them above the *Habnichts* class of those without taxable assets, and many were not even citizens.[124]

Augsburg possessed six such houses, one of which, the Breyschuh house, had disbanded by 1530.[125] The other five— the Rufin, the Bachin, the Herwart, the Gwerlich, and the Hirn houses—showed a remarkable resilience to the Reformation. Despite the virulence of the attacks on the system of paid masses for the dead, soul-women seem rarely to have been the butt of pamphleteers, though they were equally implicated in earning money through prayer for the souls of the dead. Just as it had done in the case of women's convents, the Council proceeded in at least one house, the Herwart foundation, by offering the women annuities if they left, but it does not appear to have persisted with the scheme here or in any other house. The Herwart house was not finally closed until the 1570s.[126] By this date it had become derelict, but its numbers did not appear to drop during the years of the Reformation itself: on the contrary, they were maintained at between five and six, and there was a stable flow of new recruits before and after 1537.[127] The other

---

[124] See tables 6.3 and 6.4 in my 'Work, Marriage and Sexuality: Women in Reformation Augsburg', Ph.D. thesis (London, 1985), pp. 339 ff.; and StadtAA, Reichsstadt, Steuerbücher 1534–42.

[125] A. Werner, *Die örtlichen Stiftungen für die Zwecke des Unterrichts und der Wohltätigkeit in der Stadt Augsburg*, 2 vols. (Augsburg, 1889, 1912), i. 21; A. Herberger, 'Die Seelhäuser und die Seelgeräthe in Augsburg: Aus dem Nachlasse des Archivar Herberger', *ZHVS* 3 (1876), 283–96, here pp. 287–9.

[126] The Herwarts sold the house to the Fugger in 1573 for 700 gulden (StadtAA, Reichsstadt, Stuftungen, Herwart 15/12) (the house was empty), and the land was incorporated into the vast Fugger enclave. Note also a sale (RS 30 Sept. 1557) of 8 houses by Hans Heinrich Herwart to Christoff Fugger. On the foundation's assets, see Stiftungen, Herwart 14, 15.

[127] See, however, Werner, *Die örtlichen Stiftungen*, p. 21, and Herberger, 'Die Seelhäuser und Seelgeräte', p. 288: they wrongly state that the Herwart *Seelhaus* disappears from the tax-books in 1534 and was closed by the Council in 1537 (see also Roth, *Augsburgs Reformationsgeschichte*, ii. 322 and 349 n. 61). This is not the case, as the consistent tax-book entries and names of new admissions in 1534 and beyond prove. According to StadtAA, Reichsstadt, Prot. der Dreizehn III, fo. 245ʳ, 9 June 1537, the 5 women in the house were to be

houses accommodated the Reformation by following the religious convictions of their founders: the Bachin house, supported by the Rem family, became a Protestant institution, but there was no apparent change in its membership.[128] Numbers even increased in 1539, perhaps a generous gesture by the Rem as a result of their elevation to the patriciate the previous year. Less is known about the Gwerlich foundation, but it too survived until the Thirty Years War; while the Hirn foundation maintained its numbers throughout the period. The Rufin house remained extremely active, giving shelter to a total of twenty-three women over the period 1534–42.

So far as can be ascertained from the surviving records, the existence of these institutions never became an issue of controversy, despite both their resemblance to monastic foundations and their traffic in specially reserved, bought prayer. Indeed, the new civic, enlarged foundation of St Jacob's evidenced considerable similarity to the female soul-house, though it was open to both sexes. Offering board and lodging to worthy Augsburgers, it too required them to pray, though not for individually named souls.[129]

The duties of the sisters were a strange mixture of charitable works and religious expertise. At least by the beginning of the sixteenth century the sisters had become responsible for some nursing work, and their contract of admittance committed the women to doing whatever nursing work they were called upon to do, except in cases of pox and plague. Unlike other convents, the women were responsible for seeing to the housework themselves—a provision which reflects the kind of labour it was thought fitting for women of such low social status to perform. Those unable to do such work were denied entry to a house, and once admitted, each had to promise to do her share on her allotted day of the week, or else a weekly rota was arranged.[130]

---

bought *Leibgedinge*, but there is no mention of closure. From Prot. der Dreizehn IV, fo. 19ʳ, 10 Feb. 1538, in which the Council advises against the readmission of one unruly woman, it is clear that the house was continuing with Council support.

[128] Werner, *Die örtlichen Stiftungen*, p. 21.

[129] StBA Cod. Aug. 2o, 300.

[130] For such contracts, see StadtAA, Reichsstadt, Stiftungen, Herwart 14; US 23 Apr. 1500 (Hirn); US 27 Feb. 1505 (Bach); KWA L67 (Bach) includes contracts dated 1 Aug. 1535, Margaret Niessin; 5 Dec. 1533, Anna Bältzin; 20 Oct. 1531, Bärbel Wellerin—all admitted by the Rem brothers.

But the women's chief work was that of prayer for the souls of the dead. An important part of the ritual involved in the annual perpetual anniversaries for the dead which could be purchased from local churches, soul-sisters had a particular role in the division of labour surrounding death. Though it was a male priest who must read the masses for the dead, sound the bell, and cense the church, the work of prayer over the grave of the dead person was reserved to women. Usually this involved a full night's vigil of prayer, with four candles, at the side of the grave itself. It was therefore a more private, personal devotion that the mass, which need not be said at the site of the grave. One woman only was customarily required to perform the nightly vigil, though normally the whole community of soul-women was paid to attend the morning service, mass, and sacrifice. The women were paid individually for their contribution, or else a small sum for their personal use was shared equally between them.[131] Thus their work was individually rewarded and recognized, rather than enriching the foundation, just as the priests who said mass were paid. In this sense they formed part of the clerical proletariat, and the amount they received was not much less than that extended to the priests who said mass, the sexton, and the other attendants.

None the less, the women's proportional share of the total capital was small. The amount paid for a perpetual mass varied considerably, but at least 20 gulden was usual, with some foundations involving sums of 100 gulden. This capital was passed to the church which administered the mass: the soul-house itself did not profit from the donation. Anniversaries were thus a form of pious bequest which enriched the church or monastic foundation—which then acted as semi-contractors to the soul-houses. The church or monastery appears to have had a more or less consistent arrangement with one or another house: the Hirn house was normally associated with anniversaries from the adjoining Carmelite priory at St Anna, though masses for St Peter's are recorded as well. The Herwart house, on the other hand, was customarily associated with Franciscan masses. Here geography

---

[131] For examples, see ibid., US 8 Aug. 1501; US 24 Mar. 1505; US 8 Apr. 1507; US 8 July 1521; US 26 June 1515; US 24 Jan. 1519; Stiftungen, Herwart 13 (collection).

was not so evidently the determining factor, since the house, opposite the church of St Maurice, was some distance from the Franciscan monastery. All of the houses, despite the poverty of their female inhabitants, were situated in the prosperous regions from which the donors of perpetual masses were mainly drawn. The Ruf, Herwart, and Bach houses clustered around the area near the current Maximilianstrasse; the Hirn house nestled against the Carmelite priory.

However, between the soul-houses themselves there were subtle gradations of prestige, class, and style. Soul-women might be paid as little as 5 pence per woman for attending a mass, or as much as 15. Surviving documents show that women from the Hirn house tended to receive more than those from the Herwart foundation. Though the Hirn foundation housed only four women, the church of St Anna enjoyed considerable popularity among the richer urban élite in the late fifteenth and early sixteenth centuries, while the Franciscan church which provided most of the anniversaries at which the Herwart women prayed, catered for some who were not quite so well off. The Hirn house took citizen women almost exclusively, and its membership remained the most stable during our period, while the Rufin house, despite its comparatively large assets, housed many women for short periods only.

For admission a woman required sponsors, and the extant lists indicate that most women were sponsored by craftsmen or low-ranking church officials such as sextons—low-level patronage which reveals yet more clearly their rootedness in the world of the petty tradespeople and day-labourers.[132] So also, as we saw, if the money paid to the soul-sisters was in some sense a pious donation, in another sense payment for their work of prayer, it was not a fixed fee but a gratuity for service. On the other hand, the institution itself was seldom the object of pious bequests—unlike the convents, monasteries, churches, and charitable institutions of the city. Thus, if the social origins of soul-sisters appear to have been fairly homogeneous, their social peers were not the people for whom they were paid to pray. Even as serving-

---

[132] Professions of witnesses include the stockman at Our Lady's cathedral, a former baker (twice); 2 sextons, 1 satchel-maker, 1 cobbler, 1 purse-maker, 1 weaver, 1 tax-collector. See n. 131 above.

women, the occupation they might otherwise have chosen, they would have been more likely to service people from, or nearer to, their own class. The manner of their payment separated them clearly from convent life. Without a powerful institution behind them, devoid of wider ecclesiastical or monastic links, the patterns of the women's lives identified them rather with the class they had left.

So also, soul-women escaped the convent women's ambiguities of sexual status. Some were married (at least after the Reformation),[133] many were widowed, and many left to marry again. The qualities of the 'good soul-sister' were also cast less exclusively in holy terms, and were couched more often in the language of civic respectability. According to the contract of admission, a soul-woman was to be strong enough to do her own share of housework, God-fearing, peaceable, good-tempered, and quiet.[134] Jakob Hausstetter specified in his testament that he wanted a soul-woman 'of widow's estate, but if there be no widow, a woman who is otherwise pious and God-fearing'.[135] She need not, therefore, be an untouched, virginal woman. It is interesting that Hausstetter first envisaged a widow, for 'the good widow' is both the standard image of the deserving woman devoid of kin resources who is therefore worthy of charity, and the mature, post-sexual, post-maternal female. Her incorporation in the house of soul-women includes her in the community and removes her from a position which might otherwise be viewed as insecure and threatening. By praying for the families of others, she is drawn into a network of households and kin just as a servant might be 'adopted' conceptually into the household in which she is living. Yet the soul-woman was also perceived as less holy than the nun. Her less exalted sexual status, her markedly lower class, her involvement in menial work, all combined to situate her more closely in the world of the urban and mundane.

As a mode of charity, soul-houses seem to have been particularly favoured by women. Thus, though the Bachin house

---

[133] Thus Anna Pruncktucher from Herwart soul-house is listed in the 1539 tax-book as 'dt heurnil', an indication that she married in that year; while she paid 30d 6d in 1540 (StadtAA, Reichsstadt, Steuerbücher 1540, fo. 55d; 1541, fo. 56b).

[134] See ibid., Stiftungen, Herwart 15/7, 1470.

[135] StBA Jakob Hausstetters Testament, revised in 1496: Kiessling, *Bürgerliche Gesellschaft*, p. 237.

was administered by the Rem family, it bore the name of the foundress, a Rem by marriage, and the Herwart house continued to be known during the early fifteenth century by the name of an earlier administrator, the Vogelerin.[136] Many of the houses were referred to by the female form of the family name. Women seem frequently to have been in control of the administration of the foundation. Most of the documents from the Herwart foundation are sealed by a woman guardian, most commonly a Herwart by marriage, and documents from the period of the dissolution of the institution mention the practice of awarding guardianship to 'the oldest of the Herwart women'; that is, the wife of the oldest Herwart man.

One long dispute over the control of the Herwart foundation illustrates the complexities of this form of pious charity, controlled to a large extent by women, yet considered to be part of the charitable patrimony of a male-defined family. In 1453 the Herwart family succeeded in wresting full control of the house from the claims of the Nördlinger family and a woman called Sighart.[137] The Herwarts argued that they had taken over the house from the Eulentaler family. A woman named Ehinger, a Herwart on her mother's side, had run the house for a period of thirty years—on the family's behalf, the Herwarts claimed. When she died, control had reverted to the family. Sighartin did not contest Ehingerin's control of the house, but asserted that Ehingerin had bequeathed the soul-house and all relevant documents to her and to Jörg Nördlinger as her nearest kin. Sighartin had then run the house, delegating authority to one of the Herwart men on occasion, or to one of the Nördlingers. As the vehemence of the dispute suggests, the patronage which it afforded the women who were its guardians was not inconsiderable—indeed, the court case had been sparked off by Sighart's determination to admit a woman to the house who had been rejected by the Herwarts.

Since the Herwarts complained that they did not have the house's documentation, it does seem probable that Ehingerin had indeed bequeathed the foundation to her own nearest kin, treating the institution which she had run unhindered for thirty

---

[136] StadtAA, Reichsstadt, Stiftungen, Herwart 14, 31 Aug. 1482.
[137] Ibid., Stiftungen, Herwart 15/4.

years as her own rather than as the charity of the Herwart family.
But the judges ruled in favour of the family's claim, and in so
doing, strengthened the view that the charity was one which
remained in the male line of the Herwarts, to be run by their wives
rather than transferred from mother to daughter. Identified with
familial largesse rather than with individual feminine piety, their
transmission in the line was henceforward much more
rule-bound.

Indeed, the lay, familial aspect of the houses' administration
also helps to account for the ease with which the soul-houses were
loosely incorporated into the civic administration, and their
exemption from the type of Reformation polemic used to such
effect against the convents. Though they too were a group of
women, soul-house inhabitants had little sense of being a
collectivity and no authority whatsoever over their institution's
administration or policy, or even over its religious alignment.
Unlike convents, soul-houses almost never feature in diaries or
chronicles of the city, and even their architecture was so
undistinctive that it is hard to locate them on contemporary maps
of the city. Viewed as unfortunate individuals, the objects of
charity rather than as an active group of self-determining subjects,
the soul-house women's lot harmonized with their prescribed
class and feminine roles. Since it was a commonplace of sixteenth-
century charity that poor women were a deserving category, soul-
houses could easily be subsumed under the umbrella of civic
charity and citizen largesse.

7

The Holy Family

IN the Augsburg of the Reformation era, the notion of civic righteousness provided the yardstick for individual and collective moral behaviour. The Council called for a city which would be without sin. It believed that the social, economic, and moral order of the miniature cosmos of the household workshop should become the pattern for all Augsburgers, whatever their social status. Economic well-being, civic security, moral purity, social order, and true belief were considered to be inseparably connected; so much so that in 1546, when the city faced the grave crisis of the outbreak of war, the Council responded by publishing a mandate intensifying sexual discipline, exhorting the citizens to a modest, God-fearing, and sober life, and calling for civic prayer. The danger and disorder which threatened from without was to be countered by perfecting the citizens' inner lives, trusting in God.

Discipline and order, qualities which the Council elevated to the status of moral and religious values, were thought of as the defining characteristics of the pious household, where the distinct offices of master, mistress, children, and servants were structured in a hierarchy of benign authority of age over youth, master over servant, and man over woman. It was a patriarchal ideal which sanctified the existing exclusion of women from independent household-workshop enterprise, and from political power. It glorified the relations of property which made married women's rights to property uncertain by evoking the ideology of joint control. Yet if the Council did little to protect women's interests, even when (as in cases of marital violence) it claimed to be most sympathetic to them, this does not mean that it was impossible for women to enjoy satisfying lives in the household-workshop economy.[1] Often, the value placed on marital sharing could give

---

[1] S. Rowbotham, 'What Do Women Want? Woman-Centred Values and the World as it Is', *Feminist Review*, 20 (1985), 49–70.

the mistress of a household considerable responsibility and involvement in an enterprise in which her work was essential and valued. The fusion between work and domestic space, between adult labour and child care, could produce warm emotional relations and, on men's part, a familiarity with children and how to care for them.[2]

Evangelical religion was the faith of the guild and the household. Even the manner of its initial dissemination in towns, through guild friendships and drinking-circles, suggests how closely it was bound up with the world of the crafts. Its distinctive place can best be grasped by comparing its success with other, more diffuse movements of religious renewal: Anabaptism and spiritualism. What even contemporaries could not fail to notice was the remarkable involvement of women in such sects. The records of interrogation and punishment reveal that half or more than half of those dealt with in the great campaign of 1527–8 and in the 1530s and 1540s were female, and women were amongst the most persistent reoffenders. Particularly in view of the tendency to under-report women in such 'crimes', their frequent appearance before the Council is unusual. Religious unorthodoxy was one of the rare categories in which women came close to outnumbering men.[3]

But Anabaptism and spiritualism remained small, scattered groupings of enthusiasts. Women's involvement was not unrelated to this fact. Both Anabaptism and spiritualism, which rejected the formal institutional Church of buildings and office-holding, were primarily based on household forms of association, the arena over which women had most control. As many of the male Anabaptists became involved with missionary work or were exiled from the town, the local movement came increasingly to depend on the women who remained, often the wives of the male

---

[2] See e.g. StadtAA, Reichsstadt, Urg. 6 Mar. 1534, Walpurg Frosch: she describes first asking Lienhart Numenbeck's *Knecht* to go to her house and quieten her child; and then Numenbeck himself undertaking to go to her house to comfort her child. See also Chap. 1 above, on children and work.

[3] On Anabaptism in Augsburg, see F. Roth, 'Zur Geschichte der Wiedertäufer in Oberschwaben', *ZHVS* 27 (1900), 1–45; 28 (1901), 1–154; and F. Uhland, *Täufertum und Obrigkeit* and on the importance of women in Anabaptist meetings, see e.g. in addition, StadtAA, Reichsstadt, Urg. 21 June 1533, Gall Launer; 3–6 Mar. 1533, Elisabeth Laux; 7 Mar. 1533, Sixt Bartholome; 3 Mar. 1533, Sabina Hieber; 5 Mar. 1533, Barbara Nessler; RB 19/II, fo. 1, 1 Aug. 1545.

Anabaptists. By holding meetings in their houses, they kept the congregations together and themselves became crucial figures in the movement's cohesion—a doubly important role in a Church so fragmented and clandestine. Conversions often followed household rather than guild lines, in striking contrast to the patterns of the spread of the early Reformation.

Whether through force of circumstance or by design, women occupied a pivotal place in unorthodox religious sects which they never attained in mainstream evangelicalism. Christ himself appeared to the spiritualist Katharina Kunig, holding the Cross in his hand and speaking with a human voice. God told her that she must run about in all the streets, calling on everyone to change their ways or else he would punish the world. Even though, on consideration, she decided this would only make her look a fool and would do God's cause no good, and that it was better to lobby the preachers to carry the message for her, she prophesied that there would be great bloodshed in Augsburg and in all Germany unless people repented and reformed.[4] Kunig was interrogated by the Council on suspicion of Anabaptism. At one level, her theology, with its preoccupation with moral regeneration, repentance, and divine vengeance, rang the same changes as that of the Council. But Kunig had no respect for the now established rituals of the new Church in Augsburg or for its baptisms, which she saw as mere externals—one must be baptized in the blood of the Spirit. For their part, the reformed preachers would accept neither these feminine visions nor a woman's claims to special communication with the Almighty, who had, after all, made his views plain in the Scriptures, and these were best interpreted by the learned civic clergy.

Moral discipline in reformed Augsburg was a matter for Council concern and not for self-appointed female enthusiasts' exhortations. With the Reformation, the vision of morality which had its origins in a pre-existing civic mentality was given new force and confidence by the mainstream religious movement. Now religious and lay authorities concurred, broadly, in the images they invoked and the conception of morality with which each of them operated; while the actual responsibility for disciplining the expanded group of moral subjects rested with

---

[4] Ibid., Urg. 6 May 1544, Katharina Kunig.

the new, powerful institutions created by the city Council. The new moralism found its fullest expression in the Discipline Ordinance of 1537, which proceeded by undertaking a full-scale moral reordering of all human relationships, particularly sexual relations.

While acceptable sexual practices in the sixteenth century were heterosexual, this does not mean that other varieties of sexuality went unrecognized. In a brief paragraph on sexual offences, the 1537 Ordinance condemned 'damned, forbidden copulation', which it did not define further.[5] It referred instead to the provisions of imperial law, which more clearly define such transgressions 'against nature' as commingling of humans with beasts, man with man, and woman with woman.[6] Despite the ordinance's reticence, one ring of men who had committed homosexual acts had been discovered, interrogated, and sentenced in the early 1530s. These trials had involved the Council in a protracted and detailed investigation of male homosexuality and its forms and practices in Augsburg.[7]

The trials of these men in the 1530s uncovered a domesticated homosexuality. Michel Will, a weaver, was married; his partners were other craftsmen; and their recreations were those of other disorderly Augsburgers—drinking, travelling to villages for recreation, dalliances with women.[8] One of the offenders was a

---

[5] 'Solt yemand zu sollicher gotlosen vnsinnigkait geraten | der sich wider die Natur | oder Satzung der Kaiserlichen Recht | vnd also mit verdampter vermischung vergriffe | der soll nach erkanntnus ains Erbern Rats | am Gut | leib | oder leben | ernnstlich gestrafft werden': *Ains Erbern Rats | der Stat Augspurg | Zucht vnd Pollicey Ordnung*, Augsburg, 1537, fo. b/iᵛ.

[6] See *Die Peinliche Gerichtsordnung Kaiser Karls V von 1532*, ed. A. Kaufmann, 4th edn. (Stuttgart, 1975), p. 78, headed: 'Straff der vnkeusch, so wider die natur beschicht.' It reads: 'Item so eyn mensch mit eynem vihe, mann mit mann, weib mit weib, vnkeusch treiben, die haben auch das leben verwürckt, vnd man soll sie der gemeynen gewonheyt nach mit dem fewer vom leben zum todt richten.'

[7] See StadtAA, Reichsstadt, Urg. 1 May 1532, Christoff Schmid (priest); Urg. 1 May 1532, Bernhard Wagner; Urg. 6 May 1532, Jacob Miller (executed and burnt, 8 June 1532); Urg. 11 May 1532, Hans Purckhart; Urg. 4 June 1532, Bernhart Wagner (executed and burnt, 8 June 1532); Urg. 4 May 1532, Philipp Zeller (schoolmaster at St George's; now married; involved ten years before; left hand cut off and exiled); Urg. 19 Mar. 1534 and 1 Dec. 1533, Michel Will. The case is also mentioned in Achilles Gasser, *Annales des vetustate originis, amoenitate situs . . . (Scriptores Rerum Germanicarum*, ed. G. Menck, 3 vols.; Leipzig, 1728–30: vol. i, no. xvii), p. 1793.

[8] StadtAA, Reichsstadt, Urg. 16 Nov. 1529, Wolf Keck: both Georg Rumler and Bernhard Wagner were involved in this case, both being accused of adultery with Keck's wife.

priest, and several of those named were 'from St Maurice's', but while this could fuel anticlerical feeling in the town, it could not obliterate the manifestly lay, civic location of the crime.[9] The threat which male homosexuality posed was directed at the household, for it subverted the canons of masculinity. Michel Will was punished for murder and attempted rape as well as for homosexual acts, but his interrogation and those of the other men concentrated on discovering the exact details of the men's sexual encounters: whether anal penetration had taken place, but also what had been the precise course of events, even in manual masturbation. Both literally and metaphorically, male homosexual acts inverted the sexual division of labour. They undermined the hierarchies of the household and the boundaries between male and female—hence the Council's obsession with the details of a kind of sexual stimulation which did not accord with its notion of the male sexual role.

Men who repeatedly engaged in homosexual acts offended against the civic community to the point where they had to be destroyed, literally reduced to ashes. Execution followed by burning was a form of punishment which, though it was not coupled with an explicit denunciation of homosexuality as blasphemy, reproduced the pre-Reformation categorization of it as a variety of heresy for which the punishment was burning. The language of 'nature' which the 1537 Ordinance also adopted, cast the homosexual as a freak of nature, a kind of monster.[10] Interestingly, the ordinance wavered on the issue of responsibility, describing such men as 'falling into such godless insensibility', language which is reminiscent of its description of

---

[9] Of those named in the 1532 trials, 1 was a priest and a further 3 named by Jacob Miller were 'at St Maurice'; while Philipp Zeller was a schoolmaster at St George's. Miller was a baker; Purckhart made *Lebzelten*; Will and Rumler were weavers; Wagner was a fruiterer. Note also that Sigmund Welser, a patrician, was implicated—he was not, so far as the records reveal, interrogated or punished. On priests and homosexuality in pamphlet literature, see also Bartholomaeus Bernhardi, *Schutzrede vor Bartholomeo der ein eehweib so er priester ist gen umen hat*, Erfurt, [M. Maler], 1522, fo. B/iii, where he complains of the 'ergerniss' caused by priests to 'Junckfrawenn | Frawenn | vnnd knabenn'.

[10] On the meanings of monsters, see K. Park and L. Daston, 'Unnatural Conceptions: The Study of Monsters in Sixteenth- and Seventeenth-Century France and England', *Past and Present*, 92 (1981), 20–54; and note especially the Reformation image of the monk-calf. See R. Scribner, *For the Sake of Simple Folk* (Cambridge, 1981), pp. 129–36.

drunkards and implied that even God-fearing Augsburgers risked falling.

Female homosexuality did not excite the same overt response. Though the barrage of anti-convent writings may have been driven by the spectre of lesbian nuns, and was certainly directed against all-women institutions, it was explicitly expressed as a fear of the nuns' heterosexual lusts only.[11]

But, as Judith Brown's fascinating book about the seventeenth-century Sister Benedetta Carlini, *Immodest Acts*,[12] has reminded us, lesbianism was a known sin. Indeed, the contemporary chronicler of the Counts of Zimmern casually reports the death of a serving-woman thus:

There was also at that time a poor serving-girl at Mösskirch, who served here and there, and she was called Greta . . . She did not take any man or young apprentice, nor would she stand at the bench with any such [i.e. work with them as husband and wife and sell his goods], but loved the young daughters, went after them and bought them pedlars' goods, and she also used all bearing and manners, as if she had a masculine *affect*. She was often considered to be a hermaphrodite or androgyne, but this did not prove to be the case, for she was investigated by cunning, and was seen to be a true, proper woman. To note: she was said to be born under an inverted, unnatural constellation. But amongst the learned and well-read one finds that this sort of thing is often encountered among the Greeks and Romans, although this is to be ascribed rather to the evil customs of those corrupted nations, plagued by sins, than to the course of the heavens or stars.[13]

The chronicler's matter-of fact recording of this curiosity indicates that the idea of 'unnatural acts' between women did not lie outside his mental map. So, too, although unnatural love between women made no appearance in the rhetorical armoury of the evangelical pamphleteers, it may appear in submerged form in the accusations made against the procuress, the corrupter of young maidens who, stealing the place of the virtuous mother, initiated young innocents into venereal arts. Using the language

[11] See e.g. Bernhart Rem, *Ain Sendtbrieff an ettlich Closterfrawen zu sant katherina vnd zu sant niclas in Augspurg*, [Augsburg, P. Ulhart], 1523.

[12] J. Brown, *Immodest Acts: The Life of a Lesbian Nun in Renaissance Italy* (Oxford, 1986).

[13] *Die Chronik der Grafen von Zimmern*, ed. H. M. Decker-Hauff, 3 vols. (Stuttgart, 1967), ii. 212. See E. Hobby, 'Seventeenth Century Lesbianism: First Steps', forthcoming, for an analysis of this passage.

of sorcery usually reserved to the passionate love felt by men for women, Catharina Ziegler's mother claimed that the procuress who had kidnapped her daughter had predicted that Catharina would not stay with her; and from this, both Ziegler and her mother concluded that 'if she did not stay with her then she must have somehow bewitched her'. The Council, too, viewed this charge very seriously and demanded of the procuress: 'Since Catharina Ziegler complains that she cannot remain without her, Lemplin, she must reveal what she did to her, and whether she has not bewitched her.'

But such allegations remained submerged rather than open currents of anti-monastic or misogynist polemic. Lesbian relationships, if they existed, are unremarked; and even two nuns who lived together for over a decade after the dissolution of the convent of St Katherine were never, apparently, accused of 'loving the young daughters' or 'having a masculine *affect*'. Sexual acts between women were not unthinkable—they were named in the Imperial Law Code of 1532 to which the Discipline Ordinance of 1537 explicitly referred in the statute on 'damnable, forbidden commingling'. The Italian humanist pornographers, with whose works some of Augsburg's merchant élite must certainly have been acquainted, imagined lesbian nuns engaged in orgies using dildos,[14] a persistent male fantasy; and a satirical New Year's-greeting etching of three naked witches, sent to a cleric by the painter Hans Baldung, teased its male viewers with hardly disguised hints of female perversions.[15]

More commonly, however, popular culture exploited the theme of the rapacious woman who stole men's codpieces and unmanned them. One woodcut of about 1533 by Erhard Schoen even depicts this metaphor literally—a woman is shown whipping a pitiful man who is harnessed and pulling a cart laden with washing. Over her arm is slung the codpiece she has captured, while at her side she clutches another phallic symbol, a sword. She exults in her power and raises the whip with undisguised glee (see Plate 11). Such woodcuts tickled their audiences not by depicting a woman tyrannizing other women, but by inverting

---

[14] See e.g. *Aretino's Dialogues*, trans. R. Rosenthal (London, 1972).
[15] S. Schade, *Schadenzauber und Magie des körpers* (Worms, 1983), pp. 112 f.

11. Erhard Schoen, *The Prize of the Devout Woman*. (Geisberg no. 1176, *c*.1533).
The accompanying verses have a speech for each character. The woman who
whips her husband points out how difficult it is for beautiful young women to
put up with poor clothes, hunger, and housekeeping: if the man wants a pious
wife, he should stay at home and work, or else he will be forced to wash and
sweep. The man bewails his fate and warns those who marry before they have
a trade-skill and money: his life is a misery and his wife has made off with his
purse, sword, and codpiece. The young man on the right is worried by this scene,
but the virgin reassures him that if he is a man in all things, then she wants no
such power over men. The woman-fool advises the man to avoid marriage
altogether, to live it up and take a concubine; but the old man warns against the
wiles of such women.

the natural order as she lorded it over men. She was pictured as
obtaining her mastery through her sexual energy, and shown
dressed in rich clothes and jewels. The ultimate representation
of her conquest was her riding of men, an image redolent with
sexual significance. *The Power of Womanhood* by Peter Flötner
(see Plate 5) illustrates a poem by Hans Sachs, and shows the
'woman on top' subjecting even the most rational of men, an
Aristotle, to her own boundless lust, while he is made foolish by
his susceptibility to her charms. Yet her lust was imagined as
heterosexual lust. In the secular world, the effect of the
Reformation was to enshrine marriage, the union between the
sexes, as the foundation of social existence, while simultaneously

presenting women as a perpetual threat to order—economic, social, and moral. These were the overt themes of Council prescription and popular culture; but they hid an uneasy recognition that lust might not always be 'natural'.

THEMES OF FEMININE PIETY IN CATHOLIC AND EVANGELICAL RELIGION

If reformed moralism might be described as determinedly patriarchal and heterosexual, reformed religion was relentlessly Christocentric. The range of saints' days and the long cycle of Marian feasts were dropped, and only the Christ-cycle of feasts (including the Annunciation) continued to be celebrated in reformed Augsburg.[16] In place of the diverse multitude of saints' cults, the range of objects and places which were holy, and the variety of ways of expressing devotion, evangelical Protestantism, whether aligned with 'Lutheran' or 'Zwinglian' tendencies, made the boundaries between holy and profane more precise and centred devotion on the figure of Christ. Paradoxically, a religious understanding which at first rejected the sacrament of ordination and the religious hierarchy of priesthood which was based upon it, came to define the central religious act of worship as the hearing of the Word of God; that is, the sermon. This conception of the Christian life made the preacher as indispensable as the priest had been; in fact, more so, since holy images and objects, once blessed, were efficacious without the presence of a priest. Prayer, on the other hand, was a perpetual exercise to which all Christians were called. But its effects were unknown and uncertain. Religion entered daily life in a different fashion—for Protestants, the prayerful attitude was a permanent state of mind. But it also had to be consciously welded into older, familiar rituals. So, in the middle and late years of the sixteenth century, Protestant divines tried to protestantize such rituals as the rites of passage, exhorting Christians to pray before the bed on their wedding-night rather than participate in traditional rough foolery.

---

[16] StadtAA, Reichsstadt, RB 16, fo. 126ᵛ, 3 July 1537. So also Straf auf den Stuben, 1538(?), Fasz. Zuchtordnungen: swearing in the name of Christ, God, the Incarnation, or communion were punishable; but oaths using the name of Mary or the saints were not mentioned.

Catholics and Protestants used the register of sexual difference very differently. Catholic Augsburg was a city whose topography was a grid of historical reminders of holy men and women. One could walk from the area near the cathedral where St Hilaria had first settled with her daughter, past the site of the convent of St Martin where Hilaria had stayed, to the area near St Ulric and St Afra where St Afra had lived.[17] The sense of civic pride and tradition rested on the part which women saints as well as male saints had played. St Afra, the ex-prostitute, one of the two patrons of the city, had appeared to the town's troops in the famous battle of the Lech in 955 and saved the city;[18] the first investigations of the crypt of St Ulric and St Afra, so important to a monk like Johannes Frank in discovering a sense of the civic past, brought to light the bones of St Digna and the other virgin martyrs as well as those of St Simpert.[19] A church like St Ulric and St Afra, which advertised its great stock of holy relics in a late fifteenth-century broadsheet, listed thirty-one reliquaries containing relics of male saints, and a further twenty containing relics of female saints;[20] relics which were powerful in relation to specific female experiences, such as childbirth, menstrual disorders, and breast diseases. Perhaps it is not remarkable that women should have so outnumbered men in the lists of those punished for attending Catholic services in the villages around Augsburg.[21]

---

[17] Die *Chroniken der deutschen Städte vom 14. bis ins 16. Jahrhundert*, 36 vols. (Leipzig 1862–1931), iv. 290.

[18] Ibid. 295.

[19] Ibid. xxv, Franks Annalen, pp. 302 f.

[20] *Ursprung und Anfang Augsburgs* [Augsburg, Johann Bämler, 14]83, bound with Hagiologium of St Ulric and St Afra. A further 3 reliquaries contained unidentified holy remains; 3 contained relics of both male and female saints and martyrs; and 6 only of the reliquaries were Christocentric, containing relics related to Christ's passion, birth, etc. However, a comparison of the number of mentions of saints and martyrs presents a slightly different pattern: while 8 were Christ-related and 3 Marian, 91 were male individuals and only 39 were female. The male saints reveal a much broader range of individuals. By far the most frequently represented female saint was St Afra. 'Companies' of women associated with particular female saints— St Afra, St Ursula, St Glisa—are mentioned, though they are not in the case of male saints. Thus, in this collection at least, the female relics are marked by a weaker sense of individuality, and a correspondingly greater sense of feminine collectivity.

[21] See e.g. StadtAA, Reichsstadt, Prot. der Dreizehn V, fo. 77, 17 June 1539: Frau Ehingerin, Weispronnerin, Dichtlin von Munchen, Enndlin kindtpet kellerin and Schenckin are named as having gone to Lechhausen for a Catholic baptism; Prot. der Zuchtherren III, fo 34, 31 Mar. 1544: Barbara Sundau punished for attending 'papal ceremonies'.

Catholic religion was lived out in a series of small customs and rituals which permeated daily tasks. Blessed herbs, gathered at Mary's Ascension and blessed in the church, were on hand to use as cures; holy water might be kept for domestic use; fasts and feasting followed the calendar.[22] The women who had to orchestrate this religious expression within the household were involved in a series of decisions which became highly fraught in the early confused years of the Reformation. And in the pre-Reformation period, they had given household objects and daily rituals a patterned significance. Catholic religious practice had echoed and enhanced household order, yet its dramatization in the domestic sphere was women's work. Thus, at Candlemas, male household heads brought large candles, women carried red tapers which would be used at childbirth, and children brought small candles to the church, the ritual of blessing making the household order tangible as each member of the house held the candle suited to their place. But once taken home, the blessed candles would join women's household stocks to be used as they saw fit.[23]

Catholicism nurtured a peculiarly female style of devotion. Some of its features can be discerned in distorted form in the career of a fraudulent female 'saint'. This hoax was perpetrated in late fifteenth-century Augsburg, and has even been credited with hastening the advent of the Reformation as the scales fell from disillusioned Augsburgers' eyes.[24] Anna Laminit's spiritual election was signified by her refusal to eat, a continence in relation to food which was an exaggerated metaphor for sexual abstinence. (By contrast, Hans Vatter, a spiritual con-man working in Nuremberg, suffered physical contortions and escaped from them miraculously.) Though Laminit was judged a fake, her cult echoed that of Dorothea of Montau, who fasted frequently and

---

[22] For the Augsburg formula, see *Obsequiale ssm ecclesia Augusteñ*, Augsburg, E. Ratdolt, 1487, fos. xlv^r-xlvi^r. On the blessings elsewhere, see R. Scribner, 'Ritual and Popular Religion in catholic Germany at the Time of the Reformation', *Journal of Ecclesiastical History*, 35 (1984), 47–77; A. Franz, *Die kirchlichen Benediktionen im Mittelalter*, 2 vols. (Freiburg, 1909), 393–413.

[23] Scribner, 'Ritual and Popular Religion', p. 62.

[24] On Laminit, see F. Roth, 'Die geistliche Betrügerin Anna Laminit von Augsburg (c.1480–1518)', *Zeitschrift für Kirchengeschichte*, 43/2, NF 6 (1924), 355–417; and *Chroniken der deutschen Städte*, xxiii, Sender, pp. 116 f.; and xxv, Rem, pp. 11–20, 85 f.

finally died of starvation.[25] The themes of both these women's piety—genuine and false—met a deep response in popular piety.

By not eating food, Laminit used the language of the body to escape the tyranny of female bodiliness—she was holy because she was a woman freed from the shackles of female flesh. From this paradoxical status she earned herself respect and a large following attentive to her prophetic remarks. Her spirituality took the form of calling for penitential processions, and she acted through ritual rather than resorting to preaching, the usual mode of spiritual revivals led by men. Exploiting the coincidence of a remarkable rainfall which left cross-like shapes on Augsburgers' clothes, she led a vast penitential procession through the city, in which the élite of the town and even the wife of Emperor Maximilian I took part. Her following began to disintegrate, however, not because people started to doubt these divine portents, but when it was proved that Laminit did indeed eat secretly; and her support evaporated when she was implicated in a series of sexual scandals. Her 'holiness' and authority had to be destroyed not only by denying her non-corporeality in relation to food, but by presenting her as a whore, a nice demonstration of how intimately whoredom and virginity—the opposite ends of the spectrum of female existence—were linked. That she should subsequently be suspected of witchcraft hints at the ambivalences felt to be present in any exercise of female charisma—if its source could not be proved to be divine, it must stem from the Devil. It points, too, to the close nexus between perceptions of sexual attraction and accusations of witchcraft.

None the less, the cults' initial success shows the response of Augsburgers to this distinctly feminine spirituality, attractive largely because of its female voice. The effects of this feminine devotional register were double-edged, however: holiness could be attained only by divesting oneself of the sexual, feminine 'bodiliness'.

With the Reformation, the saints' cults which had allowed women some female figures with which to identify gave way to a more unified concentration on the Christ-figure alone, imagined not so often as a helpless infant towards whom the worshipper

---

[25] On Dorothea von Montau, see *Die Akten des Kanonisationsprozesses Dorotheas von Montau von 1394 bis 1521* (Cologne, 1978).

might express feelings of protectiveness, but as a grown man or judgemental Father. The expression of motherhood, so elemental a part of the popular cults of St Anna, whose church in Augsburg was among the most fashionable,[26] and of the Virgin, was not such a strong constituent of the christocentric religion. Robbed of much of the sexual ambiguities which the devotional forms had fostered—Christ was at once baby, youth, and man; and he could appear feminine, too, in his suffering—Reformation forms of devotion were not so much based on the individual's identification with the sufferings of Christ or the saints as concerned to establish a relationship with the Christ who appeared in biblical text alone.

The Protestant churches made the boundaries between men's and women's ecclesiastical roles yet more defined, as they had also marked the differences between sacred and profane more clearly. In the new church hierarchy drafted according to function by the Strasbourg preacher Martin Bucer, there was no post for women amongst the range of clerical officials. The radical implications of the early Reformation doctrine of the priesthood of all believers, the theological tenet which offered at least the conceptual possibility of a ministering role for women in the Church, were lost—indeed, the slogan itself was one of the forgotten doctrines of the Reformation.

Interestingly, one of the issues which absorbed much evangelical energy in Augsburg and in other evangelical towns was that of emergency baptism by midwives. Together with communion, baptism remained the only sacrament of the new Church, and its significance rested on its function as a rite of public incorporation, carried out before the congregation, rather than as a rite of exorcism. Yet where the Catholic Church had regarded baptism as a rite which was effective in itself, and which midwives could carry out in an emergency, Protestants were extremely uncomfortable about midwives performing baptism. Catholics, too, had not been without anxiety about how midwives

---

[26] On the St Anna brotherhood attached to this church, see W. Schiller, *Die St. Annakirche in Augsburg* (Augsburg, 1938); P. Lengle, 'Spitäler, Stiftungen und Bruderschaften', in G. Gottlieb *et al.* (eds.), *Geschichte der Stadt Augsburg*, 2nd edn. (Stuttgart, 1985); and R. Kiessling, *Bürgerliche Gesellschaft und Kirche in Augsburg* (Augsburg, 1971), p. 292.

[27] StadtAA, Reichsstadt, Lit. 1538, July–Dec., no. 11.

baptized and at what precise moment a baptism could be undertaken: but evangelicals insisted that though midwife baptisms were valid, a child baptized in this manner must be brought before the church for a special ceremony of incorporation.[28] In Augsburg, as elsewhere, the period saw increasing regulation of midwives, and the institution of a board of élite women charged with the duty of superintending the midwives' behaviour. Midwives were warned to baptize only in emergency cases. A few years later they were being suspected of spiriting babies away to the Catholic priests for baptism in the old style.[29] Not quite excluded even from the margins of cultic activity, the figure of the midwife was not to be trusted—she might involve herself with popery and superstition of all kinds.

For all the women who covertly remained Catholic, there were many more who adopted the new faith with enthusiasm, whether this took the form of mocking priests (like one girl who threw nuts at them from her window as the pompous processions of the clergy passed beneath[30]), or developing a Bible-reading circle (like the women in the groups surrounding Caspar Schwenckfeld), or creating the role of a Protestant pastor's wife. By the second half of the century, Protestant women may have been able to develop a female-centred piety, a language which would allow them to express spiritual yearnings and convictions in a mode based on their own experience as mothers. But this subject lies

---

[28] See e.g. ibid., Prot. der Dreizehn III, fo. 231ʳ, 27 Mar. 1537; and the baptismal ordinances for Augsburg in E. Sehling *et al.* (eds.), *Die evangelischen Kirchenordnungen* des 16. Jahrhunderts (Leipzig, 1902–11), Bayern II, pp. 39, 72–9; 85 f. In Augsburg in 1555, however, the evangelicals determined that midwife baptism should indeed be recognized (ibid. 99–102); but the vigour of the language betrays the sensitivity of the issue. An added difficulty was that to have a second ceremony after baptism might appear to be a 'rebaptism', thus laying evangelicals open to the charge of 'rebaptizing' and, by (misguided) association, Anabaptism. All these issues emerge clearly in Stadtarchiv Ulm, A [1790], 1535, in Martin Frecht's handwriting, which also condemns the 'aberglabische papistische' custom of midwives baptizing the first limb of the child to appear.

[29] StadtAA, Reichsstadt, Prot. der Dreizehn III, fo. 231, 27 Mar. 1537; RB 16, fo. 122ᵛ, 26 Mar. 1537.

[30] Ibid., Urg. 15 Apr. 1531, Ursula Rieger. It is possible that there may have been a sexual innuendo in the choice of missile—hazel-nuts were a symbol of sexual desire, and were used to represent randiness—thus, a good year for hazel-nuts presaged many illegitimate births: H. Bächtold-Stäubli, *Handwörterbuch des deutschen Aberglaubens*, 10 vols. (Berlin and Leipzig, 1927–42), iii. 1534 f.

beyond the scope of this book. In its early years, Protestantism formally denied there to be any differences in the kind of spirituality appropriate to men and women, symbolically expressing this position in its rejection of those passages in the Catholic baptismal rites which had prescribed slightly different formulas of exorcism and prayers to be spoken over girl and boy babies.[31] Implicitly, Protestants rejected the view that women's bodies were inherently evil or polluting, and insisted that sexual expression, in the context of marriage, was no more evil than any other human act. The 'churching' of women after childbirth, linked to ideas of female impurity, was held to be unnecessary.[32] If the early Protestants created a more exclusively male-run Church, this could perhaps be said to relate to external offices alone, not to religiosity itself. Nevertheless, this religiosity was far more closely aligned with men's social experience than with women's.

Parallel to Luther's theology of the two kingdoms, evangelical reformers may be said to have developed a two-kingdom theory of sexual difference—men and women were spiritually equal, but their offices in life on earth were different.[33] By locating the

---

[31] *Obsequiale ssm ecclesia Augusten̄*, fos. xxiiij^r–xxx^v; and note especially fos. xxvi^v and xxvii^v; and xxvii^r and xxvii^v. The prayers over the two sexes differ: whereas that over boys refers to the people of Israel being led through Egypt, and invokes a sense of continuity of heritage, that spoken over girls refers to the God of archangels, prophets, apostles, martyrs, and virgins—a wider heritage which did not involve the concept of the line. The second exorcismal prayer for boys refers to Christ's miracle of walking on the water and greeting Peter. For girls, Christ's healing of the blind and the raising of Lazarus are mentioned. Thus, even at this early point in the child's life, religious ritual associated the female gender with healing, the male with a more active expression of belief. For similar differences between the formulas of exorcism used for boys and girls, see H. Reifenberg, *Sakraments, Sakramentalien und Ritualien im Bistum Mainz seit dem spätmittelalter*, 2 vols. (Münster, 1971), i. 167–99, Mainz, Würzburg, and Bamberg; A. Dold, *Die Konstanzer Ritualientexte in ihrer Entwicklung von 1482–1721*, (Münster, 1923), pp. 1–48, comparing esp. pp. 7 and 16, 8 and 17; and B. Mattes, *Die Spendung der Sakramente nach den Freisinger Ritualien* (Munich, 1978), pp. 141–70. Note also F. Hocynck, *Geschichte der kirchlichen Liturgie des Bistums Augsburg* (Augsburg, 1889), pp. 119–28—boys were baptized before girls in pre-Reformation Augsburg. I am grateful to Charles Zika for suggesting this point.

[32] For blessings of the mother after childbirth and the ritual of churching, often carried out at the entrance to the church and involving the use of stole and blessed water, see Hoeynck, *Geschichte der kirchlichen Liturgie*, p. 427; Dold, *Die Konstanzer Ritualientexte*, pp. 47 f.; Franz, *Die kirchlichen Benediktionen*, ii. 208–40. In Augsburg the ritual is one of re-entry to the church, involving the use of stole and blessed water: *Obsequiale ssm ecclesia Augusten̄*, fo. xlviii^r.

differences between men and women in the secular world, however, Protestants both confirmed and elaborated the distinct duties of men and women. In this new understanding of the proper relation which ought to hold between husbands and wives, the work patterns and civic moralism of the craft workshop became the touchstone for an entire society. In Augsburg, by supporting civic definitions of honour, reputation, piety, and femininity, the clergy contributed to the new moralism and its particularly potent effects on women. This sea change constitutes one of the Reformation's most significant and abiding legacies.

[33] On Luther's doctrine of the two kingdoms, see W. J. Cargill Thompson, *Studies in the Reformation: Luther to Hooker*, ed. C. Dugmore (London, 1980), 'The "Two Kingdoms" and the "Two regiments": Some Problems of Luther's *Zwei-Reiche-Lehre*'.

BIBLIOGRAPHY

ABBREVIATIONS

BayHStA	Bayerisches Hauptstaatsarchiv München
BMB	Baumeisterbuch
EWA	Evangelisches Wesensarchiv
Fasz.	Faszikel
HWA	Handwerkerakten
HWO	Handwerksordnungen
KWA	Katholisches Wesensarchiv
Lit.	Literalien
Prot.	Protokolle
RB	Ratsbuch
RS	Realitätensammlung
StadtAA	Stadtarchiv Augsburg
StBA	Staats- und Stadtbibliothek Augsburg
SKUK	Stadtkanzlei Urkundenkonzepte
US	Urkundensammlung
Urg.	Urgichten
ZHVS	*Zeitschrift des historischen Vereins für Schwaben (und Neuburg)*

UNPRINTED SOURCES CITED

Stadtarchiv Augsburg

Reichsstadt

Ratsbücher

    1 (Frickinger) 1332–1471; 2 Ratserkenntnisse des 15. Jahrhunderts 1368–1534; 3 (1392–1441/1449); 8 (1474–8); 9 1479–81; 10–38, 1482–1573; 277 Eidbuch des 15. Jahrhunderts 1434–73.

Schätze

    16 (Civic notary's collection of civic ordinances); 36/1, 36/3, ad 36/4, ad 36/5 Zuchtordnungen; 46b Schmiede Zunftbuch; 63 PH Mair Memorialbuch; 72a Malerzunftbuch.

Steuerbücher

    1500–50.

Protokolle der Hochzeitsherren
I 1563-9.

Ratsämterlisten
1520-35, 1536-48.

Protokolle der Dreizehn
I 1524-6; II 1525-9; III 1530-; IV 1538; V 1539-40; VI 1540-2; VII 1542.

Baumeisterbücher
1500-48.

Einnehmerbücher
1500-48.

Protokolle der Einunger
5 vols., 1535-53, missing 1540-3; 1549-51

Scheltbücher
5 vols., 1509-50, missing 1529, 1544.

Strafbücher des Rats
I 1509-26; II 1533-9; III 1540-3; IV 1543-53.

Protokolle der Zuchtherren
(I) 28 Sept. 1537-30 Apr. 1539; (II) 5 May 1539-29 Nov. 1540; (III)
1 Dec. 1540-7 Oct. 1542; (IV) 11 Oct. 1542-29 Dec. 1543; (V) 3 Jan.
1544-9 Mar. 1545; (VI) 9 Mar. 1545-18 Jan. 1546; (VII) 18 Jan.
1546-28 Apr. 1547; (VIII) 20 Apr. 1547-6 June 1548.

Ein-und Ausgabebuch der Zuchtherren
1537; 8 Oct.-Dec. 1557; 1558.

Ehegerichtsbuch
1537-46.

Fasz. Ehegericht
1548-78, I.

Stadtgerichtsbücher
1500-50; missing 1514, 1524-6, 1529, 1530, 1534-8, 1540, 1541, 1549.

Urgichten
(I) 1497-1522; (II) 1523; (III) 1524; (IV) 1525, 1526; (V) 1527-9; (VI)
(1530 missing), 1531; (VII) 1532; (VIII) 1533; (IX) 1534; (X) 1535,
(1536-8 missing); (XI) 1539 (1540 missing); (XII) 1541, 1542; (XIII)
1543, 1544; (XIV) 1545, 1546.

Faszikel Musterregister
I 1520-1539; II 1520-1582.

Handwerkerakten
Bader und Barbierer 1535-80; Bäcker 1549-67; Bildhauer 1509-1699;
Bierbräuer 1549-77; Bier- und Weinwirte 1520-81; Briefmaler,

Illuministen, Formschneider 1529-1645; Buchbinder 1528-1642; Büchsenmacher und Büchsenhefter 1536-1743; Drechsler 1549-1654; Fischer 1429-1551 (1552-78); Gerber 1548-84; Glaser 1548-1645; Goldschläger 1556-1690; Goldschmiede 1532-80; Haffner 1507-1658; Kartenmacher 1520-1806; Käufler 1524-1698; Kistler 1548-66; Kramer 1524-76; Kürschner 1472-1587; Lederer 1548-1654; Maler 1515-1603; Fasz. Maler, Glaser, Bildhauer, Drahtzieher ordnung; Messerschmiede (Schwertfeger) 1490-1542; Messerschmiede (Schwertfeger) 1550-1736; Metzger 1417-1554; Metzger 1561-1798; Metzger 1550-1675; Müller 1511-82; Nadler 1549-1721; Nestler 1534-1794; Obser 1530-1632; Plattner 1530-1643; Riemer 1548-1826; Säckler 1550-1638; Sailer 1454-1615; Salzfertiger 1536-1807; Sattler 1548-1600; Schäffler 1548-94; Schleiffer 1548-1662; Schlosser 1550-1647; Schmiede 1530-69; Schwertfeger 1548-1735 u. 1779-1808; Schneider 1443-1564; Schuhmacher 1548-69; Segmüller und Flossleut 1524-1712; Sporer 1549-1810; Steinschneider 1530-1795 u. 1736-1802; Taschner 1482-1809; Uhrmacher 1544-1602; Wachsmacher 1533-1831; Waffenschmiede 1541-1811; Wagner 1548-1732; Zimmerleute 1548-99; Zinngiesser 1549-1610.

Zünfte

22, 1530-48 Maurer, Zimmerleute, Kistler, Hafner; 49, 1507-8 Zunftbuch der Bierbräuer; 50, 1560-1723 Zunftbuch der Bierbräuer; 129, 1452-99 Zunftbuch der Hucker; 130, 1456-1535 Zunftbuch der Hucker, Obstler, Sailer; 147, 1463-1536 Zunftbuch der Kaufleute; 148, 1537-52 Zunftbuch der Kaufleute; 158, 1456 ff. Kürschner Zunftbuch; 161, 1500-45 Zunftbuch der Lederer; 162, 1555-1866 Einschreibbuch der Weisgerber-, Rotgerber- und Pergamentierergesellen; 163, 1577-1878 Meisterbuch der Lederer, Weissgerber und Pergamentierer; 208, 1474-1547 Zunftbuch der Müller; 209, 1519-48 Zunftbuch der Müller; 210, 1554-1843 Gerechtigkeitsbuch der Mahlmüller; 222, 1397-1430 Zunftgenossen der Weinschenken; 223, 1480-98 Zunftbuch der Salzfertiger; 224, 1453-63 Zunftbuch der Salzfertiger und Weinschenken; 226, 1465-80 Zunftbuch der Salzfertiger; 227, 1480-1503 Zunftbuch der Salzfertiger; 228, 1503-44 Zunftbuch der Salzfertiger; 229, 1544-53 Zunftbuch der Salzfertiger; 223, 1565-1783 Handwerksgerechtigkeit der Schäffler; 245, 1453-1534 Zunftbuch der Schlosser, Schmiede und Schleifer; 266, 1471-1592 Weber Zunftbuch; 276, 1415-79 Zunftbuch der Zimmerleute; 277, 1440-87 Zunftbuch der Zimmerleute; 278, 1496-1548 Rechnungsbuch der Zimmerleute und Kistler; 279, 1537-47 Strafbuch der Zimmerleute.

Handwerksordnungen

A (*c*.1500-33); B (1548-51); C (1548-*c*.1570).

Kaufleute Stube
Fasz. I 1, v 5-9.

Kaufmannschaft und Handel
3, 4, 5, 6, 10, 11, 12, 13, 13a, 16, 17, ad 18.

Faszikel Zuchtordnungen

Faszikel Bürgerrecht

Faszikel Bürgeraufnahme
1507-1779.

Faszikel Sammlung von Ordnungen, Statuten und Privilegien

Faszikel Städtisches Regiment

Stadtgerichtsordnungen
23 vols., 1509-1806.

Ratserlasse
1507-99

Faszikel Hochzeitsordnungen
Faszikel Hochzeiten 1463-1729; Faszikel Hochzeitsamt: Generalia 1552-1777, und Verordnungen 1504-1804; Hochzeitsherren 1562-1806; Hochzeitsschreiber 1603-1794; Hauscopulationen 1548-1648; Vermögensansagen 1563-1797; Hochzeitsmahle und Einschlagendes 1551-1606, I; Hochzeitslader und -laderinnen, Leichensager und -sagerinnen 1550-1629, I.

Anschläge und Dekrete
1522-1682, nos. 1-100, I; 1490-1640, nos. 1-86, I.

Literalien
1500-48.

Personenselekt A-Z
(I) Adelman-Ehem; (II) Endorfer-Fröhlich; (III) Frundsberg-Grumbach; (IV) Fugger; (V) Guiccardini-Hörwart; (VI) Herwart-Höchstetter; (VII) Höchstetter; (VIII) Honold-Manlich; (IX) Maximilian I; (x) Marsch-Regius; (XI), (XII) Peutinger; (XIII) Rehlinger-Rentzer; (XIV) Rosenberger; (XV) Roth-Zapf; (XVI) Welser; (XVII-XIX) Autographensammlung.

Urkundensammlung
1500-50.

Realitäten
1500-70.

Stadtkanzlei Urkundenkonzepte
1.1, 1500-49 Kaufbriefe; 2.1, 1522-69 Schuldbriefe, Schadlosverschreibungen, Schuldquittungen; 2.75, 1473-1579 Schuldbriefe; 5.1, Testamente; 8.1, 1493-1569 Verträge und

Vergleiche; 9.1, 1500–49 Pflegbriefe, Abkommbriefe, Teilbriefe; 9.2, 1559–79 Pflegbriefe, Abkommbriefe, Teilbriefe; 9.26, 1554–1649 Pflegbriefe, Abkommbriefe, Teilbriefe; 9.29 undatierte Pflegbriefe, Abkommbriefe, Teilbriefe; 21.1, 1434–1767 Reverse verschiedener Art.

Kirchen und Klöster
Dom
  Hochstift 2.
St. Margaretenkloster
  Güterbeschreibung 1538.
Stiftungen A–Z

Evangelisches Wesensarchiv
Akten
  480, 481, 488, 496, 633, 634, 635, 529 ɪ, 1715.

Katholisches Wesensarchiv
ad B25/xɪ St. Kath; B26/ɪɪ; B26/ɪɪɪ; G47 Horbruck; ad H45 Bächin Seelhaus; L67 Bächin Seelhaus;

Staats- und Stadtbibliothek Augsburg
Cod. Aug. 2o; Peutinger Selekt, 73, 74, 382, 383, 384, 385, 386, 387, 388, 389, 390, 391, 392, 393, 394, 395, 396; Cod. Aug. 2o, 300.

Ordinariatsarchiv Augsburg
Protokolle des bishöflichen Konsistoriums
  1535, 1536.

Hauptstaatsarchiv München
Hochstift Augsburg
  Münchener Bestand Lit. 527; Neuburger Abgabe, Akten 3564.

Staatsarchiv Neuburg
Klöster Augsburg
  St. Katherine, Akt 81.

Staatsarchiv Ludwigsburg
B207 Büschel 68; B207 Büschel 76.

Stadtarchiv Ulm

A (Reichsstadt)
[1790]; [8989]; 3988; 3669 Zweites Gsatzbuch; [6543] Aid- und
Ordnungsbuch; [8983] I, [8983] II; 3971.
U (Ulmensien)
5307.

Strasbourg, Archives Municipales

Archives du Chapitre de Saint-Thomas
Varia Ecclesiastica II 167.

WORKS CITED: PRINTED SOURCES

Ains Erbern Rats | der Stat Augspurg | Zucht vnd Pollicey Ordnung,
Augsburg, 1537.
*Die Akten des Kanonisationsprozesses Dorotheas von Montau von 1394
bis 1521* (Forschungen und Quellen zur Kirchen- und Kulturgeschichte
Ostdeutschlands, 15; Cologne, 1978).
*Aller dess Heiligen Romischen Reichss gehaltener Reichsstag Ordnung
. . . 1368-1603*, Mainz, Johannes Albin, 1607.
AMBACH, MELCHIOR, *Von Ehbruch vnd hůrerey. Item. v. Christliche
predige S. Augustini*, Frankfurt, Cyriakus Iacob zum Bart, 1543.
*Antwurt Zwayer Closter frauwen im Katheriner Closter zů Augspurg
| an Bernhart Remen | Vnd hernach seyn gegen Antwurt*, [Augsburg,
P. Ulhart, 1523].
Aretino's Dialogues, trans. R. Rosenthal (London, 1972).
BAADER, J., *Nürnberger Polizeiordnungen aus dem 13. bis 15.
Jahrhundert* (Bibliothek des Litterarischen Vereins in Stuttgart, 63;
Stuttgart, 1861).
Beichtbüchlein, Augsburg, Johann Schobser, 1491.
*Bekandtnuss der Euangelischen Leer | in Zehen Haupt Articulen
kürtzlich begriffen*, [Augsburg, P. Ulhart, 1546].
BERNHARDI, Bartholomaeus, *Schutzrede vor Bartholomeo der ein
eehweib so er priester is genůmen hat*, Erfurt, [M. Maler], 1522.
BINTERIM, A., *Pragmatische Geschichte der deutschen National-,
Provinzial- und vorzüglichsten Diöcesanconcilien, von dem vierten
Jahrhundert bis auf das Concilium zu Trient*, 7 vols. (Mainz, 1835-48).
BROSTHAUS, U. (ed.), *Bürgerleben im 16. Jahrhundert: Die
Autobiographie des Stralsunder Bürgermeisters Bartholomäus
Sastrow als kulturgeschichtliche Quelle* (Vienna, 1972).

BRUCKER, J., *Strassburger Zunft- und Polizei-Verordnungen des 14. und 15. Jahrhunderts* (Strasbourg, 1889).

BUCER, M., *Martin Bucers deutsche Schriften*, ed. R. Stupperich (Gütersloh, 1960–).

BUGERNHAGEN, JOHANN, *Der Ehrabaren Stadt Hamburg Christliche Ordnung 1529*, ed. H. Wenn (Hamburg, 1976).

[CAROLINA], *Die Peinliche Gerichtsordnung Kaiser Karls V von 1532*, ed. A. Kaufman, 4th edn. (Stuttgart, 1975).

Die Chroniken der deutschen Städte vom 14. bis ins 16. Jahrhundert, 36 vols. (Leipzig, 1862–1931).

Concubinarij: Vnderricht ob ein Priester ein beyschläfferin haben mög, [Strasbourg, J. Cammerlander, 1545].

CULMAN, LEONHARD, *Iunge gesellen Iungkfrawen vnd Witwen so ehelich wöllen werden zu nutz ein vnterrichtung*, later edn., [Augsburg, M. Francken, 1568].

Der Curtisan vnd pfrunde fresser, [Augsburg?, 1522].

Dialogus von Zweyen pfaffen Kochin, [Erfurt, M. Buchfürher, 1523].

DIEPOLD, JOHANNES, *Ein Sermon an Sankt Mariae Magdlenae Tag . . .*, n.p., 1423 (Köhler, *Flugschriften Microfiche 456/1233, q.v.*).

EBERLEIN, JOHANN, *Die ander getrew vermanung an den Rath der stadt Vlm*, [Augsburg, M. Ramminger, 1523].

FIRN, ANTON, *Supplication des Pfarrers vnnd der Pfarrkinder zu sant Thoman*, [Augsburg, P. Ulhart, 1524].

FRANCK, SEBASTIAN, *Weltbüch, spiegel vnd bildtniss des gantzen erdtbodens*, Tübingen, V. Morhart, 1534.

FUCHS, JACOB, *Ain schöner Sendbrieff an Bischof vō Wirtzburg darinn Priester Ee beschirmbt wirdt*, [Augsburg, H. Steiner, 1523].

GASSER, ACHILLES PIRMINIUS, *Annales der vetustate originis, amoenitate situs, splendidore aedificiorum, ac rebus gestis civium Reipublicaeque Augustoburgensis* (*Scriptores Rerum Germanicarum*, ed. G. Menck, 3 vols.; Leipzig, 1728–30: vol.i, no. xvii).

GEISBERG, M., *The German Single Leaf Woodcut 1500–1550*, 4 vols. (New York, 1974).

GREIFF, B. (ed.), 'Tagebuch des Lucas Rem aus den Jahren 1494–1541', *Jahresbericht des historischen Kreisvereins im Regierungsbezirke von Schwaben und Neuburg für das Jahr 1860*, 26 (1861), 1–110.

HAEMMERLE, A., *Die Hochzeitsbücher der Augsburger Bürgerstube und Kaufleutestube bis zum Ende der Reichsfreiheit* (Munich, 1936).

—— *Das Necrologium des Benediktinerinnenklosters St. Nicolaus in Augsburg* (Munich, 1955).

—— *Das Necrologium des Dominikanerinnenklosters St. Margareth in Augsburg* (Munich, 1955).

HOFFMANN, H. (ed.), *Würzburger Polizeisätze, Gebote und Ordnungen des Mittelalters 1125-1495* (Veröffentlichungen der Gesellschaft für fränkische Geschichte, 10/5; Würzburg, 1955).

KÖHLER, H. J., *Flugschriften des frühen 16. Jahrhunderts* (Microfiche series; Zug, 1978–   ).

KOLB, HANS, *(Ein) Reformation notdurftig in der Christenheit mit den Pfaffen | vnd ihren Mägten | wil Gott haben entlich | wan jr schentlich leben mag Gott nit mer leyden* (Köhler, Flugschriften Microfiche 312/924).

LÖTSCHER, V. (ed.), *Felix Platter: Tagebuch (Lebensbeschreibung) 1536-1567* (Basler Chroniken, 10: Basle and Stuttgart, 1976).

LUTHER, MARTIN, *D. Martin Luthers Werke* (Weimar, 1883–   ).

MELISSANDER, C., *Ehebüchlein: Item die Schöne Œconomia Matthesij*, Nuremberg, L. Heussler, 1594.

MEYER, C., *Das Stadtbuch von Augsburg, insbesondere das Stadtrecht von 1276* (Augsburg, 1872).

Obsequiale ssm ecclesia Augusten, Augsburg, E. Ratdolt, 1487.

Von dem Pfründmarkt der Curtisanen und Tempelknechten, n.p., 1521 (Köhler, *Flugschriften Microfiche* 279/796).

REM, BERNHART, *Ain Sendtbrieff an ettlich Closterfrawen zu sant katherina vnd zu sant niclas in Augspurg*, [Augsburg, P. Ulhart, 1523].

——*Ain Christlich schreiben | so ain Euangelischer brüder seiner schwestern | ainer closter iunckfrawen zugeschickt*, [Augsburg, n.d.].

RHEGIUS, URBANUS, *Ain predig von der hailigen iunckfrauwen Catharina*, [Augsburg, Silvan Othmar, 1521].

——*Ernstliche erbietung der Euangelische Prediger an den gaystlichen Stand | die yetzigen leer betreffend*, [Augsburg, P. Ulhart, 1524].

SACHS, H., *Ein Rat zwischen einem Alten man vnd jungen gesellen dreyer heyrat halben*, [Nuremberg, G. Merckel, 1553].

——*Der gantz Haussrat bey dreyhundert stücken* G. M[erckel, Nuremberg, 1560?].

SACHS, M., *Nutzer Bericht von der bedeutung der Schnur vnd Crantze*, [Mulhausen, A. Hantzsch, 1589].

SAM, K., *Handtbuchlin darin begriffen ist die Ordnung vnd weiss, wie die Sacrament vnnd Ceremonien der kirchen zu Vlm gebraucht vnd gehalten werden*, [Ulm, 1531].

SCHÜTZINN, KATHARINA, *Entschuldigung Katharina Schützinn für M. Matthes Zellen jren Eegemahel*, [Strasbourg, W. Köpfel, 1524].

SCHWENCKFELD, C., *Corpus Schwenckfeldianorum*, ed. C. Hartranft, E. Johnson, and S. Schultz, 19 vols. (Leipzig and Pennsburg, 1907-61).

SEHLING, E. *et al.* (eds.), *Die evangelischen Kirchenordnungen des 16. Jahrhunderts* (Leipzig, 1902–11; continued by the Institut für evangelisches Kirchenrecht der evangelischen Kirche in Deutschland, Tübingen, 1963–   ).

SPANGENBERG, C., *Ehespiegel*, [Strasbourg, T. Rihel, 1570].

Der spiegel des sünders, [Augsburg, A. Sorg, 1480].

STRAUSS, JACOB, *Ein neüw wunderbarlich Beycht büechlin*, [Augsburg, S. Grimm, 1523].

——— *Ein Sermon in der deutlich angezaiget dye pfaffen Ee in Euangelischer leer nit zu der freyhayt des fleyschs gefundiert*, [Augsburg, G. Nadler, 1523?].

SURGANT, J., *Manuale curatorum predicandi prebens modū*, [Basle, M. Furter, 1503].

Ursprung und Anfang Augsburgs, [Augsburg, Johann Bämler, 14]83, bound with Hagiologium of St Ulric and St Afra.

WUTTKE, D. (ed.), *Fastnachtspiele des 15. und 16. Jahrhunderts* (Stuttgart, 1978).

[ZIMMERN], *Die Chronik der Grafen von Zimmern*, ed. Decker-Hauff, 3 vols. (Stuttgart, 1967).

WORKS CITED: AUGSBURG

BAER, W. (ed.), *Augsburger Stadtlexikon* (Augsburg, 1985).

BÁTORI, I., *Die Reichsstadt Augsburg im 18. Jahrhundert: Verfassung, Finanzen und Reformversuche* (Veröffentlichungen des Max-Planck-Instituts für Geschichte, 22; Göttingen, 1969).

BAUMANN, I., *Geschichte des Stern-Klosters Maria Stern in Augsburg 1258–1828* (Munich, 1958).

BELLOT, J., 'Humanismus—Bildungswesen—Buchdruck und Verlagsgeschichte', in G. Gottlieb *et al.* (eds.), *Geschichte der Stadt Augsburg*, 2nd edn. (Stuttgart, 1985).

BLENDINGER, F., 'Versuch einer Bestimmung der Mittelschicht in der Reichsstadt Augsburg vom Ende des 14. bis zum Anfang des 18. Jahrhunderts', in E. Maschke and J. Sydow (eds.), *Städtische Mittelschichten* (Stuttgart, 1972).

BOBINDER, M., *Kunstuhrmacher in Alt-Augsburg* (Abhandlungen zur Geschichte der Stadt Augsburg, 18; Augsburg, 1969).

BROADHEAD, P., 'Politics and Expediency in the Augsburg Reformation', in P. Newman Brooks (ed.), *Reformation Principle and Practice: Essays in Honour of Arthur Geoffrey Dickens* (London, 1980).

——— 'Internal Politics and Civic Society in Augsburg during the Era of the Early Reformation 1518–1537', Ph.D. thesis (Kent, 1981).

BUFF, ARCHIVAR, 'Verbrechen und Verbrecher zu Augsburg in der zweiten Hälfte des 14. Jahrhunderts', *ZHVS* 4 (1878), 160-232.

CLASEN, C. P., *Die Augsburger Steuerbücher um 1600* (Augsburg, 1976).

—— *Die Augsburger Weber: Leistungen und Krisen des Textilgewerbes um 1600* (Abhandlungen zur Geschichte der Stadt Augsburg, 27; Augsburg, 1981).

—— 'Armenfürsorge in Augsburg vor dem Dreissigjährigen Krieg', *ZHVS* 78 (1984), 65-115.

—— 'Arm und Reich in Augsburg vor dem Dreissigjährigen Krieg', in Gottlieb, *Geschichte der Stadt Augsburg* (Stuttgart, 1985).

—— 'Armenfürsorge im 16. Jahrhundert', in Gottlieb, *Geschichte der Stadt Augsburg* (Stuttgart, 1985).

DIRR, P., 'Kaufleutezunft und Kaufleutestube in Augsburg zur Zeit des Zunftregiments (1368-1548)', *ZHVS* 35 (1909), 133-51.

—— 'Studien zur Geschichte der Augsburger Zunftverfassung', *ZHVS* 39 (1913), 144-243.

FRENSDORFF, F., 'Ein Urtheilsbuch des geistlichen Gerichts zu Augsburg aus dem 14. Jahrhundert', *Zeitschrift für Kirchenrecht*, 10 (1871), 1-37.

GAMBER, O., 'Besteller, Erzeuger und Liefernormen des Augsburger Harnisches', *Welt im Umbruch*, iii (q.v.).

HARTUNG, J., 'Die Augsburger Vermögenssteuer und die Entwicklung der Besitzverhältnisse im 16. Jahrhundert', *Schmollers Jahrbuch*, 19 (1895), 867-83.

—— 'Die Augsburger Zuschlagsteuer von Jahre 1475: Ein Beitrag zur Geschichte des städtischen Steuerwesens sowie der socialen und Einkommensverhältnisse am Ausgang des Mittelalters', *Schmollers Jahrbuch*, 19 (1895), 95-136.

—— 'Die Belastung des augsburgischen Grosskapitals durch die Vermögenssteuer des 16. Jahrhunderts', *Schmollers Jahrbuch*, 19 (1895), 1165-90.

HAYWARD, J., 'Blank- und Feuerwaffen und sonstige Arbeiten aus unedlen Metallen', in *Welt im Umbruch*, ii.

HECKER, PAUL, 'Der Augsburger Bürgermeister Jakob Herbrot und der Sturz des zünftigen Regiments in Augsburg', *ZHVS* 1 (1874), 34-98.

—— 'Die Correspondenz der Stadt Augsburg mit Karl V im Ausgang des schmalkaldischen Krieges', *ZHVS* 1 (1874), 257-309.

HERBERGER, ARCHIVAR, 'Die Seelhäuser und die Seelgeräthe in Augsburg: Aus dem Nachlasse des Archivar Herberger', *ZHVS* 3 (1876), 283-96.

HOEYNCK, F., *Geschichte der kirchlichen Liturgie des Bistums Augsburg* (Augsburg, 1889).

HÖRMANN, L., 'Erinnerungen an das ehemalige Frauenkloster Katharina in Augsburg', *ZHVS* 9 (1882), 357-86; 10 (1883), 301-54; 11 (1884), 1-10.

IMMENKÖTTER, H., 'Kirche zwischen Reformation und Parität', in Gottlieb, *Geschichte der Stadt Augsburg* (Stuttgart, 1985).

JAHN, J., 'Augsburgs Einwohnerzahl im 16. Jahrhundert', *Zeitschrift für bayerische Landesgeschichte*, 39 (1976), 379-96.

—— 'Studien zur Verfassungs- und Bevölkerungsentwicklung der Reichsstadt Augsburg bis zur Einführung der Reformation', MA diss. (Munich, 1976).

—— *Augsburg Land* (Historischer Atlas von Bayern, xi. *Schwaben*; Munich, 1984).

JUHNKE, L., 'Bausteine zur Geschichte des Dominikarinnenklosters St. Katharina in Augsburg mit Berücksichtigung von Patriziat, Reform und Geistesleben', *Jahresbericht der Oberrealschule Augsburg 1957-8* (Augsburg, 1958), 60-110.

KELLENBENZ, H., 'Wirtschaftsleben der Blütezeit', in Gottlieb, *Geschichte der Stadt Augsburg* (Stuttgart, 1985).

KIESSLING, R., *Bürgerliche Gesellschaft und Kirche in Augsburg im Spätmittelalter: Ein Beitrag zur Strukturanalyse der oberdeutschen Reichsstadt* (Abhandlungen zur Geschichte der Stadt Augsburg, 19; Augsburg, 1971).

KRAUS, J., *Das Militärwesen der Reichsstadt Augsburg 1548-1806* (Abhandlungen zur Geschichte der Stadt Augsburg, 26; Augsburg, 1980).

LENGLE, P., 'Spitäler, Stiftungen und Bruderschaften', in Gottlieb, *Geschichte der Stadt Augsburg* (Stuttgart, 1985).

LENK, L., *Augsburger Bürgertum im Späthumanismus und Frühbarock (1580-1700)* (Abhandlungen zur Geschichte der Stadt Augsburg, 17; Augsburg, 1968).

LIEBHART, W., 'Stufte, Klöster und Konvente in Augsburg', in Gottlieb, *Geschichte der Stadt Augsburg* (Stuttgart, 1985).

LIEDL, E., *Gerichtsverfassung und Zivilprozess der freien Reichsstadt Augsburg* (Abhandlungen zur Geschichte der Stadt Augsburg, 12; Augsburg, 1958).

LUTZ, H., *Conrad Peutinger: Beiträge zu einer politischen Biographie* (Abhandlungen zur Geschichte der Stadt Augsburg, 9; Augsburg, 1958).

MÖRKE, O., 'Die Fugger im 16. Jahrhundert: Städtische Elite oder Sonderstriktur?', *Archiv für Reformationsgeschichte*, 74 (1983), 141-62.

—— and SIEH, K., 'Gesellschaftliche Führungsgruppen', in Gottlieb, *Geschichte der Stadt Augsburg* (Stuttgart, 1985).

PAAS, M. W., *Population Change, Labor Supply, and Agriculture in Augsburg 1480-1618: A Study of Early Demographic-Economic Interactions* (New York, 1981).

PIPER, E., *Der Stadtplan als Grundriss der Gesellschaft: Topographie und Sozialstruktur in Augsburg und Florenz um 1500* (Frankfurt, 1982).

PRIMBS, 'Das Stift von St. Stephan in Augsburg', *ZHVS* 7 (1880), 109-56.

RAJKAY, B., 'Die Bevölkerungsentwicklung von 1500 bis 1648', in Gottlieb, *Geschichte der Stadt Augsburg* (Stuttgart, 1985).

REITZENSTEIN, A. von, 'Die Plattner von Augsburg', in H. Rinn (ed.), *Augusta* (Augsburg, 1955).

ROECK, B., *Bäcker, Brot und Getreide in Augsburg: Zur Politik des Bäckerhandwerks und zur Versorgungspolitik der Reichsstadt im Zeitalter des Dreissigjährigen Krieges* (Abhandlungen zur Geschichte der Stadt Augsburg, 31; Sigmaringen, 1987).

ROPER, L., 'Discipline and Respectability: Prostitution and the Reformation in Augsburg', *History Workshop Journal*, 19 (1985), 3-28.

—— 'Going to Church and Street: Weddings in Reformation Augsburg', *Past and Present*, 106 (1985), 62-101.

—— 'Madri di depravazione: Le mezzane nel Cinquecento', *Memoria*, 17/2 (1986), 7-23.

ROTH, F., 'Zur Geschichte der Wiedertäufer in Oberschwaben', *ZHVS* 27 (1900), 1-45; 28 (1901), 1-154.

—— *Augsburgs Reformationsgeschichte*, 4 vols. (vol. i: 2nd edn., Munich, 1901; vols. ii-iv: Munich, 1904-11).

—— 'Der Augsburger Jurist Dr. Hieronymus Fröschel und seine Hauschronik von 1528-1600', *ZHVS* 38 (1912), 1-83.

—— 'Die geistliche Betrügerin Anna Laminit von Augsburg (c.1480-1518)', *Zeitschrift für Kirchengeschichte*, 43/2, NF 6 (1924), 335-417.

Ad Sanctum Stephanum 969-1969: Festgabe zur 1000 Jahr-Feier von St. Stephan in Augsburg (Augsburg, 1969).

SCHILLER, W., *Die St. Annakirche in Augsburg: Ein Beitrag zur Augsburger Kirchengeschichte* (Augsburg, 1938).

SCHMIDT, R., 'Das Stadtbuch von 1276', in Gottlieb, *Geschichte der Stadt Augsburg* (Stuttgart, 1985).

SCHREIBER, A., 'Die Entwicklung der Augsburger Bevölkerung vom Ende des 14. Jahrhunderts bis zum Beginn des 18. Jahrhunderts', Ph.D. thesis (Erlangen, 1922).

SCHRÖDER, D., *Augsburg* (Historischer Atlas von Bayern, x. *Schwaben*; Munich, 1975).

SELING, H., *Die Kunst der Augsburger Goldschmiede 1529-1868: Meister, Marken, Werke*, 3 vols. (Munich, 1980).

SIEH, K., 'Bürgermeisteramt, soziale Verflechtung und Reformation in der freien Reichsstadt Augsburg 1518-1539', MA diss. (Augsburg, 1981).

SIEH-BURENS, K., 'Die Augsburger Stadtverfassung um 1500', *ZHVS* 77 (1983), 125-49.

SIEH-BURENS, K., *Oligarchie, Konfession und Politik im 16. Jahrhundert: Zur sozialen Verflechtung der Augsburger Bürgermeister und Stadtpfleger 1518–1618* (Munich, 1986).

SIEMER, P., *Geschichte des Dominikanerklosters Sankt Magdalena in Augsburg (1225–1808)* (Vechta, 1936).

STETTEN, P. von d. Ä., *Geschichte der Heiligen Römischen Reichs Freyen Stadt Augsburg*, 2 vols. (Frankfurt and Leipzig, 1743–58).

STETTEN, P. von d. J., *Geschichte der adelichen Geschlechter in der freien Reichsstadt Augsburg* (Augsburg, 1762).

STRIEDER, J., *Zur Genesis des modernen Kapitalismus: Forschungen zur Entstehung der grossen bürgerlichen Kapitalvermögen am Ausgange des Mittelalters und zu Beginn der Neuzeit, zunächst in Augsburg*, 2nd edn. (Munich, 1935).

—— *Das reiche Augsburg: Ausgewählte Aufsätze Jakob Strieders zur Augsburger und süddeutschen Wirtschaftsgeschichte des 15. und 16. Jahrhunderts*, ed. H. Deininger (Munich, 1938).

THOMAS, B., 'Augsburger Harnische und Stangenwaffen', *Welt im Umbruch*, ii.

UHL, A., *Peter von Schaumberg 1424–1469, Kardinal und Bischof von Augsburg: Ein Beitrag zur Geschichte des Reiches, Schwabens und Augsburgs im 15. Jahrhundert* (Augsburg, 1940).

UHLAND, F., *Täufertum und Obrigkeit in Augsburg im 16. Jahrhundert* (Tübingen, 1972).

VOGT, W., 'Johann Schilling der Barfüssermönch und der Aufstand in Augsburg im Jahre 1524', *ZHVS* 6 (1879), 1–32.

WARMBRUNN, P., *Zwei Konfessionen in einer Stadt: Das Zusammenleben von Katholiken und Protestanten in den paritätischen Reichsstädten Augsburg, Biberach, Ravensburg und Dinkelsbühl* (Veröffentlichungen des Instituts für europäische Geschichte Mainz, Abteilung Abendländische Religionsgeschichte, 111; Wiesbaden, 1983).

Welt im Umbruch: Augsburg zwischen Renaissance und Barock, 3 vols., catalogue, and essays (Augsburg, 1980, 1981).

WERNER, A., *Die örtlichen Stiftungen für die Zwecke des Unterrichts und der Wohltätigkeit in der Stadt Augsburg*, 2 vols. (Augsburg, 1899, 1912).

WIEDEMANN, H., *Augsburger Pfarrerbuch* (Nuremberg, 1962).

WILHELM, J., *Augsburger Wandmalerei 1368–1530: Künstler, Handwerker und Zunft* (Abhandlungen zur Geschichte der Stadt Augsburg, 29; Augsburg, 1983).

WOLFART, K., *Die Augsburger Reformation in den Jahren 1533–1534*, (Studien zur Geschichte der Theologie und der Kirche 7/2; Leipzig, 1901).

ZORN, W., *Augsburg: Geschichte einer deutschen Stadt*, 2nd edn. (Augsburg, 1972).

WORKS CITED: GENERAL LITERATURE

ABRAY, J., *The People's Reformation: Magistrates, Clergy and Commons 1500–1598* (London, 1985).
ACCATI, L., 'The Larceny of Desire', *Memoria*, 7 (1983), 7–16.
BAADER, J., 'Nürnbergisches Rechtsgutachten über die Ermordung zweier Ehebrecher zu Ulm im Jahre 1528', *Anzeiger für Kunde der deutschen Vorzeit*, NF 11 (1864), 134–6.
BÄCHTOLD-STÄUBLI, H., *Handwörterbuch des deutschen Aberglaubens*, 10 vols. (Berlin and Leipzig, 1927–1942).
BAINTON, R., *Women of the Reformation in Germany and Italy* (Minneapolis, 1971).
BAUER, M., *Deutscher Frauenspiegel*, 2 vols. (Munich and Berlin, 1917).
—— *Liebesleben in deutscher Vergangenheit* (Berlin, 1924).
BECK, R., 'Illegitimität und voreheliche Sexualität auf dem Land', in R. van Dülmen (ed.), *Kultur der einfachen Leute: Bayerisches Volksleben vom 16. bis zum 19. Jahrhundert* (Munich, 1983).
BEHAGEL, W., *Die gewerbliche Stellung der Frau im mittelalterlichen Köln* (Abhandlungen zur mittleren und neueren Geschichte, 23; Berlin and Leipzig, 1910).
BELLARDI, W., *Die Geschichte der 'Christlichen Gemeinschaft' in Strassburg 1546–1550: Der Versuch einer zweiten Reformation* (Quellen und Forschungen zur Reformationsgeschichte, 18; Leipzig, 1934).
BERG, M., 'Women's Work, Mechanisation and the Early Phases of Industrialisation in England', in P. Joyce (ed.), *The Historical Meanings of Work* (Cambridge, 1987).
BIRLINGER, A., *Aus Schwaben: Sagen, Legenden, Aberglauben, Sitten, Rechtsbräuche, Ortsneckereien, Lieder, Kinderreien: Neue Sammlung*, 2 vols. (Wiesbaden, 1874).
BLOCH, I., *Die Prostitution*, 2 vols. (Berlin, 1912–25).
BOANAS, G., and ROPER, L., 'Feminine Piety in Fifteenth-Century Rome: Santa Francesca Romana', in J. Obelkevich, L. Roper, and R. Samuel (eds.), *Disciplines of Faith: Studies in Religion, Politics and Patriarchy* (London, 1987).
BOSSY, J., *Christianity in the West 1400–1700* (Oxford, 1985).
BRADY, T., *Ruling Class, Regime and Reformation at Strasbourg 1520–1555* (Leiden, 1978).

BRIDENTHAL, R., and KOONZ, C. (eds.), *Becoming Visible: Women in European History* (Boston, 1977).

BROWN, JUDITH, *Immodest Acts: The Life of a Lesbian Nun in Renaissance Italy* (Oxford, 1986).

BRUNDAGE, J., 'Prostitution in the Medieval Canon Law', *Signs*, 1/4 (1976), 825–45.

BURKHARD, G., *Studien zur Geschichte des Hebammenwesens* (Leipzig, 1912).

BYNUN, C., *Jesus as Mother: Studies in the Spirituality of the High Middle Ages* (London, 1982).

CHRISMAN, M., 'Women and the Reformation in Strasbourg', *Archiv für Reformationsgeschichte*, 63 (1972), 143–68.

CLARK, A., *Working Life of Women in the Seventeenth Century* (London, 1919; 2nd edn. with introduction by Miranda Chaytor and Jane Lewis, London, 1982).

CRAWFORD, P., 'Attitudes to Menstruation in Seventeenth Century England', *Past and Present*, 91 (1981), 47–73.

DAHMS, F., *Luther über Scheidung und Wiederverheirathung Geschiedener* (Berlin, 1859).

DAVIDOFF, L., and HALL, C., *Family Fortunes* (London, 1987).

DAVIDSON, C., *A Woman's Work Is Never Done: A History of Housework in the British Isles 1650–1950* (London, 1982).

DAVIS, N. Z., *Society and Culture in Early Modern France* (London, 1975).

—— 'Women in the Crafts in Sixteenth Century Lyon', *Feminist Studies*, 8/1 (1982), 47–80.

DEICHERT, H., *Geschichte des Medizinalwesens im Gebiet des ehemaligen Königreichs Hannover* (Quellen und Darstellungen zur Geschichte Niedersachsens, 26; Hanover and Leipzig, 1908).

DIETERICH, H., *Das protestantische Eherecht in Deutschland bis zur Mitte des 17. Jahrhunderts* (Jus Ecclesiasticum, 10; Munich, 1970).

DILLARD, H., *Daughters of the Reconquest: Women in Castilian Town Soceity 1100–1300* (Cambridge, 1984).

DIRLMEIER, U., *Untersuchungen zu Einkommensverhältnissen und Lebenshaltungskosten in oberdeutschen Städten des Spätmittelalters (Mitte 14. bis Anfang 16. Jahrhundert)* (Abhandlungen der Heidelberger Akademie der Wissenschaften, 1978,i; Heidelberg, 1978).

DOLD, A., *Die Konstanzer Ritualientexte in ihrer Entwicklung von 1482–1721* (Liturgiegeschichtliche Quellen, 5–6; Münster, 1923).

DROSS, A., *Die erste Walpurgisnacht* (Hamburg, 1981).

DUBY, G., *A History of Private Life*, ii. *Revelations of the Medieval World*, trans. A. Goldhammer (*A History of Private Life*, ed. P. Ariès and G. Duby; Cambridge, Mass., 1988).

DUGGAN, L., 'Fear and Confession on the Eve of the Reformation', *Archiv für Reformationsgeschichte*, 75 (1982), 153-75.

ELSAS, M. J., *Umriss einer Geschichte der Preise und Löhne in Deutschland vom ausgehenden Mittelalter bis zum Beginn des neunzehnten Jahrhunderts*, 2 vols. (Leiden, 1936, 1940).

ENNEN, E., 'Die Frau in der mittelalterlichen Stadtgesellschaft Mitteleuropas', *Hansische Geschichtsblätter*, 98 (1980), 1-21.

ERLER, A., and KAUFMANN, E. (eds.), *Handwörterbuch zur deutschen Rechtsgeschichte* (Berlin, 1964-   ).

EVANS, R., *The Feminist Movement in Germany 1894-1933* (London, 1976).

—— 'Religion and Society in Modern Germany', *European Studies Review*, 12 (1982), 249-88.

FRANK, K., 'Die Franziskanerterziarinnen in der Ulmer Sammlung', in H. Specker and H. Tüchle, *Kirchen und Klöster in Ulm* (Ulm, 1979).

FRANZ, A., *Die Messe im deutschen Mittelalter: Beiträge zur Geschichte der Liturgie und des religiösen Volkslebens*, 2 vols. (Freiburg, 1902).

—— *Die kirchlichen Benediktionen im Mittelalter*, 2 vols. (Freiburg, 1909).

FRIEDRICHS, C., 'Capitalism, Mobility and Class Formation in Early Modern German Towns', *Past and Present*, 69 (1975), 24-49.

—— *Urban Society in an Age of War: Nördlingen 1580-1720* (Princeton, 1979).

GEIGER, G., *Die Reichsstadt Ulm vor der Reformation* (Forschungen zur Geschichte der Stadt Ulm, 11; Ulm, 1971).

GLENZDORF, J., and TREICHEL, F., *Henker, Schinder und arme Sünder*, 2 vols. (Bad Münster, 1970).

GOODY, J., *The Development of the Family and Marriage in Europe* (Cambridge, 1983).

—— and TAMBIAH, S., *Bridewealth and Dowry* (Cambridge Papers in Social Anthropology, 7; Cambridge, 1973).

GOTTLIEB, B., 'Getting Married in Pre-Reformation Europe: The Doctrine of Clandestine Marriage and Court Cases in Fifteenth-Century Champagne', Ph.D. thesis (Columbia, 1974).

—— 'The Meaning of Clandestine Marriage', in R. Wheaton and T. Hareven (eds.), *Family and Sexuality in French History* (Philadelphia, 1980).

HACKER, B. C., 'Women and Military Institutions in Early Modern Europe: A Reconnaissance', *Signs*, 6 (1981), 643-71.

HARTINGER, W., 'Zur Bevölkerungs- und Sozialstruktur von Oberpfalz und Niederbayern in vorindustrieller Zeit', *Zeitschrift für bayerische Landesgeschichte*, 39 (1976), 785-822.

HEIMBERGER, H., 'Schwangerschaft, Geburt und Frauenkrankheiten in der mittelalterlichen Volksmedizin', *Württembergisches Jahrbuch für Volkskunde*, 8 (1951), 111–22.

HELMHOLZ, R., *Marriage Litigation in Medieval England* (Cambridge, 1974).

HOULBROOKE, R., *Church Courts and the People during the English Reformation 1520–1570* (Oxford, 1979).

HOWELL, M., *Women, Production and Patriarchy in Late Medieval Cities* (Chicago, 1986).

HUGHES, D. O., 'From Brideprice to Dowry in Mediterranean Europe', *Journal of Family History*, 3 (1978), 262–96.

ISERLOH, I., *Geschichte und Theologie der Reformation im Grundriss* (Paderborn, 1980).

JÄGER, C., *Ulms Verfassungs-, bürgerliches und commercielles Leben im Mittelalter* (Heilbronn, 1831).

KARANT-NUNN, S., 'Continuity and Change: Some Effects of the Reformation on the Women of Zwickau', *Sixteenth Century Journal*, 12/2 (1982), 17–42.

—— *Zwickau in Transition 1500–1547: The Reformation as an Agent of Change* (Columbus, 1987).

KLAPISCH-ZUBER, C., *Women, Family and Ritual in Renaissance Italy* (Chicago, 1985).

—— 'Women Servants in Florence during the Fourteenth and Fifteenth Centuries', in B. Hanawalt (ed.), *Women and Work in Preindustrial Europe* (Bloomington, 1986).

KOEBNER, R., 'Die Eheauffassung des ausgehenden deutschen Mittelalters', *Archiv für Kulturgeschichte*, 9 (1911), 136–98, 279–318.

KÖHLER, W., *Zürcher Ehegericht und Genfer Konsistorium*, 2 vols. (Quellen und Abhandlungen zur schweizerischen Reformationsgeschichte, 7, 10; Leipzig, 1932, 1942).

KRIEGK, G. L., *Deutsches Bürgerthum im Mittelalter*, 2 vols. (Frankfurt, 1868–71; rept. Frankfurt, 1969).

LE GOFF, J., *Histoire de la France urbaine*, ii. *La Ville médiévale des Carolingiens à la Renaissance* (*Histoire de la France urbaine*, ed. G. Duby; Paris, 1980).

LIEBMANN, M., *Urbanus Rhegius und die Anfänge der Reformation* (Reformationsgeschichtliche Studien und Texte, 117; Münster 1980).

LORENZEN-SCHMIDT, K. J., 'Beleidigungen in schleswig-holsteinischen Städten im 16. Jahrhundert, soziale Norm und soziale Kontrolle in Städtegesellschaften', *Kieler Blätter zur Volkskunde*, 10 (1978), 5–20.

—— 'Zur Stellung der Frauen in der frühneuzeitlichen Städtegesellschaft Schleswigs und Holsteins', *Archiv für Kulturgeschichte*, 63 (1982), 316–39.

MACLEAN, I., *The Renaissance Notion of Woman: A Study in the Fortunes of Scholasticism and Medical Science in European Intellectual Life* (Cambridge, 1980).

MASCHKE, E., 'Die Unterschichten der mittelalterlichen Städten Deutschlands', in E. Maschke and J. Sydow (eds.), *Gesellschaftliche Unterschichten in den südwestdeutschen Städten* (Veröffentlichungen der Kommission für geschichtlichen Landeskunde in Baden-Württemberg, 41B; Stuttgart, 1967).

MAZZI, M., 'Il mondo della prostituzione nella Firenze tardo medievale', *Ricerche storiche*, 14 (1984), 337–63.

MEDICK, H., 'Village Spinning Bees: Sexual Culture and Free Time among Rural Youths in Early Modern Germany', in H. Medick and D. Sabean (eds.), *Interest and Emotion: Essays on the Study of Family and Kinship* (Cambridge, 1984).

MOELLER, B., *Imperial Cities and the Reformation*, ed. and trans. E. Midelfort and M. Edwards (Philadelphia, 1972).

MONTER, E. W., 'The Consistory of Geneva 1559-1569', *Bibliothèque d'humanisme et renaissance*, 38 (1976), 476–84.

MÜLLER, MARIA E., *Der Poet der Moralität: Untersuchungen zu Hans Sachs* (Bern, 1985).

NAUJOCKS, E., 'Ulms Sozialpolitik im 16. Jahrhundert', *Zeitschrift für Geschichte des Oberrheins*, 33 (1953), 93–7.

OBERMAN, H., *Luther: Mensch zwischen Gott und Teufel* (Berlin, 1982).

OBSER, K., 'Zur Geschichte des Frauenhauses in Überlingen', *Zeitschrift für Geschichte des Oberrheins*, 70 (1916), 631–44.

OTIS, L., *Prostitution in Medieval Society: The History of an Urban Institution in Lanquedoc* (Chicago, 1985).

OZMENT, S., *The Reformation in the Cities: The Appeal of Protestantism to Sixteenth Century Germany and Switzerland* (New Haven and London, 1975).

—— *When Fathers Ruled: Family Life in Reformation Europe* (Cambridge, Mass., 1983).

PARK, K., and DASTON, L., 'Unnatural Conceptions: The Study of Monsters in Sixteenth- and Seventeenth-Century France and England', *Past and Present*, 92 (1981), 20–54.

PERRY, M., '"Lost Women" in Early Modern Seville: The Politics of Prostitution', *Feminist Studies*, 4/1 (1978), 195–214.

POSERN-KLETTT, Dr. von, 'Frauenhäuser und freie Frauen in Sachsen', *Archiv für die sächsische Geschichte*, 12 (1874), 63–89.

QUAETERT, J., 'The Shaping of Women's Work in Manufacturing: Guilds, Households, and the State in Central Europe 1648-1870', *American Historical Review*, 90/5 (1985), 1122–48.

REIFENBERG, H., *Sakramente, Sakramentalien und Ritualien im Bistum Mainz seit dem Spätmittelalter*, 2 vols. (Liturgiewissenschaftliche Quellen und Forschungen, 53, 54; Münster, 1971).

REINCKE, H., *Die Bilderhandschrift des hamburgischen Stadtrechts von 1497* (Hamburg, 1917).

REYNIZSCH, W., *Uiber Truhten und Truhtensteine, Barden und Bardenlieder, Feste, Schmäuse . . . und Gerichte der Teutschen* (Gotha, 1802).

RITZER, K., *Formen, Riten und religiöses Brauchtum der Eheschliessung in den christlichen Kirchen des ersten Jahrtausends* (Liturgiewissenschaftliche Quellen und Forschungen, 38; Münster, 1962).

ROBISHEAUX, T., 'Peasants and Pastors: Rural Youth Control and the Reformation in Hohenlohe 1540-1680', *Social History*, 6 (1981), 281-300.

ROPER, L., 'Luther: Sex, Marriage and Motherhood', *History Today*, 33 (Dec. 1983), 33-8.

—— 'Housework and Livelihood: Towards the Alltagsgeschichte of Women', *German History: The Journal of the German History Society*, 2 (1985), 3-9.

—— '"The Common Man", "the Common Good", "Common Women"': Gender and Language in the German Reformation Commune', *Social History*, 12/1 (1987), 1-22.

ROSSIAUD, J., 'Prostitution, Youth and Society in the towns of South-eastern France in the Fifteenth Century', in R. Forster and O. Ranum (eds.), *Deviants and the Abandoned in French Society*, trans. E. Forster and P. Ranum (Baltimore, 1978).

ROTH, F., *Weibliche Erziehung und weiblicher Unterricht im Zeitalter der Reformation* (Leipzig, 1893).

ROWBOTHAM, S., 'What Do Women Want? Woman-Centred Values and the World as it Is', *Feminist Review*, 20 (1985), 49-70.

RUBLACK, H. C., 'Reformatorische Bewegung und städtische Kirchenpolitik', in I. Bátori (ed.), *Städtische Gesellschaft und Reformation* (Stuttgart, 1980).

RUDECK, W., *Geschichte der öffentlichen Sittlichkeit in Deutschland* (Jena, 1897).

RÜTHING, H., *Höxter um 1500: Analyse einer Stadtgesellschaft* (Paderborn, 1986).

RUSSELL, PAUL, *Lay Theology in the Reformation: Popular Pamphleteers in Southwest Germany 1521-25* (Cambridge, 1986).

SAFLEY, T., *Let No Man Put Asunder: The Control of Marriage in the German Southwest: A Comparative Study 1550-1600* (Kirksville, 1984).

SCHADE, S., *Schadenzauber und Magie des Körpers* (Worms, 1983).

SCHAMA, S., *The Embarrassment of Riches: An Interpretation of Dutch Culture in the Golden Age* (London, 1987).

SCHILLING, H., '"History of Crime" or "History of Sin"? Some Reflections on the Social History of Early Modern Church Discipline', in E. Kouri and T. Scott (eds.), *Politics and Society in Reformation Europe* (London, 1987).

SCHÖNFELDT, G., *Beiträge zur Geschichte des Pauperismus und der Prostitution in Hamburg* (Sozialgeschichtliche Forschungen: Ergänzungshefte zur Zeitschrift für Sozial- und Wirthschaftsgeschichte, 11; Weimar, 1897).

SCHRANK, J., *Die Prostitution in Wien in historischer, administrativer und hygienischer Beziehung*, 2 vols. (Vienna, 1886).

SCHRÖTER, M., *'Wo Zwei zusammenkommen in rechter Ehe': Sozio- und psychogenetische Studien über Eheschliessungsvorgänge vom 12. bis 15. Jahrhundert* (Frankfurt, 1985).

SCHULZ, KNUT, *Handwerksgesellen und Lohnarbeiter: Untersuchungen zur oberrheinischen und oberdeutschen Stadtgeschichte des 14. bis 17. Jahrhunderts* (Sigmaringen, 1985).

SCHWARZ, I., *Die Bedeutung der Sippe für die Öffentlichkeit der Eheschliessung im 15. und 16. Jahrhundert (besonders nach norddeutschen Quellen)* (Schriften zur Kirchen- und Rechtsgeschichte, 13; Tübingen, 1959).

SCRIBNER, R. W., *For the Sake of Simple Folk: Popular Propaganda for the Reformation* (Cambridge, 1981).

—— 'Reorientating the Reformation', *History Workshop Journal*, 14 (1982), 2–22.

—— 'Cosmic Order and Daily Life: Sacred and Secular in Pre-Industrial German society', in K. von Greyerz (ed.), *Religion and Society in Early Modern Europe* (London, 1984).

—— 'Ritual and Popular Religion in Catholic Germany at the Time of the Reformation', *Journal of Ecclesiastical History*, 35 (1984), 47–77.

SEGALEN, M., *Love and Power in the Peasant Family* (Oxford, 1983).

SHARMA, U., 'Dowry in North India: Its Consequences for Women', in R. Hirschon (ed.), *Women and Property: Women as Property* (Oxford, 1984).

SIEBENKEES, J., *Materialien zur nürnbergischen Geschichte*, 4 vols. (Nuremberg, 1792–4).

STAEHELIN, A., *Die Einführung der Ehescheidung in Basel zur Zeit der Reformation* (Basle, 1957).

STEWART, A., *Unequal Lovers: A Study of Unequal Couples in Northern Art* (New York, 1977).

STRAUSS, G., *Nuremberg in the Sixteenth Century: City Politics and Life between Middle Ages and Modern Times* (Bloomington and London, 1966).

—— *Manifestations of Discontent on the Eve of the Reformation* (Indiana, 1971).

—— 'Success and Failure in the German Reformation', *Past and Present*, 67 (1975), 30-63.

—— *Luther's House of Learning: Indoctrination of the Young in the German Reformation* (Baltimore and London, 1978).

TENTLER, T., *Sin and Confession on the Eve of the Reformation* (Princeton, 1977).

TREXLER, R., 'La prostitution florentine au XVᵉ siècle: Patronages et clientèles', *Annales ESC*, 26/5 (1981), 983-1015.

TROLL, J., *Geschichte der Stadt Winterthur nach Urkunden bearbeitet*, 6 vols. (Winterthur, 1840-7).

VANJA, C., 'Klosterleben und Gesellschaft: Lebensläufe von Nonnen und Stiftsfrauen in spätmittelalterlichen hessischen Konventen', in W. Schröder (ed.), *Lebenslauf und Gesellschaft: Zum Einsatz von kollektiven Biographien in der historischen Sozialforschung* (Historisch-Sozialwissenschaftliche Forschungen, 18; Stuttgart, 1985).

—— 'Bergarbeiterinnen: Zur Geschichte der Frauenarbeit im Bergbau, Hütten- und Salinenwesen seit dem späten Mittelalter, I; Spätes Mittelalter und frühe Neuzeit', *Der Anschnitt*, 39 (1987), 2-15.

WEBER, MARIANNE, *Ehefrau und Mutter in der Rechtsentwicklung: Eine Einführung* (Tübingen, 1907).

WEINHOLD, K., *Die deutschen Frauen in dem Mittelalter*, 2 vols. (3rd edn.; Vienna, 1897)

WENSKY, M., *Die Stellung der Frau in der stadtkölnischen Wirtschaft im Spätmittelalter* (Quellen und Darstellungen zur hansischen Geschichte, NF 26; Vienna, 1980).

WESOLY, K., 'Der weibliche Bevölkerungsanteil in spätmittelalterlichen und frühneuzeitlichen Städten und die Betätigung von Frauen in zünftigen Handwerk (insbesondere am Mittel- und Oberrhein)', *Zeitschrift für Geschichte des Oberrheins*, 128, NF 89 (1980), 69-117.

WIESNER, M., 'Paltry Peddlers or Essential Merchants? Women in the Distributive Trades in Early Modern Nuremberg', *Sixteenth Century Journal*, 12/2 (1981), 3-13.

—— *Working Women in Renaissance Germany* (New Brunswick, 1986).

—— 'Luther and Women: The Death of Two Marys', in J. Obelkevich, L. Roper, and R. Samuel (eds.), *Disciplines of Faith: Studies in Religion, Politics and Patriarchy* (London, 1987).

WINTER, A., 'Studien zur sozialen Situation der Frauen in der Stadt Trier nach der Steuerliste von 1364', *Kurtrierisches Jahrbuch*, 15 (1975), 20-45.

WISSELL, R., *Des alten Handwerks Recht und Gewohnheit*, 2 vols. (Berlin, 1929).

WUNDER, H., 'Zur Stellung der Frau im Arbeitsleben und in der Gesellschaft des 15.-18. Jahrhunderts', *Geschichtsdidaktik*, 3 (1981), 239-52.

WUSTMANN, G., *Aus Leipzigs Vergangenheit: Gesammelte Aufsätze von Gustav Wustmann*, 3 vols. (Leipzig, 1885-1909).

WYNTJES, S. M., 'Women in the Reformation Era', in R. Bridenthal and C. Koonz (eds.), *Becoming Visible: Women in European History* (Boston, 1977).

ZIKA, C., 'Hosts, Processions and Pilgrimages in Fifteenth-Century Germany', *Past and Present*, 118 (1988), 25-64.

Index

Printed in the United States
32379LVS00003B/49-138